First Edition 1972

ISBN: 978-81-2082-650-2

Also available at:

MOTILAL BANARSIDASS
41 U.A. Bungalow Road, Jawahar Nagar, Delhi 110 007
8 Mahalaxmi Chamber, Warden Road, Mumbai 400 026
120 Royapettah High Road, Mylapore, Chennai 600 004
Sanas Plaza, Subhash Nagar, Pune 411 002
16 St. Mark's Road, Bangalore 560 001
8 Camac Street, Calcutta 700 017
Ashok Rajpath, Patna 800 004
Chowk, Varanasi 221 0011

PRINTED IN INDIA
BY JAINENDRA PRAKASH JAIN AT SHRI JAINENDRA PRESS,
A-45 NARAINA, PHASE I, NEW DELHI 110 028
AND PUBLISHED BY NARENDRA PRAKASH JAIN FOR
MOTILAL BANARSIDASS PUBLISHERS PRIVATE LIMITED,
BUNGALOW ROAD, DELHI 110 007

PREFACE

The busy life of an administrator leaves little time for collecting worthwhile thoughts on topical events and problems in the environment. However, as the level of responsibility rises, sharing one's thoughts with others interested in the fields to which the responsibility relates becomes a necessity, and the form in which these thoughts are expressed is most conveniently a lecture. Thus it came about that after resigning from the Indian Civil Service on appointment as Deputy Governor of the Reserve Bank of India in 1941 I had occasion to speak on Finance, with a frequency which grew as I rose to be Governor of the Bank (1943—1949) and Union Finance Minister (1950—1956). On demitting the latter office I entered on the career of an educational administrator (Chairman of the University Grants Commission—1956-1961, and Vice-Chancellor of the University of Delhi—1962-1967) and was frequently called upon to speak or invited to deliver a Convocation Address. During the earlier period the University Grants Commission thought it worthwhile publishing two Volumes containing such addresses. But subsequent speeches and addresses have remained unpublished, except to a limited extent, and it is many of these that are presented in this Volume.

A couple of years ago I accepted the chairmanship of an Editorial Committee appointed by Shri L. K. Jha, then Governor of the Reserve Bank of India, to edit the History of the Reserve Bank of India from 1935 to 1951 prepared by one of its Senior Officers, Shri S. L. N. Simha. During the course of this work Shri Simha was able to discover copies of a number of speeches other than formal ones delivered by me during my tenure of office as Governor of the Reserve Bank. He thought that despite the lapse of over two decades some of these were worth publishing as likely to be of possible interest to serious students of the monetary and economic history of our times. Following his advice I have agreed to the inclusion of two of these in the present Volume, one on War Finance and the other on Finance for Industry. For the rest the matter comprised under the topic Finance relates to developmental problems of the last decade and includes two memorial lectures reprinted by the courtesy of the two Universities which had invited me to deliver them.

The residual portion of the Volume contains the reprints of speeches on a variety of the aspects of our social life which does not lend itself easily to classification. The general heading of Reflections on Society will, it is hoped, appropriately cover them.

I take this opportunity of thanking Messrs. Motilal Banarsidass, for having undertaken to publish these speeches and addresses on diverse aspects of finance, education and society and for the care with which they have carried out this job.

Hyderabad, A.P. C. D. Deshmukh

CONTENTS

WAR FINANCE

Address on 'War Finance' delivered by Rotarian Mr. C. D. Deshmukh, C.I.E., Governor, Reserve Bank of India, before a meeting of the Rotary Club, Bombay, on Tuesday, the 31st August 1943.

Rotarian President and Fellow Rotarians.

1. Just as everyone is a military strategist these days, everyone is also a financier—sometimes *malgre lui*—and it is perhaps rash on my part to have undertaken to address you on the subject of War Finance. Moreover, owing to my day to day connection with Government finance, I must maintain my reserve—in more senses than one; I shall, therefore, try to confine myself to facts and figures and avoid dogma or controversy.

2. In this total war, the elaborate administrative regulation of economic life and the direct physical control of economic resources have rather pushed finance into the background, but it remains important, particularly in countries where direct controls are relatively less effective or successful.

3. I shall first state a few figures, which where they are in foreign currency will be given in equivalent crores—just to make your flesh creep ! In the United Kingdom the actual public expenditure has increased from 1400 crores in 1938-39 to 7500 crores in 1942-43, i.e., six-fold. During the same period, it has gone up in the United States from 3,000 crores to 26,000 crores i.e., 8 to 9-fold, in Canada, from 167 crores to 1131 crores, in Australia, from 101 crores to 583 crores, in Japan, from 634 crores to 1896 crores; and lastly in India from 85 crores to 322 crores, or if expenditure on account of His Majesty's and Allied Governments is included, to 660 crores, i.e. nearly 8-fold, which compares favourably with the measure of increase in any other country.

4. The predominant part of these considerably enlarged public disbursements is, of course, constituted by defence expenditure, which comprises over 50% of the national income in most of the major belligerent countries, on the basis of approximate estimates. In the case of India, nothing more than a rough guess is possible, according to which the proportion of total national income expended by the State during, say, the last

financial year, would appear to have been in the region of 15 to 20%. No direct comparison of any such proportion with the proportions attained in the richer industrial countries is however reliable; for the spare margin of income, that is to say the surplus over and above the essential minimum of individual needs, is disproportionately small in this country, with its low per capita income, measured in real goods and services available per head.

5. It is useful as a background for a survey of war finance to have an idea of the relative level of economic welfare in different countries. An ambitious but creditable attempt to present a comparative picture in this respect is made by Colin Clark, a well-known statistically-minded Australian economist, who has estimated average real income per head in terms of an international unit, which is defined as the amount of goods and services which one dollar would purchase in the United States of America over the average of the ten-year period 1925-34. Thus measured the approximate estimate of annual average real income for India for the 10-year period is placed at 200 compared with 1381, that is about seven times for the United States; 1069 or over five times for Great Britain; and about six times for Canada, New Zealand, Australia, etc. Our own economists will probably challenge the correctness of these estimates, as according to their calculation, the ratio is more likely twenty to one between England and India and perhaps thirty to one between U.S.A. and India.

6. The average daily expenditure perhaps affords a simpler and clearer idea of the relative national expenditure. During the last year, the figure was the equivalent of Rs. 21 crores in the United Kingdom, 73 crores in the United States and 1.8 crores in India, including expenditure on account of other governments.

7. It appears that an outstanding feature of the finance of the present war as compared with the last war is the greater dependence of many countries on taxation than, on borrowing of all kinds. The proportion of total revenue, mostly tax revenue, to total expenditure during 1942-43 was 50% in the United Kingdom, 55% in India; round these figures in other Empire countries and 26% in the U.S.A.

8. Of taxation, again, the increase in direct taxation,

has been far greater than in indirect taxation so that the proportion of direct taxation to the total has undergone significant increases in many countries. In the United Kingdom, this proportion has increased from 56% to 64% between the pre-war year and 1942-43, while in India the proportion of total taxes on income to total tax revenue increased from 24 to 61%. In Canada, the percentage of direct to total taxation has increased from 37 to 64% and in the United States from 50 to 73% in 1942-43. Both these tendencies, which result in giving to direct taxation a much more important role than it occupied hither to, in the finance of war, point to the essentially sounder basis of public finance in the present than in the last war.

9. Great as have been the increases in taxation in most countries, it could never be hoped that the entire additional expenditure necessitated by a war of the present dimensions could be financed without resort to borrowing. The controversy as regards the relative merits of taxation and borrowing has, in the context of the present war, become somewhat academic, for conditions have called forth at once the maximum increase in taxation and the largest possible borrowing. It has been necessary, on the one hand, to tap the reserves of taxable capacity and additions to such capacity during the war to the utmost possible extent and, on the other hand, to borrow heavily and continuously out of the genuine savings of individuals and corporations, out of the credit created by commercial banks and often directly from the ultimate reservoir of credit. i.e. the Central Bank of the country itself.

10. At one time borrowing used to be regarded as a means of throwing the burden of war on to future generations. The fallacy of this belief has, it appears, been understood from the very beginning of the present war, and perhaps the sounder basis of present-day war finance in general derives from a clearer realisation of the inescapable fact that the burden of war is in the main borne here and now by those who fight and live during the conflict. There have to be produced here and now the resources necessary for victory, and whether the Governments tax or borrow, the civilian populations have to reduce to a minimum their consumption of essential goods—and drinks—so as to make the maximum supplies available for the fighting services. So long as borrowing is internal, it involves a direct

burden on the population as much as taxation, for it increases the resources at the command of Government at the direct expense of those at the command of the people; after the war, the repayment of principal and the payment of interest on the national debt involves only an internal transference of wealth from the tax-payers to the bond-holders of Government, who are often the same parties.

11. It is interesting to note the colossal amounts of borrowings and increases in internal national debt that have occurred during the present war. The public debt in the United States has in three years nearly trebled and had by the end of March 1943 risen from 16,803 crores to 45,210 crores. In the United Kingdom the pre-war figure of 10,373 crores was more than doubled to 20,827 crores by February 1943. In Japan the rise was from 1398 crores in June 1939 to 3557 crores in June 1943. In Germany 5062 crores (at pre-war rate of exchange) in December 1939 increased to 22,720 crores in December 1942. Compared with these figures the increase in the public debt of India must be regarded as exceedingly moderate, from 1206 crores to 1439 crores by March 1943.

12. An interesting change in the composition of public debt which is uniformly noticeable in most countries, but is particularly marked in some, is the increase in the proportion of short-term or floating to total public debt. This proportion increased between the end of 1939 and 1942 from 32 to 52% in Germany, 20 to 26% in the United Kingdom, 3 to 16% in the United States and has gone up from 10 to 20% in India.

13. I have observed above that the burden of war falls mainly on the present generation. There are methods of finance, however, which do not place the major burden on the present generation. One of these methods is to appropriate for the use of Government the funds allocated towards depreciation of a country's domestic capital. This is in effect to draw upon the domestic accumulations of past generations. Another method is to draw upon the accumulations of overseas investments, if any, and a third is to borrow abroad or run into debt to foreign countries. The London Economist in a recent issue has summed up the elaborate White Paper Statistics on war finance and described in real terms how the cost of the war in 1942, or the additional Government expenditure in the

United Kingdom since the year before the war, was derived. Though the conclusions are directly relevant only to the British national economy, they give a clear statement of the essential sources of war finance in any country. The first conclusion is that the cost of the war in 1942 was in real terms almost half the gross national income of 1938, that is, the expenditure for war purposes in goods and services was equal to half their gross total output before the war. Secondly, this total cost was met, as to rather more than two-fifths, by increased production, as to rather less than a quarter by reduced consumption; as to one-fifth by failing to maintain the domestic capital of the country; and for the rest, by drawing upon the accūmulations of overseas capital or by running into debt to foreign countries (largely through the accumulation of sterling balances). The third conclusion is that about two-thirds of the real economic burden of the war is being borne by the generation that is fighting it, by working harder and consuming less, while one-third is the share of posterity. Similar analyses made for the United States show that a greater proportion of the cost of war has been met out of increased production and smaller proportions out of reduction in consumption or drafts on capital, for the amount of industrial slack and unused capacity has been greater in that country than in Britain. No precise estimates have been made as regards the relative contribution of increased production, and reduced consumption to the war effort in our country, but it would appear that the net magnitude of the last element relating to domestic and overseas disinvestment of capital, which is roughly the measure of the burden shifted to posterity, may well be insignificant in the case of India.

14. A mention may be made here of the liberal scale on which credit has been extended by the Allied nations to one another to the end that the full utilisation of the economic resources is not impeded to any extent by limitations of finance. Finance has become, as I have already hinted, a subsidiary aspect of economics during the war. Some idea of this is given by the fact that the total amount of lend-lease aid extended to the Allied nations upto the end of July 1943 reached the impressive sum of \$. 14,000 million or nearly Rs. 4,700 crores, of which somewhat over one-third was received by the United Kingdom. As to the return expected, President Roosevelt in his 11th Report

to Congress is reported to have stated that "victory and secure peace are the only coin in which we can be repaid" and mentioned that "Congress in passing and extending the lend-lease Act made it plain that the United States wants no new war debts to jeopardise the coming peace." On the other hand, also the United Kingdom has accumulations of sterling measuring the extent of current credits granted to Britain by the Empire countries amounting to over $ 1000 million or over Rs. 1,300 crores, as estimated recently by the Economist, of which India's share stood roughly at $. 500 or over Rs. 650 crores.

15. When considering the contribution of borrowing to the finance of war, it is as well to point to the distinction of quality between borrowing of different kinds from different sources, which is perhaps not commonly appreciated. Borrowing from private individuals and corporations is deflationary in the sense that it constitutes a net withdrawal of purchasing power (in the form of cash or credit) from the community; borrowing directly from the commercial banks increases in due course the balance of bank deposits owned by the public proportionately and is therefore inflationary; and thirdly, borrowing from the Central Bank of the country involves a primary as well as a secondary process of credit creation and is therefore very actively inflationary. It is of the highest importance, therefore, that the maximum receipts of borrowing are secured from private individuals and corporations with a view to preventing the expansion of the cash and bank deposits, that is, credit, at the disposal of the public so as to minimise the degree of monetary inflation, and the pressure on the price level.

16. At this point, I advert to a description—the technique of currency expansion—as it is possible that it is the subject of some misconceptions. The increase of the Reserve Bank's sterling balances and the expansion of currency are commonly regarded as inevitably and proportionately related. There is, indeed, a relation between the two but it is desirable to have an idea of the process through which one is reflected in the other. Sterling accrues to the Government of India on account of the services and goods made available to His Majesty's and other Allied Governments. The Government of India

require rupees to pay for the services and goods supplied to other Governments and obtain the same in exchange for sterling from the Reserve Bank. Sterling is also acquired by the Reserve Bank from banks and other parties, arising out of any surplus in the balance of payments of the country on private account. The sterling received from Government like the sterling acquired from banks is first reflected in the returns of the Banking Department as an addition to the "balances held abroad" on the assets side, with a corresponding increase in Government deposits on the liabilities side. The Government draws, say, cheques on the Reserve Bank against its increased deposits almost as soon as the increase accrues and the parties who receive Government cheques send them to the credit of their accounts with the banks thus increasing the figure of bank deposits; the banks in turn pass on the cheques to the credit of their balances with the Reserve Bank, which, in the result, increase as Government deposits go down. When cash payments are made by banks or Government, reduction in bank or Government deposits is accompanied directly by a reduction in the portfolio of cash with the Banking Department. The amount of cash, viz., notes and rupees, in the Banking Department is maintained at a level found convenient from experience—round 10 crores. When it tends to decline below that customary level, a part of the sterling securities or 'balances held abroad' is transferred to the Issue Department and the till of cash is replenished. In the Issue Department, there occurs a corresponding increase on the liabilities side in the 'notes held in the Banking Department' and/or the 'notes in circulation' if paid-out, as the case might be, against an addition to sterling securities on the assets side. These several processes may not all be clearly reflected in the returns from week to week as changes are continual and a weekly return may include the results of various changes at the same time, but the broad trends over a period of time do readily appear. Government deposits are being replenished and depleted continually through receipts and disbursements on Government account for all purposes. And currency expansion occurs not immediately, automatically and proportionately as sterling assets accrue to Government, but through the deficit of total Government cash receipts by means of taxation and borrowing over total Government disbursements. So that the process may be arrested or, at any rate, retarded only if Government receipts can be made to increase more nearly in proportion to the scale of Government disbursements *on all accounts*, that is to say, through an increase in taxation and borrowing, assuming that a reduction in the scale of Government expenditure is ruled out. There is no natural or necessary relation between the growth of foreign assets and internal expansion or monetary inflation, and the link between the two phenomena is optional. Inflation may, and generally does, develop without any growth in foreign balances, and foreign balances may in theory grow without causing a corresponding degree of inflation. In practice, the real question is how much Government can withdraw from the purchasing power that has been placed in the hands of the public as a result of its disbursements, and this in turn involves an enquiry into whose hands the additional income has gone. There is only one country in which the whole of the amount disbursed can be withdrawn by Government by means of taxation and borrowing, and, that is, Utopia.

17. The allocation of war expenditure between India and England does not essentially affect this question of inflation, so long as the total size and volume of resources to be withdrawn for war purposes from public consumptions is fixed, since if currency is not expanded against sterling it would have to be expanded against borrowing from the Reserve Bank. The crux of the matter is the volume of resources withdrawn from public consumption. Where the bulk of the population lives on a margin of subsistence, the scope for tightening the belt is obviously limited.

18. In considering the total amount of money in circulation, one must include bank deposits, which do not arise out of the increase in currency circulation, but from the same cause which gives rise to it, viz., the large excess in Government disbursements over receipts.

19. What then are the remedies for a state of affairs in which a continuing increase in the supply of money threatens to raise the level of prices to a point where the balance of the social and economic system might be upset ? Broadly, there are only two categories of remedies. One is measures such that

the essence of inflation, which is the growth of the community's money income, unevenly distributed, is prevented; the other, in so far as monetary expansion remains unavoidable, is diect measures such as price control, rationing etc. Among the monetary methods suggested is the floatation of loans by the British Government in the Indian market with a view to securing Indian finance for that Government's purchases in this country. This involves the tricky question of the relative financial credit of the two countries and the possibility of confusion in the money market in regard to appropriate rates of interest for the Indian Government's borrowing. Alternatively, a suggestion has been put forward by some that an increase might be made in the rate of interest on Government loans to attract greater contributions. There are important considerations that have to be borne in mind. Apart from the advantage of a low rate of interest in terms of the burden of unproductive debt, a rise in the rate might have serious repercussions on the banking and insurance worlds and might handicap industrial expansion in the post-war period, if not current production. In any case a wider and more general perception of the inherent and potential deflationary factors in the present situation, however, should restrain the rise in prices as the end of war comes more clearly into sight, and the assurance of victory becomes complete. The fact that with an immediate deficit of receipts in relation to governmental disbursements in the country, there are being built up at the same time claims to acquire, after the war, resources for an expansion of the basis of our economy and the development of our productive system should, under the conditions, act increasingly as a salutary influence. Apart from the adventitious aid of these favourable psychological factors in the fundamental situation, however, there seems no alternative to a wider extension and more intensive and stringent application of physical controls on the prices and distribution of commodities, principally rationing, so as to curb speculation, profiteering and hoarding of commodities—which is an effort to safeguard oneself against the sacrifices which other members of the community are making by way of rising prices. The stimulation of production must alsor emain a prime and immediate object of policy.

20. In considering the subject of war finance and the

elements of a proper financial system during the war, reference may be made to the aftermath of the huge public expenditure and public employment of men and resources when the time comes to break up the economic apparatus of war. A sudden reduction in the scale of public expenditure might throw a country's economy, faced with the difficult tasks of adjustment to the conditions of peace, completely out of gear and bring about a slump. The lines of economic demobilisation therefore require careful thought, and considered plans of capital development are indicated as necessary to smoothen the course of the transition, as well as to prepare the ground for an even and uninterrupted economic development on a level of full employment at home and expanding international trade abroad.

21. I may pass on, in conclusion, to make a reference to the subject of post-war monetary plans. The natural complexity of the problem has been aggravated by the number of different plans offered and their revision from time to time as a result of expert examination. Broadly, they are all aimed at ironing out fluctuations in international trade by means of international credit and they all bring out the obvious truth that if a country does not choose to get paid for its goods and services in the same way, it must agree to forego its claims if the structure of international trade is not to be disrupted again. The layman will need to be assured that the broad purpose of any plan that may finally be evolved will accord with the ends of genuine international economic co-operation. Progress towards this goal requires that no scheme is framed with a view to the narrow and immediate interests of the more powerful and richer nations which have the natural leadership of any new international financial organization, in opposition to the interests of the poorer and more populous countries. There is no reason why these two ends cannot be reconciled since the promotion of the common interests of the international community will also mean, in the long run, the promotion of national economic welfare. For, experience has shown the futility of trying to keep one's own corner of the garden pretty at the cost of the neighbours. There must accordingly be a conscious and deliberate attempt on the part of the more advanced nations to improve the standards of living in the less advanced ones, although this might, for the time being, mean

the standing still of national amelioration. A cynic has defined war as a byproduct of the arts of peace, and, in the words of Anatole France, civilization rests on the patience of the poor. The arts of peace will not endure unless civilization is broad-based on men's contentment.

FINANCE FOR INDUSTRY

Address on Finance for Industry delivered by Sir C.D. Deshmukh, CIE., in Bombay, on Monday the 7th May, 1945, at a meeting of the Bombay Branch of the Indian Council of World Affairs, New Delhi.

The object of this talk is to indicate how the internal financial requirements of industry are provided in the various countries; what facilities India has or is likely to have in that respect; and what new agencies appear to be needed in order to make up any deficiency that there may be in the country's existing scheme of finance for industry. There will be no attempt to define precisely the constitution and size of any such new agencies, but some reference will be made to the conditions which must be fulfilled if they are to be established and operated with success.

2. The division of the financial requirements of industry into block capital, i.e., finance for fixed assets, and working capital, i.e., finance for floating assets, in now generally recognised. Block capital is required by newly started industries for fixed assets, such as land, building, machinery, and appliances of a durable character, and by established industries for the purposes of extensions and replacement. Working capital is required for the purchase of raw materials, and working them up into finished products, for stores, for marketing and for day to day requirements. Broadly, the sources of industrial finance in the various countries under a capitalist economy fall under one or more of the following groups, viz., (1) the investment market, (2) commercial banks, (3) special institutions, and (4) the State. These sources are not necessarily mutually exclusive and there is almost always a blurring of functions.

3. So far as direct State finance is concerned, it is necessary to make a distinction between enterprises managed by the State itself, and enterprises under private management, even though controlled and assisted by the State. The provision of funds for nationalized enterprises run on the basis of a collectivist economy—for that is what a State enterprise amounts to—is a matter of public finance and is not included within the scope

of this talk. It is only relevant in so far as the demands on capital of State enterprises make an inroad on new capital available for private enterprise, and obviously the larger the sector of nationalized enterprise, the less will be the slice of capital available for private industry. How the claims of the two should be reconciled and co-ordinated is by itself a very important issue requiring separate treatment, which it is not possible to attempt here.

4. Before this aspect of the matter is left, however, it might be of interest to note how the very character of finance for industry alters where the entire economic structure is collectivist, as in the U.S.S.R. That country provides a striking example today of a closed economy, an economic structure in which world prices and world markets play practically no direct part. The monetary and banking system has no contact whatever with world money markets, and interest rates are governed entirely by internal conditions. It is the Production Plan backed by the real resources of labour and materials available that determines how fast new factories can be built or new tanks turned out, and not the money standing to the credit of the Finance Commissariat in the books of the State Bank. The ordinary man receives his wages in money and can spend it within limits, or may purchase State Bonds on which interest is paid. But he cannot put his money into private business enterprise. The State's earnings are directly tied up with the pricing policy of the Government. The State orders the means of production and fixes all prices, with insignificant exceptions. And the State's earnings represent the difference between the price and the cost of production. On the expenditure side, an important item in the Russian Budget is the item "finance for national industries." Investment in industry, which is to varying degrees the concern of the private capital market in capitalist countries, is in the U.S.S.R. entirely the responsibility of the State. The level of economic development and the physical resources that are available for the production of consumer goods and services are determined by the Government's general economic plan. As the people cannot buy more than the output of sales and goods and services produced according to the Government's plan, Government investment is carried out automatically as a result of the

allocation of physical resources no matter how it is financed. Such a plan is not disturbed by any financial forces. Bank credit there is, but the banks are entirely owned and controlled by the State, and though some freedom of initiative may rest with the banks, and, in particular, with the branches that maintain the contact with individual trading and industrial organizations, it is a measure of freedom duly foreseen and provided for. Credits are distributed by the Soviet banks according to the dictates of the higher authorities. The credit-worthiness of the borrowers emerges not from the security they can put up, nor from the prospective profit which their enterprises seem to command, but from the place apportioned to them in the plan. The borrowers are in the main Trusts and trading organizations which themselves are owned and controlled by the State. The deposits, other than those of the Savings Bank, are derived from these State organizations. The banks are not liable to meet large and unexpected encashments of deposits, and have no necessity to observe the canons of orthodox structure and distribution of banking assets as in capitalist countries. Banking in Russia constitutes an essential part in the planning machine which determines to a large extent the character and volume of production, commerce, investment and consumption in the whole country.

5. Turning now to the capitalist countries, the character of industrial finance is determined largely by conceptions current in regard to the part that commercial banks can play. Until recently, an almost universal feature of commercial banking in the Continent and the U.S.A. was what has been called "mixed banking", i.e. commercial banks combining industrial banking with ordinary banking business. A striking development since the world economic depression was the displacement by legislation in most of these countries, including Germany and the U.S.A., of the formerly prevailing "mixed banking" in favour of a division of functions modelled on British practice, mainly as a result of the experience gained during the period of depression. The underlying theory is that as the liabilities of commercial banks are mostly in the form of deposits, withdrawable on demand or at short notice, it is desirable that they should keep their assets in rather liquid form, easily realizable in case of need, and the wisdom of following this

policy would seem to have been demonstrated time and again in the past by the experience of countries which have pursued a different course.

6. The legislative restrictions on "mixed banking" just mentioned have the general object of prohibiting commercial banks from undertaking long-term industrial financing. Thus, in Belgium, the law of 1934 prohibited banks, which accept deposits on interest repayable within two years, from holding shares in or participating in any commercial, agricultural or industrial enterprise, with certain exceptions. In Sweden also, where commercial banks had played an important role in long-term finance of industry, usually through the formation of subsidiary companies or by way of advances against industrial shares, the 1933 Bank Act prohibits banks from acquiring shares, except to protect an advance, and from lending on securities without a reasonably wide margin between the amount of the advances and the market value of the securities. In pre-war Germany, assets consisting of shares other than permanent participations, or of Bonds not quoted on the German Stock Exchange, could not exceed a given percentage of liabilities, while permanent participations and real estate holdings could not exceed capital and surplus. In the U.S.A., where banks were mainly interested in the issuing of shares and carrying them on to the market at a profit (sometimes the interest of banks in such business being available by the formation of security affiliates completely owned by the banks themselves) the Banking Act of 1933 prohibited member banks from being affiliated to or controlling any corporation engaged in the issue, floatation, underwriting sale or distribution of stocks, Bonds, debentures, and other securities. Nor may bank officers act as officers or directors. Further, under this Act, and that of 1935, member banks may only deal in securities for account of customers, and even then not more than 10% of capital and surplus may be invested in the securities of any one maker, apart from Federal or State Bonds, nor may banks underwrite new issues. In the Argentine, as a result of the law of 1935, no bank may hold for a period longer than two years, after their purchase, shares or debentures of a business concern to an amount exceeding 20% of the concern's capital, or 10% of its own capital and 25% of its surplus. Also, no

bank may under any conditions participate,directly or indirectly, in a commercial, agricultural, or industrial enterprise of any description whatsoever. Before the war, there were only three countries, viz., Denmark, Switzerland and Czechoslovakia, where comparable restrictions were not imposed on banks in their relations with industry.

7. The corollary of the discouragement or prohibition of "mixed banking" by commercial banks is the establishment of special institutions for the finance of industry. These may be either separate classes of banks, as in France and Japan which have devoted themselves specifically to industrial finance, or investment trusts and finance corporations as in the United Kingdom and the U.S.A. or again, bond issuing institutions as in Canada.

8. In England, the provision of long-term capital for industry has never been one of the significant functions of the banking system. The great deposit banks provide working capital in the form of loans and overdrafts, but are reluctant to become partners in industry, owing, no doubt, to their realization that their financial structure makes them unsuitable instruments for industrial financing. It is true that some of them have, of recent years, been constrained to have closer relations with industry, because the chronic depression in some of the staple trades left a legacy of frozen advances. Since 1930 they have also participated in the Bankers' Industrial Development Co., which was formed to assist in the rationalization of certain industries. Very recently, they have, in a manner which will be described later, associated themselves with the formation of the Finance Corporation for Industry Ltd., and the Industrial and Commercial Finance Corporation Ltd,. for the purpose of providing finance, directly, or indirectly, for British industry in the post-war period. Nevertheless, the aloofness of Britiish banks from long-term industrial financing is still in sharp contrast with the relations between banking and industry in many other countries.

The explanation of the attitude of British banks towards industrial financing indicated above is largely due to historical reasons. Before large scale industry appeared in Great Britain, merchant capital, i.e., capital in private hands resulting from profits earned in foreign trade, was available for investment in industry when the opportunity appeared. Throughout the 19th century, moreover, firms starting in a small way built up their resources by the ploughing in of their profits, and, even in modern times, many concerns have expanded their size slowly by this means. The private banker also played an important part in the chief industrial areas in providing small but promising firms with the capital by which they could expand their business; and the development of many of the newer industries in the inter-war years owes much to his agency. The large established companies, of course, raise money by public issue on the London capital market, and the existence of the the London and Provincial Stock Exchanges provides an opportunity for the outside investor to participate in them. But the raising of capital by public issue is expensive and is an unprofitable process for amounts under $ 100,000. The London market has, therefore, concerned itself mainly with foreign lending, with Government loans and with the issue of public utilities and of very large companies. Till very recently, for the great mass of small and medium-sized firms, the process of raising capital initially, or increasing it, remained loose and informal. Solicitors and accountants played their part in bringing together would-be investors and business in search of capital for expansion. There are also local peculiarities; thus, when the cotton industry was expanding, it was common for a mill in need of capital to issue shares which were largely unpaid and then to borrow money at call on the security of these unpaid shares. Many of these shares were taken up by small investors including workers in the mills.

9. For some time past, it has been recognized in Britain that the traditional method of industrial financing left something to be desired. With mounting rates of taxation on undistributed profits, the capacity of established business to plough back profits has diminished, and taxation has also made inroads into the resources available to the private banker for investment in small, new enterprises. During the 'thirties, several new financial institutions, including the Bankers' Industrial Development Co., mentioned before, were established to fill the gap, and some of the insurance companies invested heavily in industrial securities. There was a tendency for an increasing proportion of industrial investment being made

through institutional investors including, for instance, the Great Building Societies, which financed the major part of the housing developments of the last two decades.

10. On the 23rd January 1945, the Chancellor of the Exchequer announced that he was informed by the Governor of the Bank of England that discussions which had reached an advanced stage, had been taking place among the banking and financial communities of the country on the financial needs of the country in the post-war period, and that, as a result, it was proposed to set up two companies, one to be named the Finance Corporation for Industry Ltd., and the other, a smaller one, to be named the Industrial and Commercial Finance Corporation Ltd. The former is to have a capital of £25 million and borrowing powers of four times that amount, making the total resources of the company £125 million. The capital is to be subscribed roughly in about equal proportions by a consortium of the insurance companies and the investment trust companies and by the Bank of England, and arrangements are contemplated whereby loan capital is to be supplied to the company by the clearing banks and the Scottish banks. The purpose of this capital will be the provision of temporary or longer period finance for industrial businesses of the country with a view to their quick rehabilitation and development in the national, interest, thereby assisting in the maintenance and increase of employment. The Chancellor added that the company's primary purpose will be to provide finance and not itself to reorganize industry. The other company will have a capital of £15 million and borrowing powers of twice that amount. The capital is to be subscribed by the clearing and Scottish banks together with a token subscription by the Bank of England, and the loan capital will be available from these banks in the same proportions as they subscribe for the shares of the company. The total resources of the company will, therefore, be £45 million and the object will be to supply medium and long-term capital for small and medium-sized businesses of the country in amounts, say, from £5000 to £200,000; amounts of less than £5000 being usually procurable in the ordinary way from bankers. Both these companies will be managed as units in themselves, entirely independent from the banks, with their own Boards of Directors and perma-

nent staffs of men experienced in finance, commerce and industry. The larger company will have the assistance of a special Industrial Advisory Panel. In order that the policy of the company may conform to the general economic policy of the Government, the appropriate Government departments will be kept informed of the nature and extent of all major developments being considered by the company. In an announcement to the public made by the banks in regard to the proposals for the creation of the Industrial & Commercial Finance Corporation Ltd., i.e., the smaller institution, intended to provide medium and long term capital for small and medium-sized businesses, the authors observe: "the gaps which are frequently alleged to exist in the present arrangements for the provision of credit are the absence of financial machinery specifically designed to provide (a) business, large or small, with

(i) temporary finance in anticipation of and issue of capital and/or

(2) medium term finance (say, up to periods of five years) in connection with long contracts at home or abroad ; and

(b) smaller and medium-sized industrial or commercial businesses with long-term capital where the amounts involved (say, up to £200,000) would not justify, or possibly permit of, the making of a public issue."

Given solvency and creditworthiness, the small man is adequately catered for by the joint stock banks. The provision of intermediate credits for periods ranging up to the quota of 5 years "presents no problem provided commercial justification and reasonable safety can be demonstrated. The existing banking machinery is adequate for all requirements apart from the provision of long-term capital. As a matter of principle, a deposit bank should not advance money on long-term, but its lending policy should have as its main object the temporary augmentation of a borrower's floating capital rather than the provision of funds to be invested in permanent assets. The strength of the deposit banks in this country and public confidence in them has been such that they have been able, in many cases, to assist their customers by advancing funds in the manner and for the purposes somewhat outside these normal functions; they fully intend to continue this practice after the war, but in the situation which is then likely to exist, it would appear that the medium and long-term requirements of industry and commerce may be so great that it would be advisable to provide an additional channel for this type of borrowing. It is with this factor largely in mind that the banks have decided to form, capitalize and lend substantial sums to the projected company."

11. In the U.S.A., the formation of investment trusts was sanctioned by the Federal Government under the amendment of the Federal Reserve Act adopted in 1920 and known as the Edge Act. The various States Governments permit the organization of investment trusts under their general corporation laws, there being in the case of a few States special acts governing their operation. These corporations are modelled somewhat after the British type of investment trusts, but are more diverse in form and method of operation. Their purpose is to enable the small investor to obtain access to the higher rates obtainable from the possession of stock in American industrial enterprises, and at the same time, the protection which such organizations would afford. Since 1920, a large number of investment trusts have been organised. Some of these issue both preferred and common shares as well as debentures. Others do not issue debentures, but borrow from banks any temporary accommodation required.

12. Mention should also be made at this stage of the special legislative measures taken in the U.S.A. to broaden the powers of the Federal Reserve System in making industrial loans for working capital purposes. Such measures resulted from criticisms of the commercial banks for their unwillingness to make loans to borrowers. The first such step was taken in the summer of 1933 with an amendment to the Federal Reserve Act authorizing the Reserve Banks to make loans to individuals and corporations on eligible paper. That particular amendment did not liberalize the lending powers of banks, except as to whom the loan could be made, whereas the demand was for long-term, not short-term credit. A year later, in June 1934, the Reserve Act was further amended by the addition of Section 13 (b) which had the effect of removing most of the restrictions as to the type of paper and its self-liquidating character. The loans were not to be used for

capital, for building a plant, and were permissible only in cases where finance could not be readily obtained elsewhere on reasonable terms, and only for a period of 5 years or less. Moreover, loans could not be made to finance a new industry. When operations began, the Bank was besieged with applications, and within a year's time, 358 loans for an aggregate amount of about $ 26 million had been made. About half of these loans were made directly to the borrowing institutions of business, and the other half was made by a commercial bank, with an arrangement under which the Reserve Bank shared the risk, at least 20% to the commercial bank making the loan, and not more than 80% to the Reserve Bank. It should be remembered that this was during the early stages of the world depression. As the depression lifted, credit became easier, and this was evidenced strongly by the falling off in applications for industrial loans, and in 1940, there was not a single application on file in the Federal Reserve Bank of New York.

13. In Canada, the Industrial Development Bank of Canada was brought into existence in August last year, as a subsidiary of the Bank of Canada, and its object is to ensure adequate credit to industrial enterprises which may reasonably be expected to prove successful. The authorized capital is $ 25 million, to be subscribed by the Bank of Canada, of which $ 10 million was payable forthwith. The Bank is empowered to borrow by the issue and sale of bonds and debentures, an important condition being that the aggregate liabilities, including debentures given or underwriting agreements entered into by the bank, shall not exceed three times its paid-up capital and reserve. The bonds and debentures do not bear Government guarantee but are eligible investment to be held by the Bank of Canada. The amount of such bonds and debentures maturing after ten years, which the Bank of Canada may hold, is not to exceed twice the paid-up capital and 'rest' of the Bank of Canada. The Industrial Bank is authorized to underwrite or purchase shares with a view to resale thereof, the maximum in each individual case not exceeding $200,000. The Bank is not permitted to accept deposits from the public. Profits in each year, after provision for bad debts, depreciation, etc., are to be credited to a

Reserve Fund until the fund equals the paid-up capital, and thereafter a dividend not exceeding 4% may be paid, the rest of the profits going to the Reserve Fund.

14. In introducing the Bill to incorporate the Industrial Development Bank, the Government representative in charge made it clear that the Bank is intended to supplement the activities of existing lending agencies rather than to displace them, and that the Industrial Development Bank was not being set up to finance enterprises which are obviously doomed to end in failure, as, in the opinion of Government, it would not be in the public interest to subsidise uneconomic activities in this concealed manner. It is intended that the Bank will be of particular value to small business which has laboured under a certain handicap in obtaining medium and long-term capital. These small industrial establishments are regarded in Canada as an essential part of the country's economy and an important source of employment and production. The main purpose of establishing the Bank was to fill a gap in the country's financial structure and to ensure that adequate financing was forthcoming for desirable projects which were not in a position to make an issue such as would attract the investing public, or would justify the expenses of making it.

15. In the latest proposals of the Australian Government introduced in Parliament on the 9th March 1945, an Industrial Finance Department of the Commonwealth Bank will be established to provide finance and assistance for the establishment and development of industrial undertakings, particularly small undertakings, and to provide advice on the operations of industrial undertakings with a view to promoting their efficiency. The capital of the Department will be £4 million, consisting of £2 million to be transferred from the Special (gold profit) Reserve in the Note Issue Dept., and £2 million to be transferred from the other assets of the Bank. The General Manager of the Department is to be appointed by the Governor-General. The Bank is empowered to make loans to individuals and to Building Societies for the erection or purchase of homes, or for the discharge of mortgages on homes, at the lowest practicable rates of interest. Loans to individuals will be made on credit-foncier terms for periods of from 5 to 35 years and will be secured by first mortgage on land. The loans must not exceed

85% of the Bank's valuation of the security or £1250, whichever is the less. They will be repayable by monthly or quarterly instalments of principal and interest. Loans to Building Societies in respect of a home on the security of which they have already advanced moneys, must not exceed 90% of the Bank's valuation of that property.

16. To turn now to a non-Empire country in which the progress of industrialization attracted a good deal of the world's attention prior to the outbreak of hostilities, viz., Japan. In Japan there was a very striking growth in industrial output after 1929, which was accompanied by a large diversification of manufacture, reflected in the altered composition of Japan's export trade. The normal course of industrial development was accelerated by the special circumstances of the last decade before the outbreak of hostilities, among them, the world depression being of primary importance. After 1931, the State abandoned the deflationary policy which it had been pursuing and greatly enlarged its expenditure, financed mainly by borrowing, although much of the new expenditure was incurred in connection with re-armament or with development of Manchurian resources. There was also a quickened movement towards State intervention; such intervention had as its primary object in the initial stages the abatement of economic distress, but there was a gradual movement towards a quasi war-time economy. In the summer and autumn of 1937, numerous acts were passed which were aimed at encouraging the expansion of the munitions industries and restraining the development of peace-time trades. One of the most important of these Acts was the Temporary Capital Adjustment Law which was intended to force the country's savings into the heavy industries. Under this law, industrialists had to obtain official permission before they could raise capital for establishing, extending or improving their plants; while at the same time the banks and investment institutions were required to set up machinery for controlling the underwriting of new capital issues. Three classes of trade were distinguished in the administration of this law. The first consisted of the heavy industries and the munitions trade in general. Companies engaged in these industries were free from many previous legal restrictions on the issuing of fresh capital or debentures,

provided official sanction was obtained, and the semi-official Industrial Bank of Japan and the Hypothec Bank of Japan were allowed to increase their loans to such companies beyond the limits set by earlier legislation. Cheap credit from other sources was also made available to these firms. In the second class, industries, stigmatized as "non-essential", such as the textile industries, were practically debarred from raising fresh capital during the emergency period. The third group of industries consisted of those not specified under the first two heads, and applications from them for capital expansions were to be considered on their merits. Centralized control over investment was particularly noticeable in the affairs of the Industrial Bank of Japan, which is a semi-official bank to which the Government has granted special privileges and over which it possesses large powers of supervision. Before the war it had a paid-up capital of 50 million yen, and it was empowered to raise funds, out of which it could make loans to industry, by issuing debentures to an amount equal to ten times its paid-up capital. Shortly after the war began, the Bank was authorized to issue further debentures guaranteed by the State up to 500 million yen, so as to be in a position to extend its advances to the munitions industries. In April 1939, the capital was increased four-fold, i.e., to 2000 million yen, and this carried with it the power of making a corresponding increase in its ordinary debenture issue; while the supplementary issue of officially guaranteed debentures was increased to 1000 million yen. Apparently, the Bank has now become the central financing organ for industry and has a monopoly of war-time industrial financing.

17. Having looked round the world, we are now in a position to review the facilities available from time to time in our own country for industrial finance and the formulation of the State's attitude to such matters. As a starting-off place, we may recall the recent announcement by Government of its industrial policy. In that announcement Government have set out the three-fold fundamental objectives of industrialization as conceived by them and observe that they have decided to take positive steps to encourage and promote the rapid industrialization of the country to the fullest extent possible. This announcement may be regarded as the culmination of a long

period of popular aspiration and authoritative recommendation on the one hand and relative State inaction on the other. Although the Indian Industrial Commission had made recommendations based on the principles that Government must play an active part in the industrial development of the country, by a strange trick of fate, under the changes made in the Indian Constitution in 1921, the main responsibility for the develop ment of industries by the State passed to the Ministers in the Provinces, with their limited resources, which made it impossible for the Governments concerned to give effect to any appreciable extent to the recommendations of the Commission.

18. The Commission recommended, among other things, the adoption of a scheme of industrial banks, and pending the establishment of such banks, the grant, by Government of guarantees of credit, guarantees of dividends, loans, agreements to purchase output, contributions to share capital and facilities for the hire purchase of plant. Financial assistance was given in some provinces before the Reforms, e.g., in the United Provinces. But it was not until the Reforms were introduced that Provincial Governments found themselves in a position to formulate their own policy in the matter. Since then, several Provincial Legislatures have passed Acts regulating the grant of financial assistance to industry, the pioneer in the field being Madras which passed its State Aid to Industries Act in 1923. This was followed by the Punjab Industrial Loans Act, a much less elaborate measure than the Madras Act, and the Bihar & Orissa State Aid to Industries Act. About the time the Central Banking Enquiry Committee was appointed in 1929, bills on similar lines had been prepared in Bengal, the Central Provinces and the United Provinces. In the last named Province, the question of establishing an industrial bank was examined in 1921-22 by a Committee appointed by Government. The Committee decided against the establishment of such a bank, but they were of opinion that the task of supplying small industrialists with capital upon easy terms in approved cases should be undertaken by Government, and recommended the appointment of a Board of Industrial Loan Commissioners who would be responsible for making advances from a sum placed annually at their disposal by Government. The Government established such a Board in 1922, but its functions

were advisory and the responsibility of deciding what loans should be given rested with Government. In addition to loans, grants were also made, the allocation resting with the Board of Industries.

19. The Central Banking Enquiry Committee reviewed the administration of the various State Aids to Industries Acts, and recommended that Provincial legislation on the lines of the Madras Act to provide credit facilities to new and nascent industries, or industries newly introduced into an area, or cottage industries. They also recommended that any Government assistance in regard to provision of capital in such legislation should be given through the Industrial Corporation, if and when one is established in any Province on the lines suggested by them.

20. As a result of the Reforms, the powers of the Central Government to give financial assistance to industrialists were severely limited. The steel industry received bounties to an extent far exceeding the amount given or lent to any industry by all local Governments up to that date, but, apart from the bounties granted in pursuance of a policy of protection, asssistance was given by the Government of India only in one or two special cases. The Calcutta Soap Works were granted in 1923 a loan of Rs. 25,000 in order to enable it to undertake the manufacture of dynamite glycerine; the loan was to be repaid in ten annual instalments. Plant was secured from abroad for the purpose, but, before it was erected, the company became involved in financial difficulties and it went into liquidation in 1927. In 1924, an arrangement was made with a Paper Mill company which, in essence, involved the loan of public money for a limited period. The paper industry was in difficulties at the time, owing partly to foreign competition, and the extent of its claim to protection was under consideration. This loan affords perhaps the only example of a substantial loan to industry (up to Rs. 8 lakhs) which has been repaid on the terms originally arranged, having achieved the purpose in view, but the period of the loan was extremely short and the money was advanced against actual material of an equivalent value.

21. The whole question of State Aid to industries was discussed at the 5th Industries Conference held in Simla in

July 1933, and the Conference came to the conclusion that experience had shown that, except in some Indian States, larger loans had nearly always been unsuccessful but that smaller loans had been successful in probably the majority of the cases. On the whole, there is little indication that industrial development in any Province has been stimulated to any appreciable extent by the grant of State aid. The results have in no way fulfilled expectations; the cause of the failure of the Acts appears to be that in financing the larger enterprises the Government concerned took undue risk, as it was without the means of determining correctly the soundness or otherwise of the enterprise, and was not in a position either to supervise its working or to take charge of it in case of mismanagement. This conclusion is substantiated by the failure of the Carnatic Paper Mills and the Indian Steel Wire Products Ltd., where the Madras and Bihar Governments respectively, invested heavy amounts. Bureaucratic delay and incompetence on the part of the various Boards of Industries must also have contributed to these failures.

22. Only in one Province was an industrial corporation brought into existence on the lines of the recommendation made by the Central Banking Enquiry Commmittee. In July 1938. a corporation with the primary object of giving long-term loans to small industrialists was established in the United Provinces, and a prospectus setting forth the aims and objects of the corporation and inviting applications for shares was issued. Among the provisions was the important power to obtain any provisional order or act of Legislature to facilitate the enforcement of the objects of the corporation, or for effecting any modification in the company's constitution, or for opposing any proceedings that will prejudice, directly or indirectly, the interests of the corporation. Under clause 3(i) of the Memorandum of Association, the corporation has an agreement with the United Provinces Government whereby it is to receive from the Government an amount equal to 4% of the paid up capital, but not exceeding Rs. 60,000, for a period of 15 years, to supplement its profits and enable it to declare a dividend of 4% each year. There are also detailed provisions for a contribution the aggregate of which is not to exceed Rs. 1½ lakhs. In terms of the agreement,

three of the Directors are to be nominees of the Government. Also, the corporation is not at liberty to increase its subscribed and paid-up capital beyond Rs. 15 lakhs or issue debentures or mortgages or to receive deposits for a period of less than three years. The Chairman of the Board is appointed by Government. Of the issued capital of Rs. 15 lakhs, only Rs. 10 lakhs has been subscribed and it appears that the response from the public, despite a guarantee by Government of 4% dividend on shares, was not very satisfactory. The available Balance Sheet and Profit & Loss Account of the Corporation for the year ended March 31, 1941, shows that loans and advances, a major portion of which has been made to small industrial concerns and which have been considered good, amounted to Rs. 4, 86, 000 against a paid-up capital of Rs. 5 lakhs. After deduction of working expenses, there was a net profit of only 1%. It would appear that the Corporation exists mainly on Government subsidies for the fulfilment of its requirements in regard to the declaration of divident and transfers to the Reserve Fund and the progress achieved up-to date is far from satisfactory. The Corporation has recently been authorised to receive long-term deposits for over three years, and if from this source additional funds are received, it may have some scope for the development of its activities.

23. The Central Banking Enquiry Committee reviewed exhaustively the whole position in regard to the financial requirements of industries, apart from State-aid; and recorded that a considerable amount of feeling existed among the intelligentsia of India that the State and particularly the Central Government, was not taking as much interest as it ought to in the development of India's industries. They referred, in particular, to the failure of the Central Government to take action on the recommendation of the Industrial Commission suggesting the appointment at the earliest possible date of an expert committee to examine the possibilities of establishing industrial banks in India. They pointed out how although since the outbreak of the Great War there had been a marked increase in the amount of Indian capital invested in Indian industries a not inconsiderable amount of capital invested in Indian industries still remains non-Indian, with consequent vesting of control and management in the case of some of the important

industries in the hands of non-Indian firms. They contrasted this state of affairs with that existing in certain other countries, like the U.S.A. and Japan, where the State actively intervened in the development of the national industry, particularly in the field of provision of long-term finance. They also referred to instances of special financial assistance to industry even in Great Britain with its tradition of laissez-faire, as, for instance, the raising of aggregate loans between 1921-27 of more than £74 million under the Trade Facilities Acts for approved purposes on behalf of private concerns with the guarantee of the Government, such guarantee being given free of any charge, In regard to major industries, they noticed various handicaps, such as unavailability of finance for block capital from banks or from the public. They referred to the system under which a great deal of the capital required by the cotton mills in the Bombay Presidency was obtained direct by means of deposits from the public, but suggested that this system of finance was like a fair-weather friend, since when times are bad these deposits are liable to be withdrawn from good as well as bad concerns, thereby aggravating the position at a time when all resources are required to carry over what may be only a temporary period of depression. In regard to public investment for industrial development, they referred to the absence of any recognized method in India by which the general public can obtain advice and assistance, the Stock Exchanges functioning only in the large sea-ports and an upcountry investor having little chance of getting in touch with any reliable or recognized member of these Exchanges. They also referred to the reluctance of institutional investors to invest their surplus funds to any significant extent in debentures of first-class concerns. Finally, they referred to the managing agency system and stated that although it was reported to have done a great deal for industrial development of Bombay, it had many serious drawbacks such as a tendency on the part of the agents to trade and speculate and the resulting weakness in their position to react on the financial position of the concern managed by them. They were of opinion that attempts should be made to make industrial enterprises in India less dependent on the managing agency system for future development.

24. After a careful and comprehensive review of the whole

position, the Committee made certain recommendations. They accepted the basic principle that generally speaking, initial block capital for industrial enterprises should be put up by private or public subscription and not by commercial banks, but that block capital for subsequent improvements and extensions as is not provided out of undivided profits, could be supplied, temporarily on adequate security by these banks pending the increase of share capital or the issue of debentures. They proceeded to observe, however, that this new class of business required large experience and an established policy of sound banking and could only be attempted by leading banks in a strong position. It is possible that the experience gained in other countries during the depression, had it been available to the Committee before their recommendations were made, might have made a difference. The German banking policy, which seems to have impressed the Committee deeply, was proved by experience to have been faulty, and there is little controversy now in regard to the soundness of the general opinion prevalent all over the world, with minor exceptions, against "mixed banking." Apart from the role assigned by the Committee to the banks, they came to the conclusion that, as to a very large extent initial capital for promotion of industries must come from private investment, and since the existing facilities in India were inadequate, special institutions were required. On the assumption that the development of industries within their territories will continue to be the functions of the Provincial Governments under the Constitution which was then under revision, they recommended that Provincial industrial corporations should be established, with capital initially or permanently supplied by Provincial Governments. Following the Indian Industrial Commission they held that the advisability of giving assistance in any particular case through such corporation should depend on the extent to which the enterprise will be of benefit to the public, and will add to the productive power of the Province and provide employment for its people, and not merely on its probable advantage to the promoters of the industry. They realized that there were, and would be, certain industries, mostly of a national or important character, the development of which would fall within the functions of the Federal or the Central Government and that, in any case, an all-India Corporation might be required for the purpose of securing proper liaison between the Centre and the Provinces in the matter of finance. They thought that there would be cases in which the vehicle of giving financial aid to industries should preferably be an all-India Industrial Corporation, and they did not rule out the formation of such an institution, although they did not recommend its immediate establishment.

25. On a tentative consideration of the question of the machinery of industrial finance in this country, it would appear that the present stage of development of the ordinary commercial bank in India does not warrant its undertaking a substantial interest in the long-term financing of industries, alike in view of the character of its resources and the lack of knowledge on the part of the ordinary bank management of the problems and prospects of industrial investments. Where and when (1) the prospects and profitability of industries are relatively more assured, (2) the position of the banks becomes more impregnable, and (3) the knowledge on the part of bankers of the profitability of industrial propositions is more sound, it may be possible for ordinary commercial banks to venture into a limited partnership with industry by supplying a part of its capital requirements and having a share in its management. Until these conditions are fulfilled, however, experiments in the direction of "mixed banking" would seem premature and likely to do more harm than good to the cause of development of banking and industry. Until then, a special type of institution deriving its resources from long-term deposits and debentures and share capital, participated in by the state, if necessary, would appear to be a more suitable agency for the supply of industrial finance.

26. The case for an all-India institution would appear to have been reinforced by the latest announcement of Government's industrial policy. In the pattern of economic planning foreshadowed by that announcement, there would be need of some institution to finance industries which would be the concern of the Central Government. An examination of the models available elsewhere would seem to indicate that it would be wise policy to restrict financing by such an institution to only those concerns which are run by private enterprise,

and that if any kind of central corporation is necessary for canalising the finance on behalf of Central or Provincial Governments for State-owned or State-managed enterprises, it should be entirely separate and financed entirely by capital provided by the State.

27. The development of industries except of industries "where development under federal control is declared by federal law to be expedient in the public interest" is at present a subject under the Provincial Legislative List, and it appears reasonable to expect that the care and development, at any rate, of small-scale and certain medium-type industries will remain the concern of the federal units under any likely constitutional arrangements. The State Aid to Industries Acts in the various Provinces have provided some needed financial assistance to industries but their working has suffered from the inelasticity of official procedure and possible lack of sound business knowledge of officials; the formation of Provincial industrial credit corporations, participated in by the public as far as possible, and with the requisite Government guarantee of dividend and interest on share and loan capital or other necessary support would, therefore, still remain a desideratum. There will, nevertheless, remain the large sphere of large-scale industries with inter-provincial ramifications and having all-India importance the requirements of which for long-term capital over and above what could be supplied through the ordinary investment channels, will be considerable under the tempo of a development plan, and indeed far wider than could have been envisaged 15 years ago by the Central Banking Enquiry Committee. It is here that some form of an all-India industrial finance institution possibly with a few branches so as to have an office each in the main industrial zones of India and participated in by the Government, the Reserve Bank and perhaps an element of institutional and other private capital, under suitable partnership arrangements, may fill the gap.

28. Apart from the question of the form of any special institution that may be regarded as necessary for industrial finance, a fundamental approach to the whole question is called for. The cultivation through modern organized financial channels of the new and unfamiliar field of real industrial capital requirements will, however, not be free from serious initial

handicaps and will call for a high degree of perspicacity, financial acumen, diligent investigation and assiduous study of the technical and business aspects of industries by a new race of industrial bankers. There is need for closer knowledge of the prospects of industrial projects and propositions on the part of men of finance who must apply their minds more and more to a closer study of the means of fruitful association of finance and industry, if finance is to yield greater profits, or if, in the language of the economist, the marginal productivity of capital is to be increased or maintained. The whole question of State financial assistance to industry is also full of pitfalls, and particular attention must be given to the establishment of the conditions necessary for the successful development of industries receiving assistance in the way of grants and loans. Unless industry is placed on a profitable footing and is assured of an environment favourable to growth, no solution of its difficulties on the financial plane can ensure successful results in working. If the other conditions of successful industrial development are fulfilled, the problem of financial aid is rendered considerably easier of solution. It is possible that, under certain conditions, what industry lacks and requires is not finance so much as technical knowledge and inventive ability, business or commercial intelligence and financial guidance and encouragement through temporary fiscal protection or other means. These would appear, by and large, to be the major desiderata of sound industrial development in the country. In any case, the problem of industrial finance must be viewed in its proper perspective as part of the wider problem of the economics of industry in the country and the role of the State in industrial development : Encouragement through providing, or providing machinery for, financial assistance, long-term or short-term, is only one of the ways of fostering industrial development and may be more or less important according to conditions in respect of different industries or types of industries. There is ample scope in the India of the future for the best in private enterprise combined with the best in State encouragement, direction or activity.

PURCHASING AND MATERIALS MANAGEMENT

Address on Purchasing in Industry at the Inauguration of the National Association of Purchasing Executives, Bombay on July 15, 1961

I am very appreciative of the honour that the National Association of Purchasing Executives, Bombay, have done me by inviting me to inaugurate their newly-formed organization. In the letter of invitation Dr. Vakil, the President, was good enough to say that you have been influenced in this decision by the awareness of my keen interest in the purchasing activities of Indian industry. In a sense it is perhaps correct to say that I have started taking an interest in all matters connected with the purchase of industrial materials, but this has been very largely due to my contacts, which now extend over more than a decade, with Mr. A. R. Palit, the Editor of the Eastern Purchasing Journal, New Delhi, who formerly used to be the Head of the India Supply Mission in the U.S.A., in which capacity I first came into contact with him. Having been connected with economic and monetary developments in the country for over 20 years now, I have had occasions to pay attention to many aspects of industrial activities, but I must confess that my awareness of the importance of purchasing amongst these is a fairly recent one. Nevertheless, I do now feel that it is a very important activity and it was because of this that I took the opportunity of drawing attention to this aspect at an address that I delivered a few months ago at the last annual meeting of the Bombay Management Association, under the Presidentship of Shri N. Dandekar.

It is in the fitness of things that there should have been a very noticeable widening of the horizons of responsible people at different levels in the public or private sector in regard to many formerly neglected aspects of industrial activity. The last 12 years have indeed witnessed very noticeable intensification of professional interest in different important aspects, such as standards, statistical quality control, production engineering, time and motion studies and industrial psychology, and I suppose all these are legitimately within the province of bodies such as the National Productivity Council. In this context, I should like to take the opportunity of paying a tribute to the very valuable work that is being done by the Indian Standards Institution under the dynamic direction of Dr. Lal C. Verman. Indeed, it was under the joint auspices of the Indian Standards Institution and the Indian Statistical Institute, of which Prof. Mahalanobis is the creator as well as the Director and I have been the President for the last 15 years or so, that the first attempt was made to interest Indian industry in statistical quality control by inviting Dr. Walter Shewhart, the Father of Statistical Quality Control, to come to India to educate us in the matter. Although Dr. Shewhart lectured in most important industrial centres during a period of over two months and an association for the promotion of statistical quality control was formed in Calcutta as a result of his visit, it took some time before this aspect of the economics of industry began to attract attention in the quarters that mattered. Today I am happy to say, in my capacity as Chairman of the Advisory Committee on Statistical Quality Control, that this particular branch of critical examination of industrial activity has taken root in the country and there are active semi-official units or private practitioners carrying on both promotional and advisory work in most of the important industrial cities of India, particularly, Bombay, Calcutta, Bangalore, Coimbatore and Kanpur. Other aspects like time and motion studies and production engineering have also been receiving attention, and now that there is a National Productivity Council to take note of all relevant and related aspects I have no doubt that everything that is of importance from the point of view of economic production and energetic sale of industrial products will receive intensive attention. It is in this context that I welcome the emergence of an organization like the one I am inaugurating this morning, viz., the National Association of Purchasing Executives, Bombay.

I notice that there are also similar organizations springing up in other industrial centres and the time will perhaps not be distant when one of these, perhaps yours, will expand, or they will all be federated, to form an all-India organization.

It is symbolic of this fast-growing interest in all that is connected with purchasing of materials and equipment for industry that there should be a series of seminars on the subject as well as dissemination of all relevant information in regard to purchasing activities through estimate journals like the Eastern Purchasing Journal. I have received copies of the volumes produced so far of this journal, two in number, and I notice that already scores of important aspects of purchasing have been the subject of articles written by competent experts concerning both the principles as well as the practice of purchasing. The first volume, to take a few random examples, published articles on 'Bulk Purchasing of Imported Raw Materials', 'Central Purchase and Indigenous Development', 'Cost Production through Value Analysis', 'Essential Requirements of a Sound Purchase Organization', 'Management of Purchase Functions', 'Market Research for Purchasing', Purchase for the Public Sector', 'Purchasing and Materials Management in Japan', 'Standards Guide Purchasing, etc.', in addition to specific studies of purchases for a number of industries in a number of countries. Volume 2 also carries many valuable articles on subjects like 'Central Purchases during the Third Five Year Plan Period', 'Purchasing and Value Analysis' (by your President), 'Some Thoughts on Inventory Control in Industry', 'Stock Controls, Stores Accounting and Provision Review', in addition to giving information about a seminar on purchasing or activities of the National Association of Purchasing Executives. I have referred to these matters, which must be very well known to you as well as to both purchasers and suppliers generally in the industrial world, to disavow any intention to attempt to add to your already extensive knowledge of the subject as well as to draw the attention of the public to these significant developments.

It is hardly necessary for me to refer to some of the basic facts of the situation, such as that out of the total investment of some Rs. 10,500 crores in the Third Five Year Plan creation of physical assets like buildings, plant, equipment, etc., materials and equipment will account for Rs. 5,000 crores' and even if, as your own letter of invitation to me pointed out, a five per cent reduction of purchase cost is set up as a modest goal for efficient purchasing it would mean in this context a saving of Rs. 250 crores. Since inefficient purchasing could, on the other hand, lead to a waste of an almost equal sum, as you yourself point out, the difference between efficient and inefficient handling of purchasing can easily be more than Rs. 500 crores. You recognize that the purchase of raw materials, equipment, machinery, spares and accessories, either local or from foreign countries, could involve serious loss of funds, especially foreign exchange, unless people with the right type of experience, qualifications and character are engaged in this activity and are not only adequately equipped for the task but are also endowed with the proper sense of commercial morality and are given appropriately high status.

In this context, I take the liberaty of quoting from a brief attached to an invitation which I received from the United States of America Technical Co-operation Mission to India to participate in a Workshop due to be organized in association with the All-India Management Association and the Delhi Management Association on Industrial Purchasing and Materials Management in New Delhi, on September 8 and 9, 1961, an invitation which unfortunately I could not accept as I have planned to be abroad during the period. The brief points out how greater efficiency in purchasing and materials management in the public and private sectors could help reduce the total cost on materials and equipment by Rs. 500 crores, in addition to saving substantial foreign exchange and giving an impetus to exports by reducing prices and improving quality. The average of material costs for all industries in Japan and India is about 60% of the production cost as against 58.9% in the U.S.A. The brief quotes Heinritz, a recognized authority on purchasing, as follows: "Purchasing and materials management are increasingly recognized as an integral and important part of industrial policy and operations. Together they constitute the latest, and possibly the last frontier on which management can seek any considerable cost-reductions". The brief points out how industrial purchasing, stores-inventory-control and materials management in India need modernization in the public and private sectors and asserts that the principal responsibility lies with the top management. It points out how the emphasis has shifted from bargaining to value analysis, market research for purchasing, rationalized store-keeping and selective inventory management, linear programming, etc. The following are regarded as desiderata to be worked for actively, viz., (1) rapid modernization of Purchasing and Materials Management function in the public and private sectors; (2) conducting and co-ordinating research on materials economy and value-analysis on a national basis, and (3) arranging instructional courses on modern methods of Purchasing and Materials Management for senior and junior personnel. There are two interesting notes given below the brief. One of these informs us that simplification alone can pay dividends. For instance, in the case of metal widths U. K. reduced 73 widths to 6; in the case of grinding wheels U.S.A. reduced 715,200 sizes and types to 254,200; and in the case of tacks and nails the U.S.A. reduced 421 sizes to 182 sizes.

In this context, every competent authority on the subject attaches the greatest importance to value-analysis which, according to the other note, has been known to reduce materials costs by 70% to 90% in many instances, 40% being quite common.

As Dr. Lal C. Verman has succintly pointed out in his article 'Role of the Indian Standards Institution' in volume 2 of the Eastern Purchasing Journal, the objective of Value-Analysis is to promote the use of cheaper or more readily available materials for a given purpose or end use. The concept, as another article points out, involves the asking of the following questions, viz., (1) on analysis of the construction or design of material being purchased, is it established that all the features are needed or whether simplification can be introduced ? (2) does its use constitute value, that is to say, can it be dispensed with or is its value proportionate to its cost ? (3) an analysis of the manufacturing processes of the supplier, is it found that an equally good product can be made by a cheaper method ? and (4) on analysis of the market, is it found that something cheaper and equally good is available in the market, particularly in relation to what is known of the materials used and the payments made by competitors in the industry ? The article goes on to indicate the precautions to be taken in the practice of value-analysis, viz., (1) substitution of purchasing as a service by purchasing for profits; (2) conferring on the Purchasing Officer a status befitting the importance of the job he does, and (3) appreciation by the top management of the value-analysis and co-ordination by it of the activities of the various departments in the exercise of value-analysis. It also points out how the Purchasing Officer has helped to achieve economies to compensate for the increase in the cost of certain indigenous materials which had to be used on account of import restrictions.

The last point concerning the duties of the top-management is very important. No longer is it enough or safe for the boss, however hard-bitten, to take upon himself the sole responsibility of purchase of the important raw material, e.g. cotton for textile mills. His supervision on expert purchasing organization, assisted by intelligent analysis of value, will yield far more worthwhile results.

I have quoted heavily from the journal in order to draw attention to what one might call the vast ramifications of purchasing activities. Indeed, in a larger sense purchasing is connected with the working of the whole economic machinery of a nation, affecting and being in turn affected by important economic decisions in connection with the control of imports, the promotion of exports and the conservation of foreign exchange. It should not be a matter for surprise that this is so, as conditions in the world are never static and the continuous application of the advances in science and technology that are taking place with such breath-taking rapidity constantly poses problems for and demand readjustment on the part of all connected with the purchase and supply of industrial raw materials.

It is worthwhile bearing in mind the truism that every purchase has a corresponding source of supply, as also that the competitive efficiency of purchasing organizations in their own fields necessarily implies the creation of fresh problems for suppliers, that it has an inevitable reaction on the scope of operations of purchase organizations themselves. For instance, it is well-known that gunnies or jute bags have long been threatened by paper bags or specially-made cloth bags, as well as by changed methods of transport or changed specifications of transport vehicles. The success of the purchasing organization in the sugar industry, for instance, substituting cotton bags for jute bags must mean either a contraction of possible markets or a great deal of rethinking on the part of the suppliers of jute bags. Again, only the other day Shri Manubhai Shah, the Minister for Industry, expressed the hope that India would as rapidly as possible become self-sufficient in the matter of non-ferrous metals, either by increasing its own indigenous production of these materials, or, more probably, by switch-over from one specification to another, an example being increased use of aluminium, say, in place of copper. Here again, the success of our manufacturers and our purchasing organizations must mean a temporary set back or dislocation to the usual suppliers of non-ferrous metals. But this ding-dong struggle is the price that has to be paid for modernization in industry. Many synthetic substitutes are now being manufactured in place of traditional industrial materials in Europe and the U.S.A. holding serious threats to the prosperity of the producers of these traditional materials, for instance, rubber. Even in the case of metals many a synthetic product is being used on an increasing scale and that indeed is a marked feature of the overall world trade situation, in which whilst the trade of industrially advanced countries has increased, proportionate advantages have not been reaped by the suppliers of traditional industrial materials in South and South-East Asia.

I think I have said enough to give at least to lay people some idea of the importance of the activities which your Association is going to undertake. I notice that the objectives set out in the Memorandum are broad enough, comprising as they do the following :

(a) To foster and promote interchange of ideas and co-operation among its members by co-operative professional efforts with all its policies and activities designed for the advancement of purchasing and purchasing executives and devoted to the principles of—

  (i) Loyalty to his Company
  (ii) Justice to those with whom he deals
  (iii) Faith in his profession.

(b) To evolve a code of conduct and purchasing ethics.

(c) To develop and apply more efficient purchasing methods and techniques and stimulate among the members of the Association thought and efforts towards the development and elevation of the purchasing function in the country and to collect and to disseminate information of benefits to its members regarding marketing, producing and manufacturing practices, various products and their uses and sources of supply and distribution by organizing lectures, conferences, roundtables, seminars, demonstrations, exhibitions, visits and provide library facilities to its members.

(d) To formulate a curriculum of study and training and to sponsor examinations or otherwise determine the competence and to award certificates and diplomas and distinctions with a view to attain the professional calibre of persons engaged in purchasing or persons aspiring to make purchasing their career.

(e) To maintain constructive liaison with all organizations interested in purchasing management in India and abroad for the benefit of the members of the Association.

(f) To strive for a wider recognition of the importance of the efficient purchasing in industry and to elevate the professional status of the purchasing executives, and to bring into association friendly relationship of those engaged in purchasing or allied function for industrial firms or companies or public undertakings.

(g) To publish or sponsor any periodicals, books, pamphlets, news bulletin, etc., that the Association may think desirable for the promotion of its objectives.

(h) To do all such other things as may be necessary for or incidental or conducive to the attainments of the above objectives or any of them.

The broad angle of just relations and ethical conduct commends itself particularly to me. It is no secret that malpractices abound in the field of purchasing, for which the consumer pays in high prices and the country pays in stagnant or uneconomic exports. Of course, sometimes public policy helps to keep our exports out of the markets of the world, e.g. overhigh cane prices in the case of sugar.

I have no doubt that if your Association succeeds in keeping these objectives steadily in view and in conducting the activities of the Association so as substantially to fulfil them, it will be rendering an invaluable service to the nation. In inaugurating your Association it is my hope that it may be successful in the sense I have just mentioned and occupy a prominent place in the gallaxy of industrial organizations in the country.

With these words I have great pleasure in inaugurating the National Association of Purchasing Executives, Bombay.

OXFORD CONFERENCE ON TENSIONS IN DEVELOPMENT

Factors in tensions on economic and social development urgently in need of examination by western countries as well as the developing areas, including a critique of technical and economic aid in the past.

Theme of the Conference

The participants in this conference have been informed that the object of the conference is to improve communications among countries in different stages of development, so that they may recognize that development is a co-operative partnership. The representatives of the developing countries will be invited to express their views on how this partnership has worked (or failed) in the past, and how to make it work better in the future; in particular how aid programmes have appeared to them, and what changes they would like to see made to reduce tensions which can arise from the 'donor-recipient' relationship. The hope is expressed that the channels of communication and co-operation will remain even after the conference is over, and that the developing countries may hold similar conferences in their own countries on which they will act as hosts to people from the other countries.

Main Topics

Three main topics will be discussed :—(1) Economic—how the development partnership referred to above can help economic growth, and what action is necessary by both partners in the organization of aid. (2) Education—this topic will include the problems of communicating know-how in administration, industry, commerce and agriculture. (3) Political—the problems and tensions involved in adapting democratic institutions and procedures while accelerating economic and social development.

What exactly are tensions ?

A great deal of light has been thrown on the meaning of 'tensions' by the papers prepared for and the discussion held at the Seminar on Tensions of Economic Development in South-East Asia, held in March last under the joint sponsorship of the University of Bombay and the Council on World Tensions, over which I had the privilege of presiding. I assume that copies of the report on that seminar will be made available to the participants in the present conference. A copy is appended to this paper. A glance at this paper will show that throughout the words 'tensions' and 'problems' have been used as if they were synonymous. In my opinion this is correct. Any fine distinction between tensions and problems of development is likely to confuse the issue, and possibly circumscribe unnecessarily the range of the discussions. Indeed, I wish that the use of this somewhat specialized word 'tension' could have been avoided, since the participants in this conference will be academic, administrative or political leaders and not professional psychologists. A psychologist would define 'tensions' as undesirable strains and stresses in human relations, but so defined tensions might appear to psychologists to be only natural and normal mechanisms for the fulfilment of needs in some respects, although in certain other respects or conditions, like lack of past experience, lack of skill, absence of constructive goals, presence of destructive goals or frustrating conditions in the environment, tensions might be converted into problems. Psychologists hold that in man's behaviour 'tensions act as built-in realizing devices to achieve a certain goal, to satisfy a certain need, for reducing the intensity of a certain drive'. Tensions may exist in the individual as well as in groups. In the individual they may be caused by the need to adapt oneself if one's striving for a certain goal is blocked by obstacles. It is only failure that could in such a situation lead to frustration. As tensions appear in social situations the question of rewards and punishments becomes important. If group standards are healthy and democratic the individual working in such groups may also function with a minimum of normal and adaptive tensions. In dealing with tension systems in groups the factors that have to be borne in mind are the different degrees of cohesiveness of the group, their communication facilities, the structure of the group and the position of members within the group and the attitudes of the group as a whole to forces of change and many oher factors. Where there is a wide disparity between the forces of inertia in a group and the forces of change operating from outside tensions might indeed become torsions. In such situations group discussions and participation in analysing the need of change could be found to be effective, according to one psychologist's analysis. This indicates the need for decentralization, inducing voluntary co-operation or even enthusiasm. However, as has been observed before, the purposes of this conference would be best served if tensions are interpreted generally in the broader sense of problems so that they may be more amenable to fruitful discussion by the non-specialists.

Current Extent of Co-operation in Development

It was not so very long ago that attention to the problems of under-developed countries was conspicuous by its absence on the part of the economists, administrators and politicians of the advanced countries. But the last decade has witnessed a most remarkable change for the better in this respect, a change the pace of which has within the last three or four years increased so much that despite the best will in the world it has now become almost impossible to keep abreast of all the co-operative discussions and practices that have been instituted amongst nations either bilaterally or multilaterally. Apart from the vast poliferation that has occurred in regard to the establishment of international institutions to help in the process of the economic or social development of developing countries, the number of seminars or conferences is now legion and a very large number of organizations for economic co-operation amongst nations promoted by private enterprise has also sprung up. An instance in point is the Afro-Asian Organization for Economic Co-operation, of which the members are the various chambers of commerce, which has already an impressive out-turn of work to its credit in the form of discussions and documentation. I have before me copies of annual reports of well-known and well-established international bodies such as the International Bank for Reconstruction and Development and the International Monetary Fund. Then there are the excellent reports published by the various United Nations Commissions for the different regions of the world, such as Far East, European countries, Africa and Latin America. Amongst the most notable and promising of more specialized efforts are the meetings of distinguished economists, such as the International Non-Governmental Conference on Economic Advancement of Under-Developed Countries, preliminary meeting, to be held in Geneva between the 6th and 10th June, 1961. The purpose of this preliminary meeting, which will have been held by the time the Oxford seminar is due, is to explore whether it may be useful to convene a larger international conference on economic development at a later date. Some of the papers prepared for this conference have been seen by me in my capacity as the President of the Indian Statistical Institute, Calcutta-New Delhi, which is providing the secretariat for this conference, and whose director, Prof. P. C. Mahalanobis, will have attended the preliminary meeting at Geneva. I find that the experts will have addressed themselves principally to the questions of what are the high priority issues in development policy today. I hope to be able to send a statement containing the gist of these discussions as a second appendix to this paper.

Three reports seem to me in the present context to call for special attention, viz., (1) fifteenth annual report of the International Bank for Reconstruction and Development, 1959-60, (2) annual report for 1960 of the International Monetary Fund, and (3) the ninth annual report (1960) of the Consultative Committee of the Colombo Plan for South and South-East Asia. The last mentioned report has in chapter 2 entitled 'the tasks ahead' drawn attention to some important desiderata of development emerging from a review of the progress achieved during the ten years of the existence of the Colombo Plan which are in my opinion important enough to deserve a somewhat extensive quotation. The following are the main conclusions set out in this review :—

(i) Whilst intensive efforts have been made and significant progress has been achieved and there is awareness of conscious efforts towards more economic development, in spite of some increase in gross national product and some rise in income levels, the *per capita* income ranges in the countries of south and south-east Asia remain distressingly low.

(ii) A particularly disturbing situation exists in regard to the trade of this region which lags behind the growth of world trade, leading thereby to a continued pressure on their balance of payments.

(iii) There are wide areas in which the techniques are inefficient and the numbers of trained people in administration, management and production are inadequate. The situation in regard to the shortage of food is still such as to cause anxiety, largely as a result of these factors.

(iv) Such problems as the need to stimulate investment capital, increase exports and mobilize domestic resources remain insistent, i.e., largely unresolved.

(v) There is greater need for wise and efficient use of available resources, including individual energies and initiatives, willingness to change outmoded traditions while preserving human dignity, and willingness to have and invest, these being some of the fundamental determinants of the course of progress.

(vi) Whilst many of the countries of the region are making systematic and determined efforts to attain a future in which sound economic growth and rising living standards are not dependent on extraordinary external assistance, success is yet not perceptible.

(vii) There are no short-cuts to success in the task of raising the tempo of economic growth and stimulating the various centres of economies so that the same growth may continue. The tasks ahead call for such difficult attainments as financial stability and physical and monetary discipline, so that savings could be maximised and resources mobilized for development.

(viii) In most of the countries of the region there is still an unfinished task of containing inflationary pressures and avoiding disruptive changes in the volume of money.

(ix) There are patent difficulties in maintaining in this region rates of economic growth greater than the rates of population increases and, in consequence, of keeping employment opportunities abreast of rises in labour force.

(x) Accordingly, measures of the utmost urgency are

needed to slow down the rate of population growth, although the basic need continues to be a stimulation of investment and the rising of production volumes.

(xi) In spite of a greater awareness of the significance of external resources for enabling the developing countries to gather the necessary momentum towards a self-sustaining economy, the spread and volume of foreign aid needs to be more extensive, and there is always the room for evolving new techniques in the allocation and administration of such aid.

(xii) The sharp movements in the prices of primary products , often to the disadvantage of the countries in this region, which are largely dependent on their earnings from them, lead to wide fluctuations in their foreign exchange earnings. Whilst the need for the diversification of their production as well as of increasing their export of the existing commodities and developing production for export is recognized in the developed countries, political pressures lead to the creation of artificial impediments in the way of the freest possible flow of world trade, which impediments call for urgent elimination.

(xiii) Whilst the problems of attracting foreign capital are better understood and national policies and practices are more in line with creating reasonable inducements for foreign capital to come in, there is yet insufficient recognition of the truth of the proposition that if foreign capital is to be used fruitfully the recipient country must make every effort to generate savings systematically to reduce its dependence on Government-to-Government measures and devise ways of attracting capital both from public and private sources by generating increasing confidence in its political and economic management.

Political Factors

Sometime towards the beginning of February last and a couple of months before the Bombay seminar, a seminar on 'South and South-East Asia has a Second Look at Democracy' was held (over which also I was privileged to preside), under the joint auspices of the Congress for Cultural Freedom and the Indian Institute of Public Administration. This was one of the most fruitful seminars that could have been held at this juncture and the calibre of the participants from the various countries of the region was exceedingly high, with the result that a great deal of light was thrown on the problems and tensions involved in adapting democratic institutions and procedures in the countries of this region, especially in connection with accelerating economic and social development. An especially wise decision in deciding on the participation of people in the seminar was that each country should be represented by two leaders, one representing the Government in power and the other the Party in opposition. There was in consequence a remarkably fair, free and full exchange of views, without rancour of any kind, and I wish that the proceedings of this seminar had been available to the participants in this conference. It is impossible to compress in a few statements the outcome of the deliberations of this seminar and one can only state impressions.

The general impression was that there was a deep-seated urge for democratic life in south and south-east Asia, a pressing quest for appropriate institutional expressions, together with a subdued optimism that a viable form of democracy will emerge out of the passing reverses, retrospects and preparatory experimentation, even as was the case in an earlier period of history in western Europe. This thought was a corrective to the impression that it is only in Asia that democracy has faltered and even passed out in its nascent stage. The more sophisticated observers from the West pointed out, however, that in Asia there is an almost jejune tendency to idealize democracy or wax romantic over it. The discussions often-ranged round the search for the centres of power in a democratic society or the degree of involvement in the practice of democracy by the majority of the populace. The struggle for freedom and the manner of the advent of democracy were recognized as a patent factor in conditioning leadership or attracting non-democratic forces on the failure of imperfect leadership. For such failures the usual causes were non-oriented administrative services, non-professional or jingoistic defence forces and the lack of capacity to govern soldiers turned politicians. On the other hand, there was a conflict of views in regard to the place and performance of intellectuals in politics. The tendency to abuse public funds for perpetuating political power or to draw heavily for electioneering resources on business or trade unions was stated to be a fairly common feature of democracies in Asia—where they are still working. In these countries a growing toleration of the opposition was recognized as a good augury for the health of the democracy concerned. How with determination public administration can be cleansed within a very short space of time was the lesson of a non-democratic set-up in one important country where only a sort of basic democracy is at present practised. But perhaps the most imminent danger to democracy was felt to be lack of urgency and speed in the process of economic development, or the lack of total involvement of the population at large in the process of such development, and in this context I had myself pointed to the desirability of a national government in India as demanded by the imperatives of rapid economic development.

It was left to an acute and trained outside observer to draw attention to democracy being not only a way of life but also a complex of appropriate institutions, adaptable to changing social and economic environments. Leaders, for instance, politicians, civil servants and intellectuals, were important, but by themselves they do not make up democracy; the people, particularly the peasants, matter, and so do their aspirations. But views and attitudes are not constant and that is where influencing of public opinion by those capable of doing so has its importance.

Where then there is at present an eclipse of democracy in Asia it may be regarded as temporary and one may justifiably hold that the general will is bound finally to assert itself in the establishment of a workable form of democracy. Where economic development has reached a fairly advanced stage and has yet a large and steady potential, as in Japan, the future of democracy seems assured. It also seems assured where the people are under a steady democratic influence as in the Philippines, although there much dross of partisan political practice yet needs to be refined. The testimony from prosperous Singapore was also very encouraging. In Burma out of the long ordeal of disorders the polity seems at last to have emerged into a stable democratic political order, two notable features of which are (1) self-denial on the part of the politicians in power and (2) respect for the opposition, together with (3) determined effort on the part of both to eschew non-constitutional means in gaining their ends. In Ceylon the situation is more fluid, but the impression left on our minds by the contribution of their representative was of a steady under-current of genuine democratic sentiment. In this context, the smallness of a country has an obvious advantage, and it should not be a matter for surprise if ultimately democracy struck roots in Thailand also for that reason. In North Vietnam democracy has already made way for a totalitarian system whilst in South Vietnam things would still seem to be uneasily balanced between dictatorship and democracy. But the big issue is what the future of democracy is in the more populace countries of Asia, viz., Indonesia, Pakistan and India. It appeared to me from the observations of the representative from Pakistan that there is a prospect of a return of democracy from the present basic democracy, although this is somewhat overloaded at present with nomination by the State. On the other hand, it is not clear if the guided democracy of Indonesia will lead within a measurable period of time to the return to more standard forms of democracy. In regard to India observers of all shades of political opinion seem to feel that the existing functioning, but not perfect, parliamentary democracy will gradually improve in its practice, particularly as a result of prudently supervised democratic decentralization. However, it would be rash to indulge in prognostications in matters of this kind where the course of history is often influenced by powerful individuals or their absence. Already in India positions are being taken up by the various parties against the possibility of the break up of the existing ruling party, and in the short term perspective there might be a severe struggle for power-which might interfere with the smooth implementation of plans for economic and social development.

There was no lack during the discussions of statements of the basic essentials or stigmata of democracy, viz., fundamental human rights, as for instance equality of status and opportunity, the dignity of the individual, the vesting of ultimate sovereignty in the people *via* universal suffrage and representation leading to participation of the people in governmental activity, opportunity for free expression of opinion, freedom of association, the unquestioning rule of law and the potency of the constitutional processes, minimum social and economic well-being, conscious training in citizenship and leadership, an effective opposition, social cohesion, appropriate institutional framework, etc. An examination of the actual situation led to the uncovering of the lack of some of these conditions owing tto backwardness as the cause of the eclipse of democracy.

It seems to me that Asian countries have historical economic and sociological handicaps in the establishment of a democracy. The old feudal or colonial regimes were destructive of the dignity of the individual, whilst they made no efforts to raise it by education. The citizen is therefore uninformed and in a poor state of readiness to exercise the franchise and hence his sovereignty. Often there is not a large informed middle-class to imbibe enlightened views and influence others. Moreover, whatever independence of opinion there is can soon be overwhelmed by pelf in an environment of near-destitution for the bulk of the population. The few that climb to leadership lack the ordinary correctives and learn to serve themselves rather than the people. In the economic field, moreover, the countries of Asia have to achieve industrialization, so to speak, with their hands tied behind their backs, on account of extensive labour legislation, whereas nearly all the western countries completed their industrialization unencumbered by strict labour laws and often unhindered by considerations of international ethics.

I am one of those who hold that the Communist remedy to a situation of this kind amounts to throwing the baby out with the bathwater. I believe that there would have to be a series of relapses before reforms can be firmly established and these relapses could perhaps be minimized if resources from outside helped in economic development.

Whether all developing societies can successfully, or tolerably successfully, practice democracy is a large question. Current instances seem to indicate the necessity for some sort of international and supra-national supervision of the preparatory or probationary stages. Local leadership alone may be too narrow-based to lead a people to the right practice of democracy. *A fortiorai* reversion to a feudal order or slipping through a coup-de-tat to a dictatorship is probably the wrong turning for reaching democracy.

Systematic authoritarianism, wh ch seems to ensure the elimination of personal gain by those in political power, has many striking and impressive achievements to its credit, but I do not believe that it could be the subject of democratic evolution. In other words, a revolution cannot first be decided upon in a parlour discussion and then introduced. It just happens. But there is little likel'hood of its being a native growth in any of the countries of south and south-east Asia, and if a totalitarian order arrives it will be so much under foreign guidance as to amount to a form of colonialism.

An asset in the bigger countries of Asia is that people are largely civilized, shrewd and intelligent, even if unlettered, and they are willing to be educated and led. Essentially, therefore, the issue is good and enlightened leadership. We are too near the events which led to independence and the formal introduction of democracies into these countries to be able to say whether a competent normal leadership will arise or not—there is no reason why it should not, given some imagination and rectitude on the part of the existing leadership and an adequate measure of foreign assistance in their efforts to raise standards of living in the quickest possible time. It is particularly for the top leaders to give up the trade union sort of attitude, enlarge their ranks by talent from outside—which is available—and consciously build up the echelons of second rank leaders. Particular care should be taken to give a sense of participation in the national effort to everybody, by encouraging the development of an effective opposition party. This necessarily means the abandonment of the many questionable devices now used for the perpetuation of power by small group in power because of some historical circumstances.

So far as India is concerned I am convinced that Mahatma Gandhi was right in advising the dissolution of the Congress Party and the formation of more natural parties according to important social and economic principles. The present governmental struggles often range round persons because there are hardly any principles round which they could range. One of the great weaknesses of the present situation is the absence of a real or effective parliamentary opposition. The internal party disputes are often necessary, nevertheless, in order to bring up leaders of the required calibre, and too much interference from the central party organization in such processes seems authoritarian and anti-democratic. In the final analysis the conduct of human affairs is conditioned by leadership at all levels and that order of society will flourish in the long run which gives ample opportunities for the growth of leadership at every level.

The general significance of political problems and tensions however extends over a much wider front. Briefly, totalitarian political organizations, accompanied by a good deal of regimentation of the individual or over-persuasion by means of the mass media of communications (which latter is not confined only to totalitarian countries, as Aldous Huxley has pointed out), could probably yield much more striking results in the short run, especially where the global problems of industrialization are concerned, and where in any case global planning gives an overall command of the whole national situation; but experience has proved that even in totalitarian countries there is a limit to successful nationalized management, particularly in sectors like agriculture, where the individual or small man and his incentive are matters of great moment and where decentralization has thrown up problems for which even totalitarian economies have yet failed to find a solution. Within the four corners of some form of parliamentary democracy, the less developed a country is the more complex and intractable are the problems of distribution rather than that of production. Indeed, the concentration of power and wealth in the hands of a few which is characteristic of some kind of feudalistic or oligarchic or imperfectly democratic order of things, provided the cost in human misery could be ignored even in the short run, might result in an impressive growth of the gross national product and this could be reinforced by the injection of foreign resources into the system, the accretion of these resources having been influenced less from rational humanistic or altruistic motives than from the motives that are the mainspring of action in the current cold war. Again, where massive gains have already been secured on the national front even under a feudalistic order, they can be quickly reinforced by the introduction of a new or extended democracy with, again, very impressive rates of increase not only in the gross national product but also in the *per capita* income, as in Japan during the last few years.

In the typical under-developed country of south-east Asia, however, such as India, Pakistan or Burma, the right sort of polity of the democratic model is a pre-requisite of progress, the importance of which cannot be exaggerated. In this region governance in accordance with any kind of ideology is hardly possible and some kind of pragmatic attitude has to be adopted, an attitude which represents an equipoise between the capacity of the bureaucracy to manage affairs and the amenability of private enterprise to curbs and restraints—again, perhaps, a matter of practical politics. When we say that a country is under-developed we mean that it is under-developed in every aspect, including education, the general cultivation of civic consciousness, the availability of trained personnel and, above all, a capable but flexible agency for implementation of plans and policies. But all these are simultaneously lacking in an under-developed country, and it follows that if such a country elects on doctrinaire grounds to run some kind of socialistic system of government it is riding for a fall. The weakness of national democracies shows itself in its most devastating form in the poor calibre of its political leaders, which fails to obtain its natural rectification through the exercise of their franchise by the people. Even a country like India, with a reasonably good tradition of bureaucratic government, can proceed only painfully slowly along the road of socialism because of both the incapacity of its bureaucratic agency to cope with the progressively complex tasks of developmental governance and of the weakness, vacillation, lack of purpose and pre-occupation with politics, not to speak of occasional lack of integrity, of its political leaders placed in seats of power both in the central and in the state governments more by historical accidents and political expediency than merits. Those who have a long experience of administration and who, therefore, are competent to judge, feel that the time has already come in India where the inability of the ministers to put matters right after an intelligent study of an issue has created a situation in which justice and equity are denied owing to lack of recourse. In other words, most secretaries can now pretty much do what they like in the day-to-day conduct of affairs, provided they can keep on the right side of ministers by means of judicious flattery and ensure that nothing that is of political significance to the minister is as far as possible allowed to go wrong.

Apart from these inherent difficulties, the greatest difficulty is created for the developing countries by the perpetual state of cold war that exists in the world today between the eastern and the western blocks. No country, not even the least experienced, the smallest and the least offensive, is spared by these contestants, as has been amply exemplified by the cases of Korea, the Congo and Laos. Where the cold war is at its hottest as in the last-named country, there can be no possibility of any orderly economic development, the current political conflicts consuming all the energies of the people and the rulers alike. Where the cold war is in its colder stages and can hardly be felt on a superficial examination, as in India or Indonesia, the situation is not only not desperate, but has a certain amount of advantage in that courting by both sides has in the past led to the maximization of foreign assistance. Obviously, this can only be a transitory good fortune—if it can be so described—and it would be the wish of everyone genuinely concerned with the human aspects of the problem that the cold war was allowed to rest and thereby make possible a widely co-operative and a long-term plan for accelerating the development of developing countries to the stage where they can be said to have reached a self-propelling economy. Any such long term arrangement would have to be assisted in order to ensure that the backwardness of the country concerned in its administrative agencies is made up and supplemented as far and as well as possible, so that the measure of foreign aid available can reach its optimum fruitfulness.

Education

With this we have reached the second of the three topics for discussion—the problems of communicating know-how in administration, industry, commerce and agriculture. There is by now a vast body of literature on the subject, the world having travelled quite a long way since the now dim distant days of Point Four programmes and the scheme of technical assistance initiated by the Colombo Plan. There is, for instance, the Eastern Regional Organization of Public Administration (EROPA for short) which was founded in June 1958 at the Manila Conference on Public Administration. This organization is an international association of semi-governmental nature, formed to help improve the economic and social development of the countries located in its areas by various means, consisting primarily of the promotion of the study, practice and status of public administration and also in the adoption of an adequate administrative system. The United Nations agencies have from time to time examined programmes of technical assistance in order to establish firmly what the objectives are and how they have to be achieved. The United Nations Office of Public Information in collaboration with the Technical Assistance Board issues regular technical assistance news letters, each issue dealing with some special problem, for instance, What Went Wrong in regard to Problems in Technical Aid in issue No 53 of May 1959, or, A Statistical Summary of Activities of the Expanded Programme of Technical Assistance, in the issue No. 64 of June-July, 1960.

Certain conclusions have been reached in India as a result of long experience, which are indicated below :—

(i) It is essential that all requests for technical assistance should be clearly and specifically linked with economic development projects. It is, of course, needless to point out that the requesting country should have a well-planned programme of economic development extending over a reasonable number of years. Technical Assistance must be related to projects in such a programme. In the absence of this the donor country has no assurance that the technical assistance being offered by it will be used to the best advantage and will result in a self-sustaining growth of technical skills. As a matter of fact, even the recipient country cannot, if it does not link requests for technical assistance with specific economic development projects in the programme, be sure that it will be applying technical assistance to needs strictly in accordance with its scheme of priorities.

(ii) It is essential that the technical assistance offered is both flexible and certain. It should be certain in the sense that the total quantum of assistance available in a given period should be more or less firmly committed. It should be flexible in the sense that the utilization of such assistance as between different acceptable schemes of the recipient country should not be programmed with such rigidity that it is incapable of subsequent adjustment in the light of changes required subsequently to meet, for instance, emergencies or a shifting of priorities. In India, for instance, we have the experience of the United Nations programme of technical assistance where the country allocation is announced in advance and the country is left free to frame a programme divided into two categories, the second of which is to be implemented if there are savings in the programme. Requests can be moved between categories two and one by the recipient country as required by its needs and new requests can be added by the country whenever it becomes necessary. At the other end we have the experience of the T.C.M. programme where the entire programme amount is divided between a given number of projects which are thereafter implemented with a certain amount of rigidity. We have also the experience of the other Colombo Plan countries where no programme whatsoever is framed but requests are sent in from time to time and met, if possible. This, however, has the disadvantage that the total quantum of assistance available in a given year is never known to the recipient country.

(iii) It is essential that each recipient country should become a donor country at least in a small way as soon as it can. This is necessary not only in order to enable the lesser developed countries to get the benefit of a bigger pool of aid but also in order to enable the recipient country to understand the attitudes and dealings of a donor country.

(iv) In regard to the technical assistance offered by way of training the nationals of the recipient country in various fields it is essential that more and more training facilities are developed within the recipient country itself by the donor country. In other words, instead of sending a large number of trainees to the donor country for training in a given subject, technical assistance is better applied if it is used to start a training institution in that subject within the recipient country itself. This is not only cheaper but also results in a permanent addition to the technical assets of the recipient country. It also enables the recipient country to offer technical assistance in the form of training in that subject to other developing countries in that region. In practice, however, this encounters two difficulties. In the first place, if the language of instruction differs from country to country in a given region it is not possible for the training facilities to be fully utilized by the region as a whole. Secondly, unfortunately, more prestige is attached to the training acquired in a developed country in the West than to similar training available in institutions set up by such developed countries in other developing countries.

(v) There have been instances where the donor country has expressed its inability to provide a particular technical skill for reasons which, although not expressly stated, appear to be in the nature of protection of trade secrets. Often the the donor country itself has no choice in such matters since the particular technical skill is available with some private firms in the donor country who are unwilling to share it.

(vi) While it is generally agreed that if a recipient country is to ask for technical assistance which will eventually go to the private sector the donor country should have no objection to it, there are instances in which certain donor countries are in principle opposed to technical assistance given to the private sector and only make an exception if strong justification is provided for it. The U.K. is an instance in point.

(vii) Considerable difficulty is encountered in proper planning of technical assistance on account of the different financial years of the different countries and agencies concerned and on account of the need to prepare plans sufficiently in advance to enable the donor countries to obtain requisite authority for spending the required amount of money while at the same time to make the programme fairly firm in the sense that the recipient country's own countrpart expenditure is covered by appropriate budgetary authorization.

In regard to administrative agencies, perhaps the most important for the purpose of formulation of plans and policies is the planning organization. India can well be regarded as a case study in this respect, although it is realized that planning can be and has been done through the employment of *ad hoc* agencies or with the assistance of special international agencies. The Indian example will not be claimed to be perfect by any means by those who have been closely associated with it, but with the largest effort at objectivity it can be claimed that in concept the Indian Planning Commission was an agency on the right lines, consisting as it did largely of men and women who could be regarded to have cultivated some kind of expertise in the subjects handled by them and who, with just two exceptions, had freedom from the distractions of a parliamentary life and accountability. The two exceptions were the Prime Minister who acted as Chairman and was therefore the liaison with the central cabinet, and the Finance Minister who in those early days supplied the necessary link between planning and the prospects of raising the necessary resources. Even in its early days the Planning Commission, so organized, ran into difficulties on account of suspicions, largely unjustified, entertained towards them by the ministries of the intention to encroach on their spheres of authority. In the course of time it came to be realized that the Planning Commission advised even in regard to current governmental policy only as a technical body, leaving an official decision to the cabinet or its committees. Hardly had this misunderstanding been removed when the States, gradually feeling their own strength inherent in the constitution, claimed to be consulted before plans were finalized. This was also conceded at an early stage by the formation of the National Development Council on which are represented the Central Government, the State Governments and the Planning Commission, so that all possible authorities have had their say before plans are put into their final shape for submitting them for the approval of the legislature. Even so, as may be expected in a quasi-federal constitution like India's the Planning Commission has had an increasingly hard and rough time of it in satisfying all demands and meeting all objectives. The situation has also been complicated by the elaboration of the theory of 'planning from the bottom'. Whilst this was a necessary stage in planning in the absence of which a somewhat apathetic population entertained excessive expectations of plan projects of development dropping on their areas like manna from heaven without their being expected to take any active part in implementation or indeed utilization (as in the case of developing irrigational facilities), in the event it has been proved that there are limits to the so-called 'planning from the bottom' and that the different sections of the plan have to be formulated at different levels, so to speak, so as to have any functional significance. It was not too difficult for the Planning Commission to deal with the more extravagant demands accumulating as a result of uninhibited planning from the bottom, and at the present stage it is not so much the bottom that is proving troublesome as the region on account of increasing political pressures. It has so happened that in India the end of the plan period coincides with the penultimate year of the five year period of election span so that on the eve of election plan formulations have a special political significance. However, since these pressures are not confined to any single State and since there is a limit anyhow to total resources, including foreign assistance marked by increasing understanding and munificence, occasional plums have been taken out of the pie only by a few of the more important political potentates and by and large rough justice may be said to have been done. Just as in the international sphere there is a limit to the sacrifice which people are prepared to put up with for the sake of improving the lot of their fellow beings, so also on the national scene disparities of development, stemming from historical causes, as between the different States or regions, can only be rectified a little at a time, although there may be justly said to be a conscious attempt to bring up the more backward areas, unless the cost in terms of national resources is judged to be excessive.

Economic

It is now time to consider the all-embracing economic issue. Had more time been alloted for the preparation of the basic papers, it might perhaps have been interesting and possible to preface a discussion of the issues included under this topic with some factual or statistical information, although the statistical apparatus of the countries in South Asia is not well-developed. It would have been of interest in the shape of a benchmark survey to indicate the precise place occupied by the countries in south and south-east Asia and indeed all the developing countries of the world in the scales of total and *per capita* national income. Next it would have been necessary to set down the current rate of domestic saving and investment, as well as the dimensions of the foreign assistance helping to convert these into higher rates. Lastly, it will have been necessary to compare the actual rates of growth of income achieved both as a whole and *per capita* for every country, in comparison with similar rates recorded for the developed countries, in order to reach some conclusions on whether the current disparities are being diminished or are, despite all efforts, increasing, and if so what are the likely political and economic consequences to be in the long run.

The only figures of some relevance that I have been able to get hold of are those showing the Government expenditure in Pounds Sterling on development per head representing the budget estimates for 1960-61 for most of the countries of south and south-east Asia represented on the Consultative Committee of the Colombo Plan. The figures are as follows :—

	Population (1959) (*in million*)	1960-61 *budget estimate of Government expenditure on development* (£ *Sterling*)	
		Per Head	*In Million*
Burma	20.5	1.8	36.8
Cambodia	4.8	1.8	8.8
Ceylon	9.6	4.1	39.0
India	402.8	2.0	810.0
Indonesia	91.7	1.6	144.0
Laos	1.8	4.9	8.9
Federation of Malaya	6.8	12.6	85.6
Nepal	9.0	1.7	15.2
Pakistan	86.8	1.9	165.5
Philippines	24.7	5.8	144.1
Singapore	1.6	11.4	18.3
Thailand	21.9	1.5	23.0
Viet Nam (South)	13.8	2.9	40.1

It will be noticed that the lowest range is roughly between

£ 2 to 3 Sterling per head, shown by the following countries: Burma, Cambodia, India, Indonesia, Nepal, Pakistan, Thailand and South Vietnam. The countries in the next range have development expenditures which are roughly double of the first, possibly, however, bearing the same ratio to the national income; these are Ceylon , Laos and the Philippines. Singapore and the Federation of Malaya are in a class apart with expenditure nearly twice the second group and four times the first group leading to an inference that they are probably as well developed now as a country like Japan whose national income is about four or five times that of India. In human terms, again, it will be seen that the vast bulk of the problem is still formidable as the countries in the lowest range have the largest aggregation of population, viz., India, Pakistan, Indonesia and Burma. The serious challenge of the situation will be realized when it is noted that all these countries have a rate of growth no greater than 3-1/2 per cent recorded during these ten years in spite of some ten years of planning, with the result that on the fast increasing population the advance in national income per head or the relateable rise in the standard of living is so negligible as hardly to be perceptible.

In India, thanks to the National Sample Survey and the annual national income computation, figures are available to show the stratification of society as classified by income ranges. These figures keep changing in detail from year to year, but the general features and trends are quite distinct. About 45 per cent of Indian families have an income of between $ 120 and 240 per year, which gives an average per head of about $ 45 per year, i.e. about 15 cents a day per person. The average *per capita* national income within the ranges of above $ 240 and below $ 360 is enjoyed by some 30 per cent of families, the average per diem therefore being about 20 cents per head. There is another 24 per cent families with an average income between $ 350 and 600, coming to about 33 cents per day per head. There is only one per cent of the families who have income above $ 600 per year, the family having a membership of between 4 and 5. These are payers of income tax and these are the only citizens who can be regarded to live in some kind of affluence. The average income of this class of families might be in the neighbourhood of

$ 2000 a year, or about $ 400 per person. Putting it in another way, these figures mean that out of some 438 millions there are only a little over four million people in India whose *per capita* income is about the same as the *per capita* income of an average U.S.A. citizen.

It is obvious that with a configuration of incomes of this kind the raising of the necessary savings for investment is a forbiddingly difficult task. Indeed, a little less than half the population has, instead of contributing anything, a right to receive something from the other groups in order that some improvement might be effected from year to year in their sub-human existence. The 30 per cent who have average incomes can only be expected to yield the average savings, which in all conscience will be pitifully small. Some degree of privation would have to be imposed on the other 24 per cent, who incidentally constitute the better educated and more vocal sections of the population, the middle classes or the more well to do peasants or the workers in organized industries. This glaring contrast lends force to the rancourous debate that goes on in India all the time in regard to the relative merits of and justification for direct and indirect taxation, and it is in this context that a somewhat powerful but microscopically small section of the community, viz., those who are responsible for running organized industry, both indigenous and foreign, talk in reproachful terms of the existing levels of taxation depriving them and their ilk of all incentives.

Public savings are therefore in the nature of things bound to be small and insufficient for the current developmental effort in India, and it is for this reason that for three or four plan periods India has been or will have to be dependent on the assistance from abroad. Even with such assistance, as has been stated earlier, the increase in national income or the rise in the standard of living is painfully slow or small. That is why it is of the utmost importance that every possible effort is made by India to gear its administrative machinery to the progressively difficult tasks of developmental planning, and it is for this reason that any avoidable short-comings or failures deserve to be sharply denounced, so that under democratic pressures the necessary improvements are brought about and maintained and optimum rates of progress established. In concrete terms, there does not seem to be any ground for hope in the Indian situation unless the current rate of annual increase in the national product is raised from the present pedestrian 3-1/2 per cent to seven, it being assumed that the recent re-thinking under President Kennedy's guidance of the philosophy of assistance to developing countries reaches its optimum volume.

I may be permitted to quote here the philosophy of world economic aims as given in the speech of the U.K. Prime Minister, the Rt. Hon. Harold Macmillan, M.P., at the Massachusetts Institute of Technology on Friday, 7th April, 1961 :

> Happily the present struggle in the world is not primarily a military one. The real test will not be on the battlefield but in the market place. It is now almost 15 years since the main structure of our present system for world trade and payments was designed. That was in the heyday of the East-West war alliance. The founders of GATT, the signatories of Bretton Woods and all the architects of our post-war system could not foresee the full economic effects of the great divide. World economic unity would have been hard enough to achieve in a world of 19th century nation States; it became impossible as the full effect of the Sino-Soviet system manifested itself. At the same time a new economic force has appeared in the world. The second Industrial Revolution has already swept through our developed economies. It is still only in its early stages and I am sorry to have to tell this audience that it is largely your fault. For this revolution is of a scientific and technological character. And these technical developments overlap national frontiers. They require for their effective exploitation even larger economic units. I readily admit that in spite of these two factors our international trading and financial arrangements have somehow or other managed to carry a great increase in world production and trade. But no wonder they are now beginning to creak and groan. For they are really an old model. Sooner or later they will have to be traded in. There are now three main problems to be resolved. The first is how to maximise world trade. This is essential

to the prosperity of developed and undeveloped countries alike. Secondly, how are we best to organize assistance and capital to build up the less developed countries ? Our common humanity cries out to us to help here, and our economic interest in new markets encourages us and finally political necessity compels us. Lastly, how are we to finance an ever increasing volume of trade and aid ? If our monetary arrangements are bad, or outmoded, we shall not succeed. We shall stagnate instead of expand. And Capitalism must expand or perish. Even Marx knew that.

In the same address the importance of new and extended patterns of trade for the less industrialized countries has been stressed and a preference has been expressed for more trade rather than for greater aid. The necessity has been pointed out of the advanced countries receiving from the less industrialized ones not only primary products but also manufactured goods on an increasing scale with due precautions to prevent a disruption of domestic industry. That the world needs more and more schemes for ironing out violent fluctuations in the short-term and to give some stability to prices for primary commodities has long been recognized, although in practice it does not prove too easy to devise enduring schemes in this respect. The necessity of improving the rudiments of a central banking system for the international community has also been recently recognized, particularly as a corrective of the imbalance in payments as also for expanding the total volume of money to match the expansion in world trade. Within the specific field of external aid there has been of late a great deal of advance in thinking on the part of responsible political or institutional authorities, and many of the points that India has been making, for instance, out of her now fairly long experience of the receipt of such aid, have been accepted by the industrially advanced countries, at least in principle. Despite their own budgetary and other difficulties it is recognized by almost all of them—

(i) That external assistance for development is not to be regarded as temporary assistance, as something intended to enable a friendly country to get over a crisis ; it has to be part of a well-considered policy of long period assistance designed to meet the needs of the developing country;

(ii) Nor is external assistance something incidental to the foreign economic policy of a country; there should be no question of strings of any kind;

(iii) The recipient country should be able to depend on getting this assistance for a continuing period; there has to be an informal if not formal commitment on the part of the donor country;

(iv) This assistance is in the nature of investment although because of the exigencies of the international capital market it takes the form mostly of loans; these loans will have to be long-term and the repayment obligations will have to be matched with the growth in the recipient countrie's capacity to create an export surplus;

(v) The 'monumental' approach is all right up to a point but a developing country needs assistance for a large number of small projects and also for imports that cannot be linked directly to projects; external assistance has thus to be linked to the development programme as a whole;

(vi) The needs of developing countries will grow and it must be recognized that the provision of a sufficient outflow of resources from the surplus countries to the needy ones has to be accepted as an international responsibility; the recovery of Europe should make it possible for Western European countries to take a large share in this task;

(vii) Some of the external assistance made available has to be in the form of soft loans or grants. We now have the I.D.A. India has been pressing for a U.N. Capital Development Fund. The point is that not all development is bankable in the traditional sense.

In this context it is worthwhile quoting the concluding portion of an address by Mr. Eugene R. Black, President of the International Bank for Reconstruction and Development, before the 12th International Banking Summer School, Burgenstock, Switzerland, in June 1959. Apropos the idea of the International Development Association, he said that the following fundamental questions arise :—

(i) Is it possible to administer this association with the same regard for sound fiscal policies and sound project preparation which guide World Bank lending ?

(ii) Is it possible to administer this association in ways

which will strengthen, not weaken, our links with the private markets ?

(iii) Is it possible to administer this association in a way which will insure that it contributes a net addition to the flow of development capital rather than becoming merely a substitute for effective capital now flowing ?

He added : 'I am optimistic about the chances of working out affirmative answers to these questions'. It is now realized that not all balance of payments difficulties in developing countries lend themselves to correction in the short-term without destroying much of the structure necessary to attain self-sustaining growth, although there would always be cases where they can demonstrably be the result of bad economic management. The perspective therefore must be a long-term one, involving the test of how a developing country is building into its society the many and varied institutions and policies necessary for sustained growth.

Lastly, perhaps it is my duty to attach as an appendix synopsis of tensions received at my instance from some of the representatives who attended the Bombay Seminar. So far the number of papers received is only one or two.

Social and Cultural Factors Underlying Development Programme

As stated above, all-tensions cannot or should not be eliminated or reduced because conflict is a pre-requisite of progress. But in order that the right lines of action may be followed in this difficult field one needs the assistance of many more social scientists and the cultivation by them of new social science techniques. They will also require more data, more tools and a greater body of general principles as well as specialized knowledge.

Tensions of *social mobilization* arise out of the loss of the old norms in traditional societies and the immediate non-emergence of new norms in their place. Generally speaking, such tensions can only be eased by appropriate educational policy as well as well-timed legislation.

The break up of the *traditional groupings* of society is facilitated by the conscious development of new groupings, as, for instance, by the development of trade unions or workers' associations or by the growth of co-operation or by the development of technical and social skills, e.g. use of banking institutions.

But over and above this, social mobilization means understanding of national aspirations by the people and the acceptance by them of national goals and all that this implies, for instance, thrift, the necessity of more individual decisions etc. Special attention has also to be paid to key groups such as intelligensia or businessmen, technicians, officials.

In the field of *education* the tension involved is in the *change of concept of education* itself from transmission of cultural goods to acquisition of new knowledge and skills. Modern education in South-Asia has been noticed by a distinguished social scientist (from the Philippines) to weaken filial piety and, by the difference that exists between the school language and the home language, to lead to conflict between parents and teachers. Then there is the strain of examinations and deteriorating standards; also the emergence gradually of a reluctance to return to work soiling the hands. The medium of instruction also needs attention, because if the education is to be effective the medium has to be emotionally satisfying. It has been found that tension in village reconstruction can be eased if needs are prominently brought to the attention of the people and felt by them. The value of co-operative work or innovations can also be enhanced if these are linked with existing religious or social values.

The tensions that are involved in the process of *urbanization or industrialization are now fairly well understood*. The necessary change of mentality to turn a peasant into an industrial worker takes time, and even in the secondary and tertiary employment fields the lack of skilled personnel in the various trades often leads to tensions. Here again educated public opinion could do a lot to help minimize tensions. Industrial psychologists are also needed in adequate numbers and in appropriate positions as much as chartered accountants, auditors, directors or business managers.

Labour legislation in recent years has helped a good deal to reduce tensions in organized industry, tensions which on analysis are found to arise from the loss of a sense of creativity. In mass production the machine becomes ubiquitous and the machine is almost always a breeder of monotony. The remedy in this situation is that the worker should be enabled to have more fruitful leisure and encouraged by appropriate institutional changes to take greater interest in at least some aspects of management.

So far as the Indian scene is concerned, there are various other specific social or cultural tensions leading to a loss of a sense of integrity in the nation. In so far as this is due to the weakening of a common medium of communication like English, the situation can be regarded as transitory, as in course of time Hindi is bound to be developed into both an official language and a *lingua franca*.

The *social reforms* that are being undertaken when the State judges the time ripe for their introduction also constitute a unifying factor. Amongst Hindus religious revival also is tending to be a culturally unifying factor. In this context it may be noted that the States Reorganization Commission (1955) urged greater interplay of different regional cultures, inter-State co-operation and accord through special Machinery like Zonal Council's and Regional Committees and the reinforcement of the links between the Centre and the States.

Nevertheless, there are certain areas in which tensions have not yet been brought under control. Such is the case in regard to *acute Brahmin and non-Brahmin* tension in the South, although it may be fairly safely prognasticated that in view of the very small percentage of Brahmins in the total population and their perception of the new situation created by adult franchise the Brahmins themselves are taking steps which are likely to remove the causes of friction by turning to other occupations than land holding or government service.

The *linguistic* reorganization of the country led to the spread of regional self-glorification and an exaggerated State patriotism, in some cases to the point of the development of 'Homeland' or 'Sons of the Soil' or 'Key Posts' theories. Here again better cultural understanding, beginning with the schools, supplemented by radio and films and by the spread of education at all levels, particularly university education, as well as by intensifying efforts to pull up the backward communities, much can be done to ease the tensions. In other countries of the region group conflict has sometimes been found to be due to the excessive prestige attached to the ruling class and the endowment by them of monuments and artistic work in the cities instead of procuring more industrial equipment for the country.

R. B. BAPU RAO DADA KINKHEDE LECTURES FOR 1961-1962

THE APPROPRIATE POLITY AND INSTITUTIONAL STRUCTURE FOR OPTIMUM DEVELOPMENT

In a fundamental sense the existence of an appropriate political organization of society is the prime requisite of development. The appropriateness will obviously be judged in the light of the capacity of the polity to undertake and implement successfully the numerous measures which the State is called upon to take in an under-developed country in order to promote optimal economic growth. But there are conditions of a political nature, for instance, colonialism, in which the question is more of willingness to develop rather than capacity. In a colonial economy there is every natural temptation to exploit the resources of the subjugated country for the enrichment of the ruling country. It may therefore be taken as axiomatic—although somewhat platitudinously in the present-day world—that no development that will give any satisfaction is possible without independence.

But the existence of independence is no guarantee that optimum economic growth will take place in the under-developed countries. For instance, Thailand, the Land of the Free, is not very much in advance of its neighbours in South and South-East Asia, most of whom have till recently been under colonial regimes, and Korea's economic development has been sadly retarded because of the political struggles between North Korea and South Korea under the stress of the East and West conflict. Similarly, the Arab countries, most of whom have been free for about half-a-century, have made no notable economic progress. Even Latin America, independent for a longer period, can still be included in the under-developed regions of the world. Many of the newly-independent nations of Africa are, as one may expect, hardly on the threshold of economic development. These last, moreover, have some very special psychological tensions to overcome in planning their developmental efforts, such as fear of neo-colonialism, i.e., of strongly entrenched economic power of foreign nations, even where they offer to assist in the developmental process, in place of the former political domination.

Except as a matter of exceptional good fortune, a feudal polity is inimical to satisfactory and socially acceptable development. Even where a form of democracy is in operation, that democracy has genuinely to satisfy the sort of pre-requisites that are laid down in the preamble to the Indian Constitution, viz., Justice, social, economic and political; Liberty of thought, expression, belief, faith and worship; Equality of status and opportunity; and the promotion of Fraternity—assuring the dignity of the individual and the unity of the nation.

The view generally accepted outside the totalitarian countries is that some of these elements, for instance, liberty of thought, expression and belief, does not exist in the politics of these countries. The individual therefore is deprived of one of his most precious attributes. That spectacular levels of amelioration of the standards of living have been attained in these countries during the last fifteen years cannot be denied. It is also possible, although not to be taken for granted, that as material conditions improve, the restraints on liberty will be slackened and may ultimately become unnecessary. But the suppression of personality is, outside the totalitarian block, regarded as too big a price to pay for a better life, especially when it involves a conscious suppression of the religious impulse or belief in God. The violence that is inherent in the totalitarian ideology of revolution and the elevation of the primacy of ends over means are similar arguments against the adoption of that sort of polity for bringing about optimum economic growth in the quickest possible time, in spite of its proved efficiency, at least in the short run (i.e. a generation or two).

It is for these reasons that the newly free nations of Asia and Africa adopted in the first instance some kind of a western parliamentary democracy, such as that prevalent in the more advanced West European, North American or Oceanic countries of the world. In Latin America, a special type of democracy, marked by frequent revolution, developed before the totalitarian form was evolved after the first World War in

Russia. The aberrant features of Latin American democracy, as also the present nearly universal eclipse of Western parliamentary democracy in South and South-East Asia, as also the immense difficulties experienced in some African countries in planting democratic constitutions, make it worthwhile to consider the basic conditions of democracy itself as the supposedly ideal form of political organization for nations generally and the under-developed nations in particular.

Superficially there would seem to be no flaw in the forms of democracy—all variants of a common theme—practised in the most advanced countries of the world. The level of prosperity is high both relatively and in an absolute sense in that nearly all the conditions that are needed for a stable, civilised and carefree existence for the citizens seem to exist, with leisure a bye-product of growing dimensions. It has to be remembered, however, that this situation is the culmination of decades of political, economic and social evolution, which often took place at the cost of weaker sections of the community or weaker and therefore inhumanly exploited foreign communities. A great advantage of such slow evolution was that democracy in its modern form succeeded universal or near-universal literacy. Another favourable factor was the great scientific and technological advance of the preceding fifty years, giving a tremendous fillip to industrialization and urbanization. Whilst newly developing nations are heirs to all this and need not, therefore, have to accept the same slow tempo of development, literacy and the other mental skills or habits of mind can only be cultivated through an inevitably slow-naturing educational process. Moreover, the social costs of development are now reckoned with more meticulous attention to social justice, and the facility of deploying modern technological and scientific advances is counter-balanced by the scores of restraints that by choice or international convention the State has to impose, as for instance, in labour relations, the operation of laissez faire and the like.

It is assumed too facilely that advanced nations lead a carefree existence both politically and economically. But a little observation and reflection will show that the facts are otherwise. Certain problems, e.g., unemployment or inflation, have always been hard to tackle in these countries, the

U.S.A. and U.K. being instances in point. In addition, what is a far more serious matter, in the absence of the discrimination and self-restraint that education in its widest sense confers on men, there is slow and imperceptible lowering of the ethos of these advanced societies which is traceable to the location of ultimate political power in the multitude. Some sage observers have even felt that the intellectual, (i.e. the Brahmin) is gradually on the way out in these societies, even though he is not suppressed as in totalitarian countries.

That democracy, not flawless in advanced countries, is proving tardy in taking root in the under-developed countres is therefore not to be wondered at. For the institution of fashionable western forms has not eliminated the unfavourable traditional factors of feudalism, land-lordism, authoritarianism or petite bourgeoisie. Many thinkers in these countries have begun to wonder if the conventional forms of western parliamentary democracy are the final answer to problems of polity or whether it is not time seriously to think of evolving special forms more suited to backward nations, such as personalism, greater resort to indirect election, decentralization to the smallest possible units, et cetera. Basic democracy or guided democracy seems to be variations of personalism, whilst extreme and often injudicious decentralization would appear to be desperate expedients for improving the patently inferior quality of democratic government.

The lack of restraint which is characteristic of a low level of culture and civilization is tending to be agggravated by recklessly handled democratic functions, such as those of the opposition parties, leading inevitably to an erosion of the respect for the lawful or the constitutional. In this process mole-hills of grievances are often made into mountains and an odious amount of just plain slanging takes place in both intra-national and international relations. The tone and quality of democracy as practised therefore often frequently impede the proper implementation of developmental plans or measures.

But even where, as in India, a recognizable and on the whole apparently successful form of democracy is in operation, plan achievement is rendered difficult by the form of government, which is quasi-federal in the case of India. The Constitution provides ample powers for carrying out the wishes of the Centre, but the political arrangements are such as to make central ministers very much dependent on the goodwill of local party leaders. Many decisions are taken not so much on the merit as on the insistence of strong local leaders, and, vis-a-vis planning the States are tending to have their own way, thus interfering with the balance and orderliness of plan formulation.

India is at least fortunate that it has the resources necessary for establishing a planning organization, although even here recent trends have not been very reassuring. In the other under-developed countries of the region the machinery for planning may not be as effective, and in Africa most of the newly-independent countries have so heavily to rely on outside, preferably international, organizations that in the Oxford Conference on Tensions of Development (September 1961) a suggestion was put forward, and not inhospitably received, that international agencies should build up special cadres for assisting developing countries in formulating plans.

If the formulation of socially acceptable and functionally effective plans in non-totalitarian developing countries is difficult, the implementation of plans is still more so, both in the governmental and non-governmental spheres, owing to the administrative machinery not being well-geared to the manifold and complex tasks of development and to the absence of entrepreneurial enterprise and organizational ability. For instance, a recent report presented by the Finance Minister of Ceylon to Parliament admitted that 'one of the greatest handicaps in attaining plan targets has been the lack of mature projects and the skills necessary for their execution'. This is so pronounced there that much foreign aid is reported to remain idle and unproductive.

Even in India, much better situated in this behalf, the situation in regard to sound administration is such as to cause serious anxiety, although every possible care is taken to recruit and train staff well. The fact appears to be that at all levels of political offices there is an insufficiency of leaders with a modicum of education, intelligence, industry and integrity, with resultant demoralization of the staff and cadres. In spite of much 'organization and methods' effort and much learned study of every possible problem of public administration, as well as helpful review and criticism by the Committee on Plan Projects and its sub-committees, there is a steady deterioration of the efficiency and expeditiousness of public administration, whether in the Plan or the non-Plan sector, whether in pure administration or the management of public enterprises. The virtues of functional devolution have not been recognized in practice, and pin-pointing of responsibility is often absent. Accountability to legislatures often has the unexpected result of irresolution, shifting of responsibility or recognition of functionally irrelevant considerations. Despite much apparently successful activity on the part of the Special Criminal Investigation Department, there is reason to believe that corruption continues to be rampant, for the main reason that, in the nature of things, subordinate departmental scrutiny cannot touch the highest political levels or concern itself appropriately with the more insidious forms of political corruption.

Apart from doctrinaire considerations, it is this weakness of political leadership that furnishes the best justification for the so-called mixed economy. Presently in India one could even affirm with some justice that whilst business administration is improving, public administration is deteriorating.

According to the Planning Commission—and no one will disagree with this—mere reforms in organization and procedures may not yield enough results without a concerted attempt to make the administration much more 'action-oriented'. This implies fixing specific individual responsibility for the execution of any programme and delegation of financial powers so as to avoid meticulous scrutiny of minutiae by financial experts, whose advice should be reserved for more intelligent financial guidance *via* scrutiny of the annual budget. Devolution is also not properly understood or appreciated, and it is not uncommon to find ministers rebelling against too tight a Finance Ministry control whilst hugging on to authority again those whose proper business is execution of policies, viz., departments and authorities specially designated for the purpose.

The most callous aspect of financial control appears to be the frequent delays in authorizing payments of dues, like leave-salary, pensions and even pay after a transfer. This can only be eliminated if payment of salary of the official responsible is proportionately delayed, to generate some fellow-feeling as a stimulus to quicker disposal. Arrangements whereby responsibility can be fairly and squarely fixed have an obvious merit in this context.

The planning of projects obviously leaves still much to be desired. This involves not only delay in execution and increase in estimates, but also makes evaluation of performance difficult.

The Planning Commission also suggest the working out of a system of incentives directed to accomplish reduction in construction costs, reduction in foreign exchange expenditure, improvements in methods of maintenance, the use of substitutes and bye-products and simplification of work procedures. Indeed, over the whole field of public service the system in vogue for rewarding efficiency and punishing slackness needs to be thoroughly reviewed and strengthened. Material incentives should be judiciously added to the non-material, especially various forms of appreciation and recognition of worth, a sense of partnership in a common endeavour, and human relationships based on natural respect and friendliness. Only a reference need be made in this connection to the many concrete suggestions that have been made by the Planning Commission of India (Pp. 280-290) to the specific administration or management reforms called for in the planning and execution of projects in the public sector or for securing greater economy in construction, with special and pointed reference to noted failures in the course of the implementation of the Second Plan. Some of these are: too head-long and drastic an expenditure of foreign exchange resources in the initial years with its adverse repercussion on the power-development and the production of fertilizers, the considerable lag in the utilization of irrigation, the failure to counter shortages and imbalances in production or transport of coal and the inability to moderate the intensity of fluctuation and the rise in prices during the first two years.

A new development in the administrative field in India is the decentralization of planning and execution that goes under the somewhat grandiose name of Panchayati Raj, meaning the delegation of powers to local bodies at the level of blocks of hundred villages, on an average. It is not that local bodies at this level were unknown in the past, and indeed even in pre-Independence days the Madhya Pradesh Government had devolved a great deal of power to similar bodies called Janapads. But there was no planning then and the financial resources needed for development hardly existed. What is new is the enlarged scope of authroity now entrusted to Panchayat Samitis and the altered relation of these bodies to the bureaucracy, comparable to the situation existing in municipal areas. The record of achievement of the urban local bodies in India is not too good and there is no reason to believe that in the rural environment greater efficiency will be shown by local bodies. But the experiment is well worth trying for fostering the growth of local leadership provided no idealistic or starry-eyed view is taken of the potentialities of the innovation.

The dilemma of all developing countries consists in inability to control the greed of vested interests on one hand and incapacity to take on new or more exacting administrative tasks through the bureaucracy, on the other. It is this dilemma which dulls the edge of extreme socialist doctrine and drives government to favour pragmatic arrangements involving a price for the incapacities in regard to undertakings outside the field of normal law and order functions and day-to-day administration. From a functional point of view there need be no marked difference in the management of industrial or commercial enterprises, whether in the private or the public sector. There has necessarily to be sufficient autonomy secured for the enterprise to enable it to run efficiently or with due regard to accepted codes of ethics and justice for the wage-earner and the consumer as well as sufficient profitability for the proprietor —be it the shareholders of a private organization or the public *via* the State, with accountability to the legislature. The sufficiency of profit has to be judged with reference to standards accepted the world over which, among other things, aim at securing sufficient internal finance for development and expansion.

When, as happens with better development in the modern environment, business shows an increasing awareness of social responsibility and a growing disposition to adopt modern scientific methods of business administration, on one hand,

and bureaucratic capabilities improve with improved political leadership, on the other, the distinction between private and public enterprise grows less and less significant and more and more amenable to well-recognized principles, such as are embodied in the current Indian Industrial Policy Resolution.

That the State has to carry a heavier burden of direction, regulation and initiation in developing countries had already been said earlier. This involves—apart from regulation and control and public undertakings—the promotion of many institutional reforms in agriculture, industry and the social set up. Thus, agencies have to be established for ensuring correct price-policies so as to avoid, to use a telling phrase of D. R. Gadgil's 'the continued discomfiture of the peasant and the consumer, and the assured good fortune of traders'; to plan agricultural production and to organize the agricultural producer through the co-operative movement at an all-India level, with special attention to marketing.

In the agricultural sector, land reforms and co-operation occupy a pivotal position. What appropriate and far-reaching land reforms can achieve is demonstrated in post-war Japan, where the production of rice has gone up by nearly 80 per cent, making the country self-supporting in regard to this special food stuff. The absence of land reforms in a situation dominated by latifundia has led to severe tensions, impeding development in some of the Latin American countries. In India, the Planning Commission admit that the total impact of land reforms has been less than had been hoped for because of (1) too little recognition of land reforms as a positive programme of development, not extraneous to community development and as an important factor in increasing agricultural production; (2) insufficient attention to its administrative aspects, and (3) insufficient realization of its importance, together with the early enforcement of ceilings on land as an essential foundation for the building up of a co-operative rural economy. Incidentally, land ceilings have no logical connection with ceilings on incomes, which can only be a matter for taxation policies but not for direct restriction of the fruits of development in the shape of rising national incomes. Whilst co-operation has immense potential for the improvement of agricultural production, it is futile to expect that it will be universal or even proceed fast enough to make an impact on the situation for several Plan periods. In the short run, it may well be that the withdrawals of personal and individual incentive and its replacement by work measured in terms of hourly wage done by members of co-operatives would lead to diminished and not increased production. Co-operative association for purposes other than cultivation has however great possibilities, the materialization of which has made the Japanese rural co-operative organizations independent of governmental assistance and enabled them to start with their own surplus resources many processing and cognate industries. But in Japan, as in U.S.A., the peasant enjoys the advantages of stable agricultural prices and equitable parities in relation to goods and services agricultural producers have to buy.

In the industrial sector India has established many specialized institutions for financing of industries, including small-scale industries, as also for promoting productivity and facilitating participation by foreign private capital. Schemes have also been announced for the promotion of industrial research through well-equipped regional institutes. There are also institutions for the training of business managers and administrators, the most important of which is the Administrative Staff College of India, Hyderabad. Management associations are taking a lively interest in refresher courses for management personnel at different levels and altogether the institutional framework is growing increasingly suitable for the rapid growth of industrialization on correct lines. But more imagination and vigorous action is needed in regard to export promotion, such as systematic and sustained market research for the more important Indian products and the energetic and determined follow-up of research findings as also special institutions for financing exports.

There is also scope for developing in India and the other under-developed countries industrial co-operatives of the type working so successfully in Japan. The basic unit in such co-operatives is not an individual, but a small-scale enterprise, employing between 25 and 200 workers, the enterprises being clustered in a region and specializing in the manufacture of some machinery, e.g. automobile parts or machines producing cardboard containers; the co-operative looks after the procurement of raw material, weighment of the product on a weigh-bridge, transport and the training of workers at different levels. This sort of co-operative involves an extension of the principles of co-operation the potentialities of which are yet to be tried out even in India, in spite of the progress India has made in planned development.

The tendency for industries to congregate in a few favoured cities and generally to aggravate the problems of urbanization is well-known, being almost universal. The strain that such urbanization causes on civic amenities is seldom relieved, with the result that slums multiply. The municipal authorities find themselves gravely handicapped in grappling with the situation by reason of legal or financial incapacity. It is for this reason, apart from others, e.g. claims of a backward region to a more evenly distributed industrial development, that governments often seek to influence the location of industries in a more dispersed fashion. The scheme of establishing a large variety and number of industrial estates, which has made considerable headway in India, has therefore much to commend it.

Apart from this, dispersal of industries, especially of the small-scale type, has an important bearing on stimulating all round economic growth in the rural areas, provided that the industries elected for the purpose do not suffer in an economic sense by lowered productivity by reason of their rural location. W. Arthur Lewis also recommends in this context the selection of some small towns for more intensive industrialization. 'Very few countries', he has said, 'have given special thought to planning geographical location in such a way as to develop a significant number of medium size towns, in order to prevent excessive concentrations in one or two large towns'. India's Third Five Year Plan Report has something to say about industrial development in rural areas and small towns (pages 434-435). 'Since one of the principal aspects of programmes in this field is to provide opportunities of income and employment in a dispersed manner all over the country, emphasis in the implementation of the programmes in the Third Plan will be on encouraging the further growth of industries in rural areas and in small towns as well as in less developed areas having a marked industrial potential'.

To the extent to which migration of labour into cities continues in spite of the successful implementation of the policies mentioned earlier, it might be cheaper to provide the necessary services if migrant labour is accommodated near or on the outskirts of big cities, which might help to reduce the costs of domestic water, light, sanitation and the like.

Increase in industrialization and the organization of markets and licensed ware-houses will stimulate the growth of the banking habit, as is happening in India. It is not often realized that the limiting factor is literacy, since the handling of bank-cheques will not be feasible in its absence. The sooner adult literacy is attained, the more rapid will be the spread of the banking habit. In the advanced countries the ratio of bank-money to cash is high, whereas in India and other under-developed countries it is so low that the volume of cash often exceeds the volume of bank-money.

This is only one aspect of education relevant to industrialization. The provision of facilities for technical training of all kinds is another. These aspects are now well-understood. For instance, India's Third Five Year Plan Report says (page 150) : 'Expansion of the general educational base through the programmes of free and compulsory education and provision of facilities for technical training is likely to make a steadily increasing contribution to the development of the less advanced regions.'

But what is not often realized is that in view of the very rapid rate of change in the modern environment, the very aim and object of the educational process has to be suitably modified. Perspicacious observers of the economic scene are convinced that the key factor inhibiting economic growth is the absence of an effective educational system in the broadest sense of that term, and this implies a redesigning of education for development. Invention and innovation play a significant role in the development process, as Max F. Millikan, Director of the Centre for International Studies at the Massachusetts Institute of Technology, pointed out in the Oxford Conference on Tension of Development (September 1961). The redesigning has to take notice of the advantage that the under-developed world has of drawing upon the accumulated experience of the advanced countries. But the aim of education, facilitating this, must not be only to transmit received knowledge, information and conventional skills; it must also pay attention to 'creating a set of attitudes and talents-conducive to finding new and more effective ways of doing things, running all the way from designing simple hand tools to constructing workable administrative and political institutions for a whole society'. At all levels greater stress has to be put on developing in the students interest in and capacity for creativity and rational enquiry. Moreover, apart from the application of a universally valid philosophy of education, educational technique has often to be 'cut to measure' to suit the unique requirements of every developing country. The supply of women teachers for encouraging the enrolment of girls, for instance, calls for special measures, such as the condensed courses for women instituted and assisted by the Central Social Welfare Board in India. By these courses women of an appropriately mature age, but with little or no education, can be recruited from the rural environment and enabled to accelerate the learning process so as to acquire the minimum educational qualifications needed for specialized training, not only as teachers, but also auxiliary nurses, village level workers, handicrafts instructors and family planning advisers.

But perhaps the most important reform in educational methods that is needed is 'education for problem-solving', in a world changing so rapidly that even the teacher is apt to become obsolescent.' A greater flexibility of mind and a greater adaptibility has therefore to be developed in those being educated than was thought adequate hitherto. As Millikan pointed out, 'this flexibility is needed not only at the top of the educational pyramid amongst the university-trained intellectuals. In agriculture the problem is not today to train the cultivator in the use of what is now considered the best practice but rather to instil in him a new attitude towards continual change and a capacity to shift his methods from year to year in response to new knowledge. It is not enough to teach the mechanic to repair today's automobile or radio. He must be equipped to grasp new technology as it comes along. Thus the key role for education at all levels is not only the transmission of a body of knowledge , though that is necessary, but also the inculcation of a spirit of enquiry, a capacity for the analysis of new problems and a willingness to set out into the unknown.'

The need of a more fundamental type of education, distinguished from a quick specialized or technical training, is felt even in the advanced countries—so rapid is the rate of change in the modern world. Professor Richard Eckans of the M.I.T. has estimated (Millikan told us) that in 1950 some 94 per cent of the U.S. labour force required seven years of primary education to be effective in their jobs and some 77 per cent required the equivalent of ten years schooling. 'If we were to rely exclusively on the education of school-age children to change our capital stock of human beings, an under-developed country with little education in the past which adopted today universal primary education and extensive secondary education would require thirty or forty years to bring its entire labour force up to the educational levels needed to operate a modern economy'. Moreover, the process of education must so operate in every country that talent, wherever it may be, will be searched out and encouraged so as to fulfil the double purpose of giving the citizens equality of opportunity and maximising the nations' stock of human capability.

According to India's Third Five Year Plan (page 72), in the field of health services, the Third Plan aims at a further extension of existing programmes relating to improvement of environmental, sanitation, control of communicable diseases, public health services (including maternity and child welfare, health education, nutrition), family planning and training of medical and health personnel. This is good as far as it goes, but special attention needs to be called for to the conscious fusion of the prophylactic or the preventive programmes with academic, scientific and curative medicine. Even in the West the tendency towards growing lack of coordination or integration has only recently been detected and attempted to be rectified. In India the two different arms of medicine tend to be developed separately. 'The attempted fusion', observes a competent outside expert, 'has been unsuccessful because neither understands the techniques or work of the other'. The lack of functional fusion is self-evident in the administrative complexity imposed on the local units. The situation calls for the fusion of the basically appropriate hospital unit with the health centre.

The requirements for a national Health Plan set out in the report recently presented by the Mudaliyar Committee include upgrading of primary health centres and adequately staffing and equipping them before multiplying them; as also the establishment of well-equipped and well-staffed district hospitals with specialist facilities, which would occupy a key position in the structure of health services, mobile medical vans attached to these reaching out into the villages.

The bottleneck in the execution of any comprehensive health plan appears to be the inadequacy of trained personnel. Thus, the Second Plan referred to '70,000 qualified doctors being available in India at the beginning of the Plan period, which number was expected to rise by 12,500 to 82,500, against 90,000 needed'. And yet the Third Plan says : 'The number of practising doctors is expected to go up from 70,000 to 81,000.' The inference must be either that many qualified doctors fail to practise or that one of the estimates was or is wrong.

It is not wrong estimates, but poor implementation that is however responsible for the marked failure to spend the funds allocated for the family planning programme, hardly Rs. 3 crores having been spent against Rs. 5 crores provided. The Planning Commission observe (p. 46); 'The programme, however, is a most difficult one to carry out and raises problems of great complexity. Sustained and intensive efforts are required over a fairly long period before family planning can become a popular movement and a part of the accepted attitudes of people generally'. It is difficult to see how against such slow progress in the past and the sense of difficulty of the task the approved programme of Rs. 50 crores for the Third Plan has been approved, although with a financial provision of only Rs. 25 crores. The detailed programme (pp. 676-678) includes a number of sound measures, but little to suggest the recognition of the existence of some fundamental weakness in the organization and direction of the Central Family Planning Board, except the vague and polite statement that administrative arrangements at the Centre and in the States will need to be greatly strengthened. There is indeed reason to believe that except in a couple of States the programme is not taken very seriously. The Mudaliyar Committee is of the view that the dimensions and urgency of the problem of population are such as to warrant the appointment of a full-time Minister of State for Family Planning. But this involves an expansion of the growing family of Ministers, and perhaps an autonomous Board with wide executive powers will be preferable.

R. B, BAPU RAO DADA KINKHEDE LECTURES FOR 1961-62

INTRA-NATIONAL AND INTERNATIONAL COOPERATION IN DEVELOPMENT

India's Third Five Year Plan Report has many wise and weighty observations, suggested by the experience gained in the first two Plans, in regard to public co-operation (pages 291 300), which has been recognized as an essential condition of success. Whilst conceding that voluntary contribution of labour by the people to local works and amenities and their participation in the Community Development movement mark a notable degree of public participation, the Planning Commission observe, 'It is evident, however, that the possibilities of full involvement of the people in the process of change and growth are not being realized to a sufficient degree'. They see greater scope for this through the establishment of Panchayati Raj (decentralization of maximum possible authority to local bodies comprising on an average about 100 villages and a population of around 66,000), but point out that for a much more massive advance a far greater organization of voluntary effort is called for. It is only by social action that the revolution of unfulfilled expectations on the advent of freedom can be avoided.

It is in this context that, as has been mentioned earlier, uneven distribution of the fruits of progress, which is associated with the early stages of development in a democratic society is a danger, giving rise as it does to a sense of deep resentment and frustration. The Planning Commission feel that this can be countered by voluntary service and constructive activities organized by the people themselves and that explosive situations can be avoided by social enlightenment. But in view of the observed recent trends in the distribution of income in India, a more positive corrective action would seem to be called for through taxation and expanding social service and social security. Pranab Bardhan has discussed this problem in the Winter 1961-62 issue of *Quest*. Short-circuiting the historical stages of economic growth has its disadvantages as well as its advantages. The classical secular savings of income distribution and marked widening income inequalities in the first instance have to be restrained by deliberate measures to satisfy democratic socialistic aspirations.

So far as the facts of the situation are concerned, there would seem to be little doubt that the P. C. Mahalanobis Committee, appointed about a year ago, but still at its work, will confirm one's worst suspicions based on random observations or impressions, such as : that there has lately been a lag in the direct tax structure, as compared with the development of the armoury of indirect taxes; the more or less well-known tax evasion assuming large dimensions; the accrual of a little less than one-third of the income from agriculture to the upper income group accounting for only 3 per cent of the rural population; the recorded fall in the share in the national income of agricultural labour households and the decline by 2.2 per cent in the average annual income per family of this social group in spite of a 10 per cent increase in the number of earners per family. It may well be that even land reforms, intended to benefit, have actually weakened the economic position of the agricultural labour through its attendant mass evictions, resumption of land for cultivation, et cetera. In the field of organized industry, it has been authoritatively pointed out that the share of labour in national income has remained more or less constant, and real earnings of workers have lagged behind the rise in productivity.

The mounting level of unemployment, referred to earlier, holds its own threats to a sense of belonging and to morale, whilst disparities in the standards of living, as evidenced by data relating to consumer expenditure continue to be striking both generally and in the urban areas, in particular, where the top 10 per cent of the population enjoy 33 per cent of the expenditure, and conspicuous consumption is rampant.

Incentives to work are certainly involved in any deliberate re-distribution of income *via* taxation. But for popular participation the incentives that are important are those of the three-fourths of the country's population leading today a sub-human existence. Too much is made of the importance of high rewards for the microscopically few who are fortunate enough to play significant roles in industrial production. These can be conditioned so as to expect less luscious rewards. With conspicuous consumption in the fashion, the savings urges are far weaker than in the old days when the advanced countries were developing. The clamant need of the hour is the steady and honest implementation by the State of frequently professed but waveringly practised socialist ideals. The inculcation of the love of the nation and faith in its great destiny in every heart and the exhortation to every citizen to work for the good life which all can share, which are two of the three remedies proposed by the Planning Commission, sound impressive, but they will prove unworkable in the absence of progressive socialisation and for the practical means by which the observance is secured of moral and social standards in political and social relations and in all our business and economic activities.

Apart from right policies, good day-to-day administration has also a significant bearing on willing and enthusiastic public participation in development. As Shri V. T. Krishnamachari observed in his preliminary remarks at the Fourth Annual Conference of the Indian Institute of Public Administration on 27th August, 1960: 'Our administrations affect the lives of many millions of families all over the country and it is necessary to ensure as high a level of efficiency and integrity as possible down to the levels at which they come into actual contact with the people. This means that at all stages there is a clear demarcation of functions; that officers are suitably trained for carrying out their respective duties; that the working of rules and procedures is watched and defects disclosed are removed speedily; that those whose work lies among the people spend most of their time living with them and getting to know them; and that there is careful supervision with strict enforcement of responsibility. All this means sustained efforts from day to day. It is a permanent process'. The only thing that needs to be added to these sagacious remarks is that this process cannot be carried out by governments which include ministers of poor calibre and indifferent rectitude.

Whilst on this topic it is just as well to count our blessings. India has a well-developed administrative machinery which has experience and potentiality and needs only peripheral support in the way of foreign technicians or technologists. But most of the African countries have to rely to a far greater extent on expatriates, involving many complex problems of adjustment and remuneration. The remedy suggested is recruitment by a U.N. agency, but even here the terms of the contracts, problems of co-operation and coordination among advanced countries providing the staff, excessive cost and international political pulls are likely to add new difficulties. A long-term, but in the end more satisfactory solution, could only lie in heavy investment in education with the highest priority given to secondary and technical training and a crash programme of management training. Public participation primarily implies a sense of belonging and it is in this connection that importance attaches to the elimination of all factors tending to cause emotional disintegration, such as a sense of neglect, injustice or oppression. Most governments have now realized, some after painful experience, that minorities of all kinds have to be fairly and even generously treated to the point of making them immune to political misrepresentation by interested opposition parties. The lack of emotional integration, if allowed to remain unremedied, may in addition to retardation of the developmental effort, even encourage incipient secessionist tendencies, to exploit which external power blocks may be ever willing for their own purposes. With self-determination being always within the range of possibility owing to external support, overt or disguised, there is no way of winning the loyalties of minorities except through genuine concern and generous treatment.

Development being fundamentally a transition from tradition to modernity, developing societies have to devise effective means of influencing the attitudes of social groups in favour of the desired changes. Psychological and social problems are paramount in development. There could be few now in the modern age of rapid and wide communication who would wish to hang on to the supposed merits of traditionalism out of conviction, and with the new means of mass-communication even relatively illiterate rural populations may be made to appreciate the need for change. But it should be borne in mind that in their circumstances of marginal existence they cannot afford to take risks with innovations. Here a carefully fostered rural leadership taught to appreciate the value of change can play a decisive role—hence the vital importance, in a new context, of adequate adult education and of a well-organized co-operative and community development movement to evoke and motivate leadership.

Problems of land tenure have an importance all their own in developing countries, but so varying are the conditions that the solution must be unique to each country. The termination of disproportionate rewards without effort involved in latifundia is amply justified, but excessive egalitarianism in the absence of concurrent organizational improvements with the new owners may actually be harmful to efficient land use. The unchecked pressure of population and the need for extra land is also bound to weaken the bargaining position of prospective lessees in regard to rentals and erode the desire to invest in recommended improvements. The only enduring solution would seem to be to diversify the occupational pattern of industries of a suitable type and with minimum economic viability.

The pre-requisities of optimum industrial production include reforms in respect of certain 'traditional' attitudes and patterns of behaviour of employers (e.g. as Barbara Ward pointed out in the Oxford Conference on Tensions of Development, excessive profits distributed as dividends, diverting profits to real estate for speculative appreciation, tax-evasion, operating by nepotism rather than merit, or by corruption rather than integrity, and keeping wages depressed so that a mass internal market never emerges). On the other hand, unduly high rates of salaries, an inflated wage structure and over-emphasis on welfare measures all involve injustice to the consumer—usually the more vulnerable sections of the urban and rural population.

The following argument of Arthur Lewis found general acceptance at the Oxford Conference on Tensions of Development (September, 1961) in connection with the bearing of agricultural advance on industrial development and is worth quoting in extenso : "Even if there were enough capital and skilled man-power to produce non-agricultural jobs for all those who wanted such jobs, agricultural stagnation would still inhibit economic development in two ways. First, the expanding sector needs agricultural produce, both food and raw materials. If agriculture is stagnant, shortage of agricultural products, and high prices, inhibit non-agricultural expansion. The expanding sector is driven to import agricultural products, but unless it can export correspondingly an increasing amount of its own products, this merely produces a balance of payments crisis, with resultant limitations on imports. Accordingly, the first disadvantage of agricultural stagnation is that it limits the rate of economic development to the rate at which foreign earnings can be increased through additional exports of minerals, manufactures or such services as tourism'.

"The second disadvantage is that it limits the markets for the goods produced in the expanding sector. Factory workers consume only a fraction of their own produce; they need to sell the rest in exchange for goods and other non-factory services and commodities. If agriculture is stagnant, it offers only a stagnant market, and inhibits the growth of the rest of the economy. The core of the doctrine of 'balanced growth' is that neglect to develop agriculture makes it more difficult to develop anything else......

"Failure to solve the problem of stagnant peasant agriculture is due principally to failure of governments to fix the responsibility for providing large sums of money for this purpose. Behind this failure has lain intellectual myopia. The most obvious features of the past century and a half of development in the West has been urbanisation with industrialisation. It took some time to realize that this was made possible only by an equally profound revolution in agriculture, which increased the average farm family's output from enough food to feed one and a half families to enough food to feed ten families. Most under-developed countries have now taken in the point but action is still slow."

It is time now to turn to the need and pre-conditions for external or international co-operation. The topic may broadly be divided into (i) external assistance in techniques and training, (ii) external foreign aid, (iii) foreign trade versus aid, and (iv) foreign investment.

The perspective to external aid for development consists

of the continuity of the process of development, with the countries of the world at different stages of it, as well as the rapid communicability of political and economic impulses. In such a setting it becomes not only an urge but also the self-interest and indeed the duty of the industrialized and more advanced countries to come to the aid of those which are at low stages of development and which are making serious efforts to develop their own resources and to improve the standards of their peoples.

A rapidly expanding world economy should be the objective of all countries, rich and poor, and all countries should recognize that they are full partners in the process of expanding the world economy. As the richer help the poorer to develop, and as purchasing power of the peoples of the developing countries increases, world markets will expand rapidly, and the more advanced countries will have much better prospects for the expansion of their trade. Otherwise, the industrial countries would stagnate through lack of expanding markets. Aid given to reach these goals is therefore properly mutual asistance and not charity.

Any cessation or unplanned contraction of the flow of capital aid from the relatively more developed to the relatively less developed countries will create serious difficulties and tensions. This is especially so as most, if not all, of the latter class of countries *ex hypothesi* depend on the export of agricultural and plantation commodities, many depending on one or two commodities only, the prices of which are unstable and the demand for which is found frequently not to expand with the expansion of the world trade owing to growing competition from synthetic chemical products. The prices of many primary commodities have been going down since 1957 and without any corresponding decrease in the prices of manufactured goods. This means a further widening of the gap between standards of living in the two categories of countries and a possible grievance, already expressed on some occasions, that industrial countries are benefitting at the expense of the underdeveloped countries.

Apart from economic arguments, in this shrinking world the advanced countries have a collective moral responsibility to help the developing ones, similar to the responsibility which a national government has for the improvement of the living standards of its poorer areas.

With regard to the methods of chanelling aid, internationally-administered agencies are preferable to bilateral arrangements, because in most cases, if not invariably, billateral aid is suspect as being aid given on political or military consideration. This is especially so as the competition or conflict between the 'Eastern and Western Blocs' tends to draw the developing countries into the arena of the cold war. Often this competition, it is complained, forces the aid-giving countries to provide funds for projects which are either economically unsound or for projects of import substitution involving excessive import tariffs and the ultimate curtailment of trade. Also, unlike multilateral aid, bilateral aid does not help the recipient country to plan its expenditure on a co-ordinated and carefully considered development programme.

At the Oxford Conference on Tensions of Development held in September, 1961, there was a consensus on the suggestion that contributions by the industrially developed countries to the resources of international agencies supporting development programmes, should not be less than 1 per cent of of their gross national product. This percentage, which has already been supported by all members of the United Nations in a General Assembly resolution, is estimated to yield between 7 and 8 billion i.e. roughly Rs. 3 to 4,000 crores a year if all the industrially developed countries in America, Western and Eastern Europe and the Far East agree to make their contributions on this scale. This figure does not include loans advanced bilaterally at commercial rates of interest or privately invested capital. If this is done a new era for the prosperity of the human race will have begun and the second half of the 20th century might well witness a standard of universal prosperity never before recorded in history. It will be possible for developing countries to make this contribution even if they have balance of payment difficulties, since contribution need not always be in foreign currencies and can be made in goods and/or services. An additional advantage of such a formal provision would be that it will not be overlooked if as aid for development it is included as an item in the budget of the donor country. As Barbara Ward pointed out at the Oxford

Conference, it was time that the developed countries accepted a concept of 'decade for development' so that aid can have an advocate through this procedure in the person of the minister in whose budget the item is included.

It is recognized that this is an ideal for the achievement of which all intelligent and enlightened men and women must work; but no one will wish to ignore the realities of the present-day situation which will retard its realization in the immediate future. The immediate objective should be to continue the efforts to obtain more funds for international agencies like the International Development Association, to establish regional and national development banks where they do not exist, and to make the best possible use of bilateral aid given by individual donor countries or by consortiums of donor countries.

Where aid continues to be bilateral, the donor countries should ensure that the aid is for the benefit of the people of the recipient country as a whole and not for the benefit of individuals or groups of individuals, that it is given for carefully worked-out plans and that it is co-ordinated with aid provided by international agencies and other individual or groups of donor countries.

In considering the provision of funds for the developing countries a distinction has to be made between aid for pre-investment needs and aid for the execution of development projects. Aid for the investigation of the natural resources, for research laboratories, fellowships and training in the various managerial and technical skill is of very high priority, because such pre-investment work not only helps in the discovery and planning of the development of the natural resources, but also provides the necessary pre-condition for development. The United Nations Special Fund has demonstrated that such pre-investment can best be channelled and utilized through the United Nations. Everyone interested, government as well as individuals, must therefore keep on urging that more and more should be pledged to the U.N. Special Fund.

It is now widely recognized that aid for pre-investment and investment purposes becomes one of the first needs of developing countries, as very few of these can set aside for development the 15 to 25 per cent of their national income—which is considered to be necessary for an economic take-off.

Industrial development cannot be achieved unless the necessary capital is provided for all pre-investment requirements and for the execution of projects. Pre-investment includes resource surveys, the creation of a suitable climate for investment, man-power surveys, skills et cetera.

Moreover, in the transitional period, as India's Planning Commission pointed out (p. 27 of Third Five Year Plan Report) : 'The effort to develop the basic and heavy industries and machine-building capacity, without which the growth of the economy would itself be retarded, accentuates the balance of payments problem. Replacement of imports is essentially a question of developing the necessary capacity for production within the country'. Indeed, in the initial period a larger strain is imposed by the necessity of importing specialized capital equipment and raw materials and components.

As the backward countries develop they will be forced to earn foreign exchange by exporting manufactures in the same way as other countries in their developmental stages in Europe and elsewhere had to do in the 19th century. But a deliberate reorientation of the theory and the practice of tariffs is required for facilitating such exports, not only to less developed countries but also to the more developed countries , which latter must be content with lower tariffs on such imports than they have to put up with on their corresponding exports. This need not be regarded a national hardship in the advanced countries, although sectional vested interests are bound to be affected adversely. For, the implications of the vanguard of science and technology is that those who occupy the position make room for others in the rear, occupying more forward positions, i.e., in the field concerned shifting to and relying on the scientifically and technologically more advanced manufactures.

That about a fortnight ago the U.S.A. and the European Common Market reached an agreement on a mutual 20% reduction in tariffs on their industrial products and also an agreement on some reduction in tariffs on agricultural products is evidence of the seriousness with which this question of lowering tariff barriers to sharpen the edge of competition and efficiency is being considered in the advanced countries. As a spokesman of the E.E.C. said then: 'It is the first time that one delegation negotiated tariff cuts in the name of six countries. Similar negotiations are going on or will start between the E.E.C. and Britain, Switzerland, Sweden, Finland, Austria, Portugal, New Zealand, Uruguay and Canada. In the meanwhile, the Common Farm Agreement among the six who form the E.E.C. is already an accomplished fact. The general verdict on this achievement is : 'But it has been clearly stated on both sides of the (English) channel that the 'Six' have displayed striking determination to promote political unity of the community as a whole even at the risk of ignoring sensitive national interests'. (In India we may ruefully ponder the fact that with political unity already achieved we should have occasion to worry about national integration !)

Arrangements for equitable commodity prices and for measures of international commodity price stabilization as in the case of wheat and sugar still remain a desideratum. Intranationally many developing countries lack adequate credit facilities for their exports, and even in a relatively more developed country among these, as India, it is only very recently that the government has accepted the necessity for providing these.

That private investment from abroad, in addition to governmental or institutional external aid, had an important role to play in the developmental effort is widely, although not universally, recognized. Some of the newly-independent countries feel that large-scale private investment could dominate the economy of a developing country so as to render its independence meaningless. There is also room for apprehending that in developing countries occasions might arise which could cause the sudden flight of private capital, a flight which would cripple the economies of these countries. A few developing countries are therefore totally opposed to private foreign investment, while some others permit it only if there is association with it of nationals or their governmental corporations. Against such apprehensions, a system of international guarantees is recommended on the lines on which such a guarantee is provided for private United States of America capital invested abroad.

The whole question has been carefully considered by the Parliamentary Group for World Government (of the United Kingdom), the conclusions being set out in a booklet entitled

'A World Investment Convention ?' The Convention of Code suggested is aimed at providing a minimal assurance to borrowing nations against exploitation and domination by foreign companies, and to foreign investors against confiscation or discrimination. It would therefore help to increase the flow of funds for productive investment, improve the relations between borrowers and lenders, and for both these reasons would be of considerable political as well as economic importance. The Code would provide, as to borrowers' rights (i) the right to nationalize industries, provided sufficient notice of the change is lodged, fair compensation is paid and there is no violation of any agreement not to nationalize for a stated period; (ii) to regulate by special arrangements appropriate to the technical requirements of the industry concerned the compulsory employment of their nationals in enterprises owned by foreigners; (iii) to regulate, again in an ad hoc manner, the proportion of foreign directors and of capital that may be employed; (iv) to impose restrictions on foreign payments when this is necessary to protect the exchange rate (e.g. in a crisis caused by sudden fall in the price of a stable primary commodity); (v) to lay down the financial conditions under which an investment may be made, e.g. indication of a 'fair return'.

It is worth noting in this connection that many of these borrowers' rights are insisted on even in the industrialized countries. Many European countries license foreign investments in order to keep them within the framework of national policies; some have regulations laying down the proportion of local directors or local capital that must be employed; most restrict the right to repatriate capital, in accordance with balance of payments needs.

As to lenders' rights, there are draft codes such as those of the International Chamber of Commerce. They provide for : (i) non-discrimination in political, legal, administrative and fiscal matters and in access to necessary equipment and materials; (ii) freedom to employ the minimum necessary foreign managerial or technical staff for efficient operation; (iii) to own a sufficient percentage of the capital to help bridge the differences of viewpoint between borrowers and lenders; (iv) to have facilities to withdraw dividends or interest and subjeet to the balance of payments situation, capital; (v) payment of fair compensation if contracts are revoked and (vi) recourse to an international Arbitration Tribunal in cases of disputes.

A convention of the above lines under the auspices of the United Nations would greatly expand the scope for fruitful, but not irksome, 'foreign private investment'. Licensing of such investment should in particular help to prevent undue exploitation of a highly protected internal market where a foreign enterprise jumps over tariff walls, a risk, which as T. Balogh has pointed out, might assume substantial proportions in course of time, in the shape of a large transfer burden on the borrowing country.

Current trends in international economy are of momentous import for developing countries. The European Common Market movement seems likely to involve beneficent potentialities as a reaction, exemplified by the U.S.A. President's move to secure an all round lowering of tariff walls. Further, cyclical movements of economic activity have smaller amplitude and the economies of most advanced-countries exhibt a greater stability through institutional change. Moreover, competition in rates of economic growth has led even a conservative nation like the U.K. to institute a Five Year Plan of Economic Development, involving conscious stimulation of the economy, although largely through exhortation and guidance of private enterprise.

The European Common Market as modified by lowering of tariff walls on both sides of the Atlantic, is, however, likely to aggravate the difficulties of the developing countries, unless differential tariffs in their favour on manufactured goods are conceded. Dr. B. K. Madan, who discussed the connected issues in his recent (December 27, 1961) Presidential Address on 'Problems of International Economic Policy', observed in this connection: 'The European Common Market has installed greater efficiency and higher productivity as guide-posts of economic advance, of which the less developed countries cannot fail to take note. These countries should indeed, be constantly concerned to improve the efficiency and competitive capacity of their economies; for without steady efforts in this direction their goals of economical development will continually recede'.

The above desideratum involve primarily a lowering of the cost of production. This involves choice of appropriate locations, economies of scale, special productivity studies and, perhaps most important of all, holding inflationary pressures in check. India's Third Five Year Plan Report devotes considerable attention to this problem and discusses in some detail the constituents of price policy, such as fiscal and monetary discipline, regulatory measures, such as increase in productive buffer stocks, reorganization of distribution arrangements and, in some cases even direct controls, and severe deterrents to detected and brought to book anti social activities like hoarding and profiteering.

But cost reduction and export promotion can only partially help developing countries to conserve their foreign balances. The development process involves a basic inbalance in payments which, as Dr. Madan rightly pointed out, needs provision for rather than circumvention. 'It does not admit of treatment through adjustment of the current balance of trade, but requires a change in the capital balance', pointing to the need not only of the reinforcement of the existing international monetary framework which relates to the promotion of long-term capital flow but also a re-orientation on the lines indicated by him of the monetary policies and procedures of international organization, like the International Monetary Fund.

Much attention has recently been bestowed on regional planning and economic integration, as for instance in a conference of planners sponsored by the ECAFE South-East Asia and the Far East. 'The broad conclusions reached were: (a) the recognition that planning is essential for Asia's Econo mic Development; (b) some definite steps have to be taken to promote effective regional co-operation considered as a means of helping economic progress within individual countries and the region as a whole; (c) techniques, administrative procedures and execution of plans have all to be steadily improved, and (d) an Asian Institute of Economic Development should be established to provide practical and theoretical training for governments' representatives in economic and social planning and there should be a regional advisory group on economic development planning consisting of experts who would be available on the request of governments to assist them in drawing up their plans. Moreover, an Asian Productivity Organization—including India, Japan, South Korea, Nepal, the Phillippines, Pakistan and Thailand—was set up last year to provide the means for co-operative action among its members and to serve as an arrangement for the exchange on wide scale of experience and know how, as well as to function as one of the channels through which foreign aid can be directed to its members collectively.

Concerted action among the ECAFE countries seems to be an imperative of development and has to be organized so as to overcome the diversities of geography, history, politics or ideology. Food production needs to be substantially increased—the rate of annual increase should be doubled to keep par with the explosion of population; limited markets have to be expanded and intra-regional trade promoted. In this effort, the industrially advanced countries of the world must help, especially by facilitating the import of manufactured goods from the less developed countries. There is a great deal of scope for regional infra-structure schemes, e.g., river valley schemes or Asian Highways. Co-operative institutions will have to play an ever-increasing role in the development of these countries.

For stepping up the rates of investment all the means available—public or private saving, deficit financing, foreign loans and grants—have to be deployed, subject to appropriate safeguards. The development may aim to be largely self-contained and autonomous in course of time as in India or contemplate more extended exchange with the outside world.

A common market for the region may not be feasible, but greater integration of long-term plans should be possible, perhaps involving some specialization and some realism in not aiming at having every adjunct of a developed economy, e.g., a steel mill.

The F.A.O. and U.N. have evolved a joint programme for stepping up world food availability through an international cash and commodity fund which will help to ease the food-problem.

On the Afrasian front also much incipient co-operative activity is in evidence, e.g. through the Afro-Asian Organization for Economic Co-operation, the members of which are

Chambers of Commerce and Industry. Aid through trade is its major objective, to be secured through ensuring better stability of prices for raw materials and improved access to foreign markets and by influencing State policies in the right directions for the common good.

Apart from regional and global inter-nation co-operation, the exacting tasks of development seem to call for yet new specialized international agencies and a reorientation of the framework and policies of some of the existing ones. This problem was thoughtfully discussed by B. K. Madan in his Presidential Address at the 44th Session of the All-India Economic Conference held at Dharwar a month ago. He suggested that over and above the borrowing arrangement finalised by the International Monetary Fund as a result of recent discussions, and apart from future increases in quotas, the International Monetary Fund should initiate some decisive steps in the direction of internationalisation of gold reserves over and above what has been achieved through the subscriptions of member countries. He has put forward a concrete measure, which seems feasible to me. But as Dr. Madan pointed out, 'steady and orderly progress and continued improvement of the basis of productivity and efficiency of the economy require constant vigilance against the corruptive and corrosive influences of insidious inflation and monetary disorder'.

The following facts and figures have a bearing on this caveat.

Whilst the per capita product at constant prices has increased between 1953 and 1958 or 1959 in India, Indonesia, Japan, Italy, U.K. and Western Germany, from 100 to 109, 106, 132, 134, 112 and 138, respectively, the cost of living index has risen from 120, 400, 116, 120, 123 and 115, respectively in these countries during the same period. The situation in Indonesia, judging from these figures, would seem to be such as to warrant anxiety. In India, while the rise in the cost of living is comparable to that in the other four countries, the increase in per capita product achieved at constant prices is unsatisfactory as compared with Italy, Japan and West Germany. India must therefore-better the production effort and keep a tighter check on the rise of the cost of living. The stability of domestic conditions and balance in the international monetary frame-work are inter-related and inter-dependent. Ineptitude at home is inconsistent with assistance from abroad. Any continuance of the former will in the long run cool the friendly ardour of the aid-India club far more than Goa has in the short run !

STATISTICAL QUALITY CONTROL

Statistical Quality Control, or SQC for short, means statistical methods of control developed by industry for the purpose of attaining economic control of quality of product in mass production. It is one of the weapons in the armoury of Productivity Organizations, concerned with factors such as improving uniformity of quality and fitting quality as precisely as possible to uses, rather than directly reducing cost of production. It has been demonstrated, nevertheless, that the institution of SQC leads to a significant reduction in cost, *via* avoidance of rejections and wastage or over-fulfilment of specification as a counterpoise to unequal quality or standard of product. The maintenance of SQC helps keeping the above losses to the minimum. It is like a steering wheel to an automobile on the road.

The control of quality involves the specification of what is needed—the production of goods according to specification and the inspection of the goods to test if they satisfy the specification. Statistical techniques, developed during the first-half of the present century, can indicate to a fairly precise extent the limitations on the attainment of uniformity of quality or product; help to attain uniformity as delimited; and, finally, to evaluate the quality of the product in the least wasteful way.

In his book, *Statistical Method from the Viewpoint of Quality Control*, Walter A. Shewhart, acknowledged as the father of SQC, has pointed out how during man's known history (including proto-history and archaeology) stretching over 1,000,000 years, evidence of some conscious attempt to attain quality of implement dates only from some 10,000 years ago, whereas the technique of mass production, characterized by interchangeable parts, can be traced back over only the last 150 years. Moreover, the initial efforts, based on exact science, were directed towards the production of piece parts to exact dimensions. The concept of 'tolerance' was introduced only in 1840 and of a range of tolerance in 1870. These concepts were the first-aid in reducing the fruitless cost of trying to do the impossible, i.e., trying to produce things *exactly* alike.

But setting limits of tolerance must necessarily be accompanied, to be effective, by methods of inspection which would be the least expensive, i.e. the cost of which would not be greater than the savings secured by minimizing the number of rejected product or parts of a product.

Where the manufacturing process consists of the production and final fitting together or transformation into numerous parts, it is clear that statistical inspection must be brought to bear at each stage. This process, indeed, becomes inevitable where the one-and-final tests for strength, chemical composition, blowing-out time (e.g. of a fuse), capacity to explode (e.g. of a hand-grenade) and so on are destructive of the product itself. This consideration necessarily implies the inspection of samples. It is here that statistical techniques, based on the theory of chance or probability, offered a solution, somewhere towards the end of the first quarter of the twentieth century and SQC was born.

What gave a fillip to the movement was the development of industrial standardization organizations all over the world, the consciousness of standards entailing the consideration in an increasingly intensive way of minimizing rejections of sub-standard products as well as minimizing cost of inspection.

SQC relies on the following proposition: that experience in the control of quality provides a practical technique for detecting and eliminating assignable causes of variability in the production process until a state of statistical control is reached wherein predictions based upon the assumption of randomness will prove valid. It helps, by elimination of assignable cause of variability, to make the most efficient use of raw materials, maximize quality, minimize cost of inspection and losses from rejection.

In specifying quality and the range of tolerance, the limitations on commercial conditions of production have to be borne in mind. Moreover, specification, production and inspection have to be coordinated, in the words of Walter Shewhart, so that, 'in fact, the three steps may be thought of as a scientific experiment in which the objective is the attainment of the most efficient use of the available material'. SQC can thus be an ever-vigilant and active scientific ally in closing up the tolerance range, improving the quality of goods and help decrease production costs. Its optimum utilization involves, on one hand, the enlightenment in this respect of the growing generation of industrial leaders, so that they will recognize the potential contributions that statistical theory and techniques have to offer, and, on the other hand, introducing highly trained statisticians into industry, as also 'creating a statistically minded generation of physicists, chemists, engineers and others who will in any way have a hand in developing and directing the production process of tomorrow.'

Despite its theoretical advantages it was not till the time of the Second World War that SQC was seriously adopted and developed for industrial production. Since then it has made considerable headway in the U.S.A. and in Japan and, to a lesser extent, in Europe. In India it attracted little attention, principally because economy and efficiency were at a discount in the seller's market that prevailed as an aftermath of the War. It was against this background that the Indian Statistical Institute and the Indian Standards Institution invited, under joint sponsorship, Dr. Walter A. Shewhart to India to give an exposition of the importance of SQC in industrial production to industrialists and others interested.

Dr. Shewhart's visit, extending over some months, introduced SQC as a concept and a possible practice to India's industrialists, but hardly any of these realized its significance. An association to promote SQC was established in Calcutta, but for many years this association also remained dormant. However, in the meanwhile, a few forward-looking industrial enterprises had introduced some sort of SQC in their organizations and a few Indians, who had studied SQC in foreign countries, were in a position to help in training Indian SQC technicians. The Bombay branch of the Indian Statistical Institute, for instance, started training courses in SQC within a short time of Dr. Shewhart's visit and helped to create some interest in SQC in Bombay's industrial world. The main Institute in Calcutta had been taking active interest in SQC and the application of statistical methods to industry since 1945, when the first training courses on SQC in India were organized by the Institute.

In 1954, on the advice of the Statistical Adviser, backed by the Ministry of Finance, the Prime Minister of India constituted a Statistical Quality Control Policy Advisory Committee with the writer as its Chairman, in order to promote the movement and to arrange systematically for the training of industrial employees at various levels, as well as technicians, in SQC. The Committee includes as its members both statistical scientists and academicians as well as some prominent Indian industrialists, as also representatives of the Indian Standards Institution and the National Productivity Council. A year earlier the Indian Statistical Institute had already established a SQC unit in Bombay with the help of a special grant from Government. Two more field units were added on the formation of the Committee, one in Calcutta and the other in Bangalore, and a branch of the last one was later added at Coimbatore.

During the last eight years a great deal of promotional work in SQC has been done in India, largely as the direct result of the stimulus given by the Policy advisory Committee. In January 1955 the Indian Statistical Institute organized a conference in Calcutta for the discussion of technical matters as well as questions of policy and in 1956, when three foreign experts on SQC were available at the Institute, representatives of all the SQC units assembled in Calcutta for a departmental review of the position.

Prof. Barnard of the Imperial College of Science and Technology, who drew up a report on the conference, pointed out at the outset that the term SQC as used in India denotes what is in U.K. called 'industrial statistics' or 'statistics in industry' and that in U.K. and also, to some extent, in the U.S.A. the phrase SQC refers to certain of the simpler statistical controls, while in the application of statistics, especially in Indian conditions, it is often the more advanced methods that are called for.

Training in SQC was put on a systematic basis as a result of the conference and the publication of its report. The training courses included courses not only for workers and foremen but also for managers, leading technical personnel, engineers and technologists. The importance was recognized of ensuring that those who give instruction in SQC should have continuing first-hand experience of its application. Improvements were also suggested in the academic or scholastic courses in mathematics or statistics.

Towards the end of 1955 a SQC unit was established for ordnance factories by the Ministry of Defence of the Government of India, with functions such as introduction of SQC methods in process control for the ordnance factories, the progressive taking over of their co-ordination work of the Works Inspection Sections and the investigation of the compatibility of specifications.

Skipping the intervening period, it seems worthwhile referring to the Report of Work and Review for the period January 1959 to September, 1961, prepared for the consideration of the SQC Policy Advisory Committee, since this will shed light on a number of important aspects of the development of SQC in India.

To begin with, the results of the SQC promotional work will be clear from the fact that whereas in 1955-56 the number of factories served by the various SQC units (now eight, those in Delhi, Baroda, Madras and Kerala having been added during the last two years) was 32, in 1961-62 it was 78. Inadequacy of trained staff is beginning to appear as the predominant case of retarding progress in this respect, although the position is steadily improving in recent years; against the normal workload for a trained technical assistant of 2.5 factories, we have now already 2.4 factories.

General promotional work consists of the holding of conferences, lectures and talks, followed by visits to top managements in their offices to persuade them of the value of SQC. The holding of training courses for industrial personnel has served to awaken the interest of managements, whilst managers also, convinced of the value of SQC, often influence other managers to give it a trial. Special set-backs, for instance, a fall in exports, often give an impetus to SQC in the search for remedies.

Another encouraging feature, concealed in the slow progress of membership statistics, is the building up of their own SQC organizations by factories withdrawing from membership. An analysis of the membership figures following investigation through questionnaires has indicated other remediable causes of lack of interest, such as want of supporting staff in the factory, actual opposition from middle management, lack of sustained management interest generally.

The National Productivity Council has been an increasingly active ally in the spread of SQC as part of its productivity drive. Many foreign experts, supplied under the various technical assistance schemes, have helped to bring more industrial organizations to adopt SQC. Nevertheless, the total picture is not yet satisfactory from the operational point of view.

Experience of the working of the SQC units indicates certain priorities for operation and plan purposes, although a more thorough investigation based on prescribed standrads for and details of reporting will be necessary before thoroughly reliable conclusions can be drawn. The problem that comes to notice most frequently is, appropriately enough, the study of quality, and very close to it are others such as dimensional control, process control and process capability. The utilization of resources appears to be of comparable importance, although it is generally regarded more a problem for Industrial Engineering than Quality. Reduction of waste, whether irrecoverable scrap or scrap recoverable by re-work, is more traditionally a function of quality control. Problems come up both as a result of reference from managements as points of trouble as through selection by the staff of the SQC unit as matters of profitable study which are not always recognized as problems by the management. Incursion by the SQC staff into the field of management accounting, dealing with the broader aspects of business efficiency, would strengthen SQC work, but this requires both greater confidence by management and greater technical resources on the part of the SQC units.

As for actual techniques used, the most frequent single technique employed is the control chart with which the history of SQC began. The variations of manufacture involve cause and effect analysis and this is followed by indication of appropriate steps for rectification. Work sampling and work study have been used largely in examining the utilization of resources, particularly in textile mills and engineering establishments. Other less common techniques are the 'design of experiments', a matter yet hesitatingly supported by engineers and technologists. Work study and operations research have long been in use by the units, although their recognition as highly specialized management techniques is only a recent development in Indian industrial circles.

The SQC units are financed by the Government of India on a deficit budget basis, through a grant-in-aid to the Indian Statistical Institute. The payment for service rendered by industries served is not yet on an economically adequate scale, and the time has perhaps come for placing this matter on a more business-like basis. But this raises the question of a dependable flow of the supply of suitably trained man-power. In the past the rate of expansion of SQC was held up for lack of trained personnel and the position is not much better today, since they are required not only for strengthening the SQC units but also for the basic quality control work in the member-factories advised. Within the last year or two a large number of young men, mostly statisticians, have come forward for specialized training in quality control, but it will be at least three years before these men become really useful either to the units or to industry. For more experienced personnel India continues to be dependent to a certain extent on senior foreign experts, who are hard to come by.

The problems of promotion, payment for services and supply of trained manpower are inter-connected and it is not easy to establish a balance as the work expands. In the U.S.A. as well as in Japan initiative in the adoption of SQC had come from industry itself, though with guidance from scientists and technologists. In India there is yet little support from industry —and it is still for the specialists to approach industrialists to convince them of the significance of SQC and to demonstrate and advise. General promotional work such as the holding of conferences or seminars has been and is being tried and in this the National or local Productivity Councils and the management associations can render yeoman service. There is also a place in promotional effort for the National Society for Quality Control, established soon after Dr. Shewhart's visit, but not active, owing to a number of organizational problems, until recently. It is this body which should undertake the main responsibility for general promotional work through periodical conferences, conventions, exhibitions, discussion groups, lectures by experts, publication of a journal, maintenance of a technical library, acting as a clearing house for experience in the application of SQC, production and circulation of films demonstrating the application of SQC in Indian industry and the like activities.

The SQC Policy Advisory Committee will be holding its meetings in different industrial cities in India so as to diffuse interest in SQC and they have also decided to hold a conference in Bombay next July for the purpose of interesting managements in SQC.

Other decisions for strengthening the SQC movement included co-ordination of the work of the SQC Policy Advisory Committee with that of the Project Co-ordination Committee set up by Government with a view to exploring the possibilities of introducing SQC in the public enterprises with which the Co-ordination Committee was concerned. The Committee recognized that in the initial period the expansion of training programmes and giving to them the necessary tone as well as strengthening the SQC units with personnel of the requisite calibre, would have to depend very largely on Government assistance, but it was felt that this would be a profitable investment in that productivity would be increased and any augmentation of subsidies at this stage was sure to bring benefits to the economy several times over in due course.

The association of National Productivity Council with the Advisory Committee is bound to be a source of increasing strength. There need be no question of overlapping and encroachment and apprehensions on this account. The training programmes of the National Productivity Council were usually arranged after consultation with the SQC units and there is room for making closer such consultations and contacts to the mutual advantage of the local Productivity Councils and the SQC units.

There is yet a great deal to be done in regard to the collection of information about the function of SQC systems in the Indian factories and to review the whole work. There is no doubt that progress of SQC in India has been uneven and inadequate because of piecemeal application of statistical quality control methods instead of adopting a comprehensive approach. By contract, in Japan it is reported that 60 per cent of the factories, having 100 or more employees, have full-fledged SQC programmes in operation. There SQC consciousness is aroused by lectures, seminars, quality marking schemes, exports promotion schemes, all of which called for the maintenance of quality and the employment of refined techniques of SQC. Indeed, unlike the old days the main emphasis in Japan is on total quality control and the national consciousness has been built up for making 'Made in Japan' synonymous with 'Quality'.

In the world generally there has been an extensive increase in the use of modern quality control techniques and in the development of formal quality control programmes. Side by side there has been a considerable production of literature in this field with respect to specialized applications of statistical methods. Edward M. Schrock in his book, *Quality Control and Statistical Methods*, in the preface to the second edition, says, 'it is becoming apparent that as important as statistical and other specialized techniques may be, they will in themselves assure the success of a quality control programme. Proper organization and sound administration are essential to the success of such a programme (and most other programmes). Groups attending quality control conventions and conferences have been showing an increased interest in how to start quality control programmes and how to make them effective'. It is very true that optimum results from SQC, as from any other employment of productivity, can only be secured by enlightened and efficient management.

FIRST LECTURE

It is indeed a great honour to be invited to deliver the first of the John Mathai Memorial Lectures series. During 1946 to 1959 events brought John Mathai and myself closer and closer together in public life and I learned to admire him as one of India's most cultured products, endowed with a rare combination of qualities, a perceptive and thoughtful mind, a sobriety of judgment in regard to men and affairs, a rare concern for principles, a delightful sense of humour with the soupcon of cynicism natural to a man of the world, scholarliness with its flame kept by regular reading, and fluency and cogency of expression which profoundly influenced those who heard him.

It was an inspired idea of Lord Wavell to have included John Mathai as one of the members of his provisional pre-independence Government of 1946. John Mathai fittingly held first the Finance portfolio, which had to be given up later to Liaquat Ali Khan when towards the end of the year the Muslim League leaders agreed to join the interim Government. John Mathai held thereafter the Railway portfolio which he continued to hold until he succeeded Shanmukham Chetty as the Central Finance Minister in the first quarter of 1949. I was then Governor of the Reserve Bank of India (August 1943 to June 1949) and I assisted John Mathai in the sterling balances negotiations of mid 1949. Owing to some domestic reasons I had decided to spend a few years in U. K. on retirement from the offices of Governor, Reserve Bank. But there happened a domestic calamity which made this plan like the Dead Sea fruit and John Mathai, aware of all this, invited me on behalf of the Government of India to assist Government as its Financial Ambassador in U.S.A. and Europe and, in particular, to negotiate the loan of two million tons of wheat. I accepted: the loan was destined to come two years later during my tenure of office as India's Finance Minister, but in the meanwhile towards the end of the year 1949 Mathai called me to Delhi for consultation. These had become necessary primarily because of the devaluation of the Indian rupee, together with the pound sterling and some 28 other currencies. But that visit for consultations was to turn into a continued residence in Delhi in various capacities upto the present day.

The principal matter that occupied Government's attention—atleast Prime Minister Nehru's—was not devaluation or monetary problems so much as planned economic and social development. During November and December, 1949 I participated in many an informal and entirely exploratory discussion on planning for development, but only with officials. The Prime Minister had not yet assigned any responsibility in the matter to me and John Mathai did not show any interest in it. Since he had been one of the signatories of the Bombay Plan of 1943 or 1944, this indifference on his part surprised me not a little. I believe that with the actual experience of financial and economic administration that Mathai had in the meanwhile, and with the post-war inflation a grim reality which forbade economic experimentation, Mathai had come to change his views about planning. We never discussed the matter, but had he asked for my advice I would have urged some considerations in favour of planned development, especially as India had paid the price of inflationary finance by devaluing the rupee. On the international scene planning was in the air, atleast in project or target of achievement form, eg. the Marshal Plan, the Monnet Plan, What is more, President Trueman had enunciated his Point Four Plan of Technical Assistance and in the World Bank and International monetary Fund on the Executive Boards of which I had continued to be Governor for India since the very inception in 1946, there was every indication that development in Asia and Latin America would receive increasing attention after the more pressing problems of rehabilitating a wartorn Europe had been successfully tackled.

Although I never knew the facts of the situation in regard to Mathai's attitude to planning, I willingly accepted an assignment from the Prime Minister to organize a Planning Commission for India, sometime in February, 1950 as I sincerely believed that planned development was called for in India and would attract substantial external assistances. Even after transferring Pakistan's share to her after partition, India had ample holdings of gold and sterling, a factor of strength in the context of providing domestic finance for development. The Planning Commission was formed and duly installed on April 1, 1950. In the meanwhile John Mathai had resigned and in May the Prime Minister invited me to join his cabinet as Minister for Finance and Economic Affairs, a responsibility which I accepted after considerable hesitation. My personal relations with John Mathai had always been cordial and this cordiality continued unabated inspite of the turn events had taken. Unlike some others Mathai and I allowed no meanness or malice to pollute our relations as predecessor and successor. Indeed Mathai was large-hearted enough always to extend his co-operation whenever requested by me. I was especially grateful to him for agreeing to be chairman of the Taxation Enquiry Commission, whose work is still the basis of our taxation policy, although not the source of any aberrations, excesses or mis-applications that critics in the legislature or outside may find in that policy.

John Mathai was also good enough to accept at my request the Chairmanship of the Board of Governors of the State Bank of India after it was nationalized in 1954, but he found the work not to his liking and resigned the office in a year or two.

When John Mathai became Vice-Chancellor of Kerala University, I had, as the then Chairman of University Grants Commission, again occasion to work with him, this time in the field of higher education, and I recall with pignancy the visit my wife and I paid to him and Smt. Mathai at their newly completed home in Trichur during my visit to the Kerala University and its widely scattered institutions.

Alas John Mathai was soon after to be stricken down by the fell disease that was to carry him off and my last visit to him was in the hospital in Bombay where they had operated on him. It was a sad parting as, although no word was said, it was perhaps realized all round that this was a very serious illness.

In the meanwhile John Mathai had expressed a desire that I should succeed him as Chairman of the Court of Governors of the Administrative Staff College of India. His wishes were respected and I was elected to, and continue to hold, that office, gratefully conscious of the splendid work that John Mathai had done in guiding the development of that institution in its difficult early years.

I have dwelt somewhat at length on these relations between John Mathai and myself both because of their relevance in the context of the topic I have selected for these lectures, as also because of the welcome opportunity it gives me of paying my heartfelt tribute to that great intellect and great-hearted gentleman.

Have the Five Year Plans of India been a success or a failure ?

Success or failure can be judged only in the light of the degree to which avowed aims and objects—not project targets—have been attained. It is also necessary to take an overall view of the achievements of 15 years of planned development. The objectives of India's planned development have been raising the levels of living of the people at large, eliminating unemployment and the removal of disparities, economic and social, so as to achieve social justice. In brief the main aim can be stated to be the building up of a new social order free from exploitation, poverty and injustice, in terms which would represent at least a partial fulfilment of the obligations laid by the constitution on the State.

Judging in the light of the criteria mentioned one is constrained to observe that planning has failed.

The overall statistical picture is depressing enough. Neither the rate of growth of the gross national product nor the increase in national income per capita has been satisfactory, being some 33 to 40 per cent short of the figures aimed at. But what is more distressing is that when a micro-analysis is made it is revealed that all the economic development of these three plan periods has made the rich richer and the poor poorer, that disparities have increased instead of diminishing and that very little in the way of social development has taken place. The first report of the Mahalonobis Committee on income distribution provided ample testimony in support of this finding, and specific investigations and surveys only reinforce it.

Taking the provision of shelter, which is one of the three necessities of life, the other two being food and clothing, sample surveys of urban areas show that 42 per cent of the houses had no latrines, 49 per cent no safe drinking water supply, 80 per cent were constructed with non-durable materials and 49 per cent had floor space less than 200 sq. ft. About 50 per cent of the households earned less than Rs. 100 p.m. and 47 per cent had floor space less than 50 sq. ft. per person. Decent family life is virtually impossible for the vast majority of citizens in the cities. Results of this nature are perhaps due as much to faulty planning as to poor implementation of plans and bad overall economic management in the face of mounting failures.

It is no answer to point in reply to project achievements. Apart from the fact that a very careful analysis, cost benefits or something of this nature, is required before one can pronounce on the success or otherwise of projects, there is the time-factor involved e.g. delays in the completion of projects and in their subsequent development, as in the case of many irrigation projects. In regard to costly projects, completed with foreign assistance and collaboration, it would not be difficult to prove that external assistance involves an increase in cost perhaps of the order of 33 percent.

Recently a note on lessons from the Five Year Plans reportedly drawn up by a member of Planning Commission has drawn attention to imperfections in plan execution, as well as to formulation. By implication one could conclude that plans have not been drawn up with as much care and thoroughness as necessary, and the means and instruments of execution have not been precisely determined. There was no unity of approach in regard to specific action and the degree of discipline in policy so essential for effective and continuous administration have been available in key areas, both at the national and the State levels. Short-term requirements problems fail to be anticipated and provided for and the States fail to observe agreed priorities and misapply or divert to other purposes assistance placed at their disposal by the Centre. There would appear to be lack of appropriate motivation and determination on the part of those who held political office—a glaring instance being the dilatory and half-hearted manner in which land reforms have been carried out. There are many other weaknesses to which the note has drawn attention, but what has been cited will suffice by way of illustration.

Sectors in which there has been wide-spread failure are agricultural production, community development, the organisation of co-operatives, small scale industries, especially in the rural areas, the education of women and girls and above everything, family planning.

There would probably be general agreement that the

organisation of planning machinery is weak in the states. But this is a weakness that is capable of being rectified.

A more serious lack both at the Centre and in the states has been in regard to the clear enunciation of a national policy in each separate field of social development. This in turn has been due to the absence of a proper focus on social development in the absence of which the bulk of the people are apt to be allowed to continue to lead a sub-standard existence. This is aggravated by the failure to instal measures that would make an impact on the growth of population. Insufficient attention is also paid to income distribution and the evils following in the wake of immigration from the rural to the urban areas, tending to produce a state of urban explosion.

About a month ago at Durgapur, about 15 years after the promulgation of the Constitution and the commencement of planned economic development and 10 years after the first official resolution to achieve a socialist pattern of society, the Congress found it necessary, even after an uninterrupted rule, to call for far-reaching social and economic policies and a speedier advance to socialism. Special emphasis is to be laid in IV Plans on social justice and prevention of economic power and monopoly in all its forms. The highest priority is to be given to agriculture, as also to adequate growth of basic industries like steel, non-ferrous metals, chemicals and cement as a precondition for achieving the new social order. Rural electrification is to receive special attention in order to boost agriculture and rural industries. The tiller of soil is to be its owner and special banking facilities are to be set up for giving credit to the weaker sections of the agriculturists. Co-operation was to be promoted, but it was not the intention to go the whole hog with it. Agro-industrial Corporations are to be set up in each state for processing industries as also units to manufacture agricultural implements. Last year's resolution, passed at Bhuvaneshwar, to nationalise rice-mills, has not been implemented and has been now declared to be impracticable. Further expansion in cities is to be checked and they are to be dispersed in rural areas. Land reforms, already enacted, are to be implemented simultaneously with the promotion of co-operative institutions. An integrated plan is to be evolved to overcome the present food difficulties, but details are not spelt-out and controversial issues, e. g. monopoly or partial procurement, are not referred to.

The Home Minister's efforts to root out corruption are applauded. So are the Finance Minister's efforts to unearth hoarded illegitimate money, which gives rise to serious distortions of the economy and an abnormal rise in prices; streamlining of the administration and maximum insistence on accountability of results have also been suggested to ensure the successful implementation of development programme.

The Congress President referred to the Party's determination to get rid of the deficiencies, mistakes and short-comings of the Third Plan.

The resolution in detail says :

Progress towards a socialist society in our country is to be measured in terms of the success achieved in creating adequate employment opportunity and in ensuring for every family a minimum standard in respect of the essential needs of life, in particular, food, clothing, housing, education and health.

In the allocation of resources in the Fourth Plan a major consideration must be the production of essential commodities, services on an adequate scale so that the promise to the people to establish a national minimum by the end of the Fifth Plan becomes possible of fulfilment to a substantial extent. Causes which have led to lower rates of economic growth than aimed at in agriculture and industry are to be analysed and remedies devised. The pace of increase in both industrial and agricultural production is to be quickened effectively.

As the economy grows, social justice is to be promoted to diminish disparities and prevent concentration of economic power and monopoly.

There are avoidable delays in the initiation and development of projects in the public as well as in the private sectors. Emphasis on improved management practices and better management planning. In the field of social services inadequacies in the facilities for education, health, housing and social welfare persist. This lag should be made up. Failure to achieve anticipated results and rise to the level of expectations lie mainly in the sphere of implementation, which underlines the need for better administration and more positive public co-operation-dynamic socialist outlook.

The official report points triumphantly to the continuing and growing faith of the people in the Congress inspite of the numerous difficulties and problems and a deteriorating economic situation. All this would have been very encouraging as an approach to the First Plan but amounts to clear confession of failure so far as the first three Plans are concerned.

As regards specific sectors, a great deal of material is available in regard to the failure of the plans both in the rural and in the urban areas.

In regard to rural areas, a study by Dr. P. N. Masaldan of the Lucknow University financed by the Research Programme Committee of the Planning Commission throws some light on what has gone wrong.

In general villagers are not showing much enthusiasm in adopting new methods for agricultural production—due to time consuming practices, lack of better bullocks, inadequate supply of seeds, poor communications, absence of irrigation and water logging. The co-operative is still not fully accepted. There is a wide-spread feeling among villagers that socially and politically influential sections of the population are likely to secure benefits from the land consolidation movement.

The development programmes in the field of animal husbandry are gaining acceptance but artificial insemination is not making headway owing to shortage of pedigree bulls and light fees. Inspite of an intensive campaign for the distribution of hatching eggs and birds of improved breed, response is not satisfactory owing to reluctance to change dietary habits, cast-prejudice and non-availability of ready markets for eggs.

There is no feeling of involvement of the people themselves-improvements are looked upon as brought by Government agencies. Hardly 20 per cent know about village plans of development or believe that the villagers had any part in their formulation.

As regards urban areas the common man appears to be ignorant about development schemes and feels neglected in general. People complain about the slow pace of development, absence of adequate programmes to meet immediate needs, as also about co-operation, inefficiency and lack of responsibility of the officials.

Regarding utility of family planning, 25 per cent did not

know anything about it. The Family Planning programmes have not rendered much service in the fields of sex and moral education, inter and inter-family relations and marriage counselling.

The problems of rapid urbanization, judging from a memorandum prepared by Dr. J. F. Bulsara with financial assistance from the Research Programme Committee of the Planning Commission, 1964 have yet to be handled effectively.
Socio-economic surveys of 9 Indian cities reveal :

(i) Increase in number of dependents with a decline in employment of women;
(ii) 20 to 30 per cent families live in destitution (annual income Rs. 150/- to 300/- per annum per adult).
(iii) 36 to 85 per cent live in poverty (range of Rs. 180 to 600 per annum per adult).
(iv) Housing conditions are extremely distressing. 27 to 75 percent of families living in one room tenements.

The conditions in Kanpur and Bombay with 62 per cent and 78 per cent in such tenements is particularly shocking morally intolerable and socially explosive.

Slums are destined to exist and grow unless: (a) migration from rural areas can be checked (b) low cost urban housing is provided.

For (a), provision of civic and social amenities eg. protected water supply, communication and electrification are essential; as also.

For (b) an energetic programme of rural industrialization—the Punjab may well be a case—study worth learning lessons from, although here the vital element is the vitality, resourcefulness and sense of self respect of the population itself—the initiative has come from them.

Proper land use and liquidation of speculation in land values is absolutely essential. Here Government is the chief culprit. Strict rationing of accommodation space as well as of the house compound is a *sine qua non*. A beginning must be made here with the houses and compounds of ministers and secretaries and other high officials in Delhi. Ordinarily, no one at any level need have more than 3 bed rooms, in addition to a drawing room, a dining room and an office room, and no room need have a carpet area of more than 224 sq. ft or 22.2 sq. meters. No house need have more site than .25 acre or .1 of an hectare. No house need have a total plinth area of more than 2250 sq. ft. or 225 sq. meters, the cost of which would be below Rs. 50,000. There is a universally applicable arrangement of this size, I believe, in U.S.S.R. and there is no reason why a self-proclaimed socialist government like the Government of India could not take up as a matter of first priority an arrangement at least approximating to this. All legal obstacles in the way should be far removed by the necessary constitutional amendment. It is only a reaching and revolutionary change of this kind that is likely to enable the state to do something substantial to improve the housing situation in urban areas. The state has been enjoined in the constitution to ensure that the minimum essentials of life are available to every citizen. Of these, cloth is not too difficult to provide, and disparities in availability are not at present leading to serious consequences. As regards food, the government will continue to fumble and to experiment, to waver and vascillate as long as food production has not been established on a proper basis. But providing shelter is a tougher problem and cannot be solved merely by the provision of industrial or co-operative low-cost housing. A revolutionary approach is called for on the lines mentioned earlier. Moreover, since, this will help to solve the problem only partially, and social services and social welfare measures would have to be organized so as to supplement inadequate incomes in the case of at least 50 per cent of the urban families.

Although the urban socio-economic surveys could not be fully informative in this respect, the broad conclusions in regard to family planning were.

(1) knowledge of family planning is negligible;
(2) mothers desire spacing between births;
(3) they prefer a family with 3 to 4 children and
(4) an effective and easy oral contraceptive is desirable.

A measure of the prevailing poverty is available in a study of urban income and savings made by the National Council of Applied Economic Research in 1960-62.

Population surveyed by random sampling in towns with 10,000 or more population was 62.4 million. Income earners were found to be 1.5 per house-hold of 5 persons, 40 per cent owned houses and 9 per cent had rent-free accommodation, 51 per cent lived in rented accomodations. After payment of taxes average income was Rs. 437/- per head. About 86 per cent had 52 per cent of the disposable income—did not save—indeed dissaved. The remaining 14 per cent shared 48 per cent of the disposable income, and here the net average saving was about 14 per cent consisting of provident fund, liquid assets, houses, life insurance, gold jewellery, consumer durables and business. It was noticed that next to the size of the income, of all the demographic and socio-economic factors that influence savings, *education had the most significant direct relation to savings.*

Concentration of Economic Power

A recent study of the private sector shows that concentration of economic power is a growing evil. The study establishes that there was an increase in the concentration of economic power in the private sector between 1951 and 1958. The sum total of net fixed assets, depreciation and inventory of all private sector companies had nearly doubled over the period from Rs. 1736 crores to Rs. 3204 crores, the proportion of capital owned by individuals and Government having declined against that owned by companies and Life Insurance Corporation. The managing agency system still predominated in the management of large public industrial companies. But, barring a few, nearly all managing agencies had poor resources, provided only a fraction of the total share capital of companies. Inter-corporate investment was the major instrument of the ownership and control of companies.

Most other countries of Asia have done better than India whether they have had stablized democracy or not and comparable, planned economic social development or not.

The following extract from a recent press report would be found to be of interest in this context :

"India and Pak : Growth angle"

Express News Service, Washington. January, 18, 1964 was for India a 'year of hunger and ideological changes' according to "The New York Times" Supplement on Economic Developments in Asia.

An article on India in the supplement said :

'Generally India's 16 years old faith in socialism—already on wane—grew dimmer still. Desperate dependence on the United States for wheat that costs no foreign exchange affected the economic ideology as well as the inter-national policy.

"The Congress Party enclaves were notable for the absence even of lip service to the old socialist ideal".

In Pakistan, on the other hand, although the population was rising at the rate of 2.8 per cent yearly, there was a 'healthy margin of economic growth'.

Pakistan's gross national product had been rising at the rate of 5.4 per cent annually for the last four years and the 'nation's output of goods and service is out-stripping the population growth", the supplement said.

The most serious lack in the Indian situation has been inadequate allocations for and attention to social services and social welfare. It is necessary to recall that what we are primarily considering is development, not as an end itself, but as the means of achieving the fundamental aims and objectives set out in various places in India's Constitution. The implication of this is that the fulfilment of basic social values and urges may well be found to transcend the field of economic and social development. But our immediate concern is contribution of social services and social welfare to development as part of the necessary investment in human capital. Even within this restricted field, social services and social welfare can be proved to have received insufficient attention in the planning done so far. In other words the priority accorded has not been high enough; nor have the allocations been adequate. It is difficult to advance quantitative proof of this as India's planners have yet to evolve in this regard success indicators, possessing the property of easy measurability. It is high time that a number of such indicators are evolved, and before they can be evolved a great deal of systematic investigation will have to be undertaken by teams of economists, sociologists and social workers.

With some such measurements the potentiality for furthering development will be found even in social welfare, that is services intended to cater for the special needs of persons and groups who, by reason of some handicap, social, economic, physical or mental , are unable to avail themselves of, or are traditionally denied the amenities and services provided by the community.

Two important considerations are involved here, which are apt to be overlooked. One of these concerns an attitude of mind. The broad goals prescribed by the Constitution e.g. social-justice, equality of opportunity, cannot be realized by a society insensitive to the handicapped or underprivileged or disadvantaged sections of the population. The view that is sometimes entertained at the highest levels of authority that India has not enough resources to develop even its normal population and cannot therefore spare any for the handicapped etc. is, besides being unconstitutional and inhuman, also invalid. The reason for its invalidity is that the proportion of the population that can be regarded as handicapped is quite large —indeed in India's present stage of development it will be found on examination to be larger than that of the 'normal'. By way of proof, one has only to think of the hundreds of millions of women so far denied even elementary education and the hundreds of millions of children in the rural areas for whom no pre-primary education is provided. This leads one to the second consideration, which is that the economic consequences of social welfare deserve attention and research, including even sophisticated investigation such as cast-benefit analysis. It will be found there are several ways in which social welfare programmes lead directly to increase in production. e.g. condensed courses of education for adult women conceived also as social welfare *via* rehabilitation to bring them up to the required minimum educational level, so that they can be trained to become elementary school teachers, especially for girls' schools, handicrafts teachers, auxiliary nurses, family welfare advisers; or to give other instances, organisations of industrial co-operatives for indigent women; craft and technical training to facilitate employment of the handicapped and disadvantaged. Apart from the direct contribution, welfare schemes considerably reduce the drag on the economy and mitigate the invisible social costs of social phenomena like beggary, delinquency, crime and the like.

During 1952 to 1962 the Central Social Welfare Board gave considerable philip to well-planned social welfare work, especially as extended to the rural areas. But over-centralization at the centre and premature decentralization on the ground and inability to get the best out of non-governmental organizations has more or less enfeebled, if not destroyed, what had been built up, and everywhere the splendid corps of voluntary workers that had been built up is now disheartened by reducing their functions merely to advising the bureaucracy. What in my opinion the situation calls for is a more enlightened view of the importance of social welfare in the development process, that will revitalize, and use more extensively, the voluntary organisations in the country. Such re-thinking has constantly to be reinforced by continuing studies and by consultation between sociologists and economists.

In this context I may be pardoned if I venture to draw attention to the Research Council for Social Development recently set up by the India International Centre. The aims and objects are :

1. The India International Centre was established with the object of promoting understanding and amity between different communities of the world and as one of the means of fulfilling that object, the Centre considers it desirable to undertake or promote the study of social development.

2. And further to that end, the Centre also intends to undertake studies :

(i) in the national/regional policies of social development;

(ii) in the process of planning in social development; &

(iii) in the interaction between social and economic development at various stages of national growth in developing countries.

There are striking instances of developing countries e.g. Puerto Rico, in regard to which evidence is available to show that substantial investment on social services led to an augmented economic development rather than retardation of it. Apart from this, new needs for social welfare measures arise, as the result of the development process itself, e.g. from the social disorganization that follows industrialization and urbanization. These needs have to be anticipated and provided for rather than left to be dealt with afterwards in their inevitably aggravated forms, e.g. slums.

But social services and social welfare will remain neglected unless there is understanding of the need of the effective organisation of social administration in India.

This aspect of public administration, which is destined to assume increasing importance in view of the ultimate accepted or avowed aim of development has not in India been receiving the attention it deserves. The whole subject was discussed thoroughly at a seminar organised by the India International Centre about a year ago, in which nearly 150 experts participated including 15 from abroad, 12 representatives of the United Nations, specialized agencies and other international organizations, in addition to appropriate representatives of Central, State Governments and voluntary organizations. A full report of the seminar is available in print and deserves persual by all those who are concerned with the improvement and appropriate evolution of public administration in a developing country. It is hoped that it has, in particular, attracted the attention of governments in India and other developing countries in Asia.

On the present occasion it is only necessary to refer very briefly to some of the more important findings of the seminar. These are :

1. In its social aspect, public administration has in substance (as Chief Justice Gajendragadkar who inaugurated the seminar pointed out) become a branch of social service and as such a revolutionary instrument of the State. The goal of welfare can be achieved only if legislative policies are wise and comprehensive and social administration is honest, incorruptible, ruthlessly efficient and fully responsive to the challenge of the times.

2. Social administration may be defined as that part of administration which provides and operates services leading to the removal of prevailing disabilities and to the creation of opportunities for the well-being of individuals and families in the community.

3. In most developing countries, not excepting India, machinery for implementing social services especially social welfare services and also for their evaluation, is inadequate.

4. There is a lack of a clear social policy; as well as gaps in legislation and programmes are unavoidable dispersal of services, with inadequate means for co-operation and co-ordination.

5. The hierarchial organization bureaucratic procedures

of the administration are particularly disadvantageous in the field of social administration as contacting people for rendering services is an essential feature. A suitable simplification accounting and auditing reporting procedures is also called for.

6. Very essential is the formulation of a national policy for social development, planning jointly by the federal, state and local governments together with voluntary organisations.

7. It is of the utmost importance that the people get a full sense of participation in the planning and implementation of all forms of community service.

8. In the organization of such extensive participation by the community in the field of social development the voluntary agencies should be given an adequate role to play side by side with government agencies at all levels. The more overpopulated a country is in relation to its resources, the more obvious should be the need for stimulating voluntary effort to supplement the needs of social development.

9. When planning is done on a country-wide scale and embraces several aspects of social services, surveys and research become necessary to determine social needs and priorities. The Universities have an important part to play in this regard, specially by means of inter-disciplinary research.

In regard to interdisciplinary university research this is the place to mention that a separate seminar at the India International Centre has studied this subject thoroughly in regard specifically to social change from November 30 to December, 1964. The proceedings are yet to be available in print, but would be well worth-while study when they become available. The participants included top level university men, both from India and foreign countries representing the major disciplines concerned e.g. Anthropology and Social Anthropology, Psychology and Social Psychology, Sociology, Economics, History, Education, Political Science, Law.

The formulation of precise and clear national policies in regard to social development is a very great desideratum over and above the provisions and prescriptions of the constitution. A group of experts who studied social development planning at Bangkok in 1963 under joint sponsorship of the Economic Commission for Asia and the Far East, the United Nations Bureau of Social Affairs and the United Nations Bureau of

Technical Assistances Opeations in collaboration with Unesco and WHO called for a clear statement of all objectives of National development policy as a pre-requisite for further programming. They recommended that to the aims and objects, usually mentioned, viz. higher levels of per capital income, reduced unemployment, improved distribution of income among individuals, groups and regions, a healthy state of the balance of payments, even sociocultural values, have to be added expanded education, better health facilities, better housing and expansion of social welfare services as ends in themselves.

SECOND LECTURE

Family Planning :—

By far the most serious failure in Indian planning has been in the field of family planning.

When the first plan was formulated the known rate of growth of the population, which was 1.46 on the basis of the 1951 census, was not such as to cause alarm. Nevertheless the Planning Commission had foresight enough to take notice of the views and activities of non-official organisations, weak and unorganised though they were, and to provide some finance, being Rs. 60 lakhs, for (1) putting family planning on an official basis and (ii) for some promotional work. Following the Planning Commission's recommendations a Central Advisory Board for Family Planning was set up. But a grave error was made in its organisation in that the Health Minister, then an unmarried woman as now. put herself at the head of this organisation. In retrospect it would appear that she was also not really convinced of the need for nation-wide family planning. It may be stated in extenuation that she shared Gandhiji's views that the only justifiable means of family limitation was continence also that demographic studies were in their infancy then in India. In the result hardly anything was done to promote family planning during the First Plan period. During the second plan period there was an increased plan provision of Rs. 6 crores, later reduced as an economy measure to Rs. 5 crores, out of which only Rs. 1.26 crore was actually spent. The Minister in-charge this time was a man and very much married, and with indeed, an outsize family. There is reason to believe that he took no real interest in this part of his official duties. He also believed overmuch in official machinery at the state level in implementing Central Government training schemes, as for instance a scheme for the training of women family welfare advisers, in effect promoters of family planning. He took an unconsciousably long time, over a year, in implementing this particular scheme, through voluntary organization, as decided by the Central Family Planning Advisory Board and he agreed finally only because the state governments took no intesest in it. Moreover, the scheme was started and run on too small a scale to make any impact. It may be mentioned here that this particular scheme, has now been abandoned and the training made part of the training of auxiliary nurses. In my opinion this is a wrong decision as the matter is not essentially clinical or paramedical. It is only as a social welfare movement that family limitation can be successfully promoted and this calls for specially trained social workers. However, inspite of the clinical approach adopted in those years, the establishment of the necessary clinical amenities, viz., the primary health centres fell far short of the plan targets in the rural areas, during the second plan period.

Despite the poor performance the Planning Commission made an allocation of Rs. 25 crores for family planning for the Third Plan period, with a promise to double this allocation if necessary. Unfortunately, the expenditure so far incurred is a little over Rs. 7 crores, and it would be unreasonable to expect more than 50 percent utilization of the original allocation, not to speak of the augmentation promised.

The departmental organisation has improved considerably with the years. It is probable that there will be a full complement of primary health centres, backed by a number of subcentres. Nevertheless, the basic organizational defect, viz. the Minister of Health heading the Central Advisory Family Planning Board remains. No substantial improvement and the necessary swing away from the clinical approach, can occur unless family planning is transferred to an autonomous board, with statutory authority and an independent competent chairman with organizational ability of a high order and preferably married.

Demographic work is now on a much sounder footing and there is clearer understanding of rates of growth of population and their interaction with rates of economic growth. A great deal of authoritative literature is now available for guidance. It is possible that experience elsewhere may indicate a slower response to efforts to limit populations, but this can be an added argument for putting this very important business of the State on a sound basis without any delay and without succumbing false feelings of departmental prestige. The stakes are too momentous for the very life of the community to permit of indulging the sensitivities of ministers in power.

Fortunately, from the technical and scientific point of view, the situation is much more favourable for a more effective, and less symbolic, system of family planning. A number of important research projects, e.g. in regard to the physiology of reproduction, are in progress in Universities and other institutions of higher learning, thanks to generous support from foreign foundations, and much surer scientific guidance will soon, as a result, be available, to the clinical or other worker in the field, in regard to which contraceptive methods to recommend or promote oral, intra-uterine, surgical or others (e.g. the rhythmic method which is too sophisticated for rural areas).

But personnel, carefully trained for promotional work, remains the most important desideratum. An all-out bold approach is called for here, as substantial proportions of urban and much more of rural populations are still very ill-informed on this topic. The importance of a social welfare approach must be reiterated here.

Targets of achievements have to be set so as to ensure that progress in family limitation is marked enough dimensionally to make an impact on the demographic situation. The problem is essentially one of appropriate, adequate and effective organization, and the maximum conceivable financial cost is, fortunately, not likely to be prohibitive. The importance of proper promotional efforts will be clear from the following press report which appeared sometime ago.

"Contraceptives Destroyed—Poor response in Bihar. Dhanbad, Jan. 4 : Mrs. Sumitra Devi, Bihar's Minister for Information and Family planning told pressmen today that 7,000 contraceptives had to be thrown away as people did not come forward to utilise them. She strongly favoured legislation of abortion to protect fallen girls. The Minister said that out of an allotment of Rs. 16 lakhs for family planning during the Third Plan only one lakh of rupees had been spent so far."

The organization of the manufacture of contraceptives is a relatively simpler, although not less important, problem. Contraceptives of popular choice must be cheap and easily available.

Whatever improved organisation is set-up and improved it must be if a population explosion is to be mitigated-one of the responsibilities to be laid statutorily on it must be to submit a comprehensive annual report to parliament, so that at the highest representative level the nation can watch the progress of this vital, nay, life-and death matter.

Size of the plan

I do not profess to have studied all the relevant facts and figures bearing on the question of the size of the Fourth Plan in regard to which there has recently been a certain amount of controversy. Such facts and figures would not be available to a non-official like myself. Governments in India have a habit of furtive and secretive working, alternating with the *suppressio-veri* kind of reassuring or tendentious talk or pronouncements that democracy is supposed to demand. There is also a relative absence of guidance to the public by experts, eg. economists who are not in the employment of Government or in semi-government autonomous institutions. The Reserve Bank's pronouncements are always available, but after the event, so far as the public is concerned. It is therefore in a guarded way and a spirit of diffidence that I venture to make observations of a general nature which may have some bearing on the vexed question of the size of the Fourth Plan.

When we talk of the size of the Plan we refer to its financial dimensions at current price-levels. Since these price-levels are about 50 p.c. above those at the beginning, say of the Third Plan, the physical targets aimed at would indicate a smaller increase over these aimed at in the Third Plan than the financial allocation, say of the order of 33 p. c. It may not be difficult to demonstrate that an increase of this order in physical achievement is fully justified by the prevailing circumstances. But before the nation undertakes to implement a plan of this size it should ask itself if the price situation is such that these achievements could be secured at the prevailing price-levels, that it would not be possible to manage the economy of the country so as to lower the price-levels and secure the same order of achievement at lower financial cost and therefore less discomfort to the citizen and that there is reasonable assurance that the required financial resources could be raised without social injustice.

Subject to the limitations of my imperfect acquaintance

with and study of the factors involved I would be inclined to answer the first and third question in the negative and the second in the affirmative.

I believe there will be general agreement at the necessary level of competence that India is in the grip of an inflationary spiral owing to persistent failure of production to keep pace with investment. In spite of the reportedly good rice-crop of this year, the less secular situation in regard to expanding agricultural production, especially of food-stuffs, remains dangerously unsatisfactory. It may be possible to tide over a bad year or two by cajoling or wheedling the foreigner, with a hint of annoyance on our part should his munificence falter (as we recently exhibited in a manner somewhat characteristic of the wielder of the begging-bowl in regard to some of foreign exchange for American tourists). But there can be little confidence arising out of past performance that we are now on the threshold of an incomparably higher level of performance in regard to agricultural production.

The situation in regard to increase in population is, as has already been explained, infinitely worse in the reverse direction, because even if we were to organise this vital activity with an efficiency hitherto not even dreamed of, the results are in the nature of things slow in showing and no immediate relief need be expected.

The prices of food-stuffs will therefore continue to rise and now that they have begun to manifest their delayed reaction on the prices of manufactured and semi-manufactured articles, the price structure is bound to rise as a whole. Adjustments will periodically have to be made in the wages or salaries of our extensive fixed income group, with further impulses communicated to the price structure.

Mr. Pierre Paul Schweitzer, the Managing Director of the International Fund, who recently visited India was too courteous and correct to point all this out, but counselled, it seems to me, circumspection by explaining in general terms the danger of allowing inflation to gain the upper hand while implementing development plans. I would urge that very serious attention be paid to the general principles of monetary propriety enunciated by him in his address at the Indian Institute of Public Administration on "Some Financial Aspects of Economic Development.'

If we are wise we should read between the lines and start taking effective steps to master the inflation before we go on at the same or increased pace with planned development. The situation is not yet entirely out of hand, although it is serious enough in all conscience and this is the proper time to take the correct step in regard to plan expenditure, viz. to make a sufficiently large cut in it so as to bring the price-situation under control within the shortest possible time.

Such a period of self-restraint would, I feel sure, be understood and supported by the harassed and steadily impoverished public and as relief becomes appreciable, their support will gain in enthusiasm.

With a lower price-level, it would gradually be practicable to raise the tempo of public spending and it may well be that for the five year period as a whole there will be little loss registered by way of achievement as compared with today's paper plans, based on the larger size and unabated rate of public spending.

The apparent case of raising financial resources in conditions of acute inflation is possibly a source of comfort to Finance Ministers (it would have troubled me, I must confess). But to the victims of taxation at the present high levels and of the present bewildering complexity must be a nightmare with the cost of living going up everyday as also annoying as the big men evade. A tax like the capital gains tax in the prevailing circumstances is the height of injustice. Values in monetary terms rise, not because of development at public cost, but simply because of exploitation, e.g. via land-value speculation, with Government as the leading monopolist and exploiter. Nevertheless Government claims a sizeable share, as a sort of reward for the fraud involved in the falling value of money brought about by its own economic mismanagement.

The handicaps :

Probably India cannot claim to be the first country in the world to undertake anything in the nature of planned development within the four corners of the Western Parliamentary type of democracy. Perhaps France can lay claim to that honour as the Monnet Plan preceded the First Five year Plan of India by a couple of years. Like India's plan the French Plan was based on a mixed economy, and indeed, the First French Plan included very little by way of projects undertaken by the State. Nor did the State assume any direct responsibility for implementation. The method followed for execution was to explain the Plan to the sectors concerned e.g. industrialists and labour unions and to discuss it with them together, relying on them for execution if they became convinced of its desirability and feasibility. In later plans, according to Dr. Hackett, the author of an authoritative book on French Planning the state has had to take a more active part in planning, especially in regard to the provision of social overheads.

France has had a long experience of working various kinds of democratic constitutions, has a thrifty, intelligent and literate population and, what is most important has a very capable and reliable bureaucracy to support her mature politicians. It is only to be expected, therefore, that the story of planning for development in France is a success story, which has attracted world-wide attention. Even countries like the United Kingdom which earlier did not believe in planning have for the last few years been adopting planning methods and setting up the necessary machinery for it.

Three things are absolutely essential for good and successful planning; (i) an effective and adequate planning organization at central and local levels which is readily accepted by the Ministers; (ii) an efficient machinery for execution and (iii) good management at the highest political levels. The process of planned development in India suffers from grave weaknesses in all these three aspects, weaknesses which interact and aggravate the consequences.

Two defects in the main characterise Indian planning machinery. Although well-conceived in the beginning it has been allowed to deteriorate by thoughtless proliferation and dilution of membership by the addition of members-politicians who could not possibly lay any claim to expertise when they were appointed. Too many Ministers have been made ex-officio members of the planning commission, probably in a mis-conceived attempt to temper their hostility to the planning commission, a hostility which has grown with the years.

Moreover there has been unconscionable delay and negligence in setting up adequate and competent planning machinery at the state level. The result has been slovenly planning, the defects of which have already been noticed in the planning Commission note referred to earlier. Another persistent defect in planning has been the failure to build plans round needs strongly felt by the people themselves. All planning more or less is regarded by the people as a gift from a benevolent Government. There is therefore no popular involvement in or commitment to planned development. This state of affairs is the most damaging testimony to the failure of the Community Development movement. Incidentally, it would, in my view be wise to wind up the Central Community Development Ministry so that responsibility for development on the spot would rest where it rightfully belongs, viz. with the State Governments.

Coming next to the quality of the bureaucracy, there is mounting evidence that it is steadily deteriorating, both at the Centre and in the States. It would take too long to go into the etiology of this phenomenon. It is the cumulative effect of a number of factors, such as poor education of the lower echelons, the growing complexity of government business, the increasing scarcities caused by erroneous economic management, the absence of any genuine attempt to cultivate a social conscience, the paralysing effect of unduly minute scrutiny by the legislatures and their committees and above all, the poor calibre of the political management at the top.

The inadequacy of the executive machinery shows itself in the endless delays that occur in the disposal of business. Instances as in relation to industrial licensing or payment of dues by government are notorious, but even in matters where private profit is not involved, the delays are maddening—unless by expenditure of personal influence some powerful intervention is sought. The public concerned dare not complain for fear of vindictive treatment meted out to them by the officials concerned. To give a few instances, there is reason to believe that of 50 licences for new cement factories pending for a long time, only 3 or 4 have been granted, and in the meanwhile most important constructional work, e.g. of universities, is held up for lack of cement. Again, the situation in regard to payment of dues by government, including authorised grants is shockingly bad. It would be enlightening for the Prime Minister to obtain a list of payments overdue (i.e. beyond say, three months) in all the Central Ministries. Voluntary bodies carrying on with the aid of private charity are driven to despair by the unconscionable delays that occur in the release of authorised grants. The Audit Report, 1963, of the India International Centre of which I have the honour to be the President contains the following remark, which speaks for itself. "...........A sum of Rs. 21500/- has been outstanding from the Ministry of Education since 1961 for the preparation of the paper on and for the supply of copies of 'Traditional values in Indian Life'. We understand that the Ministry has been reminded. Bills for work done by members of the Bar of the Supreme Court of India for the Law Ministry are known to be outstanding for months and even years. One Advocate cheerfully gave out that he had a bill outstanding against the Law Ministry for seven years.

This sort of delay is not uncommon even in Universities. In the University of Delhi I found three years ago some 4,000 bills pending. Indeed so bad had the situation become that traders had ceased to extend credit to the University departments. Thanks to the efforts of an able Finance Officer, appointed thereafter for the first time, the arrears have been cleared and the current payments are in reasonably good order, with the result that the Delhi University has regained most of its reputation. But delays continue to occur unaccountably, although in a small proportion of cases, in the disposal of day to day business, and this in spite of the introduction of organisation and methods, deterrent punitive action and closer supervision by officers concerned. Here there is no question of loss of morale on account of harrowing scrutiny by a legislature, or lack of administrative experience on the part of the Head of the Institution, or political interference. I have reluctantly come to the conclusion that the smaller Indian official shares the national ethos of shirking work. Dilly-dallying and gossip seem to have an irresistible attraction for our people even during hours legitimately to be devoted to work. The extent of supervision at all levels that is called for in India is many times more than in any civilised country, in contradistinction to Japan, where I believe the need for it is minimal.

Of failures of a worse order than dilatoriness I do not propose to say much on this occasion. I cannot, however, resist the temptation to assert that what I said about corruption some six years ago in the course of my Srinivas Sastri Memorial Lectures at the University of Madras, has been amply justified by subsequent events. I am more than ever convinced that there is need for an independent standing commission to go into complaints of political and other forms of corruption preferred by people against ministers.

There is urgent need for installing a machinery for dealing with complaints of corruption against officials as well as Ministers, irrespective of the rights and wrongs of the barren controversy regarding the incidence of corruption prevalent in India as compared with other countries. The state of corruption is no more static than unwanted pregnancy and both must in due course bear fruit. If an evil is not countered with wisdom and firmness when its suspected size is manageable and it is left to be dealt with at a later state of magnification sufficient for easy identification, the consequence will be disaster. A stitch in time in this case may well save more than nine later.

However, apart from machinery to deal with corruption, there is imperative need for the appointment of an Ombudsmen by Parliament and State Legislatures, with authority to enquire into citizens' complaints against the executive with adequate powers to question even members of Government and to call for official papers and with the responsibility of making periodical reports to the legislature. This one reform will do more to tone up the day to day administration than any number of other measures of the conventional kind. The shelves of Government Departments are groaning under the weight of reports on administration, most of the recommendations in which incidentally, have not been carried out.

But the state of inefficiency and corruption of the bureaucracy is not entirely dependent on its own composition, recruitment, training and supervision. It is powerfully influenced by the calibre and ethos of their political bosses, and where these are low, as in India, the quality of the bureaucracy is bound to deteriorate. Where these are largely devoid of a social conscience and hold their primary interest in keeping their office, without being deterred by scruples or principles, there the tone of public administration is bound to deteriorate fast. There are often no limits to the lengths that political bosses will go in order to oblige their political supporters or to save influential friends from the legal consequences of their misdeeds, as for instance, attempting to defraud the customs.

Moreover the implementation of plans of economic and social development involves far more than a reasonably efficient and pure day to day administration. It calls for managerial skills of very high order. But the stark fact is that in a nascent democracy such as that of India's, with a largely illiterate and ill-informed electorate and with an unscrupulously run party election machinery, it is virtually impossible to secure even a modicum of high managerial skill amongst those who are elevated to ministerships. Although India has a Western Parliamentary democracy, the built-in safeguards for its proper working that are present in some of the advanced democratic countries are lacking with us. The absence of literacy and social education on the part of the franchise-holder have already been mentioned. Over the years this has led to growing inferiority of the calibre of those who are elected to the legislatures. The big men who had secured independence naturally stepped into positions of power, men who had come triumphantly out of the ordeal of fire that the struggle for independence was, and they did well by the country. Under the late Prime Minister's enlightened initiative their ranks were reinforced by men of affairs, with well-tried competence in management or specialities. But that generation and that spirit have passed away, and the men now in power have as a whole less achievement during the struggle for independence to their credit—indeed some had only a minor contribution to make and that during the short-lived Quit-India movement of 1942. As the electorate has through successive general elections tasted its power, and as the party machines have worked, the tendency is to send up as elected representatives local political bosses not necessarily endowed with qualities of leadership at the state or national level. Nevertheless, such is the working of the political machine, that when cabinets are formed, even minor politicians of some local influences, able to command a sizeable block of votes have to be accommodated. Instead of conscience, apprehension of losing political support makes cowards of even good leaders. In the result the managerial machine at the top-most political levels is just unequal to the jobs that devolve on it.

As long as this state of affairs is allowed to continue, the implementation of development plans is bound to remain poor, even if we had angels as members of the bureaucracy.

The situation would not have been so desperate had the ruling party had a fixed and identifiable ideology. But this it has not, as it includes all the spectra of the political rainbow, from deep-dyed violet to flaming red. It was in wise anticipation of this that Mahatma Gandhi had advised the disbanding of the Congress after the attainment of independence, so that proper political parties could come into being based on distinguishable ideologies.

The confusion of ideologies would not have mattered so much had there been a persistent trend towards cultivating a socialistic attitude on the part of those admitted as members of Government. But despite repeated slogans there is singular lack of the right social attitudes on the part of Governments in India, judging both from affiliations and performances.

The election situation in India is characterised by two imperfections. One is the absence of any real opposition to the congress party, the result of which is that democracy in its true form is not in operation. The real tragedy of the Indian political situation is the absence of a strong and well-led socialist party. But a worse aspect, for which it is difficult to find any justification, is the utter dependence the Congress Party has shown on collections from big business for fighting elections and continuing in power to promote a socialist economy. Both big business and the Congress have been going about this business year after year with their tongues in their cheeks.

It would be immeasurably better for the promotion of right attitudes towards social development, and indeed the cultivation of a social conscience, for the party in power to depend for their election finance on small collections from millions of the citizens than millions collected and almost extorted, from big business. This was how Mahatma Gandhi operated in the old days and how he built up the Congress movement and established in process genuine mass-contact. This is how truly socialistic parties operate elsewhere, e.g. U. K. and Japan. The socialism that has to depend on money from big business to be returned to power can only be skin-deep. Governments as in India, with too small an endowment of managerial ability and over-dependent on big business and therefore beholden to it, cannot accomplish much by way of economic and social development, no matter how ambitious the planning may be.

Some critics, who have noticed Governmental failure in this behalf have advocated a unitary form of government. In my opinion this would amount to taking too much of a risk, staking too much on the possibility of having a capable unitary Govt. presumably elected by the existing type of electorate disadvantaged by lack of literary and social education.

To my mind the remedy is two-fold : one aspect of it is the cultivation of genuine mass contact as represented by the methods of collecting election finance from house to house instead of Big house to Big House. The other aspect would consist in securing a leaven of talent and ability for management from non-party persons for the Ministries at the Centre and in the States. It should be the party leaders' business to ensure that his cabinet contain persons with real capacity to manage men and affairs and with a will to learn their business, if they are new to it. Arrangements could without difficulty be made to ensure that they get elected. And there is no reason why for the implementation of a national plan, a national government could not be formed, including able men from some other parties as well as talented non-party individuals. The test would be whether all those admitted are willing to co-operate in building up the sort of socialist economy or a democratic socialistic welfare state such as the constitution enjoins on us to build up.

Implications of Socialism

With the flux of time ideas of what is not a socialist society have become more instead of less confused. One of the weaknesses of the Indian situation is the ruling party which has no economic theoretician of any standing in its ranks. The governments have their usual apparatus of economic advisers, but however able some of these men may be, they are obviously not free to express opinions which can be published. No precise statement of what sort of socialism the ruling party has in mind can therefore be available—there is no mind of any consequence and any way it has not been set to work on the problem. India has no Walter Lange or Michael Kalecki as Poland, more fortunately has. I am not competent to speak on the merits of issue of this kind, but it is my belief that no clear statement of what sort of socialism the Indian Government is aiming at is available from any professional non-official economist. One of the members of the Planning Commission is a distinguished economist and produced a few years ago a note on the implications of a Socialist economy for use in a seminar to consider the approach to the Third Plan convened by the Congress Party, a seminar which I was invited to participate in and in which I was Chairman of one of the five committees (Institutional changes) and drew up for the Chairman, Smt. Indira Gandhi, the report of another Committee (Implications of a Socialist economy). The distinguished economist's note gave good guidance in regard to the implications of socialism as understood by him. But as far as I can recall he had not considered it necessary to rise and answer the question—Why Socialism.

In the meanwhile since the socialism of our choice has not progressed appreciably beyond the establishment of a few public industrial and commercial enterprises and since the successive Plans continue to pin their faith on a mixed economy, the ideological situation remains foggy in the extreme. The situation has been made worse by the somewhat light-hearted statements made by top-ranking political leaders that marxism is outmoded and falsified by the march of history. Also the old ideas of Western European Socialism have undergone considerable change, so that it need not now imply even an all out command of the means of production so long as there is control by the state at strategic points. The theoretical justification for socialism has to be formulated by our own economic theorists, in the context of the fundamental aims and objects of Indian Society. In doing this they will have to take fully into account formulations made by the economic theorists of the totalitarian countries, as well as, by classical literary or non-literary economists, of varying biases from the extreme right to the extreme left (short of communistic socialism). There are now clear statements of the marxist economists, like Lange and Kalecki, which have to be considered and rational answers, if any, have to be given. There is, for instance, the first of the three projected volumes of Lange of his 'Political Economy' which appeared in

1959 (Lange advised the Indian Planning Commission during the period of the First Five Year Plan or at the commencement during the period of the First Year Plan or at the commencement of the Second Plan.) That economic rationality is determined by social and institutional conditions is one of the important formulations in this volume which has a bearing on 'Why Socialism'. His essay 'Why capitalism cannot solve the problems of under-developed countries' contains theoretical generalizations which relate greatly to the issue of Why Socialism. In an early essay "Price Flexibility and Employment, 1944, Lange had argued that the theoryt hat economic equilibrium is attained automatically apply only in a highly improbable set of contingencies, in view of the contrary trends of the oligopolization of the national economy (growth of savings worsening of investment conditions, labour savings innovations). An oligopolistic price policy might, for example, greatly blunt or even nullify the stimulation of the multiplier processes initiated by the State to stimulate a flagging economy. Therefore, a decidedly anti-monopolistic economic policy with a socialist orientation is essential. Lange wrote that in most cases the only means of averting the harmful operation of oligopoly is nationalization of the appropriate branches of industry and commerce.

Kalecki's 'An outline of the theory of Growth of the Socialist Economy, 1963', is another massive contribution towards the understanding of or an enlargement of view in regard to the basic economic problems and alternatives facing modern societies. Kalecki's main conclusion has a great deal of topical interest. He writes "Adherence to the rule of feasibility of the plan and consideration of the pattern of present consumption enjoin caution in fixing the rate of growth. Nevertheless avoidance of waste and concern for the effectiveness of investment make it possible to maintain it at a relatively high level." The key-stone of Kalecki's theory is the statement that the aim of socialist production is the consumed part of the national income, while the means towards attaining this aim is the productively accumulated part of it. This, it will be noticed, reverses the relationships within the capitalist economy whose aim is accumulation. According to Kalecki, a higher rate of increase in the national income favours long-term consumption, but militates against short-term consumption and conversely. A compromise is to be found between short-term and long-term consumption. Fixing the rate of increase of the national income is both the most important and the most difficult macro-economic decision in the socialist state and is a decision essentially political in nature. This in turn involves criteria, including the degree of labour mechanization and labour productivity, which may have to be subordinated to maintenance of employment. A problem of this kind is particularly acute in under-developed countries, with a large and growing surplus of under-employed manpower.

Totalitarian socialist theorists do not find it necessary to discuss the managerial ability of the state to plan globally and the bureaucracy's ability to implement. These are implicitly assumed. Unfortunately, these are the very factors likely to be weak in under-developed countries and that is their cruel dilemma, whilst there would be greater justification for socialist policies there would by the same token be less capacity to adopt them successfully.

A mixed economy would be therefore unavoidable in practice. It is an illusion to hope that private enterprise will have the motivation and conscience of Trusteeship. Vigilance and control would always be called for, and for exercising these the right kind of leadership with adequate collective managerial skill and a carefully nurtured social welfare attitude, nourished by sensitive contact with and co-operation of the people are essential. Unfortunately, it is precisely these elements that are weak in the current Indian situation. To strengthen them is the supreme task before Indian statesmanship.

CONVOCATION ADDRESS

(1965-66, Bangkok)

ASIAN INSTITUTE FOR ECONOMIC DEVELOPMENT AND PLANNING

It is indeed a signal honour to have been invited by the A.I.E.D.P. to deliver a Convocation address, and I am deeply appreciative of it, not only as the former Finance Minister (and ex-officio member of the Planning Commission) of India, but also as currently an educationist. Indeed my presence in Bangkok on this occasion is due to a UNESCO assignment to assist in the drawing up of a long-term educational plan for some 16 countries in Asia. The presence here of the Director, Dr. Narayan Prasad, and the most distinguished international personage, who is presiding this afternoon, Mr. Eugene R. Black, takes my mind back to the days when I too was counted as a colleague of them both in the world of international finance and banking. This adds a sense of gratification to my sense of privilege. I thank them both for their generous kind referrences to me in the course of their observations.

The International Bank for Reconstruction and Development over which Mr. Black presided for about a decade with outstanding success, together with the International Monetary Fund, were among the earliest specialized agencies of the U.N. to be set up after World War II, and for someone like myself who was associated with their work for over 12 years from the days of Bretton Woods and have had a great deal to do with problems of development in India it is difficult to be restrained in extolling the manifold assistance that these famous institutions have given to developing countries in planning, promoting and evaluating their developmental efforts. The passage of time has only served to demonstrate the uncanny soundness of their basic concepts—monetary stability and optimum healthy development. They have through the years promoted the establishment of new international or regional institutions for the purpose of reinforcing or complementing their own efforts. It is to the working out of the plans for the establishment of an addition to this illustrious family, viz, the Asian Development Bank, that we owe the presence of Mr. Black in our midst. I take the opportunity of felicitating that great organization which has sponsored this new Institution, viz. the ECAFE, and its eminent Secretary-General, U Nyun, on this happy event. As Chairman of the Governing Council of the Asian Institute he has a very special role to play in ensuring that the personnel at the national levels in Asia concerned with developmental planning and administration in their many aspects have cultivated the capacity to make the optimum use of the imposing array of international institutions in the course of their work on the national scene.

I should like to add a word of congratulations to the Director on the organization of the work of the Asian Institute on sound lines within such a short period after its establishment. It is not too easy to provide appropriate training facilities for senior and middle-level officials holding responsible positions in diverse activities and institutions, both public and private, playing a role in national development. As Chairman of the Court of Governors of the Administrative Staff College of Hyderabad, the only one of its kind in India, I have a good idea of the difficulties involved in getting a faculty together of the necessary eminence, expertise and experience, and in organizing the teaching and learning as well as in developing research and consultancy work. All these three aspects are interconnected and mutually supporting, although in the nature of things, advisory work will take time to develop and make its own contribution, not only to the National Governments, but also to research and training within the Institute.

Certificates will presently be awarded to some 28 Fellows from 12 countries in the region in token of the successful completion of their course of training at the Institute. They include responsible officials with diverse concerns—bankers, agricultural experts, economic planners, Finance or Economic Affairs Ministry officials, progress evaluation specialists, commerce and accountancy specialists, tariff or foreign trade specialists, statistical advisers, economic analysts and researchers, agronomists, economists and plan directors. This diversity reflects the complexity of the development and plan operations and processes. Their course of study and exchange of ideas, through syndicates, seminars and lectures, must have been a rewarding and memorable experience, augmented as it was by carefully selected study tours. I heartily congratulate them and wish them the fullest possible scope for the development of their special talents and competencies enriched by the course of training undergone here. I have no doubt that they will be prepared to give of their best on their return to their respective posts.

In the convocation addresses of the usual academic kind the Chief Guest, occasionally miscalled Orator, is expected to offer advice to the graduates. Although some speakers venture to fulfil this expectation the wise ones among them take special care to keep the dosage very minute indeed, almost on the homeopathic scale. But men and women such as the Fellows of this Institute need no advice; and enlightenment of the appropriate sort (with my own small contribution last year) they receive I have no doubt in ample measure. I shall therefore not attempt either to advise or to enlighten them : I shall try, rather, to set before them a few reflections that occur to me as a result of direct or indirect association with the problems of development and planning in India and in the region over the last fifteen years.

At the outset it is perhaps necessary to remind oneself that development does not necessarily involve planning—indeed the International Bank for Reconstruction and Development was conceived at Bretton Woods and Savannah in the forties of this century, when except in the totalitarian countries planning was not in vogue and was indeed in bad odour. Experience has shown beyond doubt that planning is called for to optimise development, and in the developing countries, with their largely unutilized resources in men and materials, planning is essential if the development process is to go forward smoothly and adequately towards its commonly accepted goal of rising standards of living.

While planning is accepted readily in principle, difficulties are immediately encountered in deciding the question—what sort of planning? By and large one may say that three models exist, viz, the global totalitarian type, the advanced guidelines type & the partial mixed economy type. Defining democracy as some sort of parliamentary democracy of the western type, one would distinguish between the first two by the total absence or presence of the democratic element that characterises the polity of the country concerned. In both types the people's participation is essential, as indeed, in all other spheres of social activity, but in the former it is secured through means other than suffrage in the parliamentary sense and is perhaps because of this all-pervasive, whilst in the latter it may or may not be so comprehensive and may even be sectoral, depending as it would be largely on persuasion and appeal to reason. Because of the importance of public participation, no matter how secured, totalitarian plans are often found to be more effectively implemented than those lacking this element in its full amplitude. In the countries of this region this could be the result of either imperfect use of the modern means of mass communication where the type of democracy prevailing is very limited in character or where democracy is practised in the western parliamentary fashion, the practitioners are inexperienced and elected representatives of the people, from among whom high political offices are filled, fail to keep in touch with the people. Planning under an experienced democracy need not necessarily mean poor execution, as the success of the Monnet Plan and the succeeding French Plans have demonstrated. But it would seem that in the countries of the region democratic planning must suffer from the unavoidable and possibly transitional weaknesses of the political system, especially in regard to public cooperation. This is an area which, it is worthwhile remembering, will require sedulous care to cultivate both in the formulation and in the execution of plans.

In another important respect also nascent democracies, especially with adult sufferage exercised by a largely illiterate and ill-informed electorate, have a disadvantage in that the men or women elected to high political office at all material levels are unlikely to have the necessary calibre and quality, and would usually be incapable of concentrating on the work of governance owing to very demanding political pre-occupations. Lack of proper direction or guidance on their part, not to speak of occasional misdirection, almost invariably affects prejudicially the morale of the public services, turning even good material into indifferent performers. In such circumstances it behoves the better elements in the public service to muster courage, advise without fear or favour and stand by their principles, in addition to carrying on their duties with a sense of dedication.

But there are other factors which are entirely beyond the control of the public servant, excepting the defence services perhaps, which are in a class by themselves and have little immediate concern with planning and economic development. One such factor is political stability. It is almost axiomatic that lack of political stability is inimical to economic growth to an optimum extent, even if it does not lead to its reverse. Essentially this involves the socio-political phenomenon of leadership—where a country is blessed with a well-consolidated and wise leadership economic progress will be maximized, no matter what the form of polity is, although, the best prospect for public cooperation will be found related to the existence of some form of democracy.

From the field of political stability one may turn to another important pre-condition of economic progress, viz, monetary stability. In this area the public servant, in the shape of a central banker has, or should have, greater assurance of his advice being heeded. This is not to say that the course of events is not influenced by extraneous political pressures. Numerous instances can be quoted to prove that almost too frequently the contrary is the case. But the Central Banker, as an expert or a specialist, is perhaps in a better position to argue a case than the common run of public servant. Mexico can be cited as an illuminating example of sustained economic growth following the pursuit of sound monetary policies advocated by the Central Bank. This is not the place or the occasion to pursue this topic in any depth. But I believe that it would be an advantage, especially to the non-professional economists, to bear in mind some of the generally accepted propositions in respect of monetary stability. They are as follows, to quote Maurice Frere, the doyen of European central bankers :

(1) monetary stability is one of the essential conditions for rapid and lasting growth because it is the most powerful force behind the formation of savings, without which it is impossible to carry out the investments that are indispensable for such growth;

(2) monetary stability is likewise necessary to encourage a rapid increase in productivity, which is also fundamental to economic growth;

(3) governments elected by universal suffrage must keep away from the temptation to avoid any direct or indirect creation of fiduciary money to cover a possible budget deficit and must find the funds required from taxation and borrowing;

(4) the discipline that monetary stability calls for also entails, in addition to the will to tax or borrow, the free manipulation of the most effective instrument for the defence of price and monetary stability = the interest rate;

(5) as manipulation of the interest rate has strong political repercussions, monetary policy occupies a place of its own in the government of a country;

6) In order to avoid the trials and tribulations of later corrective deflationary measures it is best to fight inflation wherever and whenever it raises its head; this involves the most scrupulous care in the creation of money.

(7) to ensure a better defence against the various possibilities of inflation it seems essential that the monetary authority enjoys a large measure of independence vis-a-vis the political authority;

(8) it is essential that the independence of the monetary authority be supplemented by legal provisions, giving those responsible for monetary policy a secure foundation which will enable them to resist effectively any pressure that the government may be tempted to exert on them;

(9) It would be a profound and dangerous illusion for the governments of countries to believe that of the many problems facing them that of maintaining monetary stability is of secondary importance and that it is still possible in the world of today to ensure such stability by strict exchange-price control under cover of which inflation can freely take its course; and

(10) countries in a stage of monetary instability are

generally a prey to disorders, revolutions or civil war—the precursors of a repressive system of government.

In this connection a word of caution seems particularly necessary to countries with a large export surplus and consequent ease of the foreign exchange situation. These will usually be countries dependent on large exports of a few primary commodities. They will find that the rise in prices due to inflation and consequent fall in the internal purchasing power of their currencies will inhibit the growth of the confidence in money as a store of value and therefore the emergence of a money-economy out of their predominant subsistence economy. This will come in the way of the desired industrialization as the essential imports will be gradually harder to come by as inflation gathers strength and as the sufficiency and assurance of export earnings becomes incapable of being maintained at any desired minimum level. The absence of a well-developed monetary system will mean very limited scope for the generalized creation of credit, even if this war were to be regarded as without peril. In any case, with increasing difficulty in obtaining essential imports for industrialization, even selective injection of credit for industrial projects will be impossible.

Where the economy is very largely at a subsistence level, deficit financing is bound to fail of its purpose. No additional employment could be created out of disguised unemployment, as Hla Myint has so clearly shown in 'The Economics of the Developing Countries' as the necessary surpluses could not be extracted from the agricultural subsistence economy. The out-puts from created money will in the beginning be small or slow in coming, with the result that prices will begin to rise, confidence in money will wane in favour of hoarding and turning money into durable goods and the situation will worsen as the inevitable price-wage spiral gets under way.

In the developing countries of Asia planners and economic administrators will have a great deal to do, one hopes, with the taking of correct decisions at a number of crucial points.

Generally speaking, imitative planning is full of pitfalls, against which I am sure the fellows in the Institute's course of training have been fully warned. Plan patterns have to be custom-built even more than sartorial productions and can never be used as imported. Even a unified model for the region is impossible to construct, as we consultants appointed by UNESCO to assist the drawing up of perspective educational plans for the countries in Asia have found out in regard to the field of education. Conformity in the general area of development and planning is still more chimerical to aim at. The approach and strategy will differ according as such factors differ as the pressure of population, the degree of emergence of a money-economy out of a subsistence economy and the position in regard to an export surplus. Countries with a large population pressure, but severe limitations of size and resources will have a special problem of their own to meet and solve.

In the course of formulating policies for planning certain considerations, which would seem to be valid, will have to be borne in mind. Some of these are as follows:

The cruelest dilemma of the planner, especially the outside expert , is that the same conditions that make the task of development large also conspire to make the feasibility small. While some of the missing elements such as capital, expertise and technical know-how can to a limited extent be procured from abroad, the import of political stability or general efficiency of the administrative machinery is impossible. The countries in the region will have slowly to learn how to create these favourable conditions, and until they are created to an adequate extent economic growth sustainable over long periods is bound to be slow. To hasten slowly will have to be the motto of planners in the region.

On the social side, while the transition from tradition into modernity will mean consciously promoted social change and careful designing of the institutional infrastructure, there is risk in undermining for the sake of modernity the social structures that have served as economic supports in the past, e.g. the family and its built-in social security. Any forced change of stress in this respect may well pose new problems of sustenance for the under-employed population which is to be drawn into new forms of production.

Emphasis on agricultural productivity would seem to be a key-factor in modernization and industrialisation. This involves the adoption of new and better techniques as well as judicious incentives, in addition to re-arrangement of the scale of operations of agricultural units. Land tenure reforms have indubitably been a necessity in this context, but it is safe to believe that the last word has yet to be said in regard to the size of the farm and its organization on an individual, cooperative, or joint-stock basis.

A related field full of perplexities is that of the organization of labour—intensive small-scale industrial units, as the first step in drawing population from agriculture into industry. More labour means more consumption over the subsistence level and less availability of savings for present investment. In this context again the over-whelming importance of maximizing agricultural productivity should be clear.

In the field of industry, while a rising wage-cost-price level will be a retarding factor, a steady high minimum wage level could often lead to better techniques and the search for devices to lower costs, with consequent benefit to all sectors of the economy.

I have indicated only illustratively a few of the many policy issues likely to be involved in planning for development in Asia. A word must be added in order to focus attention on what appears from experience to be a prevailing weakness in the planning in this region—that is the absence of detailed and well-thought programmes into which all plans have to be translated if they are to be implemented successfully. This would in turn involve frequent consultation with the agencies which will be responsible for execution at various levels, both in the course of the formulation of plans as well as during implementation. This process should go on *pari passsu* with consultation with the public concerned, in order to ensure their full understanding and cooperation. Many a plan has remained on the shelf or been badly implemented or proved to be misconceived on account of the neglect of these indispensable prerequisites.

Somewhere in the information literature of the Institute it is stated that the Institute is essentially a staff college for management. I would be inclined to agree if one regards public administration as a species of management. But whether it is governance or public administration or management, what the planning and conduct of human affairs need is informed and competent leadership at numerous levels, and where this is missing they are sure to languish.

It is the belief of many educationists, and venturing to speak here for a moment as an educationist, I share that belief— that the missing component in development is often education, taking precedence over injectment of investment in the form of material capital, and this is especially needed for both ensuring the maximum fructification of external aid and for providing in adequate measure the entrepreneurial and managerial, as well as administrative, personnel required by a developing economy. The lack of such personnel inhibits the absorption of capital in productive investment even if sufficient savings were to be available. But educational expansion and diversification has to be accompanied by a careful adjustment of salary differentials and a proper balance will have to be maintained between the production, through the educational system, of specialists and technologists on one hand and general scientists on the other. Moreover, in order to ensure quality at the tertiary level of education admission to the university courses, especially of the honours and advanced kind, will have to be suitably restricted, other avenues of higher education being provided both to satisfy individual aspirations and to supply to the nation the growing stock of highly educated persons that the increasingly scientific and technological world of ours will demand.

I shall conclude by re-iterating my hope that the fullest possible opportunities will be available to the Fellows to play their part to the best of their capacity and by wishing them God-speed.

Address delivered at the Inauguration of the

SECOND WORLD UNION CONFERENCE

Pondicherry, 12—16 *August*, 1967

I feel greatly privileged to be called upon to inaugurate this, the Second World Conference of World Union. The focus of the previous conference, held also at Pondicherry, in 1964, was on 'Conscious Evolution & the Destiny of Man'. The present one is centred on 'Education for One World'.

I regret that I have no precise or detailed information about the aims and objects of World Union and do not have by me the proceedings of the First World Conference. It is a non-profit, non-political organization, located at the World Union International Centre of this Ashram of Pondicherry named after the hallowed name of Sri Aurobindo. Its essential character is a movement for Unity and Peace through spiritual and scientific development. Its membership is International and it receives its inspiration and guidance from The Mother. It was Shri Aurobindo who used the phrase 'World Union' in the sense relevant to this movement. His message broadcast from the All India Radio on the eve of Independence Day in 1947, laid stress on the necessity of unity and emphasized the resurgence and liberation of the people of India; Asia has risen, said he. There India has her part to play in forming a World Union for a fairer, brighter nobler life for all mankind. A total spiritual direction given to the whole life and whole nature can lead humanity beyond itself. The World Union was his prophetic vision, based on an abiding faith that man will rise into superman. A greater destiny waits you in your front! This transient earthly being if he will : Can fit his acts to a transcendent scheme : The superman shall wake in mortal man: And manifest the hidden demi-god. Or grow into the God-Light : Or grow into the God-Light of God-Force : Revealing the Secret deity in the cave He would be the saviour of the world— "Again, He who would save the world must be one with the world". This world is a vast unbroken totality. A deep solidarity joins its contrary powers. God's Summits look back on the mute Abyss ! The High meets the low, all in a single plan.

Shri Aurobindo firmly held that the life divine must be realized on earth. Man, he said, should transcend his present human limitation and grow into fulfilment of the rich splendour of the divine. He showed in the Life Divine, his magnum opus, the strength and weakness of the human mind, which interprets the Truth of Universal existence for the practical uses of a certain order of things, but, not the power that created or manifested it. 'Reason' as he pointed out, was the helper, reason is the bar, when, as result of this next evolutionary jump, the mind of man pierces through the lid of ignorance and touches the plane of supramental consciousness, man will have passed beyond knowing. He will have 'acquired super conscient knowledge.' Sri Aurobindo's International University Centre aims at that supramental education which will result, not merely in a progressively developing formation of the human nature and increasing growth of its latent faculties, but transformation of the nature itself, transformation of the being in its entirety, a new ascent of the species above and beyond man towards superman leading in the end to the appearance of the divine race upon earth.

The Mother has explained this idea thus : it is not the welfare of humanity that we seek but the manifestation of the Divine. We are here to work out the divine will, more truly to be worked upon by the divine will, so that we may be its instruments for the progressive incorporation of the supreme and the establishment of His reign upon earth.

This consummation of man's existence obviously depends on man's evolutions as a species in the long run and his education in a right way in the short run, but continuously, as a conscious effort.

The previous conference held three years ago dealt with 'Conscious Evolution and the Destiny of Man'. That Conference adopted four statements, the outstanding portions of which have already been quoted in the papers supplied to us.

I would draw attention to four elements contained in these—

(a) need for dedication to the task of discovering our true soul, to collaborate with the forces of conscious evolution, and to contribute to the birth of a new world of harmony;

(b) an awakening of man to a new sense of his own destiny is noticeable. Millions who now respond to the world need are finding their own way towards world unity and right human relations;

(c) our united efforts in fostering an active spirit of co-operation can transform the future of mankind;

(d) in an age when all human values are threatened unless unity prevails, both men of science and spiritual aspirants should seek the largest common ground in the spirit of mutual understanding and collaboration.

It is indisputable, I think, that in the cosmic context, or even in the context of life on earth, man's evolution will have an important part to play in the constitution and nature of human society. Most of the processes involved are involuntary, but nevertheless dependent on man's habits. Every physical, mental and spiritual change will be transmitted from generation to generation according to human choices, habits, response, environment, and conscious breeding, on the basis of well recognized genetic principles. There is no hiatus between the past, the present and the future. Essentially man's destiny, unlike that of his fellow-beings on earth, is largely, although, not entirely, in his hands--it is largely enough to amount to significantly. Hence, it is of supreme importance for man to be introspective and to watch well where he is going.

That politicians are the principal authors of wars is only a superficial truth and a false alibi for the citizen. No war is possible without the citizen's active or passive, implicit or explicit support and collaboration. Indeed every successive war, big or small, shows how progressively more important the citizen is for sustaining a war. It would be as true to say that even a small nation can resist indefinitely a war with conventional weapons as to say that a powerful nuclear armament will finish a war within five minutes.

This is the reason why the more advanced (is this the right adjective to use) nations, old and new members of the nuclear club, are escalating armaments to every level of the balance of terror, and the emergence of a new member (the admission is by gate-crashing, although a weak ballot system is often sought to be operated) is the signal for a fresh burst of escalation of the engines of instant mass extinction. This is why in a war, declared or undeclared, where fighting breaks out between a big power or a small power, endless non-nuclear fighting is apt to take place, and where no great national interests are involved, small shindies are almost encouraged among the non-nuclear nations until the risk of involvement of the nuclearwise powerful nations appears, when these small fires are promptly put out by the many means available, e.g., presure in the United Nations, threat of non-supply of armaments. Once the danger recedes prodding to another rumpus begins, with the direct or surreptious supply of armament and weapons to the weaker nations. This is a kind of non-stop cockfight for the amusement of those controlling the more advanced nations.

It is clear that unless the engines are reversed here, mankind will cease to exist and all hopes of the rise of man to superman, and the establishment of a world union will be falsified. Gruesome as this prospect is, in the cosmic sense, and so far as the divine will is concerned may be that we, the inhabitants of this planet, could take a philosophic view that life in our human sense will be continuing in some other planet, in some other solar system, and in another galaxy in the incomprehensible immensity and infinity that is cosmos. But it is possible to hold that this guarantees philosophic contentment too far. If therefore, we are to continue to consider these matters purely on a mundane plane then it is easy to realise that mankind is poised on the edge of an abyss and that there is still time to retrace our steps and to reach the heights which are beckoning to us so encouragingly in the opposite direction—the heights which we seem to have missed on our way, on the degeneration of the race and human affairs that took place on the 5th August, 1945 when an Atom Bomb was dropped on Hiroshima. In restrospect, historians as well as biologists would certainly hold that that event marked the nadir of man's sub-human civilization over the last two million years or so. Scientists still working on cosmic things assure us that the earth may look forward to some 15 or 20 millions of years' life. Assuming that this is not outrageously wrong it will seem to be man's primary business, here and now, to consider the wisdom of retracing his steps.

In this perspective it is easy to see that what the World Union is attempting is something of transcendent importance. No turn in human affairs is to my mind likely to come without directing attention to the nature of man or the ways of transforming it. No amount of political organisation is likely to control the present trends of National or even International governance. It is undoubtedly within the limits of feasibility to improve the consideration and capacity for World Governance of an International Organisation and even to reinforce the beneficent tendencies of the intermittent International Co-operation that is in evidence today. But it is doubtful if measures of this kind are likely to eliminate the possibility of violence on a National or International Scale. No conceivable control of law and order situation by a reinforced or reconstituted International Organisation could possibly prevent outlawry such as that of China, and the only answer to the outlawry is by a conception of the purposive use of force by a well-organised state, which in this context will be the International State.

One has therefore necessarily to prevent the real cause of war, which may in the first instance be the politicians, and which in the ultimate analysis are the people themselves. A great deal may perhaps be achieved of the dissemination of right ideas such as those held by the World Union. Something unexpected and yet of a revolutionary magnitude could emerge as a result of the emergence of a *yuga purusha*—a prophet or a superman, "superman in the tradition of all such men that we have had in the past". History has demonstrated that the influence of such men can be transcendental and earth-shaking as well as permanent. But we have also to remind ourselves that permanency of the influence does not guarantee preservation of the original teaching. It is here therefore that duty devolves on the common man to think for himself and apply his mind to the problem of not only the preservation of his future but for the more exciting problem of the amelioration of things and institutions in his environment.

I have already indicated that human civilization does not progress consistently, it moves in an incomprehensible and illogical way. But the seeds of the present are sown in the past, and the present holds the seeds of the future. All human civilization is a continuous process, which to more than a limited extent is capable of being influenced by the acts, habits, and character of each individual of the species, and all the influence that is perpetually being radiated is in confirmation, thereby unceasingly, as well as indisputably, continuing its character.

It is here that education should play a vital part. The wisdom of the choice of the topic for the present conference, namely 'Education for one World' commends itself to me and has my hearty approbation. A basic statement for the seminar which will be concerned in detail with this, is already in the hands of the participants, and those of us to whom special responsibility has been assigned in this respect will have another opportunity and occasion to deal with more than a score of issues that arise in this context. I shall not therefore take up time in discussing in detail this aspect of this topic. It will suffice to say that the phrase World Education used in this context has the widest possible connotation. As Shri Aurobindo has said "that alone will be true and living education which helps to bring out to full advantage, makes ready for the full purpose and scope of human life all that is in the individual man, and which at the same time helps him to enter into his right relation with the life, mind and soul of the people to which he belongs and with that great total life, mind and soul of humanity of which he himself is a unit and his people or nation a living, a separate and yet inseparable member" With this I have great pleasure in inaugurating this conference.

Speech delivered at the

CENTRAL INSTITUTE OF EDUCATION

Prof. Kabir, President and Secretary of the Central Institute of Education, Alumni Association and Ladies and Gentlemen,

I am grateful to the Alumni Association for inviting me to participate in this function. My own acquaintance with the late Prof. Basu was indeed very limited although not quite so limited as we expect from the anecdote that you were told, and it was a kind of poetic justice that when I entered on my career as educational administrator one of the first books that I read was Prof. Basu's book on the history of, I think, university or higher education. In addition to that, of course, I know in a general way of the very valuable work that he did for the Central Institute of Education. And after I received the invitation, I have done a certain amount of reading about his work and achievements. All this has enhanced my sense of respect for him and therefore, I very readily join you all in paying homage to his memory on this day of dedication.

I do not know how Prof. Basu laboured to build up this institute, bringing to his task both a sense of professional competence and deduction as well as a great deal of humanism. From the accounts that have been given to me by his former pupils, amongst them Dr. Saraf, and the accounts I have read, it is very clear to me that he was one of those few people who brim over with the milk of human kindness combined with competence, a quality alas too rare in this world.

On this day, whilst recalling Prof. Basu's contribution, one cannot but express a sense of regret that invades one that perhaps the objectives for which he worked so devotedly have not been fulfilled. I believe that the basic aims of the Central Institute of Education were two; to prepare it for the higher destiny of being converted into a national institute of education as also to make it the centre of advanced research on education in the way in which the faculty of education of some universities is developed. I believe that over the years, these objectives have somewhat been obscured and indeed recently there were dangerous trends in a direction which were not likely to bring about such results. I say 'were' because I have now reason to hope that perhaps a view has been taken which is more in conformity with the original ideas. However, I fear that the first objective is never likely to be fulfilled, viz., the Institute being converted into an institute of a national institute of education, since the aim of those who are responsible for decision are already contemplating the establishment of a separate national institute in the south of Delhi. But there has been some gain and that is the trend in the direction of developing the research and faculty side and the way is perhaps clear for the institute to achieve this, viz., its operation as a faculty of the university of which it is a constituent unit, and if this process were to be carried out to its logical conclusions and to its consummation, then I think we may agree that we are paying real homage to the memory of Prof. Basu.

Now in regard to the subject matter of the memorial lecture this afternoon, I do not know that I have very much to add to which Prof. Kabir has said. Most educationists have come to the same conclusion, as he, viz. that there is indeed an abundance of writing on this subject which takes various forms, whether it is about cultures or whether it is about general education. There is never a moment, I believe, when this particular problem, of balance in higher education, is absent from the minds of reflecting academicians. On the major objective we are all agreed the objective of education is to secure a fully developed and integrated individual by means of drawing out the best in him on the basis of our past human experience and in the light of the requirements of the modern environment. Then analysing this a little further, we have noted the fact that this means not only attaining competence to the highest level to which competence can be achieved but also some other aims e.g. a sense of social responsibility or character and attitude or philosophy of life, that is to say, a preference for a spirit of service rather than advancing the interests of self. But when one comes down first to the details of this balance in the wake of higher education and one has to look through the corner of one's eyes at the genuine character of the milieu, then one is confronted with difficulties.

So far as these difficulties arise from the pace with which

things are changing and are getting obsolescent I take a little more optimistic view than Prof. Kabir has taken. For instance, we recognise that when we train a person to be, shall we say, an engineer or some other professional what we want is not a technician but a technologist. And a distinction has been made between these terms on the basis that a technologist is one who can cope with the problem of obsolescence. In other words, education will have been given in the principles rather than to details and above all he would have been taught how to learn that is to say how to turn his own knowledge to the acquiring of new skills on his own. Because it is true to say that what he has learnt becomes obsolescent almost within five years of his getting his degree. This is a problem with which we have to live, all of us have to live, that is to say, whether our educational system gives him a character or not, this is a global problem and I believe that it is being successfully handled and there is no reason why we should not be able to handle it.

But the other problem, viz., that of character, is a most baffling one and I have come to the conclusion that if there is anything which higher education does not give it is character. In other words, I have noticed the most glaring failures of character amongst the most highly educated because they have the capacity to be clever whereas the simpler people cannot think of the smart tricks which a highly educated person can think of. And it seems to me that the failure lies somewhere else. It would be very rash to enter upon an analysis of the causes of this; it may be that it is a secular phenomenon because we are taking too short a view of history and in the light of what is happening before our eyes, in circumstances which might prove to be abnormal later in historical retrospect, but what we see around us in some places is certainly very disturbing. Here on the Indian scene, for instance, we see a steady erosion of the rule of law; almost every morning when you open a paper you read about some disturbance somewhere which ought not to have taken place. And I am not talking only of those who are charged with committing excesses but also those who are supposed to deal with it. It happens at both the levels. That is to say, the salt itself seems to be losing its flavour. Then there is another element which I suppose is peculiar to the Indian scene and that is the somewhat undeveloped ego, shall we say, of the politician. He has not yet evolved something which is stabler and this can compare with what happens elsewhere—although ultimately all the politicians, I suppose, are the same all over the world. Nevertheless, if one may try to reduce it to concrete terms the balance between service of self and service of one's fellow-being seems to be titled very much in favour of service of self in this country. This, I am quite certain, is again a temporary phenomenon. After all we are practising something according to the rules of countries which have passed through a long period of trial and error and which have not introduced this on, so to speak, a clean plate. That is to say they have achieved literacy, to take an example, before their democracy came, whereas we have borrowed all the best rules again without the existence of the conditions which are implicit for the maintenance of such a system.

How to correct this is a topic which will take me much beyond the bounds of the present discussion. But in a brief word I could say that our polity ought to be regulated in accordance with the availability of reliable leadership. In other words, I believe that in our conditions, the number of leaders who could be trusted is very much smaller at the moment than in the more advanced countries and therefore we should have a kind of polity dependent arrangements in regard to devolution, decentralisation and so on which will be in accordance with this smaller availability. I have referred to this matter because I believe that the present failures are having a very serious effect on the new generation and even if education had the capacity to nurture character, this nurturing could not be successfully carried out if the environment and the milieu are not very favourable. In other words what they learnt here, if learnt is a right word, would be unlearnt as soon as they go out of our campus or out of the influence of the teachers.

This is something I am sure which is of very great interest to members of an institute like this because they will be taking on the roles of teachers. We are not considering teachers in abstract, we are considering teachers who will be entering on this profession very soon. Well, I shall leave this matter here and I come to the other point, how to achieve the balance between science on the one hand and humanities on the other.

The question is not really as simple as that of science and professions and humanities. So far as the University of Delhi is concerned, we have the smallest percentage of students I believe in India who are taking science, may be about 20% as against 35 or 40 in other places. So, one cannot say that in Delhi greater importance is given to science. But I should hasten to explain that this is due to the fact that the Delhi University is very very careful about its standards and all honours and post-graduate education in science is the direct responsibility of the Departments of the University. It is easy thus to see why there is not that scope for ready expansion that exists in certain other places. But when we come to an analysis of the students who take different sectors of humanities, then one is compelled to agree with Prof. Kabir that there is a great deal of selection of what you call soft option. I shall not particularise because that might give offence. I do not know the educational background of those present in this assembly. But most of you will realise what I mean. It is very difficult, for instance, to get good students for philosophy. You ask my old friend, Dr. N.N. Banerjee—(retired Professor of Philosophy) he had been complaining—I asked him how it is that I find great difficulty in filling his place. I asked him; why don't you, as a teacher, ensure that, you had the second level and the third level and other people ready in succession to take your place. He replied : what sort of material do I get ? The very best material goes to the professions and the next level of material goes to science and the third level goes to agriculture and veterinary and then the rest, perhaps some of them good ones, go in for economics; but for the rest you get fairly indifferent material for some of the other humanities.

Now how is this to be rectified ? You cannot rectify it by reinforcing this argument again and again that for the affairs of life what you want is not only skill and confidence but values and judgments and so on. The young persons who are under our care ask, but what good are they to us, in securing employment or a proper level of pay? In other words it all depends on what kind of prospects society offers to these people. So far as the professionals are concerned, there is, because ours is a developing country, a very great demand, shall we say, for doctors, engineers and technologists, and so on. There is also a fairly good demand for scientists. There should have been a demand for agricultural experts, agronomists and veterinarians but somehow their scales of pay have been so low that they do not feel attracted. I think that that has been a very great mistake, and we are now realising that. We also need supporting scientists, that is to say, good B.Sc. (Hons.) graduates. I think we are getting short in that particular commodity. We probably have sufficient economists and statisticians, and anyway people are prepared to take up these subjects. But I do not know who requires philosophers, historians and psychologists; some industrial psychologists are needed, as also as some labour officers of personnel officers. But many of the other subjects suffer because nobody knows what is to be done with people with competence in them. Where do they exercise this capacity to exercise judgement ? Therefore, my suggestion would be that in all walks of life people should make it clear that they do not want only scientists, but also they will also need generalists for general management or administration and supporting services they will prefer those who have graduated in the humanities. If you do so and fix scales of pay which compare with those which are given to engineers or which a doctor can make, then I think there will be a chance of correcting the balance, and the excess of which is causing a certain amount of anxiety to us. I believe that analyses have been made in other countries of who succeeds in what employment. I think Prof. Blackett once said that he found that persons graduated in the humanities do just as well, if not better, in business management as the scientists.

This of course reflects the kind of education that the universities have been giving in the past. That is to say these are the differences between the specialists and the generalists and it is the recognition of this that has led us now to this new exploration as to what place general education had in the system of higher education. But the more we examine, and we have been doing it for the last ten years, the more confusing general education has become, with the result that the latest finding is that there is just nothing that we can do about general education except integrating it with all instructions. Because it is not a subject or it is not anything that you learn, it is not good books, it is not good leaders, it is not this or that; it is almost like Brahma. And like Brahma it should be omnipresent, it should be everywhere. Whether you teach science, whether you teach anything else, they led to this idea that all this is to be practised in a world which does not consist entirely of science. And therefore, it should, to a certain extent, be reflected in our integrated courses in engineering and technology. But they have not yet started integrated course in medicine. In engineering they have a five year course so that for the students admitted as they are after passing the higher secondary—the first two years are a sort of foundation years where the student learns a lot about sociology, economics and what not in order to prepare the ground in his mind, the frame of reference against which he is going to exercise the competence which he is going to acquire later. I think that is very sound. Similarly I suppose for those who are studying humanities, there must be some way of acquainting them with the tasks that human beings have in regard to scientific and technological progress. Science and technology are now very conspicuous features of the new landscape and a historian who neglects to study the recent past or anything what science and technology has done, I am quite sure, will not be able to write proper history. This can be amplified and can be applied to other subjects. So, this, I think, is the way of bringing about a balance, bringing about a greater recognition of the humanities, of securing, of ensuring that the content of education is such that there is the optimum preparation of the student for filling any role in life, whether it is pure science, whether it is applied science, whether it is the world of values, or whether it is the world of management and so on.

So far as the teachers are concerned they have no problem. The system is a kind of self feeding system, it is a feeding back. To the extent to which the educational system is growing there will also be room for content teachers, that is to say a person who has a certain preparation, for teaching a subject. Because they know that we are looking for more philosophers, more professors and more readers of philosophy and, at the rate at which universities are going, the demand is growing considerably. It is so large that it has now become very difficult to find properly qualified people for the many jobs which have to be filled in the work of higher education.

Well, I thought I would place some observations before you following the very stimulating lecture that Prof. Kabir in the light of his very long and mature experience has given to us and with this now I shall call upon the Secretary to propose a vote of thanks.

CONVOCATION ADDRESS

at Shivaji University, Monday, October 17, 1966, *Kolhapur.*

Your kind invitation to me to deliver the Convocation Address for this year has not only greatly honoured me but also given much pleasure. It has given me the opportunity of observing the rise of a new seat of higher learning in an area which has figured prominently in the historical developments in the country over the last 350 years or so and which is the home of some of the most energetic and vigorous people in the country, gifted with a rare capacity for organizing progressive agriculture and industry on a co-operative basis.

My acquaintance with the affairs of your University is necessarily limited, but I have heard sufficient from the Vice-Chancellor to form the impression that the University has got off to a good start. The Education Commission has indicated the basic Principles that have to be kept in view in establishing new Universities. They include a responsibility for making a substantial improvement in standards and in the output and level of research and necessity of ensuring a strong core of teaching departments combined with about 30 affiliated colleges in close proximity. They have entered a caveat against creating by the establishment of a new University an undue dispersal of intellectual talent, funds and administrative ability, all of which are in scarce supply at present. Although the Education Commission have not mentioned it I regard the opportunity to try out interesting innovations in the field of higher education as one of the prime justifications for the establishment of new Universities. This point is amply illustrated by the modes of development selected for themselves by the crop of new Universities that has sprung up in recent years in Great Britain. On the Indian scene I fear there is far too strong a tendency to enforce uniformity and to discourage experimentation by means of direct or indirect regulation.

Old or new, Universities have important objectives to attain, which have concern with the pursuit of knowledge, the development of qualities of leadership, the provision of highly trained man-power to the nation, professional and of other sorts, and the development of 'the good life' in individuals and society. In addition, as the Education Commission points out, Indian Universities have special responsibilities in regard to intellectual and spiritual leadership of the community and elevation of the education level, not only of schools. but also of their total environment by means of adult education.

The tree is proverbially judged by its fruit and the University will be judged by its alumni. As new Universities have special opportunities and responsibilities so have their alumni. They constitute the foundation on which the fulfilment and reputation of a new University will rest. If theirs is a rare opportunity theirs also is a new challenge.

It is of this opportunity and this challenge that the Chief Orator at the Convocation address of a University, specially, a new University, should speak on, out of the maturity of his experience. I agreed to address you on this occasion out of mixed motives, such as a sense of natural affinity and affection, a solicitude for your career as citizens of our beloved country and a desire to share with you some of my thoughts on current trends in the hope that they might in some way help you in fulfilling your roles to come in life.

But first of all let me congratulate you graduates on the successes and distinctions that you have achieved. For a new institution such as yours, with the initial difficulties of organization, the pass percentages achieved appear to me to be very creditable, and this could not have been accomplished without the wholehearted collaboration of all concerned, viz. the College Managements, the Staff and the Students, under the wise and able direction and guidance of the University authorities.

If it has not already been formed I would suggest that you take the earliest opportunity of forming an alumni association. Such associations, apart from the satisfaction of natural sentiments such as pride and affection for the *alma mater*, serve as invaluable links between the University and its environment and between the older and newer generations. In advanced countries, especially U.S.A., an alumni association plays a significant part in maintaining the tone of the University, but in India they are not very much in evidence, except for the purpose of election of past graduates to the seats reserved for them on the Senate and other bodies of the University.

Learning, resources and standards are and have always been the prime pre-occupation of Universities. That Universities are the main source of the highly trained manpower needed for economic growth has also been fully accepted. But the emergence of a University's sense of involvement in the well-being of its milieu is a relatively modern phenomenon, which is in fact just begun to be realized in India. In matters like adult literacy and adult education Universities have a significant role to play which is as yet not fully appreciated. As the Education Commission picturesquely put it: "The image of the University as a closed academic community of scholars creating and disseminating knowledge and perpetuating its own type is a thing of the past. The walls which divide the gown and the town have crumbled and the life of the University and that of the community can be vitally linked for their mutual enrichment." How this is to be achieved has been indicated in sufficient detail by the commission. There is a place in this effort for voluntary agencies, which in effect means the private citizen, to which category some of you will belong either immediately or a few years later after completing further stages of your education.

There is, however, one field of very special importance to which pointed attention has been drawn by the Education Commission; that field is the liquidation of illiteracy for which a sustained campaign is strongly urged, a campaign which should involve, besides Governments, Voluntary Agencies, Industries and Educational Institutions, all educated men and women in the country. I suggest that whether in the University or out of it, students and ex-students form voluntary organizations for the express purpose of participating vigorously in the campaign for the liquidation of illiteracy. Maharashtra has already done much in this direction by means of its *gram-shikshan mohim*, and the trail has already been blazed, for young educated men and women to follow.

There is nothing like some over-mastering passion for public service like this to keep the flame of your patriotism burning bright. To my mind, patriotism is apt to be confused, unwittingly perhaps, with advancement of self-interest or acquisition of power, and many a seeming patriot is apt in the light of experience to be found to be a highly ego-centric individual who has convinced himself that his being at the head of affairs at his chosen level is the sole means of saving the country. Real patriotism is, however, dedication of oneself to one's more disadvantaged fellow-beings, often without recognition or reward. Indeed this dedication is both patriotism and religion, if one is inclined to be religious.

From the point of view of success, a spirit of service is the best guarantee of its success. It will draw both money and co-operation, which will flow freely, no matter how difficult the circumstances, to those who are known to be working genuinely for others, without a thought for advancing their own financial or political interests. The history of Maharashtra is full of noble examples of such servants of the people and it is these examples that ought to be emulated by young people rather than those who have achieved glamorous successes in the field of politics.

Before the advent of independence the common man, somewhat helplessly, bewailed the unethical conduct of business. The cynical answer to him in those days was 'Business is Business'. Today, with a democratic constitution of the Western parliamentary type in full operation, a new area of unethical conduct has emerged—that is politics. The lack of a high ethos is even more conspicuous in this arena than in business and even more emphatic is the cynical answer : 'Politics is politics'. While legal curbs create an illusion of restraint so far as business is concerned, because ingenious evasion is manifold and widely spread, in politics there is not even a semblance of self-restraint. The god that presides over business is, however, a god that cannot be imposed upon—it is the balance-sheet and like the lily that has blown and is no longer decorative, a spent business man quickly disappears from the scene. Not so the politician, who can flourish indefinitely long after his utility, if he ever had any, is exhausted. The voice of his God, Vox Populi, speaks only after long intervals and seldom in terms that are just or clear. The criteria for measuring success or failure are either non-existent or ambiguous and in any case our cultural milieu is such that inutility or worse in this field is seldom exposed or can rarely be established or brought home.

That a little less than three-fourths of the population of our country and therefore of the franchise holders, is illiterate and ill-informed has something to do with this stage of affairs, a situation which is aggravated by inadequate development or imperfect use of the many modern means of mass-communication. It is in this context that eradication of illiteracy should be recognized as a matter of prime importance, for education could open the gates for better understanding and more judicious exercise of the franchise.

However, I should like to sound a note of warning here. In my view it is vain to hope that education will help in the cultivation of moral and spiritual values. The general experience, on the contrary, is that education intensifies and renders more capable of misuse one's innate imperfections in the sphere of these values. The naturally cunning and unprincipled, for instance, become more unmanageably cunning or unprincipled. I have yet to be convinced that education in general or university education, in particular, helps to form character.

To my mind character is the product of innate endowment, influence of environment and constant self-introspection in the light of that indefinable, imponderable and intangible conscience. It is very much the private business of everyone, subject to a variety of influences all through life. Good acts and good habits are the basis of good character, and therefore, character formation is a continuous process from birth to death, a process in which constant introspection can play an important part.

It is also my belief that the tone of society round one can play a material role in the formation and stabilization of one's character. There are fields of human activity such as business and politics, where a noticeably depreciated scale of moral and spiritual values prevails and in these spheres character is an easy casualty. Mounting scarcities, such as exist today in India, are also destructive of acceptable moral and spiritual values, especially in congested urban conditions.

I am convinced that in the long run no society can prosper in which scales of moral and spiritual values are continuously depreciated. Such a society will be full of tensions and conflicts which are bound to entail the gradual erosion of the rule of law and to end in some sort of cataclysm. In this context

I feel no compunction in quoting what I said on a previous occasion of this kind. "The world is very dynamic and there is a great demand for scientists and technicians, yet greater is the demand for people whose character, sense of justice and creative ability can be relied upon. We are lagging behind on account of centuries of slavery and in order to line up with the advanced countries we shall have to work very hard. This task is as great as was the struggle for freedom. We have become lethargic on account of centuries of slavery. We can easily tolerate injustice, rudeness and falsehood. We shall have to give up this moral apathy and this is to be done by young persons like you. The world that you will enter with such aspirations will be lacking in comforts and amenities and you will have to struggle hard to attain them. The moral plane of this struggle will be very low. Everywhere, you will find the greed for power, crookedness, dishonesty, indifferences to justice and such other evils triumphant. In such an adverse environment, the strength of your character will be put to test. Cultured young persons like you, with strong character, will have to change this atmosphere. It is natural that each one of you may not be able to display supreme courage. However, the progress of society can be measured only by the character and efficiency of its ordinary or average citizens. It is true that the development of culture and civilization is the result of the efforts of a few extraordinary thinkers. But the extraordinary will be extraordinary after all. The common people can always do one thing. They can remain firm in their character and can thus promote the progress of the entire society. Whatever be your status or post, I advise you to work whole-heartedly and to preserve your character. Character has no connection with high or low status. On the contrary I have noticed that even a rich man does not attach as much importance to character as a poor man does. The experience of the human race to this day shows that the happiness of character eclipses all the pleasures of worldly life. And what else do we need besides maximum happiness in life ?"

We of this century are living in the midst of a heady cultural revolution characterised by explosion of population, on one hand, and explosion of science and technology on the other. Whilst the former makes tremendous demands on our resources the latter has within it the potentiality of meeting them. What is needed however, is a thorough understanding of the situation by the young and the old alike if the human community is to live harmoniously. In the conduct of human affairs, especially, the relationship between the older and the younger generation has to be re-identified and redefined. This is especially necessary in a country like ours where the population is predominantly young i.e. where the proportion of people in the lower age-groups is markedly higher than in some of the more advanced countries.

Even in the more advanced countries, where affluence is well established, the mutual relations between the young and the old are marked by lack of understanding. While the old are puzzled by unaccountably turbulent behaviour on the part of the young, the young have ceased to find any inspiration or guidance in their elders, so much so that there are instances where groups of youth have objured conversation, as useless, with anyone above 30.

The difficulty of understanding between the generations has always been noticed throughout human history, but the pace with which science and technology are proliferating and advancing has immeasurably widened the gulf between the generations. A time will soon come when the old will be dumb-founded by the behaviour of the young and when the young will find the old incomprehensible and probably a hindrance to human progress. The situation will be aggravated by the ever-increasing longevity in an over-crowded world.

What then is called for in such a situation ? For one thing, the redeeming feature will be that the young of today will be the old of tomorrow, and as we grow older we shall have to strain every nerve to fight obsolescence. In other words we shall have to remain students all our lives. Secondly, since values do not change so fast as science and technology, the young will have to think deeply on moral and spiritual values, so as to keep up a level of gainful and satisfying communication with the old, as also to prevent thoughtless upheavals in the name of modernity.

Such a value, for instance, is the rule of law. It must be the common concern of old and young alike to cherish this value, for in its absence the fabric of society itself will crumble into chaos.

It is my hope that what I have said will give some food for thought to my listeners and that they will strive to create a better world for themselves and their new generation.

Let me wish you the very best in this endeavour and in your future life generally.

CONVOCATION ADDRESS

at the Annual Convocation of the University of Madras, 26*th August*—1964.

Your invitation to deliver the Convocation-address of the University is a very great honour indeed. The University of Madras is of the ripest vintage among Indian universities and has achieved an excellence and standing worthy of its maturity. Over the years a few more universities of India have joined the vanguard of front rank universities, a few others have perhaps had their lustre dimmed, but Madras has maintained a steady preeminence, threatened perhaps only during the last few years by innovations such as the three-year degree course and the attempts of the state to hasten the adoption of Tamil as medium of instruction. Of some of these matters I may have occasion to speak a little later on.

My first duty this afternoon is to offer my hearty congratulation to the graduates, in their impressive numbers,— not only on their passing their respective degree or diploma examinations, but also on the distinction some of them have achieved or the prizes and scholarships they have secured. The academic scene in this regard is one of healthy emulation and of fitting reward to sustained effort on the part of both the faculty and the students. Some of the graduates will be leaving the portals of the university while the others will be continuing their pursuit of learning or professional skills and to all such I wish god speed and success. The first degree stage is the most difficult of all. Those who negotiate this with some distinction need entertain little fear of not making whatever grade they have set their minds on. There are some levels of achievement which are being abolished, as for instance, a III class in M.A. or M.Sc., a fact which will no doubt govern choices before any further step in one's educational career is planned. The faculty of law still remains in most universities a resort in part for the not so well endowed or for the not so serious; but there are trends observable of more rigorous admission requirements for legal education. If they gain force, as I hope and expect they will, then we may regard all post-graduate achievement in India as not only well worthwhile in itself, but also as a guarantee of reasonably satisfying employment. For those to whom their first degree will be a terminus, whilst avenues of employment will, I imagine, be open, judging from the available information, the waiting will sometimes be long or the employment secured will be below the level of their scholastic achievement. I do not know how unsatisfactory the situation in Madras is in regard to this, oddly so called, 'educated unemployment'. But whilst it is true that many graduates have to accept an initial employment below the reputed worth of their degree, it is also true that the B.A.s and B.Sc.s of Indian universities have had a shorter span of education before school-leaving, of one or two years, as compared to nearly every other country in the world, advanced or unadvanced. In U.S.A. and Japan the school occupies 12 years and is followed by 4 years of instruction in the university. In Europe, hardly anyone enters the university before undergoing 12 years of schooling of some sort. Even if we assume that other things are equal which they are not—our B.A. or B.Sc. courses include contents which would be included in high school curriculae in most countries. Our stage of university equivalence, if of a different sort, in maturity of scholarship to the Bachelor degree in other countries is the Master's degree, which should be normally achieved at the age of 22, at which age, at most European, American and Japanese universities young men and women obtain their first degree. It is for this reason that most educationists are in favour of extending the total period of education before the first degree to 15 years at least, starting school from the age of 6. My own personal predilection is in favour of 11 years of school, followed by 4 years for the first non-professional degree—our B.A. or B.Sc. The 12th year should more advantageously be entrusted to colleges than to high schools both because of the smaller numbers involved and the different methods of teaching, as well as some other advantages. If allowance is made for the inclusion in our total numbers of young persons at universities who are in reality finishing some of the unaccomplished ends of secondary education, we shall find that as compared with most countries we have too few undergoing university education, may be in the proportion of less than 2,000 per million of population as against 5,000 per million for most developed countries and 7,500 to 10,000 per million in countries, as widely different in economic achievement and affluence as Philippines and Japan or France, Sweden, Canada and U.S.A. The corresponding U.K. figure of 2,500 is small by comparison, but the Robins Commission Report has made recommendations which if accepted, as they have been or are most likely to be, will raise the proportion much nearer the continental figures. In India we shall need to double the proportion as soon as practicable. It is also often asserted by those not fully acquainted with all the facts of the problem—usually in the Press, that India is having too many universities. My own view, based on an intimate acquaintance with university education and administration is that we have far too few universities, and that even if the number were to rise to 100, on a population of some 500 million and a total university enrolment of 2 million we shall have an average strength of as much as 20,000 per university omitting the immature part of school population—the intermediate or junior college level. I am convinced that a university cannot very conscientiously undertake to have an enrolment exceeding 10 to 12,000 and that for other universities 25,000 or thereabout is the limit for competent management.

These numbers should comprise only the quality education of the orthodox type. There can be additions due to other types e.g. evening colleges, correspondence courses, lightly guided external students, especially women. While the classical purpose of university education remains above controversy, viz. the pursuit of learning for its own sake, the rapid involvement of the community in university education all over the world has brought into focus other ends of university education such as all round development of the individual for enriching life as well as the discharge of responsibilities towards the community. Indeed in the developing countries educational planning has to be geared very closely to the requirements of trained personnel for the planned or unplanned task of economic and social development. Indeed on how successfully this planning is formulated and implemented will depend the prosperity of countries. This is perhaps by now obvious, but not so obvious are some of the more obscure factors currently receiving attention.

The first of these is the problem of obsolescence which arises from the incredible acceleration of the pace of advance of science and technology, discovery and invention. The sword of learning has to be sharpened almost continuously if it is to retain the keenness of the edge. So large is the volume of original scientific or technological publication in the world today in almost any discipline or on any section one may think of that the interested scientist or technologist can never hope to be able to acquaint himself with all of it in extenso. He has to pick and choose with the help of digests and a stage may soon come when a digest itself may prove to be indigestible. The time is not far off, when the scholar will have to depend on some sort of electronic computer to help him absorb that part of current publication which has a bearing on his own discipline or specialization. It follows that mere transmitted knowledge will be of no avail and that what the pupil has to be taught is how to learn to learn. The fundamentals of a subject will have to be well-taught, but stored up facts and figures, deductions and applications would have to be rigidly limited so as to be illustrative. Again, in the field of technology, acquired professional skills would be out of date soon after the stamp of competence is placed on them in a university convocation. The final convocation will no longer be the end of the journey—it will merely be the beginning of an endless process of learning. What has been said is not true of science and technology alone. Even in the shifting sands of the humanities accepted theories soon get out of date, and in any case there will be no theory that will not have to be reconsidered in the light of changes in environment and in human society brought about not only by science and technology but also by shifting sets of accepted values or dispositions. Instances in point are economic doctrines applicable to developing societies or the theory of practice of democracy in countries that have become independent or have shaken off foreign domination in the post-war era. Even the method of teaching languages is undergoing a profound change under the impact of the developing science of linguistics as well as the availability of audio-visual aids like television.

But this is only part of the trouble. Where the whole environment is changing so fast, the task of preparing young people to live on terms with their half or quarter century is one of growing perplexity. Gone for ever are the comfortable days when notes drawn up years ago could be used by the teacher, year after year with no change, even in the jokes.

I should like to end with quoting two passages from an address delivered by Mr. J. George, Harrar, President, Rockefeller Foundation at the University of Florida in April last. These passages state what I have said at length earlier in my address :

"..Higher education should, therefore, have the principal effect of sharpening that wonderful biological tool, the human mind, to a keen cutting edge. This still little-understood living receptor, computer, and analyzer contains the power which has moved the world and will send it in whatever directons it may take in the future. Properly stimulated, the individual mind cannot only move with confidence toward the solution of the great problems of mankind; it can also make each day in life a new and meaningful intellectual experience, with its appropriate content of pleasure in new discovery, new skill, new application. Unfortunately, this does not invariably happen. The brain seems to be at once the most powerful and the least exercised of human organs. It rarely seems to give out from overwork...."

"....The world will need tomorrow, more than ever in the past, the selfless contributions of people in all walks of life. No one has the right of exclusive responsibility; and no one has the right to exclude himself from responsibility. The home, the church, the factory, the business office, the school, the laboratory, and the other institutions of our democracy provide unlimited opportunities for individual self-expression and contribution to the cause of mankind. We all have the right to vote, the freedom to exercise charitable and philanthropic impulses, the ability to continue the learning process, and the obligation to act constructively as members of the local and national community. Only if each of us seizes his opportunities and none of us abdicates his responsibilities will be able to meet squarely the challenges before us today, and those others perhaps more severe, which will confront us in the future...."

LANGUAGE PHOBIA AND UNITY OF INDIA

What sort of danger linguistic problems hold to the unity of India ? It is abundantly clear that by the unity of India one means, not so much a sense of emotional integration about which one hears so much, as the political integrity, i.e., wholeness of India as a nation. In other words, one thinks of the possibility of an area or a State with a separate language working up an agitation for secession from the nation that is India, in order to form a separate nation that would gain recognition by international bodies like the United Nations.

It is well known that before the completion of the process of independence and the integration of the States, this was indeed a very dubious and complicated issue. Apart from the general problem posed by the 560 and odd former princely States, there were the special problems created often by the statesmen in charge there, by the demand that the States be recognized as distinct nations. It is strange to recall that even the old Travancore State was one of these, apart from the two other classical examples of Jammu and Kashmir and Hyderabad. However, it may safely be said now, as a result of monumental statesmanship, all these dangers are well behind us now, except for the loss of portions of Jammu and Kashmir first to Pakistan and now to China as a result of very special factors. Although from one State one hears occasional reports of a demand for secession, there is reason to believe that this is a result of no more than political slogans and that, in practice, in any case, there would be very stern counter measures taken by the Centre and indeed by the country as a whole to prevent any such political slogans from developing into any active attempts to separate from the rest of India.

So far as the north of the country is concerned not only are there linguistic States but also in several States, superficially at least, only one language is the official language. These States are U. P., Bihar, M. P. and Rajasthan making up a total population of 175 millions. He would be a bold man who would argue *per contra* that these 175 million people have learnt to live in amity with a full sense of emotional integration, merely because the official language of the States concerned is Hindi. Indeed some of the most virulent political struggles for leadership have been staged in these very States, and although at one time there was a proposal, based on a great deal of common sense argumentation, that the State of U. P. be split up into two with consequential peripheral rearrangements, one of the most important politicians of the country is reported to have declared that the partition of the U. P. could only take place over his dead body. This clearly proves that the real culprit in the lack of this unity is not the linguistic States but something else, and unless this 'something else' is carefully traced out and diagnosed, there is an imminent danger of a false prognosis and a great deal of ineffective and possibly mischievous action.

It is not clear how the 'one language—one State' arrangement that is now in existence holds any kind of threat to the unity of India. Language is essentially a vehicle for cultural patterns and for inter-communication in regard to current affairs. Since, with the advent of Independence, and the conferment of adult franchise as a concommitant of the western parliamentary form of democracy, it is very essential that the link between the voters and their representatives, in the legislatures and in the governments at various levels, should have the closest possible intimacy, this would have its maximum strength in uni-lingual states.

Problem of Sophisticated People

The fact that the literacy percentage in India is now round about 30 and that the truly literate percentage of the population would be hardly half of this, even linguistic sentiments would dimensionally be so small as to be easily outweighed in the balance by more natural aggregations of interests, such as regional, political, religious or economic. In other words, linguistic problems largely exist in the minds of only the more sophisticated section of the community and these have been using language as a peg on which to hang other ulterior motives. I do not believe that the man in the street or the peasant thinks of language with any kind of sentiment. All he is concerned with is that he should not be inconvenienced in the conduct of his day-to-day affairs, and even in this he is prepared to be surprisingly tolerant.

My view therefore is that the perils of linguism are artificial or a creation of a very small sophisticated minority and that it is almost the red herring trailed across the path by interested groups which have other aims and objects, more material than linguistic sentiment, in view. Of all the so-called dangerous issues, at present the subject of pejoration in India, linguism is the most innocuous, for it means the desire to separate in arrangements which would make for the maximum understanding and the readiest communication in regard to everyday affairs. To cite one example applicable to the sophisticated minority, the current controversy over Hindi is to my mind really a struggle for a somewhat unrestricted market for publications. If Hindi were to be more prevalent than is warranted by, say, merely its being an official language or as a *lingua franca*, obviously the reading public and of publications in Hindi would be increasingly large at the expense of the reading public in the other languages which might be destined to be neglected from a base commercial motive. In other words, if an option were to lie before an author capable of expressing himself in, shall I say, Gujarati and Hindi, it might very well be that he would prefer to write in Hindi because of the far wider reading public that he might have and therefore of the larger rewards that he might reap. It is here that a great deal of restraint is called for. Every language has a genius of its own and mirrors patterns of culture which do not conflict with but are complementary to the sister patterns of culture prevalent in India. It is therefore in the best interests of the country that all these vehicles of human transaction and communication should be given their maximum possible encouragement so that they might together contribute to the strength of the unity in diversity that is India.

The remedy for such false self-appraisals—whether of language or of national or communal character—is to mix freely and without inhibitions with others, and this implies means of communication in the shape of a common language. In other words, the more we acquire facility in another language than our own the wider is our horizon and the more the basis of a wider understanding. The academic bodies like the Sahitya Akademi and the National Book Trust are making systematic efforts to make the speakers of one language familiar with the cultures and ideas mirrored in the other languages of India mentioned in the Constitution, by the necessarily limited and unsatisfactory method of translation, and their efforts will bear fruit only if the study of languages becomes more systematic and purposeful in the school, the university and citizenhood (among citizens).

Fortunately, as Lancelot Hogben has claimed and tried to prove in his famous book 'The Loom of Languages', scarcely can anyone have any rational basis for the belief that he or she is congenitally incapable of becoming a linguist. If a language phobia exists, it must be a by-product of formal education or other agencies of social environment.

How true this is of India, with its post-Independence language phobias, which are the result of neglect of teaching languages to pupils no less than of the slogans of politicians or of vested interests ! And yet how easy and how rewarding is the study of languages, especially in India, where they belong to two main language families, provided the aim is not perfect mastery but the more modest one of acquiring a small workmanlike vocabulary and getting a grasp of essential grammatical peculiarities.

But the private citizens' efforts have to be reinforced by the purposeful efforts of the State. It is here that I see the greatest ambivalence of the Indian scene, a profession of deep concern for the language and culture of minorities and a practice of direct, but more often indirect, (i.e. through official myrmidons) denial of opportunities, of suppression and of compulsive use of the majority languages. It is principally this situation that has even created the antithesis of linguistic problems and national unity. Its remedy can only be in the rooting out of such fissiparous politics and vested interests by every citizen who has a concern not only for national unity but also for progress towards an international society in which India will be an honoured member.

CONVOCATION ADDRESS

at the Karnatak University, October, 11, 1963.

Mr. Vice-Chancellor, Staff,
Students and Graduates of the year :

This is not the first time that I am visiting the Karnatak University, and I recall with pleasure more than one visit in the course of which I have seen this relatively new university establishing itself with assurance amongst the universities of the country under the assiduous and fostering care of the Vice-Chancellor, his colleagues and the State of Mysore behind them. I am happy to see this growth and I feel sure that it has taken place without any sacrifice of quality or standards. I take this opportunity, therefore, of congratulating all concerned on the remarkable progress achieved within a relatively short span of years.

Whilst at all times it is an honour to be invited to deliver the convocation address of a university, one feels overwhelmed when one is honoured in addition, by the conferring of a degree, *honoris causa*, by a seat of higher learning.

Now that I have been brought within the fold of this university there is a special reason why I should say something worthwhile to my co-graduands. Unfortunately, I have been called upon during the last seven years to deliver far too many convocation addresses, most of which, together with my addresses on cognate subjects, will be found in two volumes published by the University Grants Commission under the titles '*In the Portals of Indian Universities*' and '*On the Threshold of India's Citizenhood*'. I feel sorely tempted, therefore, merely to refer my listeners to these two volumes.

But, on reflection, I feel that such a course would not be in accordance with the true spirit of universities. Apart from its basic purpose of extending and deepening the frontiers or the fields of earning, the university has the essential duty of teaching those young men and women who happen to be entrusted to its care, how to live on terms with their environment. This duty does not merely refer to the production of personnel, trained in modern science and technology, for the diverse roles that have to be played by the citizen of any developing country. The process also implies an understanding of the total setting against which such duties or indeed any other duties and responsibilities have to be discharged. Moreover, the one feature about the evolution of human affairs that none could have missed noticing during the last few years, is the breath-taking pace at which our environment is being transformed, thanks, to the triumphs of science and technology. It is therefore, more than ever necessary that the university students should fully understand the world in which they will very shortly be called upon to play a role, no matter how high or low such a role might be. It is as a result of the realization of this duty that the university world of today is more or less in a perpetual state of ferment with arguments, controversies and disputations in regard to all sorts of topics which are relevant to their aims and objects, administration, motivation, conditions of work, operation and environment. University-men often feel called upon to participate in these discussions and, irrespective of this, it is always a rewarding experience to have had the opportunity of comparing and contrasting by visiting other universities, both in this country and abroad.

I have just returned from a tour abroad which lasted for over two months and in the course of which, apart from attending the World Food Congress at Washington between June 2 and June 17, I visited a large number of universities both in the U S.A. and U.K. and elsewhere, such as Princeton, Pennsylvania, Rutgers, Massachusetts Institute of Technology, Harvard, Brandeis, Cambridge and Oxford (revisited), Reading, Swansea, Leicester and Teheran. More important than this, I have also participated in the Ninth Quinquennial Congress of the Association of Commonwealth Universities held in London and at St. Andrews between 14th and 24th July last. During the course of these visits and this Congress I must have met literally hundreds of university-men and women at all levels from administrators, teachers, students and those sections of the public which are represented in the university governance. To complete the picture, I should say that I have also attended a meeting of the Executive Council of the World University Service in

Geneva and have had some discussion in regard to educational planning with Dr. Philip Coombs, Director of the International Institute for Educational Planning, only recently set up by the UNESCO.

As a result of these visits, discussions and talks I have gathered some impressions which I believe it might be worthwhile placing before my listeners.

The predominant impression that one gathers is in regard to the great solicitude which modern societies feel at all levels in regard to assistance of university education. By common consent this is regarded as by far the most critical of the stages of a nation's education, if that nation is to take its proper place in the political, economic and social advancement of the world. This realization is reflected in the ready support which the State authorities, municipal corporations and local bodies generally give to their universities as also in the great care that they take to ensure that the university world is allowed to discharge its somewhat unique responsibilities without interference either from those that wield political power or those that furnish it with the sinews for its proper running or development. There are, of course, exceptions occasionally to be found to this rule that on no account must the autonomy of universities be interfered with, but such exceptions are to be found almost invariably accompanied by a low standard of governance or economic progress. What is especially noticeable is that the great temptation to exercise indirect authority through financial sanctions is rigorously resisted. Whilst this result may, in part, be due to the maturity of political experience or innate good sense, it is often the result of the logic of events based on the peculiar nature of the work of a university, which can prosper only in an atmosphere of academic freedom. This is not to say that utilitarian aims are entirely eschewed; but they have invariably to be subordinated to the fulfilment of the higher intellectual aims and purposes of a university. Neither research nor teaching, both of which lie at the heart of all university operation, can possibly function in an atmosphere where the researcher and the teacher are required to work not under his own steam, so to speak, but in a system of regimentation. The frontiers of learning are the only frontiers which will not yield to armed and controlled cohorts, no matter how well-organized the command behind them might be. In the ultimate analysis all scientific discovery and advance can be traced to some inspiration, some felicitous flash of imagination, which will only come where the mind is untrammelled and the spirit is not oppressed or harassed by a sense of subjugation or subservience.

The controversy over quality versus quantity in the world of university education wages fast and furious, and, superficially, it would look as if even amongst advanced countries the system adopted is fraught with the danger of damaging quality in the interest of increasing quantity. But on an analysis of this situation one finds that in most well-ordered advanced countries there is a jealous regard for safeguarding standard which is not affected by the concessions that are made to the citizens' aspirations for enlarged opportunities of higher education. In this respect it would be interesting to contrast the two outstanding systems to which Indian universities owe a great deal of their inspiration, namely, those in the United Kingdom and the U.S.A.

It is well-known that in the United Kingdom the selection of students for university education has so far been extremely rigorous, a situation which is brought out by the fact that only about 1,25,000 young men and women in a population of 50 million are receiving university education in that country in some 30 universities or comparable institutions. On the other hand, in a population which is about four times as much, and where, therefore, had the British system prevailed, one would have expected a university student population of a little under one million, there are as many as four million young men and women in universities or other institutions of higher learning, including institutions equivalent to what are known as polytechnics in our country. Admission to a university is indeed a very great privilege in the United Kingdom, which is reserved only for those who can succeed in a very severe test known as the advanced level general certificate examination, and since the number of applicants is much larger than the number of seats available, only those who have achieved very high distinction stand a chance of being accepted as students in a British university. Even on the British scene, the pressure of numbers is steadily mounting, and currently there are controversies reflected in the debates in Parliament in regard to whether the number of seats to be provided for, say, in another five years' time, should be raised to 150,000 or 175,000. There is quite an eruption of new universities, some 10 or 12 being in active process of establishment. One noticeable feature of the British system, which reflects the basic autonomy enjoyed by seats of higher learning, is that there is room for a great deal of experimentation and innovation. Although there is a co-ordinating and sustaining body like the University Grants Committee, every care is exercised to ensure that the free exercise of academic choices is not interfered with when the necessary financial assistance is to an increasing measure being made available to these new universities. It is worthwhile noticing here that the cost per student in a British university incurred by all authorities together is very near £ 1,000, against hardly an equivalent of £ 100 in India. Even after full allowance is made for the higher cost of construction and by far the better conditions of service and terms of employment enjoyed by the teachers, this higher cost reflects the furnishing of far superior educational amenities for the young people of Great Britain, levels which it would be vain to hope would be reached in India even in a century.

Whilst the concern for standards is more or less built into the British system, it is not quite so obvious on the American scene or indeed in other parts of the Commonwealth, such as Australia. Here, in the more blatantly democratic spirit of the communities concerned, there is a far readier recognition of higher education not only as a means of the advancement of learning, not only as even the fulfilment of the diverse scientific, technological, professional and other needs of the nation for highly educated and trained personnel, but also as a means of fulfilling a basic urge of the citizen to the highest degree of education that the resources of the nation can sustain. In theory, therefore, in the U.S.A., as in Australia, there is no one who seeks admission into a seat of higher learning who does not find himself admitted to some institution or other at this level, but the checks and balances operate in two distinct ways, both ensuring that there is no dilution of the ultimate standard achieved. In the U.S.A., for instance, nearly all the 2,000 and odd institutions of higher education are entitled to give their own degrees and may confine themselves to as few subjects as they wish to cater for or instruct in. Over a long period of evolution of the system of higher education, the public has come to cultivate a fairly reliable sense of discrimination as to the relative value to be attached to the degrees of the colleges and the universities, the latter instructing in a very large number of disciplines, whilst the former confining themselves to much narrower ranges in arts, social sciences and sciences. There is in popular judgment a readily recognizable order of excellence of the American colleges and universities, and the standards in the top quarter would be found to be as high as are likely to be encountered anywhere else in the world. This is achieved as much by initial selection by option after tests and interview, as by a voluntary or involuntary weeding out at the end of the first year. It is in the first year of the four-year course for the first degree that both inclinations and aptitudes can be tested and young men and women enabled to make up their mind on whether they will continue with college and university education at all, or, if they do, which subjects they would like to take their first degree in. Whilst the work for the first degree even in the remaining three years may not be uniformly rigorous, in the post-graduate studies the work involved is extremely arduous and there is a provision for a degree, such as M.A. or M.Sc., for for those who cannot make their grade of the doctorate. It should be remembered in this context that the total span of school education is 12 years which, together with the four years for the first degree, make a span of 16 years, as against the 14 years, often without an honours course, in most Indian universities.

Incidentally, one may notice that the M.A. or the M.Sc. is a far more essential study in the Indian system than either in the U.K. or in the U.S.A. And in both the countries the period taken for Ph. D. is not less than three years, with the result that in most countries one with a doctorate would easily be found to have taken 19 years at least to reach this eminence. A somewhat interesting example of selective admission is to be seen in the University of California, where there are about 11 or 12 independent campuses of the university strung out over the whole of the State, which are free to determine their own quality in regard to selection and passing. There is, in addition, the State College in which there is room for any young man or woman who has graduated from school but has been unable to secure admission on any one of the campuses of the University of California. In addition, of course, there are private institutions, some of very high quality, such as Stanford.

Both in the United Kingdom and the U.S.A. the graduate is a valued member of the society, is much sought after and has great prestige. This is the result not only of academic perception but also of the social and economic conditions in which, there being full employment, many young people are tempted to enter upon a calling or a vocation without waiting to complete a course of higher education. So far as the graduates are concerned, industrial houses and other employers often make a point of locating promising young men and making them offers of employment which materialize as soon as the results of the examinations or tests are out or complete.

One feels tempted at this stage to contrast the position in the state of employment opportunities of graduates in India, and on a superficial examination of oft-quoted statistics one might feel depressed. But I have come to the conclusion that there is a great deal of silver lining to this particular cloud. In the first place, the total figure of educated unemployment given out, which, I believe, stands at some 750,000 today, includes a very large number of matriculates or under-graduates. The total number of unemployed graduates would not be more than, say, 150,000 in this total. This number is moreover to be interpreted in the light of the basis on which these figures are compiled, in particular the distinction of the term unemployment. On close examination it would be found that the period taken as a test is often somewhat low, as for instance, six months, whereas the results might be entirely different if a longer period, such as one year, has been taken. Furthermore, the phenomenon differs from place to place and from area to area. There are States, especially the backward ones, where there could not possibly be any educated unemployment to speak of, as the total number of trained manpower is woefully short of all kinds of jobs to be performed. In the more sophisticated States and in the urban areas generally, again, unemployment is largely a question of reluctance to take a lower job and a perpetual quest for a more rewarding one. It may be easily conceded that there are no standards that one can lay down in this respect, although one would feel inclined to concede that after a college or university education a young man or woman should not be called upon merely to make a simple entry or to arrange papers or to receive and despatch correspondence. But it is here that we have to remind ourselves that the total span of higher education in India is only 14 years as against 16 in most advanced countries, especially U.S.A. One might almost go on to postulate that the Indian M.A. or M.Sc. is often not very much superior to the B.A. or B.Sc. in U.S.A. or U.K., and in a sense the M.A. or M.Sc. may be regarded as the completion of the first stage of university education comparable to what is done in scientific, technological and professional fields.

I have no information in regard to the employment opportunities in the area within the jurisdiction of the Karnatak University, but it is my belief that by and large there would not be found to be a surfeit of graduates and that within a fairly reasonable period of time almost every graduate will find something worthwhile to do.

It is with this realization that I extend my hearty congratulations to those on whom degrees are being conferred today and express the hope that sooner, rather than later, they will find themselves in roles in which they can effectively further the aims and objects of our modern Indian community.

The inter-relation of university education and employment in developing countries is found to be somewhat more complex when one comes to details. In the U.K. a project has been undertaken by the London School of Economics to investigate this question systematically, and it is possible that the Delhi School of Economics may have the opportunity of collaborating in the work so far as the Indian scene is concerned.

One may expect that the newly established International Institute for Educational Planning will, when its work is sufficiently established, be in a position to assist developing countries in properly planning their educational systems, particularly the priorities.

Onerous responsibilities rest on the authorities in regard to educational planning. But in my opinion still heavier tasks await the newly educated generation. As long ago as in the days of the *Taittiriyopanishad* it was recognized that the older generation was not all virtue and merit. The graduate of the day was pointedly asked, in the course of the famous standard convocation address—which begins with *Satyam Vada*—to eschew carefully the faults and bad ways of the teachers. On reflection, this must be so, or else the movement of mankind will be retrograde.

Current political and other conditions in India do not always furnish good exemplars to youth, and it is for the highly educated section of it to improve on their Gurus. *Shishyad ichchet parabhavam* has a deeper significance than is usually imagined.

CONVOCATION ADDRESS

at the University of Kerala, November 21, 1962.

Mr. Chancellor, Mr. Vice-Chancellor, Members of the Senate, Graduates of the Year, Ladies and Gentlemen :

I feel greatly honoured by the invitation that the University of Kerala has extended to me to deliver the Convocation Address this year.

I have been closely connected with matters academic and educational during the last six years and during this period, in retrospect, I discover to my horror that I have delivered more than a score of convocation addresses. These and some other addresses that I delivered during this period have been printed or are going to be printed in two volumes, the first of which entitled 'In the Portals of Indian Universities' has already been published and the second entitled 'On the Threshold of India's Citizenhood ' is about to appear. I have brought with me a dozen copies of the first volume as a present to the library of the University in the hope that it might be read by some of the students who are listening to me or the generations of students that will be succeeding them. I should make it clear that I do this not out of any overweening conceit but out of a genuine desire to share my experience with other students. For, let me confess, I am, and have been, a student all my life, being anxious to acquaint myself with the new developing situations in the fast changing modern environment. Indeed, I feel that these are the only terms on which anyone in our modern human society can usefully continue to be a member of it.

I therefore felt some compunction at accepting the invitation to deliver the convocation address. But I finally decided to accept it for two reasons. One I have already indicated, viz., that in the intellectual and academic sphere there is always an advantage in sharing experience and in an exchange of views and I thought that this was an opportunity which I should not miss. The second reason is a more personal one, and that is that as Chairman of the University Grants Commission between

1956 and 1961 I had more than one occasion of acquainting myself with the special difficulties of the University of Kerala in developing, and as on account of my former and still continued interest in economic development, I have been taking a somewhat special interest in the economic development of this beautiful and, in many ways, unique State. Indeed, on one occasion I went so far as to express the view that the peculiar circumstances of Kerala called for a sort of a 'Package Development Programme' for the State. Moreover, since it is well-known that the spread of primary education has been more extensive and the percentage of literacy higher in Kerala than in any other State of India, there arises the intriguing question of why in spite of these Kerala should have the same difficulty as other States and perhaps even greater difficulties in the matter of reaching a high level of economic development. This led me to consider the relation between education and economic development and I thought that the present was a fitting occasion on which I could place some of my thoughts and views before the young people of Kerala represented in the convocation audience.

The Vice-Chancellor, while extending the invitation to me towards the end of July last, was good enough to acquaint me briefly with the activities of the University and its plans for future development. He has informed me that the University has affiliated to it 86 collegiate institutions of different types and is imparting instruction directly or indirectly to some 50,000 students, of whom 30 per cent are women, undergoing courses in the various branches of learning. I learn that the activities of the University, which have hitherto been concentrated mainly in the city of Trivandrum, are being extended to other places in the State by the provision of necessary facilities at those centres for post-graduate studies and research. I was glad to be informed that two such University centres are being established, one at Ernakulam and the other at Calicut, during the Third Plan period. Having had some idea of the cramped nature of the University's present campus in Trivandrum, I was happy to learn that the campus of the University is being shifted to an extensive area outside the city to provide space for an adequate expansion of its present and future activities. There is evidence that the existing University Departments of

Study and Research in Trivandrum, which are limited in number, are being developed and strengthened and that new departments are being started with the assistance received from the University Grants Commission. One item of information particularly interested me in view of all that has been said recently in regard to the medium of instruction by various academic gatherings, the last and most influential of which was the Vice-Chancellors' Conference, held recently in Delhi. That is that the University has already taken certain measures for a much-needed improvement of the standards of instruction in English and will continue them with vigour.

I heartily congratulate the University on the progress that has been achieved especially in view of the many difficulties that were experienced in the past. Those that are familiar with the affairs of the University, as I used to be, when I was Chairman of the University Grants Commission, are well aware that the development of the University began in real earnest only as a result of the passing of the Kerala University Act on 30th August, 1957. The autonomy of the University, which is bound to be somewhat qualified by the remaining momentum of the old order, began only then, and in this context I was happy to learn from the Vice-Chancellor that the State Government is actively supporting the University in the promotion of the measures mentioned above.

The Kerala University Act of 1957 had the objective of making the University a teaching agency for the conservation, promotion and development of Kerala art and culture and Malayalam language. The Act also mentions prominently amongst the objectives the provision of greater facilities for post-graduate studies and regional research in all branches of learning by establishing centres of post-graduate studies and research in different parts of the State. Although the Act mentions as ideal the gradual change of the medium of instruction into Malayalam in all educational institutions of the State, which will naturally include the university, in view of the pronouncements in this respect of the Vice-Chancellors at the last Vice-Chancellors' conference referred to earlier, I have good reasons to hope that the change will be carried out without sacrificing any important element of university education. It is in this context that I welcome particularly the measures taken by the University to improve the teaching of English and to establish University centres at Ernakulam and Calicut in addition to the growing centre in Trivandrum. I feel sure that these measures will help lay the foundation for a simultaneous and steady advance of study and research in both the fields of science and the humanities, including social studies, so as to enable Kerala to take its due share in the country's national reconstruction programme.

I have indicated earlier that of late my thoughts have centred a great deal round the connection between education and economic development. It will be realized that planned economic development—and that is the sense in which at least in the case of developing countries one uses the phrase—has a vital connection with the educational process, and that modern civilization owes its characteristic features to the widespread use of science and technology. That the advancement of both science and technology is a function of higher or university education is indeed now generally recognized. But if planned economic development is the distinguishing feature, as I think it is, of the 20th century, then one might go on to assert that a proper understanding of education is necessary if one is to survive in the current, that is to say, the 20th century. Indeed, to consider the mutual relation of education and economic development is broadly to ponder the problem of living in the 20th century with its special problems of the atom, population growth, food resources, international co-operation, race relations, etc.

Superficially, it would seem somewhat odd that one should start taking a great deal of interest in the problems of the 20th century only after half or more of the century was already over. But on reflection it would be realized that the whole character of the century has been transformed by the emergence of nuclear physics and its practical applications which came into prominence towards the end of the Second World War. It would therefore be correct to say that modern 20th century only began somewhere round the middle of the century. So revolutionary has been the impact of nuclear physics on human life in its myriad aspects that we have already started to distinguish the second half of the century as the beginning of the atomic age with potentialities which it is impossible to conceive even fractionally.

The establishment of various international institutions like the United Nations and its organs or specialized agencies has been the inevitable result of the transformation of the scene by the atom. No doubt there have been in the past attempts made by nations to come together in order to confer and evolve solutions and even to surrender some minute fractions of their sovereignty for the preservation of peace and for the supposed advancement of prosperity; but dissidents have always plagued these attempts, and some semblance of what could truly be called an international assembly could only take shape with the growing realization of the horrors of atomic warfare. The balance of terror, which according to many experts is responsible for engendering a growing bias in favour of peaceful methods of settling problems, has been rising to higher and higher levels as a result of 'refinements', if that is the right word to use, in atomic weapons of destruction. A stage seems almost so have been reached that for the sheer logical necessity of saving what one is struggling to preserve by war, nations seem to be on the verge of agreement in regard to the renunciation of nuclear armaments. In these matters, nations can either go forward and backward and cannot stand still, and it seems to me that the renunciation of nuclear armaments may well be the beginning of the renunciation of all armaments, although such a stage can only be reached after periodic or fitful use of conventional means of aggression or defence, as the case may be, as currently with China and India, respectively.

The existence of the United Nations pre-supposes the existence of national communities, each with freedom to join or to withdraw from the organization. The mouthpiece of each nation is its State or Government which exists in the capacity of trustees for its people and the general acknowledgment of the people, which is the necessary condition for existence of the Government. It follows that by and large nations will cast their votes in the manner provided for in the Charter of the United Nations and its organs or agencies in accordance with the expressed or implicit wishes of the national community and that these in turn are bound to be influenced by their own recognition of the new emerging factor in the life of the world viz., human solidarity and fellowship and the essential mutuality of the interests of human communities. It is for this reason that education about the United Nations assumes signal importance, and it is because of this that educational problems in general are now receiving attention at international levels, as well as in national institutions of education. For instance, some of the schools of the United Kingdom now hold an international course, that is, a programme of lecturers on subjects like Living in the 20th Century or the Atom in the 20th Century. Again, the British Council with the support of two large industrial companies has helped to establish an International House at one of its important schools where boys from the U. S. A., Canada, France, India, Pakistan and Iran and stateless boys from Belgium, born in Brazil, live together with English boys. It is this factor which, again, accounts for the establishment of new institutions like the International House of Japan established some 10 years ago in Tokyo, or the India International Centre established in March 1959 in New Delhi and inaugurated in January, 1962, of which latter nearly all the Indian universities are foundation members. This is a new dimension in education, in its broadest sense, which is bound to grow with the passage of time.

The principle was accepted unanimously by the 11th session of the United Nations General Conference in late 1960 that 'education is a basic factor in economic development'. According to Mr. Rene Maheu, Acting Director-General of UNESCO, this recognition has greatly strengthened the unanimous decision within the United Nations system. While the organization confined its work to stimulating research, it was called to a hitherto unparallelled extent to help apply the fruits of research, and one resulting readjustment in the structure of UNESCO'S Secretariat has been the setting up within the Social Science Department of a unit to study the role of education, science, and technology and information in economic development. In the course of a recent address delivered at the India International Centre, which is an Associated Institution of UNESCO in connection with the East-West Major Project, Mr. Maheu pointed out how the overall purposes of UNESCO was 'advancing the objectives of international peace and of the common welfare of mankind through the educational, scientific and cultural relations of the people of the world.' It is well-known that these are in their turn profoundly influenced by the pace of economic and social development in the under-privileged areas. International organizations like the UNESCO are therefore vitally interested in the drive initiated for accelerating this pace and are actively engaged in helping countries concerned to lay the foundation for progress in that direction in the shape of universal primary education and literacy. It is now universally accepted that without raising the general level of education it is not possible to achieve satisfactory economic and social development and that disparate economic and social development is a fertile soil for lack of international (on our sub-continent, even national) understanding.

But our concern is primarily with university education, and as Chairman of the University Grants Commission pointed out in his address at the recent Vice-Chancellors' Conference, 'in the modern world with its increasing dependence on science and technology, universities hold a unique place; and their role and influence in determining the pace of progress—material, cultural and even spiritual—is both powerful and, profound, and perhaps there is no other institution or agency which in this respect is of comparable importance.'

Since the days of Cardinal Newman there has been perpetual or recurrent debate in regard to the purpose of university education or the mission of universities. The mission of universities is to provide a society with good and competent men and women trained in arts, science and technology, in medicine, agriculture and other professions, and, above all, inbued with a sense of highmindedness and dedication. Equally important is their mission to seek and cultivate new knowledge and to engage vigorously and fearlessly in the pursuit of truth.

But the most critical aspect of education is the need to educate for innovation and it is remarkable how everyone in the academic world, particularly, the fraternity of economists, has begun to develop an awareness of the crucial importance of education—investment in the stock of human capital, as they call it in their jargon—in the process of economic development. But, what one spends on education will produce its economic yield only over a long time in the future. Since the production interval of human capital is longer than that of most physical plant and equipment, it goes without saying that what is spent is withdrawn for a considerable period from the production of immediately consumable items. This underlines the need for, and even more careful long-range planning of, human investment than of physical assets. But there are certain compensating features : one is that human capital continues to yield services over a considerable number of years. Recent statistical studies of economic growth in the United States have suggested that not more than half of that growth is attributable to physical capital formation. The balance reflects increases in the productivity of physical inputs, which are to be explained partly by the expansion of human capital, accomplished by education, and partly by an acceleration of investment and innovation. The development process requires above all continuous creative innovation and this has a double implication for education. Some problems of educational philosophy are universal problems, but the design of appropriate and efficient educational techniques for a particular environment calls for a special act of innovation, in order that education may be adjusted to its local limitations and may help in exploiting the opportunities of any given environment. The question of medium, for instance, obviously calls for diverse solutions according to circumstances. It goes without saying that if one of the languages commonly used in international discourses is or can be selected as the national language, there would result enormous educational advantages. On the other hand, it is impossible to conceive of a living growth in education fitted to its environment if a medium of instruction is such as to be beyond the academic reach of vast-sections of the population. In other words, even at its highest level education can yield its maximum fruit, in the form of research and success in the pursuit of learning, only if it is in live contact with its environment through the commonly accepted medium of communication, viz., the regional language.

The educational factor of unique importance in the modern or 20th century environment is that the generation now entering schools will have to cope with a world not only totally different from the one their fathers were brought into but also totally different from the one in which we now live. Thus, as Max Millikan (Director, Centre for International Studies, Massachusetts Institute of Technology) pointed out last year in an important seminar held in Oxford on the Tensions of

Economic Development, 'the educational problem is not to train this generation to substitute our present answers for their fathers' answers but rather to give them tools and an attitude of mind with which to work out answers to their own'. This in turn calls for a fundamental kind of education which equips the man, through understanding what he is doing, to adapt to rapidly changing circumstances. Every society has always required a few such people. But as economic development proceeds and change accelerates, the numbers needed who have this fundamental education are enormously expanded. At all levels in education what is important is not only the transmission of a body of knowledge—although the lower the level the more necessary that is—but also the inculcation of a spirit of inquiry, a capacity for analysis of new problems and a willingness to explore and, if possible, to master the unknown. For underdeveloped countries the rapid rate of change has other implications in respect of educational priorities. For instance for economic development to proceed rapidly these countries, must, as a matter of national policy, devote much more attention to adult education than is necessary in the United States and Western Europe. Moreover, in the underdeveloped part of the world there is one issue which can be solved through a massive educational effort, and that is how to secure equality of opportunity to all elements in the population, and select from the entire population those best qualified to fill professional, technical, administrative and political rights. Equality of opportunity is essentially a political factor and calls for treatment at the political level. The second is primarily an educational and economic factor. Moreover, whatever form of political control may prevail, economic growth requires, for technical reasons, an enormous broadening of the functions of decision-making through all sectors of society. It is for this reason that unlike the last century or even the first half of the current century the demand for competent decision-makers cannot be effectively met by relying on a small hereditary elite.

Equality of opportunity and the search for talent are the two factors that seem to me to tip the scale in favour of extensive higher education in the current controversy over quantity and quality of higher education. The search for talent cannot be complete or satisfactory unless one has made sure that the field of choice is as broad as one can possibly have it, whilst equality of opportunity postulates the provision of suitable landings at every level of education which will allow of the satisfaction of natural aspirations to the extent to which innate endowment and cultural environment permit of their fulfilment. In this context an element which has hitherto been relatively neglected in the system of education prevailing in India is the development of student counselling and vocational guidance in the light of the construction and application of intelligence tests and aptitude tests and the maintenance of a continuous record of achievements, failures and biases in respect of children or young persons going through their various stages of educational development. These factors are reinforced by the additional factor of the nation's current requirements of trained professional, scientific and technological personnel as determined by techniques of perspective planning. These techniques have only lately begun to be applied in India and are being improved only very slowly. Nevertheless, it is now quite clear that the nation's need of trained educated personnel related to the implementation of successive Plans of economic development is very much larger than one would ordinarily imagine. There is, moreover, another characteristic of the Indian educational scene which is of relevance here, viz., the wastage and stagnation as evidenced by the dropping out, the detention of students and the large percentage of failures in the several examinations. The consequence of this state of affairs is that, until an improvement is secured and the resources applied to education are used more fruitfully, the respective portions of the educational pyramid must be wider than they need be in other countries.

There seems to be an impression prevailing that unemployment amongst the educated is acute in India because of reckless throwing open of educational opportunities to far larger numbers of young people, largely unfit for receiving the particular type of education involved, than is needed. But even to the extent to which this view is correct—and it is possible that it is not correct except to the extent to which there is imperfect mobility or an unsatisfactory system of choice of types of education by young people—is only another way of saying that India is yet to emerge as a reasonably well-developed country.

What genuine unemployment amongst the educated might be existing is only another aspect of the inevitable lack of balance between ends and means in the relatively backward economy in a country which, for very good reasons, has elected to have a system of political government confined within the four corners of the western parliamentary system of democracy. So far as mere numbers and ratios go, the percentage of youth of the appropriate age-group going to colleges and universities in India is about the lowest amongst countries of any size and importance in the world. On the total population it works out to less than 2,500 per million of population, and about one-third of this number is receiving what in other countries would be regarded as part of secondary education, as the total span of education up to the first degree in India is about two years shorter than in almost any other comparable country.

In this context, I have been comparing—inevitably, because the convocation of the University of Delhi is only about ten days ahead—the relative situation in the Universities of Kerala and Delhi. I find that whereas the strength of the Kerala University was about 45,000 in 1959-60, whilst that of the Delhi University is around 25,000 in 1962, in the former year the Kerala University awarded 4,330 degrees, whereas the Delhi University is going to award 4,377 degrees. Whilst the number of B. A. and B. A. (Hons.) degrees in Kerala was 1,519, Delhi is going to award 1,987; moreover, whilst in Kerala only 37 were awarded B. A. (Hons.) degrees, in Delhi the number will be 609. Similarly, for M. A. the number was 78 in Kerala, whilst it is likely to be 869 in Delhi. As for Science, the Kerala University awarded 1,523 degrees as against only 509 in the Delhi University, but whereas there were only 16 Hons. degrees awarded by the Kerala University, 255 are going to be awarded by the Delhi University. The number of M. Sc. degrees for the two Universities has been or will be 58 and 103, respectively. Again, as against 3 Ph. D. awarded in Kerala in 1959-60, Delhi is likely to award some 40 this year. I regret that strictly comparable figures have not been used by me, but the latest figures for Kerala were not available to me when the address was drawn up, and, in any case, my object was to draw attention to the relative position in respect of quality education in the two universities. In this respect Delhi has had an earlier start and has over the years deeveloped the post-graduate side of its education in a reasonably satisfactory way, although the percentage of students offering professional or science and technological courses in the Delhi University is very much lower than either the national average or the percentage for the Kerala University. But the point I wished to bring out in particular was the relatively greater attention paid to the Honours stream in University education in Delhi. I feel convinced that the separation of the Pass and the Honours courses and the institution of evening colleges, correspondence courses, etc. furnishes the right answer and accomplishes reconciliation in regard to the tug of war between quality and quantity in higher education.

On a population of about 20 million the Kerala University has 2,500 young persons in colleges and University departments. For Delhi a comparable figure cannot be given because of its being the metropolitan town and its attracting students from not only the metropolitan area but also other states of the country, as well as students from abroad—the Delhi University currently has about 500 foreign students. In other countries the number of young persons undergoing higher education is normally between 5,000 and 7,500 per million of population, although in the U. S. A. it probably exceeds 10,000 per million of population. According to the figures given out by a high level educational administrator from the U. S. S. R., in that country this number is 2 million, out of which 60 per cent receive education through evening classes or correspondence courses.

This leads me on to consider the question of the employment situation in Kerala. According to the publication of the Government, 'Kerala 1961—An Economic Review', unemployment is considered to be the greatest menace in Kerala by one and all. But it is admitted that there is no recent appraisal of the problem on the basis of a survey conducted to study the various aspects of employment, and whatever 'guesstimates' there may be are evidently out of date. The data pertaining to employment furnished by the Employment Exchanges reflect only a partial picture, since they covered only the urban centres. In Kerala the urban population is proportionately less than that for all India, although the recent trends show a growth at a rapid rate. With this qualification, it would seem that the employment Exchange figures indicate that the number of opportunities for employment was higher in 1960 than in 1959 and it had improved in 1961. The Review states that this comparatively better employment situation is merely due to the increase in the absolute number of jobs created in the two years compared, without any reference to the annual increase in the labour force. The economic setting shows both encouraging and discouraging trends. Production in agriculture and industry continues to maintain its growing trend which was evident for the last few years, and the market for export products has been generally good. On the other hand, the consumer has had to face another year of rising prices, including a substantial rise in the prices of rice and cloth, and the terms of trade continued to work against the non-ownership classes. Developments in the economy are generally held to have vindicated those who advocated a bigger plan. Resources were growing out of past investments and the State seems to be poised to take full advantage of what had been achieved in the past decade of planning. This was the picture that could be seen before the present emergency. What reaction it will have on the size and priorities in the Plan, it is yet too early to discern, but I have a feeling that any unfavourable effects due to the emergency would be partially counter-balanced by the reaping of the fruits of the planned development of the preceding ten years.

The University of Kerala has a University Employment Bureau functioning as an integral part of the national employment service with freedom to develop on its own lines. But figures in regard to registrations and employment enquiries and placements were not available to me.

It would appear from the occupational distribution of the live register maintained at the general exchanges that the number of registered persons seeking clerical and related occupations, together with those persons who are unclassified, accounted for 70 per cent of the total registrants in 1961 as against 61 per cent in 1960. This indicates the growth of unemployment among those who have only general education as compared to that among those who seek any specialised occupation.

But I do not think that there is any good reason to feel

unduly depressed about the situation. The academic world seems generally to be moving from the Oxbridge tradition, that is to say, education for meritorious elite, brilliant products of grammar and public schools, to a system of free and multi-geared educational programmes leading on to widespread educational facilities fitting into this age of technocrats and astronauts, as to children born of illiterate peasant stock, as in U. S. S. R., or of American cabinet officials as in U.S.A., whose parents were of poor migrants. This latter tradition, subject to what I have said about the separation of the Pass and Honours streams is in my opinion undoubtedly the more justifiable and enduring, because education is here regarded as a vast humanizing process. Charles Frankel, Professor of Philosophy, Columbia University, summarising an interesting batch of critical essays on Issues in University education, observes: 'But there is a still more significant function which American colleges and universities serve and which inevitably affects their educational programmes. From a sociological point of view, the American college has one primary meaning. It is the great social escalator to contemporary American society, the major avenue by which the members of mobile society are enabled to move upward on the social scene. Young Americans come to college to learn how to behave and how to dress; they come to college to meet—and to marry—the right people ; they come so that they can leave labelled 'college graduates'. For, the college degree is one of the few symbols of status that exists in the United States, and its social-importance is all the greater as a result'. He goes on to observe that most American college students are newcomers to the environment of higher education and that the majority do not come to college out of a love of learning for its own sake and that they come to improve themselves economically and socially and that their interest in their education is likely to be practical and vocational, even narrowly so. It seems to me that there is much in this that could be considered applicable to the Indian scene, and that here too, although the motivation is, as in the U. S. A., somewhat utilitarian, the process of higher education is generally a humanizing and civilizing one and that higher education is an end justified in itself. The question that is often put to educational authorities, 'What are we going to do with so many graduates that you turn out ?' is, in my opinion, an irrelevent one. It is the duty of the State to consider what they propose to do with these highly educated persons. It is for the State to indicate in what respect they would prefer higher education to develop so far as quantity or quality is concerned. But it is not for the State or the public or anyone else to cavil at the opportunities sought by young people to fulfil their natural aspirations for the maturing civilizing process that we call university education.

As I congratulate all those that have obtained their degrees at this Convocation, I also congratulate them on having had the privilege of passing through this humanizing process and emerging, no matter what room for improvement there may be in the system of education adopted, as more mature, better informed, and generally better developed citizens and human beings. To this I would add an expression of my hope that the clouds on our national horizon would soon be dispersed and that the economic and social life of the State and the nation will develop along lines which will provide appropriate opportunities to all the graduates to play their role as matured individuals, finished citizens and well-informed human beings.

EDUCATION FOR INTERNATIONAL UNDERSTANDING

According to the preamble to the Charter of the United Nations, it was the peoples of the world who had expressed their determination 'to save succeeding generations from the scourge of war'. But integration is something more than absence of war. It denotes a positive stage of accord and harmony, which is peace in the true sense of the word. The oft-repeated proposition can bear reiteration in this context :

> 'When we talk about Unesco, we are talking about peace in our world and in our times, in the only place where it matters and where it is lasting—in the minds of men.'

The U.N. then fulfils the purpose through UNESCO, one of its important specialized agencies, and this agency in turn endeavours to bring about a state of mind among the peoples of the world which would not only abjure war but cultivate peace. Thus through UNESCO, principally, as also other direct means, U.N. strives to bring about integration through 'education'.

'Education' aimed at achieving its grand aim and objective, comprehends in addition to formal education every other type of enlightenment and development of the mind that is pertinent. It includes adult education in its many varieties, social or fundamental education and teaching about United Nations, i.e., keeping the peoples of the world fully informed of the aims and activities of the U. N. What they need is instruction not so much for a 'passive state of non-belligerency' as for a 'dynamic state of international co-operation.'

So far as formal or school higher education is concerned, the curriculae must provide room for an understanding of the six fundamental features of the Charter of the U.N. Its purposes, principles and ethics have to be widely understood even outside educational institutions, the task being performed not only by special voluntary organizations, but also through the education in this behalf of its public servants by each member State.

A great deal of preparatory work has already been done in the directions indicated above. UNESCO'S 'Education for International Understanding' contains an eight-point statement, the three fundamental parts of this statement being teaching the common heritage of humanity, cultivating attitudes necessary to achieve an overall sense of understanding and developing certain skills. All these subserve the basic need of developing a loyalty which is yet something new to the ordinary citizen of any nation, a loyalty beyond the frontiers of nations and is universal, a sense of human solidarity, fellowship and co-operative endeavours towards the attainment of man's exalted destiny.

School and college curriculae and text-book shave their importance because the child of today is the citizen of tomorrow. It is in their minds that must take root ideas leading to the realization of the common heritage of man, an understanding and appreciation of differences among peoples, a recognition of the basic human dignity which must be respected and safeguarded, an awareness of the inter-dependence of nations and the consequent need for international co-operation. The grand strategy is the building of a better world and the path is the acceptance of one's responsibility to an ever-widening circle of 'our people'.

The re-writing of history text-books is the most pressing and essential task among the measures necessary for promoting international understanding. History has to be taught as the story of the development of human civilization and not as a chronicle of the occurrence, mostly political and military, of events affecting groups, races or regions. Modern historians are no doubt realizing this but the temptation to depict the fortunes of people within 'national' frontiers is too strong to be overcome in its entirety. Partitions of countries under stress of rival ideologies or as a result of sectarian forces even leads to a further atomised history lessening instead of enhancing the prospects of understanding. UNESCO's III Major Project for Mutual Appreciation of Eastern and Western Cultural Values was a practical attempt to overcome the sense of separateness and to promote a sense of oneness.

Equally important is the place of Geography, especially Human Geography, in the scholastic curriculae. This subject has been called by some experts one of paramount importance in the teaching of international understanding. Human Geography is one of the best vehicles for developing the attitudes and skills necessary for successful endeavour to this end. The 'shrinking of the world' of which one speaks so glibly can be made to be meaningful only by means of the study of Geography against the perspective that modern science furnishes. Geography has been defined as the subject which deals with a comparative study of man and his relationship with his natural environment.

Whilst History and Geography, properly taught, could lower the artificial or natural barriers to understanding, the study of Social Science would reveal the true nature of relations in human society. The understanding of group behaviour on national attitude, especially in periods of stress and strain, can only be attained through Social Science.

A few months ago the writer had the good fortune of participating in a meeting of experts called for the purpose of advising on the guiding principles concerning International Relations and Exchanges in the fields of Education, Science and Culture—the special province of UNESCO. Such relations are not new in human history, but hitherto they have lacked coherence, consistency and universality. At times spontaneous cultural relations have come into existence between peoples. On occasions, Governments have consciously and deliberately promoted them by means of cultural diplomacy, whilst in a few cases, again of its own accord and under its own momentum, cultural diplomacy has reached the stage of collective cultural relations. All these beneficent trends need purposeful stimulation and guidance into the broad stream of world-wide understanding. But the progress towards a spirit of universality is not merely a matter of reinforcing existing trends. Thought has to be devoted to cultivating a more dynamic and intensive approach and to keeping attention well-focussed on the emergence of any new complicating or retarding factors which must be eliminated.

Then there is the question of political ambivalence, a professed adherence to right theory and a proclivity towards indulgence in wrong practice on the part of Governments. Improvement of international relations among nations is, further, not only a matter of intellectual integrity; it is also a question of building into the supporting societies a capacity to discover, disavow and rectify gaps between theory and practice in respect of international understanding. In this context, it is well to remind ourselves that the U. N. operates less by virtue of its statutory status or the letter of its Charter as by the reflection of the conscience of the world in its explicit deliberations and its concrete operations.

The basic principles already expressed or implicit in existing Charters, Instruments and Resolutions of U. N. and its relevant specialized organs or agencies comprise the following :—

1. That there is dignity and worth in every culture;
2. that all peoples have the right to conserve and develop their own culture;
3. that all cultures contain elements which can contribute to the development of all mankind and can therefore be considered inter-dependent;
4. that everyone has the right to enjoy the arts and literatures of all peoples and to share in the benefits of scientific advancement in all parts of the world ;
5. that there should be mutual advantage to all participants in international exchanges in the fields of education, science and culture; and
6. that all men have the right to participate, universally, in exchange with all others.

These principles cast certain duties on Governments, such as;

To make known abroad, among nations willing to receive such knowledge and information, experience of the ways of life of its own citizens;

to provide the means for its own citizens to be informed about and have access to the achievements of other nations;

to secure the highest possible degree of reciprocity in international relations and exchanges;

to develop educational, scientific and cultural relations in such a way as to encourage stability and continuity in the relations between nations, even where political relations may be strained;

to establish, in agreement with other nations, programmes which will lead to improvement in relations; to encourage the educational system, specifically, to be used as a means of improving international understanding.

The concrete means that are calculated to further the aims set out above will include :

International exchange of persons, directed not only with a view to facilitating the transmission of knowledge, skills and experience, but also to encouraging free and frank discussion of differences in such a way as to minimize the area of misunderstanding and to maximize that of co-operation. The programme in this behalf should lay stress on living together and benefiting from direct contacts. Foreign students are a category of visitors calling for special attention and treatment, e.g. in regard to selection, counselling, opportunities to acquire an understanding of differing social environment, assessment of methods of training and impact on parent society on completion of visit abroad. This last is an aspect of the matter which presents special difficulties both owing to vastly different sociological setting and backwardness in economic development, with its dominant characteristic of lack of suitable employment opportunities.

Technical co-operation involves special problems. It can be most effective only on the basis of the fullest possible knowledge and appreciation of the countries concerned. It involves appropriate orientation of personnel, close study of the needs of the countries receiving such assistance and precise response to requests made. The whole process has a vital bearing on the cultural relations between donor and receiving countries.

The presentation of the literary and artistic creations of other nations is a means of bringing about understanding with its own peculiar problems, as, for instance, those of prompt and adequate translation, copy-right conventions and other forms of agreement, which safeguard literary and artistic creations and otherwise promote co-operative effort. But when successful, (music is a difficult area) they are most effective in promoting the establishment of universal values.

The free exchange of scientific information is even more

important for promoting universality. The effectiveness of research is dependent upon the inter-change of ideas between scientists throughout the world, and on mutual communication among them concerning current achievements.

The most difficult area concerning international understanding is that of the free flow of ideas. Whether it should be promoted for its own sake without reserve, or only in ways which would encourage mutual understanding and peaceful relations is a debatable point. The measures taken to secure the end are apt to involve delicate questions of respect for national sovereignty. The experience of those who have participated in conferences held with a view to shedding light on current controversial concepts like co-existence, have testified to their value despite patent handicaps.

The encouragement in every possible way and at all levels of foreign languages is in principle a potent means of furthering international understanding. The field is so vast that no efforts made to stimulate it could ever be excessive.

Since maximization of human weal is the goal and since it is correlated to the quality of human culture at its highest levels, whilst conceding the dignity and worth of every culture in disseminating ideas and knowledge on the widest possible scale, care will have to be taken at the same time to ensure that man does not lose contact with the highest levels of cultural achievement.

The overall purpose of UNESCO, as its eminent Director-General, M. Rene Maheu, pointed out in a recent address delivered at the India International Centre, an Associated Institution of UNESCO, in connection with the East-West Major project was, 'advancing the objectives of international peace and of the common welfare of mankind through the educational, scientific and cultural relations of the peoples of the world.' These in their turn are profoundly influenced by the pace of economic and social development in the underprivileged areas. UNESCO is therefore vitally interested in the drive initiated for accelerating this pace and is actively engaged in helping the countries concerned to lay the foundation for progress in that direction in the shape of universal primary education and literacy. Without raising the general level of education, it is not possible to achieve satisfactory economic and social development, and disparate economic and social development is fertile soil for lack of international understanding. For international understanding, education in all its aspects and in all its variety is a medium as vital for life as water for fish. As H. G. Wells, the first writer of a systematic History of the World, wrote—"History is a chronicle of the struggle between education and chaos."

ROMANIZING INDIAN SCRIPTS

The most powerful political argument in favour of Romanizing Indian scripts is that the measure will equally displease the users of the diverse Indian scripts. For, as an article of Punya Sloka Day rightly points out, the issue is basically a political one. There will always be reputable experts who would argue powerfully against making a change at all or changing only to the Nagari script, just as there would be a considerable body of experts favouring the change. It should not be too difficult even to demonstrate that there would be a clear and significant balance of advantages in romanizing Indian scripts. But a final pronouncement, preceding the necessary statutory action, must come from the highest political level. In a democratic set up this might prove difficult, but not impossible.

The script reform in Turkey introduced almost overnight by Kemal Ataturk and a similar reform introduced in our generation by the Indonesian leaders are examples that invite emulation. But the quality of leadership that a similar step will call for under a system of Parliamentary democracy will have to be of a different and higher order. To equate the reform in question to the establishment of the decimal system of coinage or of the metric weights and measures, as Ray has done, is however to under-estimate the resistance of powerful sentiment or the pull of vested interest.

That at the last National Integration Conference there was a favourable reference to uniformity of script is proof of the supreme importance of the issue from a political point of view. There could be no possible doubt that a uniform script will facilitate materially the spread of the study of Indian languages in India. But the apparently innocuous posing of the two major alternatives, viz., Nagari or Roman, holds in it the seed of interminable discord. If one might venture to prognosticate, Nagari will never be accepted in India as the common script, whereas Roman could conceivably be. And this debate means definitely defeating the purpose, viz., emotional integration.

Fortunately, the political argument in favour of Romnizing can be powerfully buttressed by the academic and the economic. To share a script with the 800 million people of Europe, the America and part of Africa, especially the English-speaking world, would be a tremendous advantage from the point of view of international cultural exchange. It will also help in facilitating the acquisition of English in the educational field as the language most capable of helping the Indian languages to develop.

But the most objective and therefore ultimately convincing argument in favour of Romanizing is its potential for achieving significant economies in printing. Size for size Roman alphabet is easier to read than nagari and printing all our growing volume of books and other publications in Roman alphabet will certainly lead to massive economies and conservation of scarce national resources.

With literacy still distressingly low (hardly 15 to 20 per cent in the Hindi-speaking and Nagari using regions), adult education is a vital factor in the fostering of democracy, and the valuable experience gained in this behalf by the Defence Forces until recently proves conclusively that with Romanized alphabet literacy can be achieved in a matter of months and much earlier than with the use of any of the Indian alphabets.

The technical matters of detail involved in the putting into practice of the principle of adopting Romanized alphabet are properly matters for experts. Ray's proposals appear to furnish a suitable basis for discussion among experts, which should include not only linguisticians, litterateurs, but also printers, publishers, educators and social scientists. A gathering of competent men in these fields should experience no great difficulty in recommending a modified Romanized alphabet or system of spelling for use in the writing, typing and printing of Indian languages. It may be recalled *en passant* that the Romanized alphabet in Europe is not exactly identical, since there are specific diacritical marks, as well as methods of spelling and pronunciation and use suited to the requirements of each language using the alphabet.

CONVOCATION ADDRESS

Delivered at the Tribhuban University, Kathmandu, Nepal, April 1961

I deem it a rare privilege to have been invited to deliver this, the very first, Convocation Address of the Tribhuban University. I venture to think that the invitation symbolizes the close ties of history, civilization and culture that have bound together India and Nepal from the dawn of history, as also the common concern for and devotion to the task of economic and social development that presently preoccupies the peoples of our two nations. Nevertheless, from a personal point of view I regard this opportunity to visit Nepal as most gratifying, since during the last twelve years I have had occasion to take a special interest in some important aspects of the affairs of Nepal—this fascinating mountain country, occupying some 56,000 sq. miles in the hills and valleys of the Himalayas—in the shelter of some of its grandest peaks including Everest, Makalu and Kanchinjunga.

2. The first of these occasions was when as Governor of the Reserve Bank of India I had occasion to depute some officers to advise the Government of Nepal on the steps necessary for the establishment of a Central Bank for the country. I am happy to find that the project has been successfully implemented and that as a result the currency situation of Nepal has become stabilized, with the circulation of the Nepal rupee to all parts of the country, the provision of exchange services on a satisfactory scale and the achievement of full convertibility between the Nepal rupee and the Indian rupee at the stable ratio of 160 to 100.

3. The second was a series of occasions, from 1952 to 1956, when as Finance Minister of the Government of India I established close contacts with the representatives of Nepal in the Consultative Committee of the Colombo Plan, or had something to do professionally with financial arrangements between Nepal and India. Since my resignation from that post in July 1956, I have naturally not been in a position to take such a close interest in the economic development of Nepal. But I am delighted to find in the Colombo Plan Report for

1959-60 much evidence in regard to the progress Nepal is making in this sphere.

4. The Report bears testimony to the continued improvement of the economic and financial situation in the country, to increased agricultural and industrial production and to the stability of the prices of consumer goods. I find that there has been a marked increase in the tempo of development activities. I have already referred to the stabilization of the exchange rate and the completion of arrangements for the unlimited convertibility of the Nepal rupee into the Indian rupee. With a rate of revenue expenditure of less than Indian Rupees Nine per person per annum, Nepal is at a greater disadvantage than India, but substantial financial assistance from friendly countries, e.g. U.S.A., India, U.K., Australia, Canada and New Zealand, has enabled Nepal to budget for reasonable development expenditure during 1960-61, at a rate of Indian Rupees 20 per person, against Indian Rupees 12 per person during India's Second Five Year Plan period, which is coming to an end a few months earlier than Nepal's First Five Year Plan. That Nepal provided for the first time for the floating of a public loan during 1960-61 furnishes proof of her increasing financial confidence. That much (about three-fourths) of the development expenditure has to be met out of foreign aid is only natural for a country starting with such a heavy load of underdevelopment. What is important is that the aid should be promptly utilized by improving administrative and financial procedures and inculcating in all concerned a sense of urgency in development activities. The stepping up of the development expenditure from Indian Rs. 4 crores during the first three years of the Plan to Indian Rs. 5 crores in 1959-60, with an estimated development expenditure of Indian Rs. 16 crores in 1960-61 seems to be a reassuring sign of the recognition of that sense of urgency which I mentioned a little while ago.

5. On the basis of this scale of implementation of the First Plan, the Second Five Year Plan of Nepal, of Indian Rs. 122 crores, including Indian Rs. 29 crores for the private sector, does not seem too ambitious. But its implementation will put a severe strain on the administrative machinery—Governmental or directive organization. The tasks towards which the Plan is directed are heavy, viz., a 30 per cent. in-

crease in gross national income, development of agriculture, building up of an infra-structure for economic development, especially in transport and communications. But perhaps the most onerous task will be the production of appropriately trained and qualified administrative, scientific, professional, technical and technological personnel..........And that brings me to the heart of the matter, viz. education.

6. The neglect of education that occurred during the centuries prior to the Great Change in 1951 was characteristic of the then prevalent political organization of the country, as much as a consequence of its isolation from the outside world. Prior to the mid-century there were only 200 primary schools in Nepal, and these too mostly of the Gompa and Pathsala type, in addition to four high schools. It says much for the awakening that has taken place in the country that today, in the course of ten years, the number of educational institutions has gone up to about 3,000 primary schools (including Pathsalas) 125 secondary schools, and 864 adult education centres. But impressive as this expansion has been it should be borne in mind that this represents facilities, say, in the field of primary education only for 200,000 children, i.e. perhaps 25 per cent. of the children of the age-group 6 to 11, in contrast with 62 per cent. in India and an even higher percentage in most of the other countries in South and South-East Asia. Of the age-group 12 to 14 about 30 per cent. go to the middle schools in India and of the next age-group, from 15 to 17, about 15 per cent. go to high schools or higher secondary schools. I have no information in regard to corresponding percentages in Nepal, but on the assumption that some 40,000 children are enrolled in her 125 Secondary Schools, the combined percentage must be very small, hardly five per cent.

7. Where there was only one college in 1950, Nepal has now 26 colleges, 16 of them Degree Colleges (2 Science, 1 Commerce, 1 Law, 1 Women's and 1 Sanskrit Mahavidyalaya.) I conjecture, in the absence of precise information, that there are about 8,000 students enrolled in these colleges, with a small number receiving collegiate and university education outside the country, principally, I imagine, in India.

8. If this is a fairly correct guess then that would give a ratio of about 1,000 young persons per million of population

receiving higher education in Nepal, as compared with 2,500 per million in India. On this background the establishment of the Tribhuban University is none too early and the Queen Mothers deserve congratulations on the initiative taken by them in setting it up at an opportune time.

9. I mention these figures and make these contrasts in order to emphasize what I have no doubt is fully recognized by the authorities in Nepal that the most important infrastructure for economic development is education in all its branches, including the education of the adult, not only for the supply in adequate numbers, and of appropriate quality and attainments, of all types of academic, scientific, professional, technical and technological personnel, but also a better oriented population responsive to the modern environment. But above all, in this highly competitive world of ours, every country needs leaders of high calibre such as only university education can produce if the standards are set and maintained at a high enough level.

10. A very important point to bear in mind is that like life itself education is an integrated activity, divided into the compartments of primary, secondary and higher only for the sake of administrative convenience and that there is both quantitative and qualitative inter-connection between one stage of education and another. For instance, if it is desired to expand the number of admissions to technical and technological institutions, e.g. engineering, and medical colleges, one cannot do so unless a sufficient number of potential candidates who have studied the appropriate sciences, physical or biological, come out of the secondary schools. Again, it is only secondary schools that can feed colleges and universities; but the growth of secondary schools is limited by the number and quality of teachers, possessing the appropriate University degree available. These vicious circles are broken by fixing special priorities and making special arrangements, involving greater strain on the part of those who can be induced to take to the teaching profession. As between Nepal and India, perhaps to a certain extent importation of teachers is possible, although India herself is now experiencing a shortage of qualified teachers in science and technology.

11. I have referred to standards in education and

quality of its products from time to time. The importance of these is theoretically recognized by everybody, but in practice in the anxiety to extend and expand education authority is often prone to allow standards to fall and quality to deteriorate. The pressure of increasing numbers would by itself constitute a growing strain on resources which are either severely limited or which cannot be augmented fast enough. But a more insidious factor, at least in India, is popular pressure to admit anybody and everybody, with the minimum qualification of a bare pass, to the benefits of higher education, more or less as a matter of human rights. However, in India, as the dust of controversy is settling down, it would appear that the educational authorities will be taking steps to ensure that, firstly, university education is provided only for those who are likely to benefit from that education—and this involves not only talents but also motivation of the right sort—and, secondly, a sufficient number of scholarships are awarded in order to ensure that no young person of the requisite qualification and quality is bereft of the benefit of higher education because of poverty. The division of the higher education stream first into the University and the non-University channels and secondly, so far as the University channel is concerned, into pass and honours courses of appropriate duration could solve this problem without great difficulty, reconciling the two principles of fulfilling the nation's need for élite and the individual's keen aspiration for continuing his education after the secondary stage and therefore satisfying an inner urge or improving his own prospects in life.

12. For, education is a matter of concern both to the individual and to the nation. Its primary purpose is to help an individual to achieve individual excellence or to understand more and more the best of what has been thought, said or done in the world. Education must ensure that the personality of the student is developed in all its aspects, physical, intellectual, aesthetic, moral and spiritual. But it has also to turn him into a responsible citizen, with a feeling for his fellow beings and a desire to play his role as well as he can in the society to which he belongs. These two objectives are, fortunately, not contradictory. Indeed, they are complementary. Individual excellence is, in other words, almost a guarantee of good citi-

zenship. That is why apart from, or preferably as a part of, its academic aims, every university has to help individuals, i.e. students, to develop their capacity for growth and leadership. It is only thus that they might be able to make their maximum contribution to the social, economic and cultural life of their country. The students are not only to be guided in their intellectual endeavour but also helped and encouraged as they seek to lay the foundation for a socially useful life.

13. A heavy load of responsibility thus rests on the authorities of a University, especially a new University like the Tribhuban University, which has inherited a system of higher education with many imperfections of university practice. For instance, although its colleges were formerly affiliated to the Patna University, that was for purposes of a mechanical system of application of courses and syllabuses and conduct of examinations and awards of degrees, without inspection or any other academic control. I understand that your new University has already set about instituting reforms such as an inspection system and post-graduate lectures in some subjects, besides collecting the necessary statistical information from the affiliated colleges. But all these improvements must need speeding up, and the whole apparatus of the University has to be built up, including a library, class-rooms and laboratories and hostels, and staff quarters. Even in India it is only during the last five years that financially assisted by the University Grants Commission, representing the Central Government, and by the respective State Governments the Universities have made some headway in constructing these amenities and facilities, and both the teacher and the student community have a reasonable chance of showing their mettle. In detail construction work poses many intricate problems, apart from finance, such as appropriate specifications, space-requirements, building standards, economy, and, above all, avoidance of costly delays on account of an imperfectly-geared administrative machinery. A Building Committee, appointed by the University Grants Commission, consisting of experts and experienced administrators, has greatly helped to secure uniform standards and despatch as well as economy in India.

14. But something over and above these technical and administrative improvements is required if University edu-

cation is to serve its deeper purposes, and that is proper motivation on the part of both teacher and student.

15. I have already made a mention of the inter-connection of the different stages of education in the matter of the production of teachers. In this connection, I am glad to notice from the Colombo Plan Report for 1959-60 that the number of normal schools for teachers is steadily rising for training primary school teachers and that about 400 trained teachers are being added every year to the number already available. But these and the teachers in secondary schools and colleges must be enabled to provide not only routine instruction but also counsel and guidance to students by means of suitable facilities and by proper conditions of service, including scales of remuneration commensurate with the dignity and national importance of their profession. These will include well-equipped and properly utilized libraries, private rooms, laboratories and reasonable equipment for these last, in addition to suitable salaries to draw the best out of them.

16. Perhaps even more important is the proper motivation of students. It is here that we in South and South-east Asia seem to fall far short of the ethos of academic life in the more advanced countries. This is not merely a question of the existence of proper facilities and the absence of basic amenities. For, even with an imperfect apparatus of higher education a properly motivated and therefore diligent student can extract sufficient out of his university career to look back upon it with pleasure as well as pride. Also, in any case, the amelioration of the physical apparatus of education requires large outlays of money and takes time to be effective. A student who fails to make the best of whatever facilities happen to be available is doing less than justice to himself. But the motivation that I have in mind is a question of a more fundamental attitude of mind. What is it that a student expects the University to do for him ? If the answer is that the University is expected to cram some learning into him so that he may pass examinations, obtain a degree and thus qualify for a job somewhere, then the student will be hardly a better man or a better citizen for having studied at the University. He will remain essentially uneducated and uncultured, even if he does well in the examination. It is only when he regards university education

as a privilege, extended to the talented few in conditions that will help him to develop all his faculties of head and heart, free from the cares of life, that he will profit the most from that education. He will then address himself to his studies with single-minded devotion, bring to his work a sense of intellectual curiosity and learn gradually to think out problems and form his own judgments on important issues. He will then entertain a concern for greatness—great men, great ideas and great books or works of art. He will try to form his own sets of moral and social values and evolve a philosophy of life for himself. It is only then that he will qualify for the place among the élite that university education is intended to achieve for him.

17. Even in regard to development of character the inculcation of the habit of critical thought is important. Such a habit will function in regard to regulation of desires and inclinations—which is the essence of character. The good example and influence of teachers can help materially in such character formation, because young people learn not only by rational instruction but also by experience and example.

18. During the last five years I have delivered over twenty Convocation Addresses to the fresh graduates of Indian Universities. A volume containing the earlier ones, entitled 'In the Portals of Indian Universities' has been published by the University Grants Commission of India, and I have ventured to present a copy to the library of the Tribhuban University. A second volume—entitled 'On the Threshold of India's Citizenhood'—is in the Press and should be out before long. I mention this in the hope that the more curious from amongst my listeners might wish to glance through these Addresses some time.

19. I do not believe that systems of education can be articles of export or import. There is by now established a modicum of uniform precepts of higher education in the systems and patterns must differ so as to accord with unique historical and social environment. Nevertheless, the traditional links between Nepal and India have been strong and many, and so far generations of young men and women from Nepal have received their higher education at Indian Universities. It is possible therefore that what is being thought, said and done in India in regard to University education will prove to

be of special interest to the leaders, teachers and students of Nepal. I have no doubt that they will be taking notice of significant developments in India in regard to important issues affecting University education, e.g. the medium of instruction, the place of English, the reform of the syllabuses and of the examination system, whilst evolving a system of higher education in consonance with the genius of the country and the nature of the tasks that have to be undertaken by the Government and the people of Nepal.

20. In this context a new University has many advantages, although much careful planning and energetic implementation will be required before a new University is properly established. The range of models that the University can choose from as suiting the special needs of the country is extensive. In India teaching-cum-affiliating University has been found to be the most useful type, at least to begin with, although there is much to be said for a largely residential unitary University to supplement the first type. The arrangement under which the University proper looks after honours and post-graduate courses, while the affiliated colleges provide under-graduate education, leading to a pass degree, has also much to commend it. Whatever the chosen type, sufficient finance has to be made available by the State not only for establishing and maintaining seats of higher learning, but also for developing them and for the vigilant and continuous improvement of standards.

21. Before I conclude I should like to congratulate the new graduates, the very first batch, of the University on their success and to wish them God-speed in their careers as citizens. The greater the leeway in development a country has to make up the heavier will be the responsibility that will rest on the shoulders of the highly educated minority, but the more gratifying the rewards. It is my fervent hope that many who are taking their degrees today will carve out for themselves a place of honour in the history of Nepal in the fullness of time.

SELECTIVE ADMISSIONS TO UNIVERSITIES IN INDIA

Unlike many other countries in the world, in India the standards of higher education are a statutory duty of the Central Government, whilst the rest of university education is the province of the States. This concern with the maintenance of reasonably high standards of teaching and research in institutions of higher learning in India has an historical background, since the establishment of universities in India under the British rule a little more than a century ago was the result of initiative taken by the then Government of India. In recent years the question came to the forefront as a result of the recommendations of the University Education Commission under the chairmanship of Dr. S. Radhakrishnan, then the Vice-President of the Union, the report of the Commission having been received by the Government of India soon after the advent of independence. It was only natural, therefore, that the Constitution, which was promulgated with effect from the beginning of the year 1950, should have reserved to the Union Government the responsibility for "the co-ordination and determination of the standards" of higher education. In exercise of their statutory duty in regard to the standards of higher education the Government of India created an organization by statute, called the University Grants Commission, 1956, and the Planning Commission allocated a sum to this Commission in order to enable it to discharge its responsibilities for the development of higher education which might be regarded as satisfactory from Indian standards of public expenditure on the social services including education.

Of the many aspects of higher education to which the University Grants Commission devoted attention and applied the resources at their disposal perhaps none has greater importance than the question of restricting admission to universities to young persons who appear likely to benefit from university education. This question has emerged as a result of the present state of affairs in which academicians and others are united in thinking that more than any other factor the pressure of vast numbers entering the universities and their constituent and affiliated colleges has led to the steady deterioration of standards, because of the inadequacy of the resources available for expanding proportionately, not to speak of improving, the apparatus of higher education. For instance, when the University Education Commission reported in 1948 the total number of young persons in colleges and universities in India was 275,000; by the end of 1950 it had risen to 420.000 and by the end of 1955 to 750,000, and by now the number must be a little over a million. With all this, public expenditure on the multifarious amenities that are essential for a sound system of higher education has not increased in proportion.

At this stage perhaps some explanation is necessary why numbers of this order are regarded as excessive for institutions of higher learning in a country of the size of India. On its latest (1961 census) population figure of 438 million the ratio of young persons in universities and colleges is a little under 2,300 per million, whereas in the United States of America the corresponding ratio must be more than 8 times as much, and ratios four or five times as high are not unknown elsewhere, including Japan, the Asian country which leads in this as in many other directions. Curiously enough, it is only in the United Kingdom that the ratio is somewhat similar to that obtaining in India, but here again there is a significant difference, viz., the span of primary and secondary education is two years longer than in India and that admission to the universities takes place only after very rigorous qualifying tests have been applied. To put the matter in another way, of the one million young persons now in the universities and colleges of India, about one-third are studying in classes which in most of the countries that matter educationally would be regarded as part of the secondary education. If allowance is made for this situation, the real ratio for India would be a little over 1,500 per million of population, instead of 2,300. It is usual to consider the Indian figure of numerical strength in universities and colleges not so much against the total population as against the population which is literate, and this appears at present to be about 30 per cent of the total population, i.e., 131 million, of which the ratio would be 5,000 to one million, instead of 1,500 to one million. This last conclusion brings into relief the shape of the educational structure at the base of higher education, the general conclusion that emerges being that the base of the Indian educational pyramid is very much narrower than in most of the countries of the world.

On the advent of independence the makers of the Indian Constitution observed that even primary education had made only an unequal and halting progress under British rule, the percentage of children between the ages 6-11 attending school being hardly 40. They therefore inserted among the Directive Principles of State Policy a requirement that the States should use every endeavour to ensure that free and compulsory education is provided to all the children in the age-group 6-14 within ten years of the inauguration of the Constitution. But despite special efforts this has not proved practicable, and on the advice of the Planning Commission the Governments in India have set themselves a more modest goal, viz., that free and compulsory education be provided to all children in the age-group 6-11 by the end of the Third Five Year Plan period, i.e., by April, 1966. The percentages at the higher levels of primary and secondary education are correspondingly low, being round 30 and 15 per cent of the age-groups concerned, viz., 11-14 and 14-17. It is out of last group that the institutions of higher education secure their entrants.

Admission to universities and colleges in India does not require any special tests or examinations conducted by the authorities of universities and colleges. A mere pass in the school-leaving examination (which is generally called Matriculation or the Higher Secondary examination) is, in theory, a sufficient minimum. It is interesting to note at this stage that the pass percentage at the Matriculation or the Higher Secondary examination in India is round about 50, so that of all the young persons in the highest class only half qualify theoretically for admission to institutions of higher education.

Out of those qualified, again, possibly one-third do not have the means—although, perhaps, all have the inclination—to pursue higher studies. Since the span of primary and secondary education is noticeably smaller than elsewhere and since in existing conditions the students who have school-leaving qualifications do not have that command of English which is found necessary in most jobs in the public or private sector, no one who has not had at least two more years of higher education has a chance of securing employment, and for a significant proportion of posts the minimum qualification is a first degree. This being so, apart from the question of means, almost every one who can afford it wishes to enter a university (including colleges) so as to better his or her prospects of employment. In the case of girls, at least in the more sophisticated urban areas and amongst the middle classes, the marriage prospects are improved if a girl has a university degree. The pressure of numbers is a result of these factors, combined with the steady expansion that is taking place all over the country, including even remote rural areas, in regard to primary and secondary education owing to the stimulus given by the State as well as to a genuine and rising concern for education on the part of the people. This pressure would not have made itself felt had the State possessed the resources to construct, equip and man universities and colleges or if the inadequate efforts by the State had been supplemented by private organizations. Although both these agencies have made commendable efforts to meet the situation, the total resources at the disposal of the community have proved wholly inadequate for the purpose, especially in view of the many other competing priorities not only in the field of social service but also in the general field of social and economic development.

In a country where social and economic development receives special attention through a series of Five Year Plans, as in India, in addition to the desires of pupils and their parents, the growing needs of the State for scientific and technological personnel can be expected to be a dominant factor, and that, indeed, is the case in India. The concern of the State for making it possible for prospective employers to secure the necessary qualified professional, scientific or technological personnel has been evidenced by the special allocations that have been made as part of the series of Five Year Plans for establishing the necessary specialized institutions or in bringing about a deliberate increase in the proportion of pupils taking professional, scientific and technological courses as against arts or the humanities. Indeed, so vigorous have been the efforts of the State in the former direction that many a medical or engineering college constructed and equipped at great expense is 30 or 40 per cent short of qualified teachers, a situation which is being sought to be remedied by making the profession more attractive by improving the emoluments of the teachers of these colleges, as well as by *ad hoc* measures such as the institution of special pedagogical courses, supplemented to a very small extent by the import of teachers from the more advanced countries, particularly from the four countries which are extending special assistance to India in building up institutes of technology, viz., the U.S.A., U.K., West Germany and the U.S.S.R. The somewhat meagre existing system of scholarships is also being improved to the extent to which resources permit so as to attract students to these special courses. For the Third Five Year Plan period the target set before the higher educational authorities is that the percentage of pupils taking professional, scientific and technological courses should be raised from the present 30 to 40 by the end of the Plan period.

In the existing circumstances, the competition for admission to professional and technological colleges is sufficiently severe to ensure that only first class students stand any chance of admission to these institutions. Even for the pure science course in the universities in the post-graduate stages students who have secured above 60 per cent of the marks in the qualifying examination are available, and it is only in the agricultural and veterinary colleges that students who secure 50 per cent or more have a chance of being admitted. This statement has to be qualified with reference to the practice obtaining in many institutions, especially in the South, which under directions from the State Governments are compelled to admit students belonging to backward communities even though they possess lower or even the minimum qualification. In this context, it is necessary to explain that the system of examinations prevalent in India is of the year-end essay type with no credits added for any work done during the year under the guidance of the teacher. A great deal of serious thought is being given by the higher educational authorities in India, under the guidance of the University Grants Commission, to reform this system and certain conclusions have been reached according to which it might be possible for partial credit to be given for course work; but definitive measures to introduce reform in this direction have yet to be taken by the Universities.

It has been stated, probably with justice, that the prevailing system of university examinations in India puts a premium on memory, but even so the ordinary pass percentage for the first degree of Bachelor in Arts or Science is between 50 and 60. When it is recalled that for the school-leaving examinations also a somewhat similar pass percentage obtains one has some measure of the unsatisfactory teaching and/or learning in universities. It is possible to hold that if the physical apparatus of education is improved so as to bring about a more powerful motivation for and a more diligent application to studies, there would be a marked improvement in this and similar pass percentages in the Indian universities, but a study of the relevant facts and figures has brought conviction to the minds of Indian educationists that the improvement will continue to be halting because of the indifferent quality of the students admitted to universities. It is perhaps necessary to note at this stage that there is no system of vocational guidance or personal counselling in vogue in India's schools and that because of its backwardness in industrialization the bulk of those who obtain the first degree in Indian universities seek some kind of job under the State. Since the total number of such jobs available every year is very much smaller than the number of fresh graduates who have terminated their studies at university, there is always an appreciable number of university graduates unsuccessful in securing employment and not particularly qualified for undertaking some other work by way of self-employment. It is possible that this is a transitory state of affairs and that as India's industrialization advances there will not only be a diminution in unemployment amongst university graduates but also there would be greater suitability of avenues of employment for those who have graduated.

On theoretical grounds a stand could be taken that every young person who has passed out of school is entitled to have the opportunity to prosecute his studies further, if he desires to do so, in a democratic society, but by and large such a view does not have a wide acceptance amongst educationists. They are aware that even in the U.S A. where at one time a view of this kind was widely prevalent, most State universities have now had to fall back upon selective admission before the invading tide of numbers, and that today there are hardly five or six States in which the State universities are compelled by law to admit every young person who seeks admission with the necessary minimum qualification. The pros and cons of this issue have been thoroughly debated during the last few years and most representative or authoritative bodies have reached the conclusion that admission to universities must be selective, being confined only to those young persons who have given evidence of sufficient talent to warrant the belief that they would benefit by a university education. But there is a powerful body of opinion to the contrary amongst politicians, particularly those who are responsible in some measure for the governance of the country, especially at the State Government level. It is here that the impact of the general public desire to extend widely the benefits of education to classes hitherto denied this opportunity makes itself felt, and since nearly all universities are dependent on finance provided by the State for both non-recurrent and recurrent expenditure, the attitude of the Government of the day constitutes a powerful factor in the situation. The result is somewhat in the nature of a deadlock, political pressure pulling one way and academic conviction pulling another way. The crucial issue in the Indian situation affecting higher education in India is how to find a way out.

The writer has on more than one occasion propounded

a solution, which has yet to be considered in detail by the various educational authorities concerned. That solution is that the stream of university education should be bifurcated into a honours stream and a pass stream, only candidates of the requisite high talents and attainments, as may be specified, being admitted to the honours stream, whilst all possible facilities are provided for satisfying the aspirations of those not so gifted for not only an easier pass course but also a more diversified and shorter post-secondary course of education. It is felt that it is only through these means that whilst popular aspirations are met and possibly satisfied, the nation would make sure that it secures all the highly qualified academic talent that it will require for the manifold tasks of planned economic and social development.

EDUCATION IN INDIA : PROGRESS AND PROBLEMS

There is probably no country in the world which is not concerned with the progress of its educational institutions and the resolution of the problems that arise from time to time so that the educational system may be fully adapted to the modern environment. Even in th· more advanced countries of the world the pace at which scientific and technological discoveries are being made or new applications developed the rate of obsolescence in the education apparatus is found to be very great. In the less advanced or developing countries the problems are of a different character, but they are no less acute and there is less capacity in the authorities to find solutions to them without some external assistance, and when a developing country is of the size of India, with an enormous population, all its resources of organizational capacity and inventive ability are seriously strained in order to ensure that a minimum degree of progress is achieved in expanding the facilities for education and in coping with the problems that arise from time to time, so that the right priorities are fixed and that standards are maintained at a reasonable level. Moreover, the capacity of the authorities to deal with these problems or to achieve results is often limited by the ethos of the society, so that in addition to measures involing what might be termed the technique of education, there is a far more difficult problem ever present of adapting the attitudes of sections of the community at all levels in favour of a proper orientation of the educational system.

In regard to the priorities there are already certain national decisions which are embodied in the Constitution, as for instance, in the chapter setting out the Directive Principles of State Policy under one of which children of the age group of 6-14 are to be provided free and compulsory education by the end of the year 1960 (within ten years from the commencement of the Constitution). Much of the effort in the educational field on the part of the State is, therefore, devoted to the expansion of the necessary facilities for primary education and a considerable percentage of allocations under education in each of the three five year plans is earmarked for the development of at least the lower stage of primary or elementary education. There was a time when persons in authority were inclined to turn the blind eye to the importance of primary education for children between the ages of 3 and 6, but thanks to the pioneering work in the private Montessori institutions in the cities and similar but more informal facilities offered by the rural welfare projects started in their thousands under the auspices of the Central Social Welfare Board and the Indian Council for Child Welfare, which generally undertakes the responsibility for all problems connected with both education and development of children of all ages, there is in the third five year plan a separate provision for the encouragement not only of pre-primary education but also for the establishment of a number of model integrated projects of child development throughout the country. This is a very welcome departure from the hitherto conventional type of children's education, as it has been demonstrated—that children who have had the advantage of pre-primary education are far better oriented for and give a much better account of themselves in the regular lower elementary stage of education, which is critical in respect of one important desideratum, viz., universal literacy.

Although substantial progress in statistical terms has been made in respect of the spread of primary education since the advent of independence, there are serious shortcomings in this field, some of which can be traced to an inadequacy of resources, some to wrong theories and some perhaps to a lack of perspicacity or determination. So far as the fulfilment of the Directive Principle of State Policy is concerned, there has been a manifest failure to reach the targets set by the constitution, and the sights have had to be lowered in two important respects, one, in regard to the age group, which is now taken as 6-11 instead of 6-14, and, second, in regard to the time limit, which has had to be postponed from the end of 1960 to end of 1965. Apart from the fulfilment of constitutional obligations, the percentage of the age-group 6-11 or 12 going to schools in India compares badly even with the comparable figures attained in some of the other countries in south and south-east Asia. Moreover, although the average of enrolment for this age-group is now a little over 60, it has been pointed by the National Committee on Education of Women and Girls that this average masks many disparities as between State and State, as between urban and rural areas and, worst of all, as between boys and girls. There are large tracts of the country, particularly in the Hindi-speaking areas and in Orissa, where not only is the total percentage low but also the percentage of girls enrolled in schools is especially low, posing one of the most difficult problems in the field of education before the educational authorities of the Centre and the States concerned. There is also a great deal of wastage and stagnation which is apparent from a comparison of the total figures of enrolment in the different classes of the lower elementary stage. There is still an acute shortage of adequately trained teachers, especially women teachers, and even in the third five year plan allocations a sufficiently large sum has not been earmarked for financing the special measures that are necessary in order to induce parents to send their girls to the schools, as, for instance the provision of school mothers or staff quarters or hostels for girl students at the secondary stage, which provides the teachers so badly needed for overcoming the social and economic hindrances in the way of girls attending schools. The numbers involved are so large as to exceed the total population of many important countries. For instance, it has been calculated that the number of children between 6 and 11 who ought be in schools by the end of 1965 under the Directive Principle of the Constitution is over 50 million, which is the total population of the United Kingdom. Again, during the period 1961-65 as many as 18 million girls, that is, more than 1½ times the number in school today, have to be enrolled, a task which seems well-nigh impossible. Indeed, in the absence of adequate provision for the special measures necessary it would look as if the provision on the standard pattern made for the expansion of primary schools is likely to remain largely unutilized so far as enrolment of girls is concerned. This would seem to be a bad case of miscalculation and misdirection of scarce resources.

But perhaps the worst complication that has been plaguing everybody concerned in the field of primary education is the fad of what is called Basic Education. When Mahatma Gandhi, supported by some eminent educationists, first put out his ideas in respect of the reorientation of the primary system of education so as to give a very prominent place to learning by doing, i.e., on the basis of some selected crafts, there was perhaps some theoretical justification for a somewhat over-emphasized departure from the lifeless futility of the 'three Rs' primary education as practised at the time. But since then the importance of crafts at various stages of education has been amply recognized, whilst there has been sufficient time to demonstrate the truth of the proposition that the process of imbibing abstract ideas begins at a much earlier stage on the part of children than was thought possible when basic education in its pristine form first received the blessings of eminent educationists. In any case the system of teaching by co-relating a craft to what is taught is so complex and difficult and the choice of a right craft so unreliable that progress in the establishment of basic education of the genuine type has been, as might have been expected, exceedingly slow, with the result that fanaticism and bigotry, baulked of any genuine results, have driven the protagonists of Basic Education in defence of their progressively indefensible doctrine to dilute and modify the nature of 'basic' education to such an extent that one of the perhaps most distinguished of supporters to the original form of basic education felt compelled to pronounce the other day that basic education as practised in India today is a fraud. Perhaps the most signal service that educational authorities could render to the nation in the field of primary education would be to muster sufficient courage to discard basic education even as a label and to start devoting attention to the problems of primary education with greater originality and awareness of the development of education in its earlier stages in the modern world.

The progress of literacy, which is conventionally regarded as the culmination of the first stage of elementary education, has even on the figures available not been very impressive, although here again the statistics vary from State to State, being most depressing again in the Hindi-speaking areas and in Orissa, especially in the rural areas and among women. The proper measure to improve on the situation would have been an intensified campaign of adult education, but this also has made very halting progress, possibly for the lack of sufficient funds for the purpose or for want of the necessary number of trained teachers. There are important organizations in the country which have registered a measure of progress in this field but their work has been patchy and has suffered for want of steady guidance and support from the State. If literacy in its true sense, i.e., ability not only to read and write but also to absorb the main contents of simple literature put out for the purpose, is regarded as a *sine qua non* of a properly functioning democracy, then it is obvious that India is at present at a serious disadvantage in maintaining and improving upon the tone and character of its nascent democracy. The more advanced countries of the world achieved universal literacy first, followed by industrialization, unfettered by many restraints which modern civilization has imposed on it, culminating in the establishment of a democracy of the western parliamentary type. But over the large part of Asia, Africa and even Latin America this process has had to be reversed, independence having preceded industrialization and that in its turn being in advance of universal literacy. Such a situation obviously holds very grave perils for the progress of industrialization or the maintenance of true democracy. It is obvious, therefore, that here is a field of education which demands the urgent attention of the policy makers and the planners at the highest level, and calls for the proper deployment of all the resources for mass communication that science and technology have placed at the disposal of mankind.

The second stage of elementary education, that is, schooling for children from 11 to 14, is important in many ways, particularly as the stage which provides the large mass of teachers needed for primary schools, especially in the States which are more backward in this respect, or for the enrolment of girls. Only a small fraction of those who complete the first stage of primary education proceed to this second stage because of the wastage, stagnation and other difficulties mentioned above, and progress in this field is often hindered by the uncertainty in regard to whether this stage of education should be attached to the high schools or to the primary schools. From the pedagogic point of view, it would seem to be preferable to attach this stage as a preparatory stage for the high school or higher secondary school, but because of the general grouping given in the constitution and the difficulty of establishing high schools rapidly enough there is an increasing tendency to add these two or three years to the lower elementary stage with a pass certificate at the end. So far as men teachers are concerned this is only an intermediate stage since they will not be admitted to any teacher's training institutions unless they have passed their matriculation or the higher secondary examination, by which time they will also have reached an age at which after teacher training they could be employed as primary teachers. In the case of women teachers, however, even this will not be sufficient and in any case the numbers required are not available for service in the rural areas. Here lies the importance of one of the most perspicacious recommendations of the National Committee on Education of Women and Girls that women of a more mature age, in circumstances which make it desirable for them to look out for some means of livelihood in their neighbourhood, should be selected for specially condensed courses of education so that they could be enabled to attain the minimum educational qualification of a higher elementary pass certificate and be therefore qualified for admission, according to merit, in teacher training institutions. Whilst under the stimulus given by the Central Social Welfare Board a number of non-official organizations have arranged such condensed courses with impressive success, there has not been a parallel movement on the part of the State or official agencies and there is every apprehension of a serious shortage being experienced in the total number of women teachers required in the rural areas in some states or in the Hindi-speaking tracts generally.

Even in respect of the higher elementary stage of education Indian statistics do not compare favourably with those that obtain for some of the other countries in south and south-east Asia. It is to be hoped that this is only a transitional state of affairs and that within the next decade or so India will have virtually fulfilled the obligation imposed on the state in respect of education of the 6-14 year group of children in regard to free and compulsory education. It is only when this has been achieved that the country will have an adequately broad basis for the higher forms of its educational system, and it should be borne in mind that these are bound to be more and more diversified as the requirements of development become manifest and as the economic and social life of the country gets more and more complex in response to the progress of human civilization.

The field of se ondary education was surveyed comprehensively by an important Commission a few years ago and since then a great deal of money and effort has been devoted to the diversification and amplification of this stage of education. But it is already clear that whilst a great many departures have been made from the somewhat rut-like norms accepted in the past, there is a great deal of confusion, overlapping and uncertainty in regard to such matters as trade or technological education or multi-purpose schools and the justifiable expectations of the young people that undergo these courses of education at the secondary level. The confusion has partly been caused by the lack of the necessary statistical estimates in regard to technical, vocational or professional manpower that a country rapidly moving on to the take-off stage will increasingly require. It is hoped that a true perspective in regard to these non-academic streams will soon be available, but if correct judgments are to be arrived at even against such a perspective it is clear that a system of intelligence testing and vocational guidance suitable to Indian conditions be established. Here is another area in which sufficiently determined effort does not seem to have been made, with the result that there is a great deal of miscalculation and frustration, not to speak of wastage of resources, difficult to evaluate. To illustrate, it often happens that young people, whose abilities have not been tested, choose for their multipurpose secondary education some craft involving mechanical or manipulative still and yet expect that the portals of the university will not be barred to them after they have passed their matriculation or higher secondary school public examination. It is here that the importance of a properly worked out and adequately applied system of intelligence quotient testing would be valuable. It has been proved in other countries—and there is no reason to believe that India is different—that any young person with an intelligence quotient of less than, say, 110, can seldom make the grade in university education; and yet these young people may have great natural abilities which would make them good technicians or handicraftsmen, of which the country is bound to be in increasing need. There is need therefore to install at the earliest possible moment suitable facilities for the diversion of these various streams of young people to the channel of higher education, i.e. education beyond the secondary stage, which is appropriate to their natural endowment and their bent of mind as well as, necessarily, the precise nature of the higher secondary education that they may have received. Intelligent tests can usefully be employed in determining, among other things, eligibility for subjects or courses requirng a high degree of intelligence, and sections of a grade or course differentiated according to ability.

So far as the more academic streams of secondary education are concerned, there are again serious weaknesses, especially in regard to the teaching of sciences. Preliminary conclusions reveal a serious shortage of science teachers, not to speak of the methods of science pedagogy being behind the times. Very special efforts seem to be called for to make up for this deficiency, especially with a view to ensuring that at the later professional stages the necessary strength of well selected and well trained scientific and technological personnel is available to the country. The detailed estimates that have been made in the Planning Commission would seem to indicate that unless very energetic steps are taken here and now, the shortage that will be experienced ten years hence will be so serious as to stultify all the other efforts to develop the economy of the country.

Put simply, the situation would seem to be that the pace of preparing the necessary strength of scientific and technological personnel perspectively required for the country is very unsatisfactory and inadequate today.

Another serious shortcoming of the secondary education system, apart from the inadequacy of the enrolment of girls which has been referred to above, is that arising out of the language situation. Here, on the face of it, it would look as if Indian students have to carry a burden of language learning which their confreres in other countries are not required to carry. The three-language formula for secondary education, which has been now generaly accepted and may be expected to be in genuine operation, requires that in addition to the original language and the mother tongue, every child at the secondary stage must learn and pass an examination in Hindi as well as in English. On examination one would probably come to the conclusion that it is possible to exaggerate the difficulties of the situation and that in most countries of the world the attainment of a minimum proficiency in three languages is the lot of all young people at the secondary stage. Whilst no extraordinary efforts are involved in the learning of the regional language, where it differs from the mother tongue or Hindi, the teaching and learning of English has so far posed very serious problems because of the *dichotemy* of mediums of instruction as between the secondary and the university stage. For about a generation now secondary education has largely been conducted in the regional languages, whilst the medium of instruction at the university stage has been English. It has been the almost unanimous finding of educationists that young persons find it extremely difficult, almost impossible, to follow teaching in English for the first three to six months of their university education, in spite of the fact that they have been in most cases exposed to the teaching of English for about six or seven years in the higher elementary and the secondary stages. On analysis of the situation it has become clear that this unfortunate result is nearly always due to unsound methods of teaching English. It can also be established fairly satisfactorily by experience already gained that where the teaching of English is carried out according to the most modern scientific methods for the development of which the science of linguistics can be employed, the mastery of English attained by the students is adequate for the purposes of university stage of education. The establishment of the Central Institute of English at Hyderabad a few years ago is a step very much in the right direction and it is to be hoped that the advantage of the facilities that it offers will be taken by as large a number of teachers of English in the secondary schools as is possible and that if necessary the number of such institutes will be multiplied in order to ensure that the study of English, if not as a medium of instruction, at least as a language for international communication, is successfully carried on.

Whilst on this subject, it is just as well to postulate that here we are dealing not only with the transitional problem of the teaching of English as a medium of instruction but also its teaching as a language of international importance, not to speak of its significance in any secondary system of education as a mental discipline together with the teaching of other classical or modern foreign languages, an academically worthwhile end in itself.

Although the controversy over the medium of instruction at the university stage has raised a lot of dust in recent years, the basic issues are fairly simple and have been greatly clarified by the conclusions reached by the recent National Integration Conference, in the portion relating to Education, as a potent instrument for achieving or maintaining national unity. It has been accepted there that after suitable preparations which would be regarded as adequate by the academic world and after a period of phasing, if necessary, the regional languages will gradually replace English as a medium of instruction in colleges and the universities. The very important point has also been made that the pace of these preparations, the main object of which is to develop the regional languages, will be increased rather than retarded by the better teaching and learning of English, since development of the regional languages is essentially the process of adding to the vocabulary new words expressive of new concepts which, by hypothesis, are not known to those who have knowledge of only the Indian languages. In other words, this reflects the historical state of affairs where India has been left behind even in the progress of humanities and sociological sciences, not to speak of science and technology, in spite of the fact that there have been a small number of Indians who have been in the fortunate position of making their own contributions to the advancement of learning on the world front. That all new concepts cannot immediately be translated is accepted by anyone who has any idea of the dimensions of the problem involved both in regard to the volume of new ideas or inventions or the formulation of new concepts, on the one hand, or the time, energy and money which has to be expended in obtaining almost immediate translation into other languages, on the other. Even a country like Japan, which may be regarded as among the advanced nations of the world and which for years has been spending immense sums of money on translation into Japanese from the important foreign languages, particularly English, finds itself handicapped in the race and it is well-known that in spite of their best academic efforts the mastery of Japanese university students and academicians over foreign languages is not as good as is desirable. Since English is, so to speak, already an existing asset in India on account of historical circumstances, however distasteful the contemplation of this might be to some, it is only commonsense that India should make every endeavour to strengthen its grip over and mastery of English rather than allow it to weaken. Since such an attainment will ensure both the development of its own languages and the maturing of the capacity of the country to make its proper contribution to the advancement of learning, there need be no qualms about the adequate and continuous study of English at all stages of education from the secondary upwards. Indeed, so far as science and technology is concerned, it would be found that the study at least for the purposes of comprehension, is necessary of one or two other foreign languages as is customary in most of the advanced countries of the world.

One of the most depressing aspects of the educational scene in India is the large percentage of failures. Its immenstity is first noticed at the end of the secondary stage when about half the number of students fail to pass at the first attempt. Sufficient statistics are not available to show how many pass at the second or subsequent attempts and how many finally give up although anxious to continue their education and in possession perhaps of means to enable them to do so. It is clear however that here is an aspect of the national life where serious wastage and in consequence dangerous frustration and disappointment prevail. The causes of this phenomenon have been investigated, particularly by the secondary Education Commission, and it is possible that some remedies have also been applied, but any noticeable improvement is yet to take place. The improvement in the conditions of service of the teacher, including the strict regulation of the number of students he is called upon to teach, and more positively, the provision of facilities for enabling him to establish better contact with his pupils are remedies the importance of which cannot be exaggerated. It is possible that in the press of multifarious reforms and diversification this important aspect of secondary education has failed to receive adequate attention.

It is realized that with a better pass percentage at the secondary stage the problem of numbers in higher education will become more acute, but this has to be faced squarely and in relation not only to the requirements of the country bus also in relation to the natural endowments of the pupils. It is only natural that the employment situation being what it is there should be a fierce competition for the relatively insufficient number of jobs available for the educated young people, i.e., those who have passed their secondary stage of education. But if sufficient attention is devoted to the analysis of natural talent then there should be no difficulty in devising a system of higher education which whilst ensuring reasonable satisfaction of aspirations will ensure that the country's main stream of academic learning is enabled to flow strongly so that its university men would not only provide all the highly trained manpower that is academically or professionally required but will also be able to make their own proper contribution to the advancement of learning. For those who have special aptitudes for technical, trades or crafts there could be short two or three courses of higher education corresponding to the junior colleges or the polytechnics in other countries. There could also be not too difficult course of three to four years university education for students of mediocre ability to enable them to obtain their first degree and qualify for the many supporting jobs that will keep multiplying in an expanding economy. But special attention will have to be devoted to the more precise calculation of highly trained manpower, whether on the academic or on the professional, scientific and technical side, in order to enable the country to hold its own in the increasingly difficult and complex modern civilization.

Sufficient progress has not been made in the field of university education in respect of this very scientific process of discriminative higher education, with the result that there is a great deal of stultifying uniformity which imposes burdens on the less gifted and does less than justice to those students who are more gifted. The confusion that it is evidence in regard to the three years degree course is an instant in point. The original recommendations of the very authoritative commissions in this field were that the three years degree course should follow two years of an intermediate course between secondary and university stage of education, so that the total course of education up to the first degree would have a span of at least 15 years. In passing, it may be noted that this itself is a span of education one year shorter than is prevailing in most of the advanced countries of the world, which have a 12-year course of education for the age-group of 6-18 followed by a four-year course for the first degree, examples being the United States of America and Japan. In any case, in no country of the world except India are young people admitted to the university stage proper unless they attain the age of 18, whereas on account of slackness and slovenliness and the way of least resistance at all levels, quite a significant percentage of the young people in India are able to secure admission to the universities at the age of 15, 16 and 17, an age at which they still lack the emotional or intellectual maturity that is necessary for making their university education fruitful. In the education field there is no reform which is of greater seminal importance than this, namely, the lengthening of the period of pre-university education, so that no pupil is admitted to the university before he or she attains the age of 18 years. Another important reform, already adumbrated, would be to separate the honours courses, which should be confined only to the talented students from the pass or technical courses the facilities for which should be multiplied as widely as possible in order to satisfy the natural aspirations of the young people for higher education. This will be all the more effective if scholarships, freeships and other similar concessions are made available on a significanly large scale to students on the basis of merit and need so as to maximise the educational opportunities for young people in accordance with their natural endowments.

The reforms suggested above will also imperceptibly exert a beneficent influence on the situation that prevails in regard to student indiscipline in Indian universities. The main cause of such indiscipline, which has been conspicuously noticed in recent years, are two, viz., the somewhat immature age of the Indian university student and the increasingly deleterious effect of the example set by the progressively political-minded society outside. It remains to be seen if the very important recommendations made by the National Integration Conference in respect of the patterns of behaviour and eschewing of violence will be implemented. If they are implemented without mental reserves and with all the earnestness possible one could almost guarantee that the Indian university situation in respect of student indiscipline will improve to an astonishingly pleasing extent. But, on the other hand, if the older generation fails to mend its own ways, especially in the conduct of politics or business, then no amount of advice given to the younger generation will have any effect. Indeed, it might conceivably lead to a violent contrary reaction and a feeling of cynical disgust on the part of the young people, a situation which would hold unpredictable dangers for the development and advance of the country.

The total resources which India can devote to investment in human capital will always be found to be inadequate when compared with the tasks in hand. It is all the more necessary, therefore, that priorities be determined with the utmost care and the quality of the human material maintained at a sufficiently high level. The recent appointment by the University Grants Commission of a committee to pronounce on the improvement in standards, if any, brought about as a result of the efforts made to this end during the last six or seven years is a step very much in the right direction. But it should be remembered that the aims and objects of education, particularly higher education, in India transcend the mere maintenance of standards. They also comprise the re-orientation of the system so as to produce not only 'good citizens', but men and women imbued with a sense of unity or Indianness and capable of adapting their skills, their learning and their thinking to social, scientific or technological horizons which cannot even dimly be perceived today.

THE PRESENT STATE OF UNIVERSITY EDUCATION IN INDIA

In inaugurating the Vice-Chancellors' Conference at the National Defence Academy, Khadakvasla, near Poona in June last I observed that in my opinion University education in India was both inadequate and sub-standard. This continues to be my view, in spite of the efforts that have been made in the past and that are presently being made by the authorities concerned, particularly the University Grants Commission, to bring about an improvement in the situation. The inadequacy is the result of many causes, but principally the relatively short span of the previous stages of education, viz., primary and secondary, the lack of breadth in the supporting structure of secondary education and, lastly, the unsatisfactory quality of both the instruction provided in secondary schools and the nature of the qualifying tests. The lack of quality in university education, which justifies its being described as sub-standard, arises out of, again, a shorter span of instruction than is usual in the more advanced countries as well as out of the generally inferior apparatus of higher education provided in the country, the standard of which has progressively deteriorated over the years on account of the unregulated pressure of numbers.

Taking the relevant statistics into consideration and comparing them with similar statistics in other countries, it will be noticed that the span of pre-university education in India has been either 10 or 11 years, as against 12 in most advanced countries. This situation is aggravated by the commencement of the primary stage of education for a significant percentage of boys and girls, especially in the urban areas, at an age which would be regarded as immature and inappropriate for formal instruction in accordance with the best educational theory. In recent years there has been a recognition of these short-comings and at least in some of the States efforts are being made to refuse admission to the first class of the primary schools to children who have not attained the age of six. But this process requires to be extended very rapidly and supported by other measures, such as the prohibition of skipping of classes, i.e., what is called double promotion, as well as by consequential minimum age limits for admission to the higher stages, e.g., eleven for the higher elementary or the middle school stage and fourteen for the high school or higher secondary stage. An excellent opportunity of bringing about a universal improvement in this respect *via* the introduction of the three-year degree course scheme was misused on account of vacillation and unjustifiable compromise a few years ago, when the original proposal of imposing a three-year degree course for the first degree on a 12-year span of education between the ages of 6 and 18 was watered down and it its place a somewhat ambiguous arrangement of 11 years schooling with a minimum age of 17 plus for admission to college or university was adopted by most of the educational authorities in the country. This compromise was even worse than it appears on the surface, since in the south of the country generally the school span was already of eleven years, followed by a four-year first degree course, which in some universities led to an honours degree, in the north of the country whilst ten years was the span of pre-university education, in one important State, with a population of 70 million, for over a generation the secondary course is already of 12 years, consisting of ten years for high school and two years for intermediate college. Most thinking people are now veering round to the view that a way out of the present state of affairs would be either to revert to the original proposal of a total span of schooling of 12 years or to retain what is called the pre-university course, which is at present the transitional course between 11 years of schooling and three years for the first degree. There is also considerable support for the idea that at least for an honours course, about which something will be said later, the minimum period required after 11 years of schooling is four years including one preparatory year in which considerable emphasis would be laid on instruction in a foreign language, preferably English, as well as general education.

Apart from the length of the span of schooling, the shape of the educational pyramid in India appears to be such as to make it difficult for the schools to yield talent in adequate numbers for the higher academic courses in colleges and universities. To take a simple illustration: whereas in a country like the United Kingdom almost every child below the age of 17 finishes his or her high school course, only a very small fraction, consisting of rigidly selected youngmen and women can hope to be admitted to the universities. In India, however, it would probably be found that whilst the pass percentage in the school-leaving examinations is on an average 50, nearly 2/3rds of the successful candidates aspire for and succeed in receiving some kind of university education. In a sense this rush to colleges and universities is connected with the noticeably short span of schooling prevalent in India, not to speak of the relative inferiority of the instruction provided in schools on account of a variety of reasons. An employer who expects some basic qualifications in his prospective employees cannot afford to employ half educated young children often below the age of 16 even for relatively routine jobs like making entries in the despatch register or sticking stamps on envelopes.

The situation has in the past been made worse by the difficulties attending the use of the media of instruction. For over a generation boys and girls have been instructed in schools right upto the school-leaving examinations through their regional languages, leaving aside a very few schools as exceptions. English is no doubt among the three or four languages prescribed for the curriculae, but in some States the instruction has been given over a totally inadequate period and in all States generally the methods of teaching English as well as the portion of time devoted to the subject have been unsatisfactory. The result inevitably is that young persons listening to lectures in English for the first time on admission to colleges and universities feel completely lost for some months and the re-establishment of university examination at the end of the first year, i.e., on the termination of the pre-university course, in most universities, has meant that for absorbing the contents of the course and for preparing for the examination only about six months are available to the young people.

The public pressure for the introduction of the regional languages as media of instruction in colleges and universities is understandable, but in practice there are several important pre-requisites which have to be satisfied before an orderly changeover can be made without prejudice to the quality of instruction. Amongst these is the development of the language concerned by extending its stock of technological or other terms embodying modern concepts with which the speakers or writers of that language are not yet fully familiar, as well as the preparation of good standard books by talented writers. Much of this difficulty could be overcome by a commonsense approach, such as the permissibility of parallel media of instruction with the expectation that as the regional languages are developed the use of English will gradually diminish, finally to disappear so far as medium of instruction is concerned, provided that consistently effective care is taken to ensure that English continues to be used both for comprehension and expression for utilizing the holdings of the libraries and for keeping in touch with the work being currently done in the various fields of knowledge in the more advanced western countries, much of which work will always be available either in original or in translation in English.

The prevailing examination system both in the schools as well as in the universities is such as to put a premium on memorizing and to discourage reading to supplement the lectures as well as original thinking stimulated by means of seminars or discussion groups or closer contacts with the teachers. The whole question of reforming the present examination system so as to remove these glaring defects is under review by the University Grants Commission, together with a broader investigation of the appropriateness of the current syllabuses and the current methods of teaching as well as learning. The Commission has appointed series of committees to investigate and make recommendations in regard to these important matters. subject by subject, or faculty by faculty, so far as the review of syllabuses and teaching and learning methods is concerned. The work of these committees has reached an advanced stage and it should not be long before the provisional conclusions that have emerged are debated upon by the teachers in each faculty exhaustively, so that a programme of reform of syllabuses, courses of instruction and the examination system could be carried out in a phased manner over a period of years which would perhaps be between five and ten years.

The advent of independence and the introduction of a western parliamentary democratic system of government has led to wider awakening amongst the people and greater aspirations towards higher education, at least as a means of improving qualifications for the competition for jobs, principally under governments. These political pressures cannot easily be resisted, especially as, whilst so far higher education has largely been confined to the urban centres, accounting for less than one-quarter of the population, political power *via* the franchise has predominantly devolved on the rural population which has so far been left behind in educational opportunities and which is now keenly conscious of both its previous privations and its present political power in the shape of the franchise. Since the University Education Commission, under the chairmanship of Dr. S. Radhakrishnan, reported towards the end of 1948, a number of young persons in colleges and universities has more than trebled, although, if the first two years of the old intermediate course or the one year of the pre-university course is excluded, the numbers in what could be described as university class proper would be round about only 600,000. This is a very small proportion indeed, amounting to some 1,500 per million of population, for a country of any importance, the corresponding figures in most other countries, being very much higher, e.g. 2,500 per million in U.K. some 5,000 per million in Japan and most of the countries in Europe, and about 16,000 to 18,000 per million in the U.S.A. Whilst the numbers have thus increased, distributed amongst the larger number of colleges and universities, the apparatus of higher education has been very seriously strained with consequential general deterioration all round. It is only during the last six or seven years that through the University Grants Commission purposeful attempts are being made to lift the standards by improving the physical amenities on the one hand and by limiting the number of admissions per unit of higher education, on the other. In this process thousands of new classrooms have been built, new laboratories constructed, libraries established or improved and their stock of books replenished and opportunities for better personal contacts between students and students provided by increasing the number of hostels. There are also proposals due to be implemented during the period of the Third Five Year Plan for rapid development of facilities to teachers for running seminars or discussion groups so as to intensify and supplement the instruction in the classroom and to encourage a sensible use of the library facilities. Attempts are also being successfully made to break up unwieldy instructional units, for instance, the mammoth colleges in the cities of Calcutta and Howrah, as well as to prevent the numbers admitted or instructed in any single unit from exceeding from a certain optimum figure which is round about 1,200. Bearing in mind the steady and almost irresistible pressure for opportunities for higher education mentioned above, this means that accommodation for the increasing number of young persons can only be provided by the establishment of new units of instructions, i.e., colleges. In this respect also the University Grants Commission has indicated certain basic conditions which should be fulfilled so that a new unit that is established and claims affiliation to any particular university is able to fulfil certain minimum conditions. But this step alone, or the multiplication of universities themselves, will not by itself help to bring about a real improvement in the standards of university education, unless care is exercised to confine the selection for more rigorous university courses to only those young persons who are likely to benefit from such courses. In other words, a system has to be devised which, whilst providing ordinary facilities for young persons to obtain a bare pass degree, special care will have to be taken to admit for separate honours courses talented boys and girls who would be assisted by extending a system of scholarships, so that no talented young person is left without the means of developing these talents by means of education in university. Although no concrete steps have been taken in this direction, there is reason to believe that there is a great deal of opinion that would favour this sort of bifurcation of the streams of higher education into two streams, viz., one of the ordinary boy or girl somehow qualifying in the first pass degree and a more selected stream of talented boys and girls assisted by scholarships who would be given the full opportunity of all round development under proper supervision in selected colleges and in the post-graduate courses of the universities. It is only by following some such course that apart from the optimum development of the youthful talent, the country can ensure that it can have an adequate supply of suitably-trained people not only for scientific and technological jobs but also for fulfilling the urgent need of the elite or leaders in a fast developing modern society. In this context, the most important factor is that of motivation, motivation both of the teachers as well as the taught. Evidence in regard to teachers towards their profession is conflicting, and perhaps, in the nature of things, it would not be easy to arrive at a verdict which would be just and correct. Whilst it is undoubtedly true that given proper encouragement, as, for instance, by gradual improvement of emoluments and conditions of service, many a teacher can be induced to show a better spirit of dedication to his chosen profession, there would probably be found to be a significantly large mumber of teachers who would fail to respond to such stimuli. The only remedy in such situations would be to wait for this generation of teachers to pass out and in the meanwhile to ensure that the new recruits have the necessary orientation and attitude of mind, in addition to improved prospects and an assured prestige for their professional status.

The motivation of the students is much more difficult, although here again an improvement in the motivation of teachers, together with an amelioration of their conditions of service and the provision of the necessary facilities for out-of-classroom instruction, is bound in its turn to have influence for good on the spirit of application and industry of the pupils. There is an unfortunate over-emphasis on obtaining a university degree as a means of securing a job, usually in some government organization. This somewhat low utilitarian motive has to be replaced by a higher motivation, such as the development of the personality in every direction and the cultivation of innate talents and spiritual and aesthetic sensibilities. With a rigorous selection of students for the honours courses it should not be difficult to bring about such a motivation, as has been the experience of other countries such as Japan, or the United Kingdom, where because admission to a university is so highly competitive and the test so rigorous that the young people who have once succeeded in getting admission think a hundred times before by some wanton act or on account of a trifling provocation they throw away these hard-won opportunities. Such a careful selection may also be depended upon to furnish a natural solution of the problems arising out of the so-called students' indiscipline, which in this country is more largely the exhibition of some childish traits rather than display of any mature sentiment.

Lastly, as everything else, a country can only have the sort of university education that it deserves, in other words, unless the circumambient atmosphere or ethos of a country is high, the standards of university education in that country will not become or remain high. Here the remedy is largely in the hands of the existing leadership, and where there is failure, as has happened in many instances in India, the repercussions on the student community are necessarily unfavourable. But even in such circumstances the younger generation is not entirely absolved of its responsibility to do what they can to utilize to the fullest possible extent the precious interval of higher education that is conceded to them. With the efflux of time they will step into many a position which is now occupied by the senior leaders and if the apparatus of university education gives them reasonable chances they would have no excuse for preparing to occupy these places with avoidable lack of mental, physical and spiritual equipment, or lack of proper orientation towards fulfilment of the role of the elite in the new society.

Address at the Annual Founder's Day celebrations of the Doon School at Dehra Dun on 20th October 1951.

Mr. Martyn, Boys of the Doon School, Ladies and Gentlemen,

It is hardly necessary for me to say that it gives me very great pleasure to be amongst you on this occasion. As Chairman of the Board of Governors I wish I had more frequent opportunities of acquainting myself with the progress of the School and coming into contact with the boys. But official duty, alas, is a severe taskmaster and when it is reinforced by prolonged parliamentary sessions, while the longing to get away from it all and refresh the spirit by associating with the young and the unsophisticated grows, the opportunities to do so dwindle.

I share Mr. Martyn's quiet satisfaction at the progress achieved by the school during the scholastic year that is about to close. The results secured both in the examinations and in sport give evidence of the maintenance of high quality, and the range of miscellaneous outside activities is impressive. I welcome the establishment of the National Cadet Corps and have no doubt that it will attract increasing numbers of the boys. I have good authority for the statement that it is in defence training centres rather than in her high schools and Universities that India is training her future leaders on correct lines; and periodical training, however brief, on similar lines must supplement what we can offer and do a world of good to our boys. One activity which I hope very much will not languish despite the departure of an interested teacher is nature study. To my mind, in no aspect of the education of children and youth is India more deficient as compared with countries of the West than in inculcating and fostering the study of nature. To most grown-ups a tree is merely a tree, a bird a bird and a rock a rock. Few seem to realise how even apparently drab natural surroundings become interesting if one observes birds and takes note of fauna and flora, and how

The vision of the Founder, the late Mr. S.R. Das, has

the beauty of nature takes on a new meaning in the light of informed scientific observation. And all this wealth of pleasure is over and above the practical benefits of the study of wild life. Symptomatic of our national indifference to the study of nature is the sudden contraction of the membership of the well-known bombay Natural History Society after the departure of British personnel from the public services. A few enthusiasts and experts are attempting to keep the Society going, but it is an uphill task. I shall regard my present visit to the School well-worth while if these somewhat discursive observations find some response and lead to sustained and extended interest in nature study on the part of the staff as well as the boys.

Another activity which I wish I had the chance of observing at close quarters and at first hand is the work of the Dehat Sabha. Among young men and women all over the country there is at present a growing realization of the urgent need of assisting the folks in the rural areas to improve their surroundings, educate themselves and make their lives more meaningful. There are some who would make it obligatory on school and college students to undertake some such work as a prerequisite of the conferment of academic qualifications, but what is done for the love of it and with understanding is far superior in value to what is ordained, and it is for a public school like ours to set a shining example to others in this as in other respects.

Mr. Martyn's feeling reference to finance as a headache strikes an answering chord in my heart. There is nothing so depressing as the lack of finance for developing useful and essential activities and institutions. The very causes that have led to the contraction of the value of money have created conditions unfavourable for private charity. Government assistance to the School may or may not arrive, but no public school could expand its activities satisfactorily if it depended to any appreciable extent on Government assistance. It is for parents and friends or the School to consider if they could not make renewed efforts to put the School on a sound financial footing. No gift is worthwhile unless in the giving it hurts the giver.

after nearly a generation unfolded itself gratifyingly. The ten lakhs of rupees he collected in those days could buy things worth fifty lakhs today—a reflection which gives the measure of the intensity of his efforts. The measure of the success of the Institution that he founded is to be had in the fine reputation that the Doon School boy has established for himself whichever vocation he has chosen to adorn, not least in the Defence forces.

This splendid tradition of the school must be a beacon-light to its present boys and I am sure they need no advice from me to help them make the best of their opportunity. As Mr. Martyn has rightly observed, in essence a public school is a community in which a group of boys has the best possible opportunity to formulate its attitude to life and to consolidate its belief in the things that are good and its intolerance of humbug. As C.E.M. Joad has remarked, nowhere else is it possible so harmoniously to develop every side of one's nature as at a good public school. The spirit of the boy at such a school is refined and enriched as his body grows in balanced development. "For the well-nurtured youth is one who would see most clearly whatever was amiss in ill-made works of man or ill-grown works of nature, and with a just distaste would hate the ugly even from his earliest years and would give delighted praise to beauty, receiving it into his soul and being nourished by it, so that he becomes a man of gentle heart". With a well-blended development of body, mind and spirit, a public school boy can triumph over what Joad calls the disjunctions of modern life. India needs very many more and not less public schools, especially in view of its urgent quest for leadership in the fascinating vista of development that the advent of Independence has opened before the country.

For what I propose to say now about leadership, I have drawn largely on Donald Portway's "The Quest of Leadership" which I hope is available in the School Library and is read by the staff. He defines leadership as not merely the art of becoming nor even of remaining a leader, but the art of leading. The successful fulfilment of the responsibilities of leadership requires qualities different and of a higher order from those needed to obtain or retain leadership. A leader is defined as one who inspires free men with the feeling of moral obligation to follow him, which involves high purpose clearly realized and courageously pursued. The pre-requisites demanded of a leader are : (i) knowledge of the work to be done and energy to carry it out efficiently, (2) intelligence, (3) sympathy and understanding, (4) confidence, (5) determination, and (6) a philosophy, supplying the main-spring vital for success and involving moral integrity and strength of character. Important as all these are, I should like to stress the importance of knowing one's job. No man can secure the confidence of the group he leads unless he is efficient at his job, and no one will be efficient at his job unless he knows it really well.

Of what stuff shall India's future leaders be fashioned? Leadership comes but to the few—less increasingly to those few who were born for it but more to those who work to deserve it. It is very evident that education and training are vital matters in the quest for leadership, for it is in the formative years of youth that the character of a man is built up, whether for good or evil.

It will be increasingly from the alumni of public schools like the Doon School that India's leaders in all walks of life will be found in the future, as it is in such institutions that emphasis is laid on the ability to think out things and on the building up of character.

I mentioned a while ago India's comparative indifference to the study of nature. Another quality in which we compare unfavourably with many other nations is love of work. I do not think that as a nation we work hard enough. A change for the better in this attitude will enable us to fulfil plans for economic development without too great a reliance on the availability of finance. As Dorothy Sayers says in her thought-provoking pamphlet "Why Work ?"—"Work is the natural exercise and function of man. Work is not primarily a thing one does to live, but the thing one lives to do. It is, or it should be, the full expression of the worker's faculties, the thing in which he finds spiritual, mental and bodily satis-faction. In such a view, we should no longer think of work as something that we hastened to get through in order to enjoy leisure; we should look on our leisure as the period of changed rhythm that refreshed us for the delightful purpose of getting on with our work."

All this shows what a heavy responsibility rests on the teacher. It is he who observes capacities and suits his teaching to these, trains the minds and assists the manners and shapes the morals of members of the community at their most impressionable age. It is he, rather than the parents, who helps to form the child's first conceptions of good and bad, social and anti-social, beautiful and ugly. He has to furnish the vocational guidance that would help the boys to find careers where their qualities, attainments and personality would have full play. All the evidence available to us indicates that the teachers of the Doon School are doing their jobs well and I should like to take this opportunity of offering them my felicitations.

In conclusion, I wish the boys a joyful schooling that will set the hall-mark of quality on them and fruitful careers that will help them to play their part in holding up the flag of Mother India.

Address delivered at the opening of the New Science Block of Thiagarajan College, Madurai, 12th February 1959:

Sri Thiagarajan Chettiar, his colleagues and the Board of Trustees, Principal, Staff and students of the Thiagarajan College and Ladies and Gentlemen,

I am very happy indeed to be associated with this function both in my capacity as Chairman of the University Grants Commission as well as in my capacity as an ex-student of the Natural Sciences. I am very grateful to Sri Thiagarajan Chettiar for the many kind references he has made to me in the course of his address. As is usual on occasions like this, there is a certain amount of generosity, shall we say, in the terms of praise that have been chosen for the purposes of the address, but by now I have learnt to overlook this slight generosity (laughter) and to give due credit for the regard and the goodwill that usually prompt such cordial sentiments.

Whereas one or two matters in this address call for a certain amount of comment on my side, I am very glad to have some evidence that what little the University Grants Commission has been trying to achieve in discharging its responsibilities for the improvement of the standards of higher education is exerting a wholesome influence upon the educational progress in this country and in this particular field, particularly by way of giving encouragement to the teachers and to others who are intimately concerned with this process of higher learning. The leeway that this country has to make up in regard to making the apparatus of higher learning adequate, in any modern sense of the word, is immense. On account of historical reasons we have lost a great deal of ground while there has been a continued deterioration of this apparatus of higher learning on account of the pressure of numbers. It is not, therefore, to be expected that we shall be able to bring up our institutions of higher learning to anywhere within hailing distance of similar institutions in other countries, particularly the more advanced countries of the world. As against an average of the equivalent of Rs. 5,000/- per student per annum that these countries are able to spend on higher education, we, in this country, are hardly able to spend Rs. 500/- per student per annum for the same purpose. Nevertheless we have all through our long historical existence learnt to live on terms with poverty and we do not expect, at least within any brief period, our attaining equivalence or even proximate equivalence with the more advanced countries in this respect. As in other fields of life, we recognise that money is not everything and that a great deal can be achieved even where financial resources are inadequate if the right attitudes of mind are there. In other words it is the spirit of both the teacher and the taught, not to speak of the management, that matters and not the financial resources that they can command.

I am, therefore, very happy to learn that as a result of the efforts made so far by the U.G.C. and other authorities like the Ministries of Education at the Centre and in the States a spirit of optimism is gradually emerging in this otherwise somewhat gloomy atmosphere surrounding the whole field of higher education in the country. I have no doubt that if this flame of optimism is fed and kept alive then additional financial resources could be attracted to this talk of improving the standards of higher education in the country so that it may fulfil all the legitimate expectations of those who resort to it as well as those who are fostering it.

Against such a background it is a little unfortunate that certain difficulties should have arisen in regard to securing for this College the land that it so badly needs for the construction of buildings which are regarded as an essential part of any institution of higher learning worth the name. The campus of 10 or 11 acres—(I took only a round figure)—is entirely inadequate for a College which during the last ten years has reared itself almost entirely on the strength of private munificence and has nevertheless given such a good account of itself that it has secured affiliations both for the graduate and the Post-graduate courses in most of the important subjects.

It seems, therefore, very necessary that it should be helped to put up these new constructions and it is patent that this cannot be achieved unless there is the land on which to put up new buildings. This state of affairs is not, as far as I can ascertain, due to any negligence on the part of the management who moved in the matter perhaps within a year or two after the establishment of the College and I believe that an important notification under the Land Acquisition Act was passed about 8 years ago. The natural expectation therefore is that within these 8 years that notification would be followed by a valuation or a determination of the compensation to be paid and that the State Government will issue the next notification due under that Act to enable the management to take possession of the site and to start its construction. This delay has appeared to me so abnormal when it was first mentioned to me (I think perhaps it was last year) that I took some trouble to look into the facts of the case and made bold to mention this particular case both to the Education and Finance Minister, Sri Subramaniam, as well as to the Governor of the State. Now that I have paid another visit to this College and assessed, so to speak, the atmosphere engendered by the lack of construction, especially of what the report called permanent hostels, I shall try again to draw attention to this very important matter in the quarters that count. In an age where one thinks of big plans of economic development measured by crores of rupees by periods of 5 years, 8 years it seems to be an abnormally long time to enable the College to acquire some 59 acres of adjacent land and if this kind of pace were to characterise the rest of our progress then it will require a statistician of a very high order to find out what period will be required for doubling our national income. (Applause).

I have listened with very great interest to the report that has been read out of the progress of the College and it would only be perhaps a very trite observation on my part that this remarkable progress could not have been possible without the spirit of dedication shown by Sri Thiagarajan Chettiar and his family. (Applause).

I often have occasion to consider this question of the

establishment of new Colleges, because the University Grants Commission has taken the view, rightly, that so far as individual institutions are concerned, there is a limit beyond which it would not be right to admit more students, not because of any doctrinaire consideration as to the number of young people that are to be at Colleges and Universities but because of the operation of that troublesome thing which we call conscience. If this hall can seat, shall we say 1,500 people, if in his large-heartedness—Mr. Thiagarajan Chettiar tried to seat 2,000 probably there would be very dire consequences. In my opinion the same thing ought to apply to any educational institution and the final arbiter in this matter must be the academic conscience of the management and the teachers helped may be, by standard regulations made by Universities and supported by expert bodies like the University Grants Commission.

This issue is entirely separate from the issue of how many young people in this country ought to be at Colleges and Universities and how they should be selected. On the second part of this issue there is a certain amount of general agreement that since, as in many other fields, our resources are limited, we had better not waste them or use them wastefully. Now, if resources are devoted to the higher education of 100 young people out of whom only 25 come out at the other end with the minimum qualifications, then I think most sensible people would agree that there was an extravagant use of resources such as at least a poor country like India cannot afford. Therefore all thinking people seem to have come to the conclusion that these resources had better be devoted to the education of those who are likely to benefit in an educational sense from such education, and I doubt if anyone will really quarrel with this kind of conclusion.

So far as the University Grants Commission is concerned, there is also a statutory and financial responsibility. The Central Government has placed at the disposal of the Commission funds which are considerable although I have often complained that they are not adequate. In any case it is the duty of the Commission to deploy these funds in such a way as to bring about an optimum improvement of the standards of higher education in this country. One way in which we try to do this and to make up for past deficiencies is to augment the amenities and facilities for such education. Larger accommodation, establishment and improvement of libraries, construction of laboratories, improvement in the teacher-pupil ratio—all this requires finance. If then we find such finance and expect an improvement which can be statistically stated, that is to say so many square feet in a Class Room for pupils, so many square feet in the Laboratories, so much space for 100 books in the Library and so many books per student and so on and so forth, and if all the while the numbers are growing in the same institution, then obviously everything that we are trying to achieve is being at the same time neutralised. Therefore we are very vitally concerned with ensuring that if our financial assistance is accepted it is subject to a kind of self-denying ordinance which an institution is prepared to impose on itself, that the numbers will not be increased beyond an agreed ceiling.

But the second question is not quite so clear and that is apart from the general aims of higher education, that is to say, to develop personalities and sensibilities and widen the frontiers of learning and all that, there is also a utilitarian aspect of education, namely that the nation is entitled to look to a College and a University or the total number of Colleges and Universities in the country to turn out the kinds of people, professional and otherwise and in adequate numbers that are required for all the different fields of economic and social development.

The calculations are in their very nature difficult and uncertain. Also during the course of planning, with which I had the privilege of being associated at one time, we got off to a somewhat late start in reckoning our future requirements and even now I do not believe that there is anyone in this country who has a very clear idea of how many people, graduates of what kinds, will be required during the third five year plan. We have a fairly accurate idea in regard to the professional courses, the number of Engineers, Doctors, may be agricultural Graduates; but as regards the Arts course we are on uncertain ground. As a kind of escape from this difficulty we keep scanning the employment horizon and try to find out what sort of graduates are being offered and what sort have to wait for an unconscionably long time for securing employment. It would look as if most of the Science Graduates succeed in finding some employment or another, no matter what class they have passed in. Even 3rd class M.A., and to my mind a 3rd class M.A. is an anachronism, because he is—I hope I am not giving offence to anyone—a master who knows one third of the subject but not two third of his subject (laughter). Anyway there is a very great demand for M.As. of all kinds, certainly for good second class and of course first class B.As. apart from Science Graduates for the teaching profession.

Although there is a certain amount of disparity, there is an overall surplus though several states are in short supply; but in certain other States there is surplusage of men teachers as well as women teachers and mobility of labour in this country is, instead of accelerating, getting slower. Nevertheless certain provisional and tentative calculations have been made; and with Universities fairly evenly distributed over the country and with a pass percentage which is not quite so depressing as it is today in the lower reaches of University Education, we ought with the present college and university strength to be able to secure all the Graduates and all the professionals, all the Masters and the Doctors that we shall be needing during the next five years. But as I said there is a great range of inequality as between State and State and with the gradual advent of the regional tongue as the medium it is getting more difficult to have free migration of students between Universities, apart from the question of their subsequent employment. Therefore, I have no doubt that in several districts and in several States more Colleges will be required and if they are required then it is the business of the State Government primarily to ensure that they come into existence, and since our experience is that no State Government is flush of funds and would be only too glad to find that some of its duties in this connection are discharged by private effort, it logically follows that it is the duty of State Governments to give every possible encouragement to such private effort, especially where a private effort is of such magnitude as it is here. It seems to me that it is almost axiomatic that the State Government should strain every nerve to help and not to hinder an Institution like this (Applause). There is one more point in this address which I must not slur over, although the matter does not primarily concern the University Grants Commission, and that is this delicate reference to the possibility of a University being established in this University Centre. The present position is that, apart from all the figures that I have quoted, we have a little over 2000 students per million of population at schools and at Colleges and Universities in this country. Now, as figures go, that is a very low proportion; in most countries the figures are very much higher ranging, shall we say between 10,000 to 20,000 per million of population. There is one country with which we seem to compare *prima facie* very favourably and that is the United Kingdom, where the proportion is about the same, that is to say 2,000 per million of population; but there are two important differences—one is that their secondary education system is one of the best in the world and young people are kept there till they are at least 18 since they will not be taken by any University, with the result that they have an excellent grounding before they reach the Universities and there is a separate admission examination called the General Certificate Examination. The consequence of taking such well-grounded pupils is that their pass percentage for the first degree is 85 as against our 55 in this country and another 5 per cent are allowed to pass compartmentally, that is to say, if they fail in a subject or two then they are given the opportunity to pass in it after the prescribed period of interval. Another 5% are kindly but firmly told to change their course, but are permitted to stay in the College and University. (Laughter). They are not given up as hopeless cases. Therefore, it is only 5 per cent who fail to make the course on account of lack of ability or lack of facility. Now as against that, we have at the first degree perhaps a pass percentage of 50 and 60 and that is after following an initial slaughter at the Intermediate or the Pre- University stage, (laughter) with the result that we have an effective percentage of only 25 and therefore any comparison with U.K. would perhaps be misleading.

Next we have about 40 Universities now for a population of 400 million, that is to say, one University per every million and each one will now start calculating how many Uuiversities they are to have because they have a fair idea of what the population is. Suppose a State has 30 million, then, one would think it ought to have 3 Universities. Well, there are some unitarian and residential, where the numbers are by the very nature of the institution limited, may be 3,000 or 5,000. Of these some have been greatly daring and have admitted more students to their sorrow; but since the average population served is 10 million each for the 40 Universities and since there are 2,000 to 2,500 students per million of population, we should have a strength of 20,000 or 25,000 per University. It may be that in the fullness of time—how long it will take to get full, I cannot prophecy—possibly this State will require more Universities. As it is, I have no doubt, centres which are well developed as Madurai, will have to be very seriously considered as the first claimants in the field.

I say this with a certain amount of abandon because the University Grants Commission is not concerned with the establishment of new Universities. Their duty the Constitution has mercifully laid on the State Governments. The University Grants Commission has been established in accordance with an item in the Legislative list which deals with the co-ordination and maintenance of standards and, therefore, it is concerned only with standards and development of existing Colleges and Universities. It is like the difference between a parent and the teacher. A teacher comes in, even at the earliest, at the pre-primary stage, but the teacher is not supposed to give birth to a child, that is the duty of the parent. (Laughter). And therefore, it is the look out of the State Government to consider whether its apparatus of higher education is complete or incomplete in the light of the preceding circumstances. Nevertheless since the University Grants Commission is destined to come a little later the law has provided that any State Government ought to have some ante-natal consultation with the University Grants Commission. Although that is not a compulsory provision, they should like to consult the University Grants Commission. The University Grants

Commission takes into account all the circumstances, finds out the numbers involved, the efficiency or otherwise of the present management, the economic situation of the pupils—because the poor pupils from rural families, all of them, may not be able to travel to the metropolis for their education; if more girls come, it might be that they might not find it convenient to go so far away from home—there are all kinds of apparatus for the present as well as those likely to emerge in the future and all those factors will have to be carefully taken into account before, if at all it is consulted, the University Grants Commission can give any advice in this matter to the State concerned although in a large number of cases there has not been this previous consultation. In the few cases in which we have been consulted we have said "Yes, Go ahead" and "Not now"—just to say that we have shown the green signal and not the red signal. Now I shall leave this matter there.

My principal business today is to declare your third Science Block open. And I do this with very great pleasure. I have not had a look at it but the outside is very attractive. At the back is the Swimming Pool and the River. It is a very good situation and I have no doubt that this block of buildings which is for the biological sciences will fulfil all the expectations that are held of it by not only you—management—not only the teachers and students, but also the University as well as the University Grants Commission. (Laugher). Because if there is one aspect of higher education to which the University Grants Commission is at the moment giving concentrated attention, it is the post-graduate courses; because we consider that that is the seminal stage from which we get the teachers, and if we get properly qualified teachers M.As. anb M.Scs., barring the third class ones, then we shall be enabled to arrest this inbreeding, this continuous deterioration, that is taking place in the standards of higher education according to all competent observers. In the beginning, our policy was to concentrate all post-graduate development at the headquarters, but we soon realised that that was not a very practicable proposition especially in regard to a University which is looking after very large numbers—may be like 60,000 to 80,000 as your University is—and that, almost in the nature of things, selected Colleges have to be given controlled and regulated affiliations in both the humanities and sociological sciences as well as sciences proper in the post-graduate stages so that the convenience of students might be served without at the same time sacrificing quality. The arrangement is that the post-graduate teaching here as in any other selected centre—this is the first to be selected—Madurai is the first to be selected in this new Scheme—will be under the supervision of the University Professor in that subject, whose business it will be to ensure that the instruction is carried out as it ought to be in accordance with the strictest standards prescribed by the University, and I think that is a development to be encouraged although it will have to be watched with care because it is experimental; but I have no doubt that as the numbers grow as they are bound to grow even if conditionally they do not grow, this kind of scheme might have to be adopted in regard to other Universities also.

I suppose since I am opening a Science Block I have to say a few words about Science. Now in a way Science is the essence of all education; that is to say, if we define education as an adjustment to the changing scales of values, then the process of adjustment in this world of ours must essentially be Science, because if its scales or values have been vastly affected by anything during the last 300 years it is by science and technology. And therefore modern education whether you like it or not is essentially scientific education. It is true that in the life of the community of humanity which is 900,000 years old, shall we say, science is only 300 years old and that is as 10 seconds in a 24 hour day. But by this science I mean not science in the nature of observation of natural phenomena that has been known to us since historical times, not even the deduction of small laws—that also was attempted several years before A.D.; but what we call the scientific method is only 300 years old. Nevertheless in all studies of science it is necessary and profitable not only to study what is called the scientific method but also the history of science; and one very eminent scientist whose name is Bernal has observed, "In science more than in any other human institution it is necessary to search out the past in order to understand the present and to control the future". Well, we assume that this will not be lost sight of. Neverthelss for the pursuit of science, we have naturally to concentrate on the scientific method.

What exactly is the scientific method? It is the analysis by experiment, the formulation of general rules leading to wider hypotheses and finally testing the validity of these hypotheses. In modern life, Science has become an essential part of the citizens' environment, because its devices now envelope modern life and life is perpetually presenting problems which have scientific implications, not only of practical questions of technology but even deeper aspects of life. Therefore one might say that science is the new tool of the human mind and it is capable of releasing the mind from its ancient constraints or its ancient taboos. It also deepens our appreciation of the orderliness of nature. It makes us admire on discovery the orderliness of nature, which means that science is essentially humble. Each new discovery can only enhance our humility as indicating the existence of infinite complexity and even now some part of this is already recognised as beyond man's ken, or his powers of observation and measurement as for instance in Astronomy or Cosmology. Now as a tool of the human mind science requires honesty of thinking above all—than a certain amount of clarity and precision if the scientific method is to yield useful results. There was a time when one thought that science was entirely a matter of a few simple laws. Now that was perhaps correct, till very recently of Physics, Chemistry, Mathematics, Astronomy, Geology, Meteorology, Oceanography, etc., and all these sciences developed earlier than the biological science; because of this dissectability of the world around us, because scientists could take it a thesis, make experiments, observe, evolve hypotheses which were not too many or too numerous and test them—that is to say, these sciences had a greater amenability to the scientific method. But that kind of statement cannot be made in regard to the biological sciences, because there are too many variables too many complicated phenomena, and some of these inter-act on each other. The range of examination of living organisms is necessarily limited. Nevertheless, in recent times, the physical sciences have developed very special tools for the use of biological science for the purposes of what one would call a micro-investigation—investigation on very small scales.

Science is of course established in institutions of higher education as well as in institutions for pure or applied research, and so far as Universities are concerned, it is pure research that will secure concentrated attention. In all countries pure science and research receive pride of place in the Universities as it should. "The Soviet rule has bestowed on science all the authority of which it has deprived religion"—says John Gunther in his book 'Inside Russia' when he was describing the Moscow University, which you remember is essentially a university for science. There, in that University, pure science is emphasised but this is something to remember that some 15,000 students who work there—the number might have increased by now, this is two or three years old—have necessarily to take courses in philosophy, economics and a foreign language other than the one learnt or studied in school. So this primacy of pure research so far as Universities are concerned is well established. One is also to remember that although individual research will still remain important, research as a means of widening the frontiers of learning must necessarily be a collaborative affair—that is to say, somebody who is doing some piece of research must keep himself in tough with what someone else is doing, not only in order to avoid any possible duplication but also not to have any kind of waste of effort, on something which has already been attempted, and indeed now this partnership is no longer between scientists themselves. Science offers a very rich partnership to Arts, to moral philosophy and to psychology and when we come to the Mental Sciences we come across still more, still greater complexities. Mental Sciences are less settled and are essentially interrelated and we find that our understanding of human behaviour in the field of sociological science is still very tentative and fragmentary.

I referred to the quality of work and the standards, and that of course applies to every thing that is done in Colleges and Universities so far as research is concerned. Measurements are not too easy and you may be interested to know that

University Grants Commission is constituting review teams to go round at least some sample Colleges and Universities in order to evaluate the research work that is carried on as well as to get an overall picture of any requirements that there may be and then to make recommendations to the University Grants Commission. The present position of course is that we are considerably behind the rest of the world and even as between University and University or State and State there are very great disparities. Here are some figures relating to the number of research papers published—scientific papers published—between 1947 and 57. The largest number of papers was published in West Bengal with 1557, Uttar Pradesh followed with 881, Bombay: 500, Mysore: 260, Andhra Pradesh: 256, Delhi : 249, Bihar: 189, then Rajasthan : 119, Madras: 114, Punjab: 61, Madhya Pradesh : 51. Other numbers are not worth quoting. (Laughter). Well, one has to note that everything must not be measured by numbers alone; may be that quality makes up for the lack of quantity here. But it is something worth pondering.

Well then I hope that in this new block that I am opening the scientific method will be followed and, what is more, that a method once learnt will also be followed in the rest of one's career in life, because one often finds that those who investigate scientific phenomena do not always carry the scientific method into their lives. In other words it is not always practised by scientists outside their professional specialities; and yet what a scientist has to do is something that seems to be applicable to life as a whole. What is he to do? He must talk and think, he must suspend prejudices, he must find out relevant facts, he must accept facts against tradition or arbitrary authority or hear-say, he must maintain high standards of personal honesty, he must keep an open mind, he must indulge his curiosity, he must focus his vision and he must like truth for its own sake. I hope that the young men and women who will be working in these blocks will learn to do all these things in the life into which they will be projected when they leave their respective Colleges and Universities. I wish them and the teachers and the management every success.

Inaugural speech at the Third Annual General Meeting of the Delhi Management Association, 3rd March, 1959, New Delhi.

Mr. President, Members of the Delhi Management Association and gentlemen :

When your President invited me to participate in this function, you informed me that the management movement was gradually gaining momentum and that it was your belief that, given encouragement, it will definitely contribute to the development of sound management techniques, methods and processes in both public and private sectors. You expressed the hope that the inauguration of this annual session by me will help in promoting the cause of this movement, and you have repeated this hope in the observations which have just been concluded.

As you are aware, I accepted your invitation with great alacrity and that was not only because of my present official position as the Chairman of the University Grants Commission; although I vehemently protest that I am not the various things that you have mentioned in your observations, I do claim to have certain interests wider than those of the Chairman of the University Grants Commission. I am by training and tradition as well as, I suppose, by inclination an administrator and there is hardly any difference between management and administration so far as the fundamental principles are concerned. Then, as you are aware, I have been very closely associated in various capacities with the economic affairs of our country, the utilisation of its resources and plans for the economic development, having regard to the optimum use of these resources.

Now, so far as my immediate interests are concerned, namely, Chairman of the University Grants Commission, there is very little that I can contribute to this morning's proceedings.

I have spent some time in going through your pamphlets in regard to aims and objectives, your three annual reports, the two previous inaugural speeches and your two previous presidential addresses as in addition, of course, to having studied and heard very carefully what you have had to say just now; and I find that most of what is worth saying has already been said either by you or by the others, that is to say the two distinguished public men who inaugurated the previous annual meetings. And I cannot miss this opportunity of paying a tribute to one of these who is no longer with us, i.e., Dr. Ghosh, Member of the Planning Commission. I had been associated with him in one capacity or another for many years and I had every opportunity to observe the remarkable knowledge, experience, balance of mind, sincerity and sensitivity which he brought to bear on everything that he was connected with, in his academic or in his official capacity.

The University Grants Commission is connected with the setting up of the development of Departments of Business Administration and has also a certain amount of incidental interest in the other higher institutes for the study of management or business administration, although it is not within the purview of their statutory duties to extend any financial assistance to them.

You have referred, Sir, in your address to the setting up of departments of business administration in the Universities and have expressed a view that these perhaps are no longer adequate for the requirements of the country. As you yourself said in the course of your first presidential address, these departments as well as the Calcutta Institute of Social Welfare and Business Management were set up on the recommendations of a Committee appointed by the All-India Board of Technical Education which is now called All-India Council of Technical Education. And, it is the practice of the University Grants Commission to refer any question concerning the expansion or the development of these departments to that Council. Therefore, I think, your plea that management should be regarded as a technical subject can be readily accepted and indeed is in accordance with current practice. Now that some time has elapsed since the establishment of these departments and these institutes, and since there has also been a proliferation of institutes with similar objectives that the adequacy or otherwise of these departments and these institutes should be systematically reviewed, especially in view of the fact that we are now on the eve of formulating proposals for a plan of development which is bound to be far more comprehensive and onerous than its two predecessors. I am sure that those who are officially connected with the problems of productivity, particularly in the industrial world, whether that falls under public enterprise or private enterprise, will take note of your plea and set about drawing up a detailed plan so that both in the private and the public spheres the country shall not fall short of properly trained and cultivated managerial talent.

Now that the National Productivity Council has been established—an event of very great importance to which you have made a reference—I have no doubt myself that this matter, the importance of which it is impossible to exaggerate, will under the sponsorship of that Council and, of course, under the stimulus given by the Planning Commission receive attention to the relevant part of the Plan. So far as your Association is concerned, I have no hesitation in congratulating those who conceived of it and those who followed up the idea, that is to say, the Federation of the Indian Chambers of Commerce and Industry and similar bodies. It is due to the interest and enthusiasm of these bodies that today we have a team of such management organisations with a federal structure. I wholly approve of the purpose—the essential and underlying purpose—of these associations, because, I believe that, unlike poets, good managers are not born but made and it is, therefore, very necessary that deliberate and conscious measures be taken in order to cultivate and foster the varied kind of managerial talent that will be required in increasing measure for the economic development of our country.

Like the University Grants Commission itself, I suppose the main purpose of these organizations will be to coordinate and maintain standards—in our case, standards of higher education, and in the case of your Association and cognate associations, standards of management practice.

You are also right so far as these higher associations are concerned, that is to say, outside the academic sphere, that the duty of management practitioners is essentially a duty of self-education and therefore, like democracy, in regard to people, one can say that your aim also would be education of management, by management, for management. And if one considers the general law of survival in life, one would find that no organization is able to survive unless it has the capacity to adapt itself to changing environments, and this implies a constant introspection, review of various processes and bringing about a conscious change; and this is essentially a task for an association of individuals with similar interests and responsibilities.

For such an association the element of success will lie in the attention that they give to orientation, training, various mercantile practices and purposeful action in order to bring about an improvement. Indeed everything has to be pressed into service for its purposes, whether it is genius—which is very rare, talent—which is scarce, common sense—which is not quite so common, experience, education and training in service. I, therefore, welcome the growing variety of your activities like your Newsletter, your arrangement of lectures or group discussions, because amongst equals a man can seldom get away with untruth or unreason.

Then I notice that you also pay a great deal of attention to cultivating relations with institutes with similar objectives. Now there are certain points which concern me not so much as a person in-charge of university courses, but as a person who has had something to do with public affairs, and it is my belief, as it is yours, that merely university courses are not enough for achieving the purpose that we have in view and that real training is a life business and that, therefore, a great many training courses or refresher courses have to be organised. In organising these courses one would have to pay attention to the various levels of management, because management is a function which spreads, so to speak, over the whole spectrum, beginning right from top management to management, shall we say, by the foremen, and it is for this reason that I welcome the new arrangements that are in view in regard to the seminars or in regard to schools for training of top managements.

There are one or two points attention to which seems to me to be necessary if your objectives are to be fulfilled. The first is, I think, a retrospect of what have been achieved as a result of work spreading now over three years. In other words, what I suggest is some kind of qualitative or quantitative measurement of what has been accomplished as a result of this drive for securing better management techniques or better management ethics. I could not agree with you more in placing emphasis on not only techniques but also ethics, and I believe that what you had to say in this particular respect is applicable to a field which is very much wider than the field with which we are dealing this morning. I, therefore, strongly endorse your impassionate plea for a code of ethics.

You have, I think, placed moral health at the same level as physical and mental health, which means denial of self-indulgence from a long-range point of view, heightened sense of social and ethical responsibility. And you are right in saying that, above all, India needs ethical leadership from those it respects as supremely practical. But I wonder if the implication of this is fully understood. I am one of those, probably in a minority, who hold that there is only one kind of ethics, which is applicable to individuals as well as to societies and to all forms of associations and that there is no such thing as separate political ethics or business ethics and this is not because ethics is anything philosophically desirable but because in the long run it is the one safeguard for the preservation of society.

There are certain other matters calling for attention, as for instance, the activities of the National Productivity Council and the help that they can give in an organised fashion for this business of national production. I hope that at some time or the other during the course of your discussions you will have occasion to consider the importance of statistical quality control, a matter in which I happen to be personally interested as Chairman of a small Committee appointed by the Cabinet in order to guide the activities in this regard of the Indian Statistical Institute, because I am convinced that every person who has any responsibility in regard to management must take an interest in the business of the production of whatever goods he is concerned with in accordance with the optimum range of quality. I have looked through the previous records of the last two or three years and have failed to discover any reference to this important aspect of management, namely, statistical quality control.

Then I do not know that I have any other matters to which I should make a reference to which reference has not been made. One is not quite sure whether some of these matters pass beyond your sphere and fall perhaps outside your sphere. There is, for instance, a reference to the draft code of efficiency and welfare about which some news appears in this morning's Press. The heading is "Move to Improve Productivity", and the announcement is that as the sequel to the code of discipline in industry the Union Labour Ministry has now drawn up a draft code of efficiency and welfare which has been circulated to central organisations of employers and workers. While the aim of the former is to bring about greater industrial harmony, the code of efficiency will aim at improving productivity and production. The Minister in-charge is reported to have suggested that payments to workers should be linked with production and that suitable incentive schemes should be devised in consultation with workers themselves in order to create a feeling among them that they will have a fair and adequate share of the benefit of increased production.

This leads me to one important point about which there has not perhaps been sufficient discussion, and that is the size of resources that are supposed to be handled by private enterprise in relation to the general business of national development. It has always struck me as somewhat peculiar that the totality of the resources at the disposal of private enterprise is regarded as a matter of, so to speak, uninhibited economics, whereas for the purpose of planned national development, it seems to me that there ought to be a more rational distribution of resources. In other words, when certain resources are drawn into private enterprise by way of profits or reserves, it is not solely a question of the dividends to the shareholders or the benefits extended to the workers from time to time as regular payments or as incentives and not even as prices charged to the consumers. It seems to me that one has also to consider what the totality of resources is that is used in this fashion and whether the State as responsible for the whole business of a planned economic development is not entitled to ensure that only those resources are allowed to flow into private industry which are needed for keeping it in good health. In other words, in countries which are under a totalitarian regime it has been shown that what is drawn by way of prices charged to the consumer partakes of the nature of a tax, and indeed in these countries it is a very familiar form of taxing the general public by means of prices charged, the analysis of which is not as easy as in a country which runs both a private and public form of enterprise. I think that this also is a question which must be considered very seriously by those who are responsible for private enterprise. In other words, under this construction, private enterprise ceases to be really private. It only becomes a form of enterprise which is for very good and valid reasons encouraged by the public, while other loads are borne by straighter forms of public enterprise. I am sure that if this is borne at the back of their minds by the managers or by those who finally control them, then it will be possible for the country to utilise its resources to the maximum possible advantage of planned development, and indeed in this view the whole business, therefore, is part of the total national fund which is available for economic development.

I have now covered most of the points to which I wished to draw attention and to which perhaps attention has not been drawn in the past. There are many important points which have been made in the past discussions which I assume as already accepted.

In conclusion, I hope that your movement will march from strength to strength, that bodies like yours will be more intimately associated with the deliberations of the planners, especially in connection with productivity, that through your efforts the stock of managerial talent that would be required on an ever-widening scale in the country will be secured, and that, therefore, every material assistance will be given to your Association in this business of the economic and social development of the country. With these remarks I have great pleasure in inaugurating your Third Annual Session.

Address at the training centre for the I.A.S. Probationers, 1959

Shri Jha, Ladies and gentlemen ! I am very happy that I have this opportunity of meeting you. When the School was in Delhi, I believe, I visited it once or twice, but for the last three years I should imagine I have not had the pleasure of meeting the young officers to train whom is the business of the School. I understand that there has been some change now in the constitution of the School and that the change now takes care of a very much larger number of people and that it is now called, so to speak, foundation training for fresh officers who are intended for different careers, followed by the continuance of the specific training for the I.A.S. probationers. In a sense that makes it a little more difficult to make observations which would be of interest to all the listeners because when it was a question of I.C.S. or I.A.S. probationers alone, one could perhaps narrow the field a little more. Administration is such a wide subject and I have had one way or the other so much experience of it that I find it very difficult to compress in a lecture what I might find it appropriate to say. There is also this difficulty, if it can be called a difficulty, that your ordinary course of lectures includes a great many lectures covering the subjects or the topics with which I might have dealt. Then, I have no doubt that a stream of literature on administration reaches you one way or another and that you take notice, from time to time, of the researches made, or the investigations carried out, or the views expressed by experts appointed for the purpose of investigating any particular aspect of administration or public administration generally. I do not know what connection exists between the School and the Institute of Public Administration, that is to say, whether the School is a corporate member of the Institute of Administration which would ensure that you would be getting their newsletter and whatever literature they publish from time to time. I refer to this particularly because, I believe, more than a year ago they held a seminar which was very important indeed from the point of view of administration. It was called, I think, the 'Morale of the Services'. Well, I suppose, it means the public services. That seminar was attended by administrators both from the public sector as well as from the private sector and the discussion that took place or the expression of views that occurred there was very frank and great many aspects of administration were animadverted on which one does not find ordinarily discussed in administrative circles. I wonder whether the record of that seminar has reached your School. I was also wondering whether those who are listening to me have read it because, obviously, of course, I cannot follow that up by saying that I shall now explain what happened there. But I should like to draw pointed attention to that record because, as I said, it contains a very full and frank expression of opinion, on matters administrative, by those who are in a very practical way concerned with it.

Apart from this, I assume that whatever good innate abilities plus good selection plus good initial training can do for you, is being done and will be done. That, of course, is half the battle so far as administration is concerned. There may be differences of opinion on actual methods of selection, the character of the tests, whether they are written or oral, or psychiatric—if you have any such thing as psychiatric tests—and there could always be a difference of opinion or room for modification in respect of the procedures followed for carrying out the actual training.

Well, one way or the other, these things have been in existence now for the last ten years, I suppose, if not longer, and indeed even in the old days there was something in the nature of training, apart from selection, which was not as elaborate as the training which you are receiving now, but which, nevertheless, secured for many a young officer a good start-off in his career. But these initial trainees, whether they were of old model or whether they are of the present model, can finally only be tested against the performance. In other words, those who are interested in administrative training, must, from time to time, be wishing to have a measure of the kind of lasting impact the training has made on those who have gone through the process. Put in other words, it really means that from time to time someone has to take a random sample, shall we say of the administration. I am not aware that there is any such system in existence for assessing how well or how badly, as the case may be, or how indifferently, the administrative machinery is working. Occasionally, on *a priori* grounds, or on the eve of major exercises in planning it occurs to some high level authority that the field should be surveyed, and we have had during the last ten years quite a large number of such surveys brought out by every distinguished experts, the last of which were the two reports produced by Dr. Appleby. That is one way, not necessarily a very complete or a very satisfactory way of finding out what the state of administration is. In any case, those findings have to be supplemented in other ways. There are other ways, so to speak, of testing the fruit of the tree that one has planted. One way is the purely fortuitous one of each one setting down his own experience either in his mind, or if he is a very conscientious person, then in some kind of documentary way.

During the last seven or eight years and certainly intensively during the last three years, Shrimati Durgabai Deshmukh, the Chairman of the Central Social Welfare Board, and myself have been touring round the country a great deal. We have necessarily been both of us very busy people. We have to synchronise our touring because we tour so often that if we did not synchronise it we should probably not be able to see each other. This synchronised touring has a great advantage. Both of us are ex-members of the Planning Commission and have still a certain amount of lingering interest in the formulation of plans, and what is much more to the point, in their implementation. She, of course, is concerned with the current implementation of many plans in the rural areas and I am implementing in my specific field a small part of the Plan—that which is concerned with the development of higher education. One way or the other, our tours take us certainly to district headquarters and now that many tehsil or taluk headquarters have collegiate institutions, I myself have also had the opportunity of visiting some of these places. So, all in all, we have a mucn more comprehensive opportunity of finding out for ourselves what exactly is happening in the country or in the countryside in regard to the implementaion of Plans. Wherever we go we make a point of contacting the Deputy Commissioner or Collector, as the case may be. We have also been meeting the Block Development Officers, the other officers of the Block Organisation, the Development Commissioners, occasionally a Commissioner—they are somewhat *rara ovis*, so to say, rare birds with extensive jurisdictions. We ask them how things are getting on. We compare notes with them. Then we meet, to a lesser extent, other people interested in other sectors of administration, shall we say, road transport, or export promotion or things like that. Well, that is entirely fortuitous. Over and above that, in the course of our many duties our responsibilities seem to be increasing rather than decreasing with age, which is a pity. We also have occassion to judge in matters small and matters big how things are happening.

To give you an instance, I had occasion to complain to the Minister for Communications only about a week ago that it had taken ten months for a telephone to be shifted from the house of the previous Secretary of the National Book Trust, of which I am the Chairman, to the house of the new Secretary. Also it had taken that much time to get an extension from the room of the Secretary to the office which is in the same building and in the same hall. We did not make this complaint lightly and the present Secretary of the National Book Trust is a very patient man. He has quite a file of correspondence with the Communications Officers in regard to the transfer of this telephone and it was only when he felt that he was quite desperate—that he had reached the blind alley, or whatever you may call it—that he thought it necessary to report to me. It is an interesting case study. The first excuses given were that the old Secretary would not part with his telephone. This answer was given after about six months of fruitless correspondence. Now this Secretary of the National Book Trust besides being a patient man is also a very careful man. So he went to the house of the old Secretary and asked him if it was a fact that he would not part with his telephone. He discovered then that the telephone had been removed within three days of the demitting of office by the old Secretary. So he wrote to the Communications people—the Divisional Engineer, I think he is called—stating this fact to him and wondering why then they had written that letter telling him that the old Secretary would not part with the telephone. The next rejoinder of the Department was a very neat one. They said, they could not trace their letter. So the Secretary sent a copy of the letter which we had on our file, and when they found that and satisfied themselves that it was not a forgery then they said that really that was not the reason. The real reason was that copper wire was in short-supply in this country. Now that sounded really a very hard reason, metallic reason. So this Secretary man who is a litterateur and a writer really was stumped by this copper wire. He was tripped and for a few months he really did not know what to do. Finally, when he thought that even copper could be produced in three or four months, I thought in his desperation, he wrote to me. I happen to know Dr. Subbaroyan and I thought perhaps as a new Minister, he might be very anxious to help old friends over their official difficulties. I wrote a letter to him and took it to him personally in the morning while he was sipping his morning cup of coffee. He was as always in a good mood. So he said he would take immediate action. That was on the 7th of October. On the 8th of October, an army of officials descended on the Secretary's house with copper wire and telephone and everything, and on the 9th the telephone was an accomplished fact. So it took two days under some influence for something which had required 10 months; and God knows how many more months might have been consumed in this particular process.

Now that is one example. I will not multiply them, but I will deal with two or three, to show how things are held up for several months. I do not say that they do not get held up in my own office. Since I am quite prepared to receive any complaints and I do receive complaints from Vice-Chancellors—I don't think the Vice-Chancellor present here (Shri Jha, in his dual role of Vice-Chancellor of the Varanasi

Sanskrit University) has complained. (We haven't yet started dealing with him). But many others have complained. Sometimes it is a question of staff being overworked. Sometimes it is a question of their being out on tour and so on.

Now we thought that so far as it was a matter of methods and organisation something can be done, and indeed the establishment of the Institute of Public Administration as well as the establishment of the Methods and Organisation Division was in a sense, I flatter myself, a healthy growth, out of the seed which was sown by me, I took the initiative in calling Dr. Appleby. It was Dr. Appleby who in his first report made these two major recommendations, whilst I was still Finance Minister, and these were the two recommendations that were accepted right in the beginning. I believe, both these organisations are doing very good work, but both of them appear to have come up against administrative problems. I quote an instance. When I took charge of the office of Chairman of University Grants Commission and in connection with a seminar on University Administration I suggested that either the Institute of Public Administration or the Methods and Organisation Division should help universities to have 'first' their own administrative machine examined and next, if necessary, (I am quite certain that it is very necessary) improved. That suggestion was accepted by several universities and they requested the Institute of Public Administration and the Methods and Organisation accordingly. The Institute said that they did not have any personnel who could be commissioned to visit universities and to examine their administrative affairs. They, therefore, passed the book to the Methods and Organisation Division. The Methods and Organisation Division apparently now is again suffering from excessive work, that is to say it has become a little unmethodical and many of them are on the eve of going abroad for some further training or the other; the number of officials which is necessary is very limited so that, I think, more than a year, about eighteen months have passed, since that seminar took place and although several requests were made by the universities it has not yet proved possible for either the

Institute of Public Administration, who have now absolved themselves of any responsibility, or the Methods and Organisation Division, to find out what is wrong with university administrations, and, I suppose, now there must be another division to find out what is wrong with the Methods and Organisation Division. So this is how these things happen.

The other difficulty about finding out what exactly the situation, apart from the absence of any systematic examination, is that people are not very willing to talk. Many an officer will talk. Many an officer will talk only if he is sure that there is nobody within fifty yards of the place and even then he is not quite sure that it will be right for him to give names or to give too many particulars which would enable something to be identified or someone to be identified and it is all very difficult. Therefore, I return to the point that really ought to be a good periodical check of the whole of this administrative procedures and machinery. It should not be in the context of planning. It can be combined with some kind of achievement audit—the sort of thing that one hears or one reads is done every few years in the U.S.A.—because unless one finds out how the administrative machinery is responding to the ever new and fresh calls made on them, it is very difficult to know how carefully trained people are faring and, what is more, whether any adjustment or change is called for even in the methods of training because things are moving so fast in our modern world that what was good and sufficient, say perhaps ten years ago, is no longer sufficient. Even before our eyes the industrial pool now has been formed. A new kind of a no category of duty now rests on government servants which in my old district administration would have been impossible to conceive.

So in order to keep pace with this improvement, with this fast development that is taking place, I think, there ought to be some machinery for finding out what exactly is happening. In the absence of that what one says has perhaps an impressionistic or qualitative value. How good the quality is, one cannot say, because quality without any consideration of quantity might be a very misleading guide, and that is why I am sometimes reluctant to make observations which appear to be somewhat critical in regard to the state of administration. Nevertheless, no one office is spared the duty of coming to judgments on sufficient evidence apart from magistrates. I am not now referring to formal proofs and the Indian Evidence Act. For, in my relationship with other human beings, I keep the Indian Evidence Act aside; similarly, in finding out what is happening and in summing up a situation one has to form judgments which are not based on the national sample survey or any other random sampling processes, because life is too elaborate and too complex for us to take that sample, so to speak, every time in a methodical way. Therefore, what I am saying should be considered subject to all these qualifications. Although I do not apologise for what I am saying, I am prepared to keep an internally open mind. These judgments are provisional and if anything to the contrary is proved then I am prepared to admit the force of those facts or those arguments and to change the totality of my views accordingly.

Subject to all these reservations and qualifications, I do not believe that our plan is going on as well as it should, or as the country deserves, or as the national necessity, which you might almost call an emergency, demands. The failures are in many fields. The large field in which measurements are very easy, is the field of agricultural production. You are all aware that 46 to 50 per cent of our national income comes from agricultural production and you also know—you have a syndicate on planning and you must be aware-that we have been setting certain targets for ourselves like increasing our national income by 5% or 6%. People are thinking now, indeed, in terms of the 3rd Five Year Plan. It does not require a very big arithmetical exercise to discover, that any failure in this respect occurs over 50 per cent of the field. Our successes have to be very resounding indeed, speaking in a purely statistical way, over the remaining field in order to get even your 5%. Secondly, 2% more of steel cannot be consumed with the same ease as 5% of grain ! In other words, a plan assumes that everything must be increasing in its place and that the gross figures are no guide to the success of our plan. In other words, a plan would not be a plan; just as an army would not be an army, unless it marches on all fronts; otherwise you will lose the battle. And that seems to be the situation here, that is to say, we have failed signally, I think, or certainly significantly—some people will say at least appreciably, in regard to the production of food. Now the trouble in our country with these measurements, again, is that providence is a very uncertain partner in this business. When we produced 68 million tons or 67 million tons in 1954-55 or 1955-56, we patted ourselves on the back. It is not an easy exercise but we did it and forgetting that Providence helped us a great deal. Well, then, according to the plan, beginning with 65 million tons, shall we say, we were supposed to travel by stages of three million tons each year to about 80 million tons by 1961. This means by the first year of the Plan we should have had 68 million tons. That very first year, instead of going up from 65 to 68 million tons, we thought more readily of the failure of Providence. We said this was all due to floods and drought and so on and so forth, forgetting that all the time we claim to have done something ourselves which might have perhaps tempered the result. In other words, it is my belief that if we had organised agriculture in that first critical and in many points of view disastrous, year (whether it is excessive imports or running through our foreign exchange or many other ways, it was a very bad year), and it was in that very year that we failed so much in organising agricultural production. Had we been careful, may be the floods and the drought (because we seemed to get bogged and parched during the same season which is a remarkable natural performance)—we might have increased it by 2 or 3 million tons at any rate. We might have kept it at 65 million tons instead of getting the 68 millions tons which was the target. But we went down to 62 which has started various economic trends and currents of an unfavourable kind which are showing their effect even today. Well that is another story. I would not take you into that in any great detail.

But I must say this, I feel confident that had there been a failure I have evidence gathered through my wandering and our joint wanderings—that nobody went about consciously to produce any kind of results. All the targets were agreed in Delhi after six months of disputation between the Planning

Commission and the Minister for Food and Agriculture. I wish it had been Minister for Agriculture and Food, but it is the way that it is put there, that is to say, food is more important because it is easier to import than agriculture which is more difficult to grow. Well, the process is very simple. Planning is not very difficult really. We said we are going to have 10 million tons or 60 million acres irrigated. Why then, our laboratory experiments show that for every acre which is irrigated we get one-third of a ton produce. Therefore irrigation of 16 million acres is equal to 5 million tons which is imperfect arithmetic, but the round figures of that is five million tons. Then, we are going to produce 37 lakhs of fertilisers because that is put down in the Plan, in the book of words; and now we know that 30 pounds of fertilisers produce about 60 pounds of grain. Therefore, you can make the calculation, I would'nt because it is very complicated. But that is so much, shall we say, X million tons. Then we are going to start 400 seed farms each with, say 25 acres. We know again from Pusa experiments that good seed brings 15 per cent more, therefore, so much more is so and after, as I said, a sparring which went about for six months, we agreed that 16 million tons of additional food grains can easily be produced. What can a country with so much labour and manpower not achieve? So we say that 16 million tons of additional food grains can be produced. But then nobody took care to ensure that these national targets were promptly passed on to the people concerned in smaller lots. Nobody can take care of 16 million acres of irrigation. It really means 100 acres of irrigation in one particular village and if in that particular village there is no channel from the distributory to the field, then even while you are within sight of the water, the grain will not grow. That again is commonsense. So, similarly, with fertiliser, in the first place, of course, we were not able to produce 37 lakhs tons of fertilisers. I am talking of the growth, not the Nitrogen—Nitrogen content is another very difficult matter—but this is the total fertiliser requirement. We get confused, someone says Nitrogen content, because it is reduced to Nitrogen content or Phosphorous content. But let us take simple figures. I think, we have reached the figure of about 18 or 19 lakhs tons of fertilizers including 400 thousand tons imported, on which foreign exchange has been spent. Sometimes the fertiliser is available, but the water is not available. Now, you know, what happens to plants when you put chemical fertiliser without water. It is a food which cannot be digested by the plants. Then, in regard to the seed farms, the calculation is quite simple, 25 acres in one State one district; there are 330 districts, shall we say, and 400 seed farms, so that on an average there is one seed farm for a district. Now, you think, that it would be easy to pick up 25 acres for a seed farm per district, but, you know, because the owner was probably an influential person and he was not going to let go his land for under rupees five thousand per acre, although land had been selling for Rs. 500 per acre in his village before. His eyes were set on rupees five thousand per acre. So, he seeks out his contacts in high places and, represents that it would be so very inequitable or inequitous that land should be taken from him at ridiculously low price. And Government said, yes, there is no reason why our citizen should be treated like this. We would not acquire this land by land acquisition processes. Let it be done as man to man, by negotiation. The man knows his power and can hold up negotiations; with the result that in the first two or three years no land was purchased for seed farms.

However, our principal difficulty was that nobody knew what he had to do in order to increase food production. I am now coming to a very important principle. Supposing you are Collector and you were asked what are your responsibilities with regard to food production, I fear it is a chronological history of inefficiency. In the first year of the Plan, the Collector said, "Sir, 28 per cent is the national target, I shall produce the national target."Well, that means all land is exactly the same. In this country, however, there is no such thing. We call it a sub-continent and harmony of diversities, but that is all wrong. Land is exactly the same according to the Collectors and they said, "Sir, we are producing 28 per cent because that is the national average. So, the State has the national average of 28 per cent. Therefore, my district has a national average of 28 per cent and, therefore, each cultivator has also 28 per cent. "So the problem is easy, I said, "I really find it very difficult to accept this. Surely yours is an irrigated land or unirrigated land or yours is a dry tract or you may not have this and you have no irrigation here. Now will you produce 28 per cent?" No, he said, that does not matter, I will produce 10 per cent or something; I will say that it is difficult to produce more because of the vagrancies of the monsoon. I think, when we, the press and other people started asking these inconvenient questions, the Collector changed their tune a little bit afterwards and next year we got the reply, Sir, I have got to increase 40 per cent. I said it is very good. It is a good district, 40 per cent, over what ? He said, "Those figures I do not know". Over 40 per cent; so I said, "Don't you know how much your district produces." He said and it was a Collector, "Sir, there is complete lack of co-ordination in this district. The Agriculture Department would not communicate the figures to me. So, how do I know?" I said, "Well, how much did you produce last year". Sir, he said,—and this was a Commissioner—"I am bad at statistics; I can't tell you these figures," or the alternative answer was "Sir, I have been in this district only for three months and I can't tell you. You know people are transferred very quickly especially if you fall foul of somebody or the other". So, I said, "what will you do ?" He said, "about 15 or 16 per cent more will be all right". I said "over what?" He said, again "that I can't tell you, but if somebody admits that it is 15 or 16 per cent, I have done my duty. I will say the floods came, the drought came or something else or the sowing did not take place in time". You will find it difficult to believe this, but fact is stranger than fiction. This is all leading to the main point that is that responsibility must be fixed if administration is to be successful. That is to say each man must know what he has to do and I am not now going down to the cultivator, although he also must know. Really the ideal state of affairs would be for us to say to a cultivator for the Gramsevak the Block Officer to say when he comes to the village, "if your field produces ten maunds we are going to arrange that your acres, will be irrigated. We will ensure that for your ten acres, three hundred pounds fertiliser must be given to you. we are taking care that on whatever it is, 30th of June, or middle of October, whatever it is, we will see that fertiliser is delivered to you." Now, of course, it will be through the service co-operatives when they are established, otherwise it would have been through the Agriculture Department which usually distributes these things. But I am not talking of the cultivator, but at least the Block Officer must be told that his production target here is 50 thousand maunds. (I am not sure whether that figure is correct for 100 villages. Please don't catch me up on that, but I am only taking it as an instance). "Now we expect 65 thousand maunds next year. If there are bad conditions we will find out what exactly went wrong, but otherwise we shall see that we give you the fertiliser or the irrigation or the distribution channel. If you don't dig them who will dig them". (I believe even in the Sharda Canal area after twenty years only 80 per cent of the area is now served by irrigation and there was a time when only 50 per cent was covered, near the Rampur side. Twenty long years it took to get the distribution channels dug. There are difficulties—where should the Colaba be; that fellow is taking more water; somebody else is taking a little bribe, and all kinds of difficulties which district officers know. So, there must be a responsibility which enables every cultivator to know his target figure. This obviously implies that the man must be sure that the fertiliser will arrive in time, the good seed (from the non-existing seed farm?) will arrive and if things go wrong, then he can say seed did not come, the fertiliser came two months after the sowing operations were over, or whatever it is, I know cases where the seed arrived one month after the last date for sowing, with the result that it was brought up by the well-to-do fellows in the village and eaten. Instead of going into the ground it went into his bowels, not of the earth. So, unless this very close organisation of millions and millions of cultivators is made or attended to, the target will not be achieved. The one great principle in administration is proper delegation, decentralisation and fixation of responsibility. Then, all of us are not saints. Some of you may be here—the present company is always excluded—

but you know that all of us do not have a sense of mission. Some of us are just ordinary people, may be lazy, if you are allowed to be lazy. We would put forward our best for if somebody pats us on the back and says this was a wonderful thing that you did.

Now I hope you will go on working accordingly either out of ambition or for the pure love of doing this—and I would rather say that I hope it is the latter rather than an ambition, that is to say, serve somebody else rather than pursue an enthusiastic service of oneself—there is need for decentralisation. But, then, I would say that there are various types of people and each cannot be trusted with decentralisation. Therefore, there is what is called a review. In other words, somebody higher up must from time to time, find out how the devolution is working. Now in the beginning he will often not know to whom to trust and whom not, but in a little while if he is at all worth anything, he will know that X, Y, Z, can be left to his job with an occasional visit and he will do it. Then A, B, C, shall we say a B.D.O., requires a little more attention. You have to go to him oftener. Well, you have to go a little oftener to him to find out what is going wrong. So, an appropriate review must go together with a certain amount of judicious praising and not too rigorous blaming. If a fellow goes wrong, don't give him up as hopeless. Try and redeem him and it is only then that, I feel, these things will work; and these principles are irrespective of what kind of machinery you have. That is to say, whether it is a Minister or whether it is a Development Commissioner or whether at the lower level it is a Panchayat or it is a Block or whether anybody comes in between, I mean to say a union body, a zila parishad and so on, because ultimately it is men who have to do things. Bodies do not do things. The great fallacy in our country appears to me to be to believe that what one man can do crowds of people can do. Now crowds of people cannot take decisions. Crowds of people can only tell you what they want in their own sphere of authority and give an indication of what the policy should be. It is a policy decision which should be taken by them. One of the causes of weakness in our country is that from the legislatures downwards everyone is trying to interfere with the doing of things rather than with the laying down of policy of how things should be done. Therefore, it is a matter of delegation. The policy-maker is delegating something and there are occasions for review which are open to the legislature. They are of a different character. The question and answer, the resolution, the half an hour discussion, the budget discussion; there are hundred and one occasions of going into these matters, but essentially it is individuals who do things and in order that they will do it properly, they must be encouraged to have a sense of responsibility, a sense of initiative. They must be treated lightly, so to speak, if they make minor mistakes. They must be encouraged and patted on the back if they do well.

Now, these things could happen in our country as they happen in other countries. There are no very innate reasons why these cannot be done. But, I believe, it has nothing to do with you. As I have mentioned it before at all levels the administration has to be strong. You cannot say that this is a political level and, therefore, the administration need not be strong. The point that I am mentioning you have no right to argue and I have no right to enter into a discussion about it, but it is my view that in the old days the executive councillors and executive members were picked men, most of them were picked men, who had a medicum of intelligence, integrity and diligence. These are the three things that are required. Well, they had them. Then, the whole administrative machine was like an organic pyramid, that is to say, some impulse in the top communicated itself in the least possible time to the bottom and, I think, within their very narrow sphere, which was law and order, they administered well. Now that our tasks are very much bigger, we must have a more sensitive machine in our hands. We must not have a machine which is less sensitive than the rulers of old had and yet there is a kind of democratic fallacy according to which we think that a Minister need not either be educated or intelligent or diligent. I am not saying that all Ministers are like that. What I am saying is you cannot tolerate any weak element at that level. If those elements are there, then many things, at least in that sphere, are bound to go wrong; and since planning is an all-out exercise where no one can afford to fail—it is like a battle, supposing on the left flank someone was to come to your relief at 2 O'clock—I don't know battles, this is what I read from books—and they do not appear there, there is a failure there because somebody waited by the roadside and had a little smoke, shall we say; well, then, you lose the battle and you might lose the war. Similarly, here, I have argued that one must ensure that there is a good level of "administration thoughts"; I am not saying that every man should be a fit man. Probably in our present democracy that might be difficult, but at every place at high level, there must be a few fit men who will give a tone and character to the administration because if that is weak then I fear—and I hope that will not happen to you because this batch must be a very good batch—that some of you will get a little domineering because the Minister leaves too many things to you. Some of you might get a little sluggish because you see that nobody is taking much notice. Some of you will lose that pristine purity of your enthusiasm which you will take from Mussoorie down to the plains, that we will now set the Ganges or the Jamuna or Cauvery, or whatever it is, on fire. You will go with that enthusiasm and you probably find that nobody seems to bother very much. That is one great danger.

Another minor evil, of course, of the political system—I hope it has stopped now—I hope it will be stopped by the time you go back to your posts—is that that you have to meet too many important people, that is to say, I think, your permanent residence is now on the railway station. I feel, very sorry for the Collectors and the others who have to leave their duties and to meet anybody and everybody to see to their accommodation in the Circuit House, to find that additional rooms are engaged for additional entourage and whose notice was not given before and all kinds of little problems arise there. Frankly, many Collectors have told me that about two-thirds of their time is taken up in this business. I believe, there are orders now to remedy this. But important men do not mind these orders, you know, they still want some evidence of their importance. So, it is in this atmosphere that you have to hang on to whatever you have to do.

I must draw to a close now. I was given one hour and I think I have done one hour. But I was going to say finally that you will ask me, what do you do then ? I say that I have only one answer for all life's problems and, that is to say, you frame your principles and you stick to them. I am sorry to have to strike a sort of an autobiographical note. But I find life fairly easy and smooth for the simple reason that I have about five or six guide posts, shall we say of principles. They may not be very good. I am not saying that they are the best guide posts that there may be, and I am sure on discussion I may change them. But who has the time to change all these things. Anyway, I have got five or six principles. I will do this, I will not do this. Shall we say, I will not grab power or pelf; I will not tell a lie and so on. Nevertheless I believe in them. However, unfortunate you may be, finally, what do you say to yourself ? "I have got a job. May be, my promotion is going to be retarded, because I said in my note whatever I wanted to say or I give attention to an unpleasant task or I take notice of somebody's brow-beating, who was a very important person in the political field. Well, I am going to be transferred from this district. What more can they do to me ?" Well, finally, I don't suppose they do anything violent to any person, but I say even if they do, what happens ? I illustrate this by a very small instance. Supposing someone is, shall we say, attacking your mother, then what will you do ? You won't say to yourself, I might be hurt or you know, I better not do that, because that fellow is a very strong fellow. No, you will resist. Whatever power you have you will use in order to prevent that fellow attacking your mother. Similarly, I say when there are principles then don't leave them and whatever the consequences, because your satisfaction will be then that you will respect yourself and I do not believe that there can be a higher satisfaction.

Welcome Address at the 30th session of the Indian Historical Records Commission

Mr. President, Members of the Commission, Ladies and Gentlemen : It is my privilege to welcome you on behalf of the Delhi University to the 37th session of the Indian Historical Records Commission. This is the second time that the Commission is meeting under the auspices of this University, the last occasion being when the Commission celebrated its Silver Jubilee in 1948. I trust we would have the pleasure of inviting you again for your Diamond Jubilee.

The last time the Commission met was in 1961. Following the Report of Committee on Archival Legislation (1960) presided over by my distinguished friend Dr. Tara Chand, I understand there was a good deal of thinking on the advisability of continuing this body. The Government has done well in reconstituting it, and not allowing it to lapse, for while the archivists have their own problems, the views of the general body of historians, the actual users of archives, are of equal relevance and importance. The Universities and learned institutions have a major role to play. For the development of archives on sound lines, there is need for a continuous dialogue between the two, the archivists and the historians, and the Commission provides the forum. The history of the Commission shows that, by drawing the attention of the Government year after year to the many problems and difficulties which historians of Modern India face, they have helped in the past in securing a liberalisation of the rules of access to Government records, in chalking out a publication programme, in the adoption of scheme for a National Register of archives of historical value in private hands, etc.

Let me say a few words on the role the Universities have to play in the development of archives. First of all, history teaching, at least at the University level, must become more source-conscious. This is the only way of developing the spirit of inquiry, which is as essential in historical as in scientific studies. Students do not often know, or realise to the extent they should, that the categorical statements of facts made in text-books or monographs are in most cases just opinions considered most plausible by the generality of scholars in the light of all the available information. It is the general belief that Asoka was a Buddhist, but how many students know that distinguished scholars like Father Heras have held that he was a Brahmanical Hindu, and this view is not without some sound arguments in its favour. Again, in a general book on English History is stated "Whne Pym and Hampden cried 'No taxation without representation' they meant 'No taxation of the rich', of the new urban, commercial class whom they represented, and Charles I lost his head, because he sought to tax those who could best bear the burden." I do not want to go into the merits of the question, but I do ask if students are aware that there is another view of that "tyrant" king. Apart from the notorious differences among scholars, often acrimonious to the point of fighting a duel, it is now realised that the historians' point of view changes with every advance in knowledge and the changes in the socio economic pattern of society. Every generation, in fact, reconstitutes its own view of the past. It would be an interesting experience to compare standard works published at intervals of 30-40 years on the history of the Greeks or of Tudor England or any field in which there has not been much of fresh "evidence" as such. I repeat, let students of history become more source-conscious : let them not take the things they read to be "settled facts", immutable and unchangeable.

Let me pass on to another aspect in which there is need for fresh thinking in our Universities. It is now a truism to say that history is not merely a study of wars and battles or of party strife. But are our Universities paying the attention that is necessary to the other aspects of history ? How many have made specific provision for advanced studies in history where it impinges on other branches of knowledge ? Let us remember that a knowledge of the historical background is an essential preliminary in any field of study, and one has to acquire the discipline of historical research before one can enter this field as an advanced student. In such an important subject as Economics, the University of Delhi seems to be the only University in India that has a Chair for Economic History. In the Sciences, no doubt, a Committee has been constituted to write the History of Science in India, but, to my knowledge there is no Chair, in the country, for the History of Science anywhere. Again, I understand a beginning has been made in the study of military campaigns in earlier times by scholars attached to the Historical Section of the Ministry of Defence, but we do not as yet have a Chair in Military History, devoted to the study of military weapons, strategy, etc.

To take up another aspect, since Independence, there has been remarkable growth in University education, and almost every region has one or more Universities. When Universities were few and we were making a beginning in historical studies, the concentration on subjects covering the whole of India was quite understandable. In such a vast country like ours, regional studies are of the utmost importance. To an inquiring mind, there should be quite adequate materials locally available awaiting exploitation. The study of the Lingayat Mutts in Mysore or of the socio-economic pattern of the zamindari system in Orissa in the last century is as valuable as the history of the war with Afghanistan in the time of Auckland. Greater attention to regional studies would give an indigenous vigour to the research activities of scholars in the different Universities and the hitherto untapped sources would yield a rich harvest. I am quite conscious that during the last decade there has been a distinct change for the better, but the glamour for subjects of All-India nature is still very pronounced.

The matters I have dealt with so far have a direct bearing on the subject of archives, for the approach of the archivist would be, at least to some extent, conditioned by the trends in historiography, as for instance in the appraisal of records for permanent preservation. The growing interest in Administrative History, Economic History, History of Science, etc. would have a long range effect on archival development. It is highly significant that you have chosen for the subject of your seminar on the present occasion "Sources and Problems of Business History in India from 1600-1900". The question posed before the seminar is whether we have the necessary materials for a proper study of the subject in our accessible records, public or private. Are there new sources which we could tap and make them accessible to scholars ? What steps are we to take to ensure that the future historian does not labour under the handicaps we suffer from now ?

I should also like to say a word or two on co-ordination of research in historical studies conducted at different centres. I understand that the National Archives of India is bringing out shortly a bulletin of research theses and dissertations in in Modern Indian History for the period 1961-66 covering all the Universities and research centres, and similar bulletins have been issued in the past. I cannot overstress the value of such publications, and I suggest that it should be issued regularly every year.

Further, I understand that a distinguished member of your Commission Dr. N.K. Sinha has been engaged on behalf of the National Library, Calcutta, in the compilation of an exhaustive bibliography of all publications, official and non-official, bearing on Modern Indian History prior to 1900. We all realise that this is a work of a seminal nature, and historians await its publication eagerly. I should like to make only one suggestion, which must have occurred to those who have planned it. Whatever care may be taken to make the bibliography exhaustive, I have no doubt that quite a large number of books found in smaller, out of the way, collections would be left out. A conscious effort should be made to trace them out and an Addendum issued every year.

This brings me on to the question of access to books and records. It is unfair to expect scholars to move to remote libraries to consult a couple of rare books or records. The solution lies in greater resort to the system of inter-library loans; there should be greater readiness on the part of libraries to send out their books, despite the danger of their occasionally being lost. Rare books, reports and records could be microfilmed and the microfilm copies could be lent out. Microfilm is not only a means of preservation but also of making the materials more easily accessible to scholars wherever they are. For instance the National Archives of India has a complete set of the Parliamentary Papers of Indian interest from 1800 to 1900 in microfilm. It should be possible, say for a scholar at Trivandrum, to consult any paper of his interest in his own place without having to come all the way to Delhi for the purpose. But this presumes a plentiful supply of raw film, which, I understand, is in very short supply owing to foreign exchange difficulties. I should say that local manufacture of raw film to ensure cheap and plentiful supply and also the machinery for microfilming etc. are matters of urgent necessity, let me say as important as setting up of a major library. There is also need for setting up, at least in a few centres, duplicating machines such as the Xerox machine. The National Archives and some University Libraries should be enabled to own such machines within the next 5 or 10 years so that important documents and reading material for students should be available to them.

A word before I close on our own activities in the Delhi University in the field of your interest. As you know, our History Department is a major centre of historical research in Modern Indian History, and the location of the National Archives and the offices of the Government of India have greatly contributed to this. In the last few years the number of scholars registered for research has gone upto 130 this year, of which the majority offer Modern period as their field. More than a dozen scholars have been awarded Doctoral degrees. The setting up of a separate section of Economic History has been an important development, and this young Department has been conducting research. The History Department has acquired, you would be interested to know, a number of private papers of the British Viceroys, Secretaries of State and officials from the India Office Library, London, such as Lansdowne Papers, Hamilton Papers, Ampthill Papers, Temple Papers and the Minutes of the Council of Secretary of State. Orders have been placed for Elgin papers.

We have also conducted two seminars in the last two

years on Ideas influencing social, economic and political developments from 15th to 19th centuries and these have greatly helped in clearing up ideas and bringing out talent. Besides the two seminars to which scholars from various Universities were invited, the Department has been conducting seminars on various subjects which are attended by teachers of colleges and research scholars.

It is expected that the deliberations of these seminars would be published shortly. We have also accepted the principle laid down by the Commission that every University must have a trained Archivist to take care of its records and we are giving effect to it.

In conclusion, let me extend to you once again our warm welcome and wish you every success in your deliberations.

THE GOALS, TARGETS AND MEASUREMENT OF DEVELOPMENT*

At the outset I should like to express my deep appreciation of the honour done to me by the Executive Council of the Nagpur University by inviting me to deliver the series of Kinkhede Lectures for the session 1961-62. This series commemorates one of the most respected of Nagpur's great men of the past, who graced the public life of the city and this region by his exemplary life and achievements. During the 30 years and more that have elapsed since the endowment was established lectures have been delivered by celebrated savants and public men, such as, to name only a few, the late Professor R. D. Ranade, the late Dr. Sir Hari Singh Gour, the late Acharya P. C. Ray and the late Dr. J. C. Ghosh, and I feel proud and privileged to have been invited to deliver the lectures for the current session in this series.

Unlike most of the previous speakers, I cannot claim to be a specialist of any profundity on the subject of my choice, although I have had during the course of a busy and varied career of public administration a great deal to do with matters concerning the economic development of India and have also had a long connection with some of the international organizations concerned with development.

Important as the subject of this lecture series is, I am aware that *prima facie* there would seem to be little room for any dissertation on the principal requisites of economic development after the publication of the Third Five Year Plan for India a few months ago. Since its publication and indeed, whilst it was being formulated, a great deal has been or was said on this topic by professional economists and public men, as well as by spokesmen of important international institutions. Long past is the time when India's efforts in the shape of planned development appeared to be a somewhat neglected field for professional economists, especially of the West. The concentration on planned

*R. B. Bapu Rao Kinkhede Lecture for 1961-62.

economic development of some sort has now become an almost universal preoccupation in the under-developed countries of the world, and correspondingly the scope and frequency of studies, lectures, seminars, symposia and conferences on the subject has also grown immeasurably. Indeed, one might wonder whether it is now possible for any serious student of the subject to keep in touch with all the literature that has emerged in regard to the various aspects of development. Against this background, I wish to make it clear that what I propose to say in the course of the three lectures of this series is not intended to be as from any strictly professional angle. My object is rather to give a bird's eye-view of the progress and main implications of the development effort in the under-developed countries, using illustratively the particulars that are available as a result of India's experience of planned development. In other words, what I wish to expose is a bird's eye-view which will necessarily not be concerned with the minutiae of any aspect of the development process—a bird on the wing cannot gather worms.

Historically, the present century will probably be called the century of emancipation. Whether for the remaining part of the century this process will lead to the ideal goal of world union or will be cataclismically terminated by universal destruction brought about by nucleur weapons is anybody's guess. But my own personal hope and expectation is that, the many world tensions that seem to point to such a dire possibility will gradually subside and that the century may well end with universal liberation leading to a world of co-operative peace and prosperity.

It is necessary at an early stage of any discourse to define one's terms, and in that connection I should like to make it clear that in most discussions the words 'developed' or 'under-developed' or 'developing' are used only in a relative sense. In other words, it is readily recognized that even in the most advanced countries the process of development is not held to have been completed. Also, there is probably no under-developed country in which some development has not occurred in the past. This definition has some bearing on the roles that developed and developing areas of the world, respectively, are expected to play in this world-wide process of development. It has also a particular bearing on the measure of assistance that is expected from the so-called developed countries towards accelerating the process of development of the under-developed, or, to use a later euphemism, developing countries. As a result of the collective efforts that have with greater frequency recently been made, especially after the emancipation of large regions of Africa, a developing country might be at a stage at which it not only needs assistance from others more favourably situated, but is also in a position to extend some assistance to countries relatively less developed, India being a case in point.

As a result of a great deal of public discussion, as well as the series of reports published by the Planning Commission, in India, at any rate, there is a fairly clear appreciation of the goals of development. In the introductory chapter to the Third Five Year Plan, the Planning Commission, for instance, explain that the basic objective of India's development must 'necessarily be to provide the masses of the Indian people the opportunity to lead a good life' and add that that indeed is the objective of all countries and their people, even though a 'good life' may be defined in many ways. In the discussions that have taken place in regard to the objectives of India's development, reference is often made to raising the level of material prosperity by employing all the scientific and technological resources that are available in the modern environment without doing any violence to the moral and ethical values which have traditionally been handed down in the country. The task is stated to be one of bringing about a synthesis appropriate to the genius of the country between tradition and modernity.

Whilst this is probably correct, for practical purposes it becomes necessary in any process of planned development to define the material targets, as also to have at one's command the means of measuring the progress that has been achieved towards the attainment of these targets ; and for this purpose it is customary to depend upon some easily comprehensible macro-indices which would present no great difficulty in their compilation. Most knowledgeable people recognize, for instance, that a minimum economic base is necessary in modern societies for the effective functioning of democratic institutions and the creation of conditions in which the individual citizens will have opportunities for rising to their full stature. Against the present range of economic bases as measured by per capita national incomes, many authorities hold, and I am inclined to agree with them, that the level of per capita national income attained in countries like Italy or Japan may be regarded as more or less the indispensable minimum level to be aimed at in any process of development. This level lies round about Rs. 1,500. One authority, quoted by Shri V. T. Krishnamachari, former Deputy Chairman of the Planning Commission, in his book *Planning in India*, defines low per capita income as one below Rs. 750. It is only when one studies the per capita national incomes in groups of countries belonging to the under-developed part of the world that one realizes the extent of stark poverty and backwardness prevailing in them. Reliable figures in this respect are not easy to come by, but sufficiently dependable approximations are available for large regions, such as Asia, Africa and Latin America ; and, of course, the more advanced the country is the more dependable are the figures available in respect of it, although allowance has to be made for the different ways in which they are constructed. There is reason to believe, for instance, that for the best part of South and South-East Asia the per capita national varies between Rs. 300 and Rs. 500, and that for many African or Arab countries the corresponding figure would probably also lie within this range, sometimes near the lower figure, sometimes near the higher. As against this, the per capita national income for Latin America is about the same as for Italy or Japan, whilst for many European countries and the U.S.S.R. the per capita income would range about Rs. 3,000. Per capita incomes of Rs. 5,000 and over are to be found in countries which are usually classed as advanced, and in some of the most prosperous ones there is reason to believe that the figure lies somewhere round Rs. 10,000. These figures bring out in strong relief the distressing level of poverty in a large part of the globe's surface. India's own per capita national income was at the end of the First Five Year Plan no more than Rs. 282, and one of the main objectives of the Second Plan was to double it by 1975-76. According to figures quoted on page 28 of the Third Five Year Plan Report, allowing for increases in population, the income per head in India should go up from around Rs. 330 at the end of 1960-61 to about Rs. 385 in 1966-67, Rs. 450 in 1971 and Rs. 530 in 1976.

I assume that the relationship between the rate of economic and social progress and the rate of investment is by now well known, in an over-simplified way, since there are here many fine points over which professional economists wrangle. Suffice it to say that any movement of the per capita incomes at the rates mentioned above would, illustratively, in India imply a rise of the rate of investment from 7.5 per cent of the national income at the end of First Plan period, and 11 per cent as at the beginning of the Third Five Year Plan, to 14-15 per cent by the end of the Third Plan, 17-18 per cent by the end of the Fourth Plan and 19-20 per cent by the end of the Fifth Plan. Domestic savings would have to rise in corresponding measure from about 8.5 per cent at the beginning of the Third Five Year Plan to 11.5, 15 to 16 and 18 to 19 per cent of the national income at the end of the Third, Fourth and Fifth Plans. As the Planning Commission point out, these sets of figures imply that, progressively, external aid will form a diminishing proportion of the total investment and that by the end of the Fifth Plan, i.e., by 1976, the Indian economy will be strong enough to develop at a satisfactory pace without being dependent on external assistance outside of the normal inflow of foreign capital.

As has been stated earlier, the Indian Plan has been used as an illustration. This is because the process of planning amongst under-developed countries has been carried out in India more systematically than in most of the other countries in Asia, Africa, or even Latin America, although for possibly different reasons. It may be stated that the more developed a country is the less the degree of planning needed, but the greater is the availability of statistics by which to measure progress, and the less developed a country is, the more probable it is that even some of the basic statistical instruments for the measurement of economic growth have yet to be fashioned. It will be easily conceded that measurement is a necessary part of the whole effort of economic development, whether such development is a planned one or a semi-planned one or an entirely unplanned one. India may well congratulate herself in this respect on having at its disposal a fairly well-advanced statistical implement in the shape of the Indian Statistical Institute, which is now by statute an Institution of National importance, and which gives material assistance in the working out of perspective, that is, long-term planning. There are also an active Central Statistical Organization and statistical organizations of varying quality and efficiency in the States. The Indian Statistical Institute also runs an international course for the training of statisticians for the South and South-East Asia region on behalf of the ECAFE, and there is reason to believe that before long almost every country will have a reasonably efficient statistical organization that will enable the government to secure the data by which to measure the success or otherwise of the current efforts at economic and social development.

Amongst special statistical studies few could have greater importance than those concerning the accumulation of savings, on the one hand, and the variation in the population, on the other. In the case of savings, the complexity of the problem varies with the stratification of the society, and averages are less and less meaningful as the range of disparities increases. There is reason to believe that in India, for instance, about half the number of families, far from being in a position to save, would probably need assistance from the State in order to furnish to them the minimum necessary for human life in the shape of food, clothing and shelter. It is probable, from the figures available, that saving to any noticeable extent is only possible in the case of a very small fraction, perhaps less than 1 per cent, since even amongst those who pay income-tax in the lower income groups, at the present prices, it is hardly possible to conceive of a capacity to save.

As regards the growth of population and connected questions, although in India there is now an active Demographic Institute and some studies made by Indian scholars as well as by foreign scholars are available (for instance, *India's Population* by S. N. Agarwal of the Institute of Economic Growth, Delhi, and *Population Growth and Economic Development in Low-Income Countries* by Coale and Hoover of the Princeton University), there is much weakness in evidence in regard to the implementation of measures taken by the State for controlling the growth of the population. It has already been demonstrated that the original calculations of the First Five Year Plan, and to some extent of the Second Five Year Plan, have been seriously upset by the discovery that the population was growing at a rate larger than what was assumed by the planners. Indeed, this must vitiate the whole of the planning process, and not only is it necessary further to strengthen demographic studies, but it is also necessary to ensure that measures for population control are formulated in an adequate way so as not merely to be symbolic, but to make an impact on the situation, and, what is even more important, implemented to the fullest possible extent. The 10th Annual Report of the Consultative Committee of the Colombo Plan points out that population growth has far out-stripped estimates in the region of the Plan, i.e., South and South-East Asia. However, this is a subject to which a reference will have to be made in a later lecture.

Coale and Hoover have in their *Study of Population Growth and Economic Development in Low-Income Countries* discussed both the effects of population growth on economic development and the effects of economic development on population growth. As regards the former, it is probably widely known that the optimum population theory is in essence an exercise in comparative economic statistics. But the relation of population to the other factors of production is not fixed and will vary with the progress of education. Apart from this, in low-income countries the limiting factor most prevalent is lack of capital ; others may be land or natural resources generally. In such regions it is especially difficult to attain adequate levels of investment and there is no visible way by which more rapid population growth can evoke a significantly greater flow of invested resources. Such a possibility may exist only in countries with highly industrialized economies. Thus, in low-income areas, effective demand as a result of a fast-growing population being non-existent, rapid growth of population merely tends to diminish the amount of capital available for increasing the average productivity of the work force and increasing the average per capita income. Lastly, the distribution of population by age is also an important factor. A change in the growth rate caused by a change in the fertility factor will bring about a large change in the percentage distribution ; whereas a change brought about by variation of the mortality factor will have only a slight effect on such distribution. Thus in low income agrarian areas, which usually have high birth rates, no matter what the mortality levels, the age-distribution is broadly based and sharply tapering, with a large fraction of the population under 15, making the burden of dependency relatively high. This burden is not reduced by a lowering of mortality, particularly among children, although of course for many social and psychological reasons it is a highly desirable goal. A decrease in childhood mortality will no doubt yield a larger population at the working ages, but these being parents, there will also be a rise in the number of children. What is needed for a smaller number of dependents is therefore a decline in birth-rates. Thus a continuation of a more rapid population growth inevitably produces, in a closed population, such as India's, larger numbers ; a slower rate of population growth brought about by a reduction in birth rate inevitably has desirable age-distribution effects.

As regards the less commonly known effects of economic development on population growth, the first felt effect is a reduction in the death-rate. As Coale and Hoover summarize it, 'economic development involves evolution from a predominantly agrarian economy to an economy with a greater division of labour, using more elaborate tools and equipment, more urbanized, more oriented to the market sale of its products, and characterized by rapid and pervasive changes in technique. It also involves improvements in transportation, communications, and productivity'. It has been seen in the economic growth of Europe, the United States, Canada, Australia, New Zealand and later of Japan, that these improvements result in bringing about a striking reduction in death-rates. The more direct factors such as improving medical knowledge and increasingly effective public heath methods also contribute to this result, which in this aspect is not confined to fully advanced countries alone.

The theory of the demographic transition asserts that the high birth rates, as well as the death rates, characteristic of an agrarian low-income society, are affected by economic development. The custom of the small family starts to prevail in the urban groups at the higher end of the socio-economic scale and spreads to smaller cities, lower-income groups, and eventually to rural areas. This is undoutedly facilitated by the availability of effective contraceptive devices. But decline in birth rate typically occurs after a substantial time-lag, in comparison with the decline in mortality rates. This lag continues until further decline of the death rate becomes difficult to attain and the birth rate again approaches equality with the death rate and a more gradual rate of growth is established, with low rises of mortality and small families as the typical pattern. But substantial economic improvement may be a sufficient condition for a decline in mortality, although it is not today a necessary condition. Also it should not be assumed that the decline in mortality will necessarily be a cause for a substantial ferility reduction, judging from the experience of countries like Ceylon. Also, as the examples of Egypt and India show, urbanization is not always sufficient to cause a reduction in birth rate. In such countries the rapid growth rate will make it difficult to accomplish the economic and social changes that reduce fertility. (Thus two important desiderata emerge, one, that the pace of economic development must be as high as possible and, two, effective direct measures to control the growth of population must be taken.

It is against this background that the adequacy or otherwise of the rate of development in any developing country has to be judged. Judged by this criterion, the current rate of growth in India is below 4 per cent per annum and must be pronounced to be dangerously pedestrian. Japan is forging ahead at 7 to 8 per cent, Germany at about the same rate, and Russia perhaps faster. The actual rates of increase in national income in some of the Asian countries as given in the Statistical Year Books of the United Nations are as follows :—

Burma	5 per cent
Ceylon	3·7 ,,
China Mainland	12·3 ,,
Indonesia	3 ,,
Japan	8·5 ,,
Pakistan	2 ,,
Philippines	5·7 ,,
Thailand	4·9 ,,

It is clear that with rates of growth of the population over 2 per cent, not only are disparities between the developing nations and the developed nations increasing, but also, internally, there is every possibility of explosive social tensions being built up.

It is not sufficient in such a situation to claim that much progress has been achieved or that Asian or Indian traditional cultural values inculde a spiritual sense of contentment, which will indefinitely tolerate widening international disparities or a sub-human existence for nearly half the population, as is the case in India. It may be that the domestic social inequalities in India are not as glaring as, say, in Latin America (at a level of per capita income about five times as high). But with the awakening that must come with spreading education and the assertiveness that is implicit in the exercise of adult franchise, the pathetic contentment so characteristic of pre-independence India will soon be, if it is not already, a thing of the past. The consequences of such accumulated social tension are incalculable and will probably prove to be uncontrollable.

Nothing illustrates the dangerous potentialities of the situation more vividly than the statistics in regard to unemployment and under-employment. The Third Five Year Plan Report of India estimated that the backlog of unemployment at the end of the Second Plan was 9 million, in addition to under-employment believed to be of the order of 15-18 million. During the Third Plan period the addition to the labour force is reckoned to be of the order of 17 million, about a third of the increase being in the urban areas. The additional employment generated during the Plan period is estimated to be 14 million, leaving the need to find employment opportunities for three million persons, and this is expected to be found through programmes of rural electrification, development of rural industrial estates, promotion of village industries and effective re-deployment of man-power, plus a specially organized 'rural works programme which will provide work for an average of, say, 100 days in the year for about 2.5 million persons and, if possible, more'.

It is abundantly clear that targets such as those mentioned above imply 100 per cent fulfilment if a socially and politically dangerous situation is to be avoided.

It is not only the volume of employment that matters, but also the quality. One of the accepted criteria of development is the proportion of active population engaged in agricultural operations. The following figures, although they are somewhat old (1950-54), give some idea of where India stands :

Proportion of active population engaged in agricultural operation

Country	*Year*	*Percentage*
U.S.A.	1950	12
France	1954	27
Italy	1951	42
Japan	1951	48
China	1951	63
India	1951	71

It would appear that there is correlation between this proportion and development and it is desirable to include it amongst selected indicators of growth. There is evidence to show that whilst in Italy, Japan and France the proportion has steadily fallen, in India it has remained almost stationary.

It has been stated earlier that the basic objective of India's development must necessarily be to provide the masses of the Indian people the opportunity to lead a good life. This remains valid in spite of the much-affirmed Indian traditional value of plain living and high thinking—a value which appears to predominate at present only in regard to its first part. As a matter of fact, for most people in India the living is too plain to sustain life properly. Taking food stuffs alone, the shortages on even the lowest acceptable standards are as follows :—

	Percentage of shortage
Foodgrains	5
Vegetables	66
Milk	61
Oil and Ghee	65
Fresh meat and eggs	88

On any internationally applicable scale of adequacies the shortages in most of these items would be still more gloom-producing.

These shortages are symptomatic of both the rapid growth of the population and the low agricultural productivity or insufficiency of land resources for sustaining both man and beast. Unless the present trends are checked the competition for land for sustenance between human beings and cattle in India will soon assume grave proportions, with disastrous consequences to the conservation of land surfaces. Increasing population and depletion of soil resources constitute a vicious spiral, the end of which is hard to foretell—it may even mean a breakdown of the social order in a near-desert country. It is in this context that I deplore the dilatory action in evidence in regard to soil conservation measures, which are discussed at pages 367 to 373 of the Third Five

Year Plan. The provision in the First Plan was only Rs. 1.6 crores, which was raised to Rs. 18 crores (actually spent) in the Second and to Rs. 72 crores for the Third Plan period. It is to be hoped fervently that achievement will be fully satisfactory in this vital field.

The Third Five Year Plan Report states that mobilization of resources for securing an adequate rate of growth is the crux of the problem of planning in an under-developed economy. A survey of the material and human resources of the country was included among the basic functions of the Planning Commission of India when it was first constituted in 1950. But there is no convincing evidence to show that such a comprehensive survey has been carried out or that the results are available for study in one place.

The very specialized calculations of man-power resources, particularly trained man-power, had a somewhat late start in India and even now it is not clear that these requirements have been calculated as precisely as possible or that necessary preparatory steps, particularly in the field of education, have been adequately initiated. Essentially this is a matter of what is called perspective or long-term planning, since investment in trained personnel takes at least ten years to mature.

It has been assumed implicitly so far that the steady improvement of per capita incomes through the Plan periods means *pro tanto* the attainment of the goals of development, viz., improving the conditions of life for the people. But even a superficial examination of the break-down of the average per capita income and related figures leads one to suspect that even after a decade of planned development, economic disparities in India continue, even if they may not have been worsened. Shri K. N. Raj of the Delhi School of Economics, who studied the matter with some care, found that significant increases in per capita income have taken place only in a few States, and as much as 30 per cent of the increase in total income during the decade has accrued to the higher-income groups. 'Is it surprising,' he asks, 'that the bulk of the population of this country should feel that they have not benefited in any obvious way from the development of the last decade ?' Many other observers of the Indian scene have expressed the same doubt, and indeed some hold more specifically that India's planned economic development has brought no solution of the country's basic problems like rural unemployment, the depressed condition of the weaker sections of the rural population, the concentration of wealth and economic power, the growth of congested industrial centres and slums, the dissolution of social ties and moral values to which Indian culture has attached fundamental importance. The Central Government has appointed an expert committee to investigate this distribution aspect of the growth of national income. If the findings of the committee confirm these views or doubts, then obviously a great deal of re-thinking will be called for of the Plan priorities and of State policies. For the situation would then be such as not only to violate the prescriptions of the Directive Principles of State Policy laid down in the Constitution, but will also retard the implementation of the Plan itself, thereby creating a vicious circle. More will be said about this last aspect concerning public cooperation in the third lecture.

The kind of Plan that is adopted has obviously a bearing on this vital question of distribution. But, furthermore, what the situation calls for is a more deliberate influencing of the growth and allocation of national income than at present by means of appropriate wage policies, taxation measures and direction of investment. Effective means have to be employed for discouraging consumption of all goods except the bare necessities of life and certainly of what is called conspicuous consumption. All possible efforts have only to be made to induce people to work more and to greater purpose. Short of compulsion, there would also have to be a conscious channelling of the surpluses of the richer regions for the benefit of the poorer ones, both in the national and in the international spheres, of which latter more will be said later.

It is for this reason that what the Planners call the approach to the Plan and what economists call models of economic growth are of vital importance. Indeed, the justification of planning as a means of not only inducing economic growth but also of ensuring desired trends in distribution of the incomes generated lies in the solution it offers to the problem of removing disparities as rapidly as possible.

It is now widely recognized that the less developed a country is the greater is the part that the State has to play in inducing the optimal economic growth of the country. In these countries, as Dr. Thomas Balogh has pointed out, the price-mechanism, which is the main regulator of a system of capitalist enterprise, cannot bring about optimal results, which can only be secured if certain conditions are fulfilled—conditions which by definition will not be present in under-developed countries. These are a speedy elimination of unemployment and under-employment, a politically sustainable distribution of income, free play to consumer's tastes, competitive markets and supply of capital responding to relative profitability, and what is profitable must not involve disproportionate social costs. In under-developed countries the State has to regulate or consciously influence the price mechanism through allocation of resources, the economically sound location of new industrial plant, fix prices for agricultural products so as to encourage production, extract as much as possible from the prices of non-essential goods by appropriate taxation policies and generally maximize the surpluses from the public sector for maximum speeding up of investment.

Apart from the judicious control of prices the State has to furnish the social capital or the infra-structure of development, such as power, transport, communications, and is primarily responsible for providing the investment necessary for utilization of the human resources by better education and improved health, especially the development of modern industrial skills.

As the Indian Planning Commission themselves concede, 'to a greater extent than in the past, during the Third Plan the direction and management of the Indian economy will call for improved methods and machinery for planning and execution, better statistical and economic intelligence, greater appreciation of technological and other developments occurring in different fields, fuller knowledge of the country's potential resources and, generally, for more systematic analysis and research'.

There has been a great deal of confusion in India in recent years in regard to the relative importance of agriculture and industry in the process of planned economic development. It has often appeared superficially that the emphasis has shifted from one to the other in an uncertain fashion. The fact is that this changing stress is a matter only of strategy, and not of doctrine. Development undoubtedly implies increasing industrialization and a steadily diminishing dependence on agriculture as a means of living of the people. But agricultural improvement is no less necessary for development than the provision of social overheads like fuel, power, transport and the like. I quote here again what Shri V. T. Krishnamachari has quoted in his book, *Planning in India* : "As Dr. Kuznets has said, 'at the danger of stressing the obvious, one may claim that an agricultural revolution—a marked rise in productivity per acre in agriculture—is a pre-condition of the industrial revolution."

The following figures, only a few years out of date, of productivity of agriculture will, in this context, speak for themselves :

Country	*Productivity in lbs. per acre*					
	Crops					
	Wheat	*Rice*	*Maize*	*Sugarcane*	*Cotton*	*Tobacco*
Egypt	1,918	2,990	1,891	70,302	535	
Germany	2,017	-	2,828	-	-	2,127
Japan	1,713	3,494	1,392	47,534	196	1,665
U.S.A.	812	2,185	1,579	48,770	268	882
India	660	1,240	803	34,944	89	987

To conclude with, it would be of interest to reflect on the following figures relating to India's Second Plan showing the percentage of shortfall in the various industrial production targets set for 1960-61 (quoted in a recent article by Dr. B. N. Ganguli) :—

	Shortage percentage
Finished steel	49
Nitrogeous fertilizers	62
Phosphatic fertilizers	54
Textile machinery	47
Cement machinery	70
Paper machinery	100
Aluminium	26
Newsprint	88
Chemical pulp	100
Soda Ash	37
Caustic Soda	26
Dye Stuffs	50
Cement	35

In the face of continued low agricultural productivity and poor performance in the industrial sector, the conclusion seems inescapable that there has been either imperfect planning or unsatisfactory implementation or a combination of both.

PROBLEMS OF NATIONAL INTEGRATION

The phrase 'National Integration' involves a logical inconsistency. A nation is a social organism constituted by individuals or social groups, as a structure of power which is centred in an individual ruler, a feudal group, a military caste, a high bureaucracy, an economic upper class, a priestly hierarchy, a ruling committee, or committee of a parliament or a revolutionary vanguard. It is therefore already integrated. But this integration is always the subject of a tension between silent acknowledgement of the people and the power of enforcement. The ruling minority in such a social group are both the objects of the silent popular acceptance and the agents of the enforcement of the law against the wilfulness of any member of the group, or, in an organization formed by groups, of any group or groups. If the unity of the organization is to be preserved, in addition to this balanced tension of acceptance and enforcement, the ruling minority, i.e., Government, must express, the communal spirit of the groups, their ideals and valuations. The spirit of the group is expressed in all its utterances, in its laws and institutions, in its symbols and myths, in its ethical and cultural forms. The balance of acceptance and enforcement and its balance in turn with the spirit of the group preserve the unity of the power group. Any disturbance of either balance tends to weaken unity and encourage a trend towards disintegration.

These factors, making for preservation of unity or liable to encourage disintegration, are not operative entirely on their own. They are constantly affected by the encounters of other power-groups, and as a result every power-group is apt to experience growth or disintegration. Each power-group, i.e., nation, has its own geographical space and also radiates its power into the larger space of mankind, by economic expansion, spread of culture and a sense of a mission, or what Dr. Paul Tillich in his thought-provoking book, *Love, Power and Justice*, calls vocational consciousness.

'Today two great imperialistic systems fight with each other in terms of both force and vocational consciousness' which in the case of Russia is a fanatical avowed concern for equality and in the case of America is 'to establish the earthly form of the Kingdom of God by a new beginning'.

The rise of rival embracing power-groups involves a decrease in national sovereignty, and a question arises whether the world is about to witness the emergence of a united mankind. Pondering three possible alternatives, it seems doubtful if as a result of this power-struggle any decentralization will take place; the establishment of a world state appears to be impossible in the face of divergent vocational consciousness and the absence of spirit of unity, which will induce universal silent acknowledgement; there may arise one power structure, if there is a minimum of suppression and law and justice and uniting love are embodied in this power, although new situations disrupting such a universal power centre are not improbable.

As things are, therefore, the greatest danger to any nation's unity is the cold war between the world's two gigantic power blocs. In the face of this threat even a profound spirit of unity in symbols, myths, culture, language and the rest has been and is no guarantee against disruption, witness the disintegration within the last decade of Korea and Viet-Nam. Even where the cold war is not very hot, a disruption may occur, as, for instance happened recently in respect of the U.A.R. and Syria. The avowed justification in all such cases is either imagined or real group grievances or divergent ideologies of the ruling minorities in the concerned groups. The seal is set on such disruption when other powerful groups, i.e., nations, recognize the fragment from the erstwhile united nation.

It is against this theoretical background that one should examine the question of India's national integration. In doing this it is as well to recall both the disintegration that the sub-continent suffered in 1947 and the integration that took place in 1949 in the Indian portion. The partition was enforced by irreconcilable group interests and facilitated by availability of geographical space for the seceding community the majority of which professed another faith. The integration of the former princely States proved possible because of the essential unity of culture of the numerous separate groups with the other groups forming India.

It is worthwhile pausing to consider here how within barely 15 years of the achievements of independence any threat could possibly have arisen to the unity of India. It would appear that the struggle between the two power blocs has no relevance to any such threat and can furnish no part of the explanation. The overt manifestation of a separatist tendency has occurred only in one of southern States, and most political observers seem to regard it more as a move on the internal political chess-board than as the expression of any gave discontent or the indication of a serious grievance worth calling for a prompt investigation and remedy.

Problems of national integration appear to be attracting a great deal of attention in India within recent years and if one were to judge from the comments made by responsible politicians on these problems arising out of some specific incidents one might be led into the error of regarding the situation as somewhat serious. It is, however, as well to recall that similar problems are encountered in many countries and at various stages of history and that they constitute the almost inevitable concommitants of either political reorganization or economic development. It may be conceded at once that because of India's size and the diversity of its languages and religions and the traditional character of its society these problems appear superficially to be more complex and less tractable than elsewhere, even after allowing for the simplification that might reasonably have been expected from the partition of the sub-continent into two countries. It is doubtful however if this view would on detailed examination be found to be correct. Where there are sufficiently powerful forces in operation, even countries with a more than ordinary degree of racial, linguistic and cultural homogeneity, for instance Korea, can suffer disintegration at the manifest cost of any of its economic development. On the other hand, where wise statesmanship has prevailed, and the more strident overtones of the Vox Populi kept subdued, triumphant examples have emerged of national integration in spite of the existence of many factors tending in the opposite direction, well-known examples being Canada, Switzerland and Yugoslavia. Balancing all the relevent considerations it would appear that however complex and difficult a situation might appear to be, there could always be an adequate answer furnished if statesmanship can rise to the occasion and every effort is consciously and honestly made by the majority in power to deal with minorities in a just and equitable manner.

After the partition of the sub-continent it was hoped that even the two minorities that were created as a result, in place of the previous one, viz., Muslims in India and Hindus in Pakistan, would be enabled to adjust themselves to the new conditions without loss of self-respect, without fear and indeed with a new-born feeling of attachment to the new nation. It would appear as if in fact these expectations have not only remained unrealized but that, on the contrary, the position of the minorities has deteriorated. This was indeed the apprehension of many statesmen and men in public life who opposed the partition at the time that the proposals in this respect in some form or another were put forward. They pointed out that even if the dimensions of the problem might be reduced their intractability would only be intensified, although it is doubtful if any one could have foreseen the mob fury and genocide that followed immediately in the wake of partition. There is reason to believe that the Hindus in Pakistan. who form about 12% of the population on the whole and more than 1/3rd in the eastern part of Pakistan, have been reduced to a very much cowed-down and subdued minority and are allowed only such positions, privileges and representations in public life and freedom in maintaining their own cultural heritage as is tolerated by the majority. On the Indian side, although partition had been reluctantly agreed to, there was never any acceptance of the theories of racial and other deeply-dividing differences which formed the basis for the claim for partition. There was every hope, therefore, although the total number of Muslims in India was as much as round about 40 million (the third largest aggregation of Muslim population in the world), that on account of prevailing secular attitude and practices of the party and men in power, this very substantial minority would gradually be emotionally integrated with the rest of the country. All the evidence that came to notice for the first decade of independence also seemed to point in this direction, although very difficult specific problems of political organization, such as the 'Police action' in Hyderabad, had to be tackled by the State. But happenings within the last four or five years would seem to indicate that far from national integration having preceded in the desired direction there seems to be a growing feeling of alienation on the part of the large Muslim minority, which has found expression in the form of communal organizations or the holding of specific conferences like the Muslim Convention. One hears a great deal of specific grounds for complaint of unfair treatment in respect of representation, appointment to public services and opportunities in commerce and industry on the part of the Muslim leaders, but the public is not in possession of the facts on the basis of which these complaints have been made and there has been no objective statistical investigation of the facts of the situation. What all this tends to is difficult to prognosticate. If remedial measures in the direction of separate representation or of specific reservation are employed, then there is every reason to fear that the vicious circle of separatist tendencies and counteracting measures tending to reinforce them will begin again. An objective observer of the political and communal situation would be justified in asserting that there is nothing in the situation which would defy the efficacy of the well-tried remedy of fair and equitable treatment such has been guaranteed by the Constitution of India.

Although the sub-continent was partitioned on the basis of a theory of racial differentiation, which was never accepted on the Indian side, communalism in the Indian context only means the still unresolved conflict of cultures and interests between the Hindus and the Muslims. In regard to other religious minorities, for instance, Christians, the numbers involved are so small and scattered that there is no practical problem of integration that has arisen. Even in regard to the noticeable racial differences, as for instance in Nagaland, where the situation was, incidentally, complicated by the intrusion of an important religious factor, wise statesmanship seems to have pointed the way to a reasonably satisfactory solution, in spite of the apparent unwisdom of creating a senu-autonomous unit of administration within the Indian Union which would ordinarily be regarded as too small to deserve any such status. Inevitably, claims have been advanced on the part of the other clearly differentiable tribal groups for similar treatment, but it would be a safe guess to hold that the example of Nagaland is not likely to be repeated.

The other major divisive factor, at least superficially, is the diversity of languages in India and the recent (1955) re-organization of the States very largely on a linguistic basis. Here again there is ample historical evidence to show that with wise political arrangements it should not be difficult to accommodate within a federal national unity an extensive diversity of languages forming the base of the reorganized States. This reorganization was recommended by a Commission appointed for the purpose of examining the whole issue afresh after taking due notice of the qualifications subject to which States could be reorganized on a linguistic basis. That Commission, which reported in 1955, took note of the fact that a majority of the States was already predominantly uni-lingual and that linguistic redistribution of the population had been a material part of the national demands at one time. They however saw some danger to the political unity of India in the concept of 'homeland' which had received adherence before Independence, as indeed they were bound to inview of the partition of the sub-continent that had ushered in independence for both the parts. It was because of this that they urged a balanced approach which was supposed to take into consideration various other relevant factors making, up the natality of unity. But even the necessarily limited experiments of a composite State which they had advocated have not survived and today it can be said that barring very minor exceptions one-State-one-language, although not one-language-one-State, as far as possible, in the basis of the political organization of India.

Second thought in regards to the wisdom of the 1955 reoganization seem to originate in a somewhat alarmist view of the disputes that are raging either in regard to the recognition of a minority language or in the treatment of the unboidable linguistic minorities in the reorganized States. The latter problem is largely a problem of frontier areas, where the population is often bi-lingual, and it is the belief of most cool-headed and uncommitted observers that the gravity of the border disputes and the difficulties of safeguarding the legitimate interests of the linguistic minorities have been largely exaggerated. Trouble of really serious nature has arisen within the last year or so only in one State, viz., Assam, where the natute of the linguistic distribution has some special features owing to the isolation of a part of a Hindu-majority Bengali-speaking district from the rest of Bengal as a result of the partition and to the somewhat weak statistical position of the so-called majority language. But even this dispute appears to have yielded to political firmness and patience and there is reason to hope that the final arrangement that will be evolved will safeguard the interest of both the important linguistic groups in the Assamese population.* Indeed, there is reason to believe that these troubles need not have arisen at all had there not been laches on the part of the Central Government of India in ensuring that the 1956 Memorandum on measures necessary for safeguarding the interests of minorities had been conscientiously implemented.

Although casteism is frequently mentioned as one of the causes of fissiparous tendencies it is doubtful if caste in this context is more than a cloak for the formation of groups and sub-groups to reap some specific political or economic advantage. Caste undoubtedly remains a very strong sociological force, especially in the rural areas of the country, and there is no doubt that in these areas however people regard it with some emotional attachment. But its corrective lies in the emergence of other groupings, e.g., co-operative or workers' unions.

Regionalism is sometimes regarded as another divisive factor, but it is clear that in the context of ambitious economic planning it represents only the excess of fervour with which local claims are pressed, often for the justificable purpose of gradually removing regional disparities.

A word is necessary in regard to the precise implication of the phrase 'fissiparous tendencies' used in connection with the differences of race, religion, language or caste. In the ultimate analysis 'fissiparous' could only mean tending towards the partition of the nation. In this sense it can be confidently asserted that there is no threat whatsoever in any aspect of the existing situation of the splitting up of the country as a result of whatever maladjustments there might currently be existent, and even the oft-repeated threat of a separate Tamilnad can safely be discounted as a minatory empty political gesture. The only real threat to the integration of the nation lies elsewhere, that is, in the field of politics, from the cold war between the East and the West. It is only when one or more Indian States turn Communist that a situation is likely to arise where fissiparous tendencies could be regarded as a real menace to the political integrity of the country.

Positive forces in the field of education for countering any tendency of disintegration would include a variety of measures comprised within the broad term 'social education' and also include urgent national tasks, such as the re-writing of history. While it is generally felt that the linguistic reorganization of the States is a measure which would prove to be irrevocable and which, indeed, appears to some as essential for the fostering of our nascent democracy, positive measures for neutralizing the separatist and isolationist effect of this reorganization could, it is recognized, be countered by promoting mobility in the educational, professional, vocational and administrative fields. Indeed, the removal of barriers to the free movement of skilled labour and managerial personnel between the different States might prove to be a portent instrument for the removal of regional economic disparities.

Again, tensions between the urban and the rural areas could be greatly alleviated by greater decentralization and dispersal of economic, particularly industrial, activity, although parity of stages of economic development would not be immediately attainable. Economic Development is not merely a question of the investment of capital or the provision of technical know-how. There must be engendered first the capacity on the part of the community concerned to utilize capital and know-how fruitfully.

There can be little doubt that in the final analysis, unity and disintegration are political concepts; it is therefore in the political field that the positive and negative measures for promoting or strengthening the unity of the country and countering the forces of disintegration would have to be taken. In this connection, the most important objective would seem to be to ensure that the State as the power-centre of the community must give continuous proof that, although a minority in power, its interests are identical with that of the entity that is the nation from which it derives its authority. Any failure on the part of the State, either to show solicitude for the welfare of the different sections of the community or to enforce authority against unjust treatment or exploitation of some groups within that community by other groups, not to speak of allowing its overall constitutional authority to be weakened, would disrupt unity and strengthen the forces of disintegration, with consequences which it is hardly possible to forecast in the present highly dangerous situation in regard to world politics. It has to be constantly borne in mind that under any form of a democratic system of government, even where grievances are not identified by the groups affected, there are political groups in the form of parties, whose business is to identify grievance and seek to obtain redress. Indeed, in the highly surcharged atmosphere of politics it often happens that the significance of grievance is magnified beyond all justification and many a mountain is made out of the proverbial molehill. In such a situation, unless the ruling minority wielding power shows both love and justice, it is at any rate bound to forfeit the silent acknowledgement of the people and possibly to drive social groups into the vortex of ever more powerful power-centres.

While all the foregoing has validity in normal times, in an emergency, where the nation's security is threatened fissiparous tendencies tend to vanish as if by magic seven factors of disintegration become insignificant in face of the common danger. It is thus amply proved that there is basic unity in the country, which will respond to stress, as well as wise governance.

PROBLEMS OF GROWING DEMOCRACY

The Constituent Assembly of independent India adopted and gave to themselves and therefore to the country a constitution which was indisputably one of the forms of western parliamentary democracy. Thereby India definitely rejected any alternative form of democracy in vogue in the world such as was claimed to be in operation even in countries whose apparatus of Government was fashioned on authoritarian or totalitarian principles. The preamble to the constitution contained a solemn resolve to constitute India into a Sovereign Democratic Republic and to secure to all itsc itizens Justice, social, economic and political ; Liberty of thought, expression, belief, faith and worship ; Equality of status and of opportunity ; and to promote among them all Fraternity, assuring the dignity of the individual and the unity of the nation. At that time India was the only instance of an Asian nation which had on the achievement of independence adopted such a democratic constitution, and the framers of the constitution could have had no doubt in their minds that the newly adopted democracy will follow the laws of natural growth as in the case of the politically more advanced western countries, particularly the U.S.A.

Now that some 12 years have elapsed since the adoption of the constitution and the establishment of the western parliamentary form of democracy in India, it is time to review the position in retrospect and to assess to what extent the assumptions of the constitution makers have been fulfilled, and whether the seedling that was then planted gives promise of growing into a vigorous tree. In making such a retrospective examination it would be necessary not only to consider the situation in respect of democracy as it exists in India today, but also to take note of what is happening to similar endeavours in the field of political organization in the large number of other countries in the world which have emerged as independent nations after long periods of colonial rule or which have as a result of internal affairs evolved into democracies of the western parliamentary type out of feudalism or oligarchy.

Any objective observer of the Indian scene would probably come to the conclusion that the democratic machinery in India is functioning reasonably well. The two general elections, on the basis of adult suffrage, held during this period of 12 years are held by common agreement to have passed off remarkably peacefully and without any significant disturbances or malpractices. There is no reason to believe that the general conduct of election campaigns in the country has been lacking in any of the characteristics of such campaigns in the more advanced countries. The conduct of the business of the legislatures has also on the whole been fairly effective and dignified, and the relations between the legislatures and the executives do not show any features more undesirable than those in any other admittedly well-established democracies of the world. The ruling party in power almost continuously throughout this period, at least so far as the Central government is concerned, may also fairly be adjudged to have made reasonably good progress in endeavouring to secure social, economic and political justice and equality of status and of opportunity by a series of appropriate measures. Liberty of thought, expression, belief, faith and worship would appear to have been upheld to a reasonably satisfactory extent. Lastly, although the dignity of the individual may not yet have asserted itself, it could be argued that this was the result, not so much of laches on the part of the government, as of the lingering of the old feudal and authoritarian tradition despite the constitution and the conscious efforts of the government to eliminate or modify them. There has been a great deal of thinking and discussion recently in regard to the danger of disunity or disintegration of the nation, but the occurrence of these debates and recently the holding of a conference on the subject by the Central government would seem to indicate that the objectives comprised in fraternity have not been lost sight of. It is necessary to add to this statement that the defence forces of the country continue to be strictly professional and amenable to the control of the civilian authority, thereby testifying to the location of political power in accord with approved democratic principles.

Even a casual survey of relative conditions in the countries of South or South-East Asia or of the Middle East would, however, disclose that against a somewhat comparable background of the historical past, the institution of democratic forms of government, varying only in detail from the form adopted in India, has not been an unqualified success. Whilst in certain countries there would appear to be no vestige left of any recognizable democracy, semantic variants have been evolved which tend more and more to confuse the basic issues. It would perhaps be too pessimistic to take the view that in some of these countries democracy has been tried and has been found wanting and is, further, destined for ever to disappear. There would, however, be justification for taking a more cautious and less starry-eyed view of the growth of democracy in countries which have adopted this form of government for the first time in their history.

The course of events during the last 12 years seems to have made it abundantly clear that in the absence of certain basic conditions a democracy is not easy to foster. Universal or nearly universal literacy would seem to be the most important of these conditions. Another important factor is the composition and attitude of the defence forces of a country ; and yet another is the level of the standard of living prevailing in the country, the lower the standard the greater the insecurity of a newly installed democracy. It is often forgotten that in the more advanced western democratic countries, democracy was the coping stone on a national structure built upon the foundation of universal literacy and substantial industrialization, in that order. The advent of democracy in these countries also took place in circumstances which were singularly favourable, in that there were no seriously opposing ideologies of political organizations in existence, nor any national counter-checks or international conventions restraining the worst manifestations of capitalism. In other words, the labour movement had in most cases not made any headway before industrialization had been more or less completed, nor had checks been imposed by organizations like international labour conventions. On the purely political front, the subjugation of other countries and the existence of colonial empires facilitated, directly or indirectly, the exploitation of the vast resources of these countries over a large part of the globe for the benefit of a few advanced nations. A little reflection will show that the environment in which democracy is to be built up in the newly independent nations of the world is lacking in these favourable factors and the struggle for the establishment of democratic forms of government has, so to speak, to be carried on with hands tied at the back.

Perhaps the most serious prevailing threat to democracy in the world is the apparent success of the totalitarian countries in boosting up their economies and raising the standards of living of their people with relative rapidity. This is not only an ideology debate, but is also the subject of a scarcely concealed and often deadly struggle, commonly characterised as the cold war, between the eastern and western blocs. Despite the best efforts of the champions of the western parliamentary form of democracy, several countries have been drawn into the opposing ideological camp often through a partition which could not be prevented. Many other countries are presently the centre of this cold war or show trends which hold the prospects of a reverse for the forces of democracy. In this context, it is clear that abjectly low standards of living provide a particularly unfertile soil for the healthy and rapid growth of a genuinely democratic form of government. This state of affairs is sought to be countered by the governments of newly democratic countries like India by systematic economic and social planning, but the success of these efforts is limited by the low level of capital formation, uncertain availability of external assistance and the lack of efficiency and adaptability of their administrative machinery, especially in respect of the implementation of the many difficult and unfamiliar tasks that such planning requires to be fulfilled.

Even where, as in India, the administrative machinery is not totally unsatisfactory and is capable of responding to determined efforts at improvement, the very size of the country and the resulting diversity of regions, languages, cultures, religious beliefs, etc., pose a serious problem for the unimpeded growth of democracy and the evolution of healthy democratic patterns of behaviour. The recent National Integration Conference highlighted two or three basic requirements in this connection. One, a somewhat long-term aspect, relates to the adequacy and soundness of the total educational system of the country. The other is the mores of political conduct, especially on the eve of elections. So far as the reform or modification of the educational system is concerned, there seems to be no insurmountable obstacles in the way of bringing about an amelioration. The existence of diversities of language, culture, religion, etc., need also be no serious hindrance in the way of fostering the nascent democracy of the country—indeed, the newly established political unity of India implies the existence of these diversities. An encouraging aspect of the question, however, is the existence of a great deal of cultural consanguinity and a great deal of cultural synthesis over the past centuries which should furnish a dependable basis for preserving the newly achieved political unity. In this context, the signal importance of treating minorities with justice and even generosity, is, fortunately beginning to be recognized. Lastly, unlike some other countries, India has inherited a tradition of professional defence forces, and available evidence would seem to indicate that this feature is not likely to alter for the worse in the foreseeable future and that the traditions that have been inherited by the defence forces will not be lightly abandoned.

The fortunes of democracy in any country in which it has been recently implanted in the challenging circumstances, briefly mentioned above, depend not only on predictable factors but also on such imponderables as the existence of good leadership, restrained in exercising power and willing to lead as well as to take heed of the popular will. In this respect, India may justifiably count herself lucky in having had a succession of greatly respected and on the whole very capable leaders over the last 50 or 60 years generally and particularly from the commencement of its independence. There has also been a conscious attempt on their part to build up second rank echelons of leaders. It is permissible to hope that if such good fortune on good sense holds, India will have sufficient time to consolidate the position in respect of its nascent democracy and to place its democratic institutions in a strong enough position to enable them to resist both internal and external stresses. It is implicit in this situation that the leadership will, from time to time, be introspective, imaginative, and conscientious, so that weaknesses are taken notice of and sought to be removed by means of a judicious blend of persuasion, justice and authority. The coming elections will be a test of the political wisdom of India's leaders and if, despite the emergence of many deviations from the norms of civilized behaviour in regard to political questions in recent months, the political parties confine the contest within the four corners of the established law and order and abide by some of the wise recommendations made by the National Integration Conference, then there would be every reason to hope that India would have set an example to the other countries in this region of the world of how to promote the growth of democracy in the modern environment so as to utilize it for securing the objectives enumerated in the preamble to its Constitution.

TRADITION AND MODERNITY IN INDIA*

I appreciate the honour that the Asia Office of the Delhi Group of the Indian Committee for Cultural Freedom have done me by inviting me to preside on this occasion. The subject for the Seminar, viz., Tradition and Modernity in India, is of such an universal interest in various aspects of life that one cannot but feel interested in participating in any discussion by informed and thoughtful people on any of its aspects. As you are aware, the two topics which we propose to discuss in particular at this Seminar are Science and Indian Culture and Traditional Cultural Pattern of India and Industrial Change. The discussion paper on the first subject has been in my hands for some time but till yesterday I had not received a copy of the discussion paper on the other subject, which reached me only this afternoon when it was too late for me to be able to even glance at it. In any case, the observations that I propose to make will not be particularly or necessarily concerned with the contents of any discussion paper but will be such as might serve to give some general direction and guidance to the discussion of the subject matter of the Seminar.

As Shri Padhye has mentioned in June, 1960, a seminar on Tradition and Modernity that is not the title on the cover page, but inside the blue cover, was held in Berlin under the auspices of the Congress for Cultural Freedom. The record of that international round table discussion, under the title of 'the problems of Afro-Asian New Stats,' published as pamphlet No. 1, 1961, by Encounter, has been circulated by the office for Asian Affairs of the Congress for Cultural Freedom. It is my understanding that the purpose of the present seminar is to carry the discussion a little further with special reference to the conditions obtaining in India.

At the outset, it might perhaps be desirable, because I do not know how many people have been able to read this pamphlet, to give a brief summary of the trends of the

*Address delivered at a Seminar in New Delhi, 1962.

Berlin discussions as given in the introduction and post-script by Prof. Shils, the Director of the seminar, as also to indicate the main observation made on a special contribution, also referred by Prof. Shils, on Tradition and Modernity in India by Mr. Burra Venkatappiah, one of the Deputy Governors of the Reserve Bank of India, who is responsible generally for work in the field of rural development and specifically in the field of agricultural credit and co-operation.

Prof. Shils has pointed out that the main pre-occupation of the leaders in the newly independent nations of Africa and Asia is or has been how to preserve a unique identity of their traditional culture without sacrificing any aspect which is of value in accordance with universal standards. The task, therefore, is of reconciling the imperatives of modern progress with their stress on efficiency, rationality and other less clearly defined modern values with a continuity of tradition which maintains the identity of the community. The process involves continuous re-assessment of the traditional institutions of family, law, religion and tribal authority, and the aim is to discover how the whole apparatus of social organization can be modernized without violent disruption or disorganization of individual and social life. These problems are not identical for every country and differ according to the stage of development, industrialization or urbanization, that has been reached by any particular country. In this context, the advent of independence and resurgence of a sense of nationalism embedded in history is bound strongly to be in favour of tradition. The effort to modernize, therefore, involves a re-interpretation of these traditions or an adaptation of them so that traditional culture and institutions may be made to accord with the requirements of the modern environment. It has to be remembered in this connection that this interpretation and this adaptation is a duty which devolves on the political or the intellectual leaders in these countries and it is for them to ensure that after identifying carefully, the living strands of traditional culture are related appropriately to the needs of modern development, the process of identification being carried out without disregard to the rationale that must have supported any particular tradition at one time or in the past. A re-assessment of traditions handed down from the past could possibly reveal that there are viable and desirable elements in those traditions which, apart from being true to the genius or ethos of any particular society, could even enrich modernity itself. This is a desideratum of very great importance, as human dignity requires that no nation should lose its essential characteristics in the scramble for development on modern lines. The means by which the political and intellectual leadership of a country would bring about what is regarded as appropriate re-interpretation or adaptation of traditional value is education in its broader sense and the use of mass communication in the large variety of its modern availability.

Special care, it is pointed out, would have to be taken to avoid the vulgarity and crudity of certain aspects of modern popular culture whilst consciously seeking to weaken the attachment of the people to vestigial elements from the inherited past. Moreover, this responsibility will have to be discharged against a general perspective of sound ideas of what is a good life, a good culture or a good society.

Now, coming to the Paper on Indian traditional values, Shri Burra Venkatappiah in the course of his observations pointed out, what Professor Shils has also noticed, that the change from tradition to modernity is a continuous one and that in that sense there is always a period of transition. Any cross-section in time would therefore indicate that whilst a change is noticeable in certain aspects, in other aspects things seem to be very much as before. So far as India is concerned, since development has already taken some strides and the period of economic take-off is within measurable distance, it forms, i.e., India forms a traditional society which shows that given the opportunity it cannot only seize it but can also make a success of adopting its own ways of life to the requirements of a modern industrial context. Nevertheless, the area of mal-adjustment, especially in relation to the disparity between the urban and rural sectors, is still very considerable and so are inequalities in the social field, especially in regard to what is popularly known in India, viz., the caste structure. Shri Venkatappiah drew attention to the findings of a recent survey of rural credit which seemed to indicate that two major factors, viz., the operation of a colonial economy for 150 years and the employment of the centuries-old institution of caste had so affected the social and economic structure of rural India that, in spite of statistically demonstrable average economic progress, the weak had become much weaker and in comparison the strong much stronger. A powerful urban and highly monetized economy had prejudicially affected the self-sufficiency of the rural structure whilst much of the rigidity of caste institutions still remains. The saving feature was that some of the traditional values regarded as generally or specifically Hindu had made the people in the rural areas familiar with some of the spiritual concepts of philosophies of the saints, sometimes even more than the sophisticated town dwellers of western businessmen. A cultural value, for instance, which appeals to the rural Indian is a worker who has renounced wealth or power for the sake of helping others. There is also a great deal of respect for values such as toleration, detachment, loving kindness and impartial justice, although there are instances or times where tolerance becomes passivity ; detachment, indifference ; and loving kindness, sentimentality. But in fields other than religious and ethical, the traditional values, emphasizing individual development and liberation, coupled with a small group within social loyalties are exercised, may result in the lack of a social purpose and a social philosophy. There is also the tardy recognition of worthwhileness of economic objective not for individuals but for society as a whole. I quote here : "To work with one's hands, to produce, to organize production for the community, to take pride in increase in production, all these are values which are only slowly being adopted." The new values and objects with which the denizens of the rural areas are yet not sufficiently familiar are precisely those which the modern mind has most explored and to which modern development is most beholden, viz., relationship between man and the universe which has given rise to the physical science and the relationship between man and man which has given rise to the social science. The only redeeming feature is that the philosophic concepts of the Indian tradition are in no sense and at no point antagonistic to these values. Indeed, throughout the history there were reforms of the saints and religious leaders, who sought to propagate philosophical concepts more in harmony with modern values such as those prevailing in the advanced countries ; for instance, human brotherhood, equalitarianism, etc. On the part of the elite and leaders who have had western education these trends were of course strongly reinforced by direct contact with the course of modern thought, although, here again, particularly in the political field under Mahatma Gandhi, the political struggle, consummated by the achievement of independence, took a uniquely indigenous form based on non-violence. The advent of independence has given rise to a lively recognition of social and economic objectives, compendiously included in the concept of a democratic welfare state. Nowhere does the large gulf between urban and rural areas and the conditions thereon, make itself evident more than in regard to industrialization which very largely has occurred in the urban areas or has led to the creation of urban conditions, as, for instance, in regard to the problem of readjustment of labour to a city life. A process of adaptation here will obviously lie in the direction of decentralization of industries within the limits of economic feasibility.

It is pointed out that the conversion of the illiterate into educated is in this context a bigger task than the conversion of the unskilled into the skilled. The main difficulties in the way of adaptation is not the will so much or the knowledge as the lack of incentives and the lack of resources on the part of the mass of the people.

It has been pointed out by more than one observer that whilst in many elections the voting tends to take place along the line of caste, despite protestations and professions to the contrary, the forces of economic development, including urbanization, are on the whole hostile to caste. To the extent to which mobility can be encouraged, the hold of caste could be weakened although the disappearance of old loyalties to caste and sub-caste must depend on the efflux of time and extent of economic change. In the light of this it is recognized that caste is something that needs to be recognised and dealt with in an understanding way rather than in the spirit of an econoclast and this holds also in regard to many other strongly-held social or religious beliefs. Caste loyalties can often be replaced by class loyalties which ignore the frontiers of castes and purposeful economic legislation has, for instance, in the agrarian field bringing about radical re-adjustment to agrarian right without recourse to violence, could create and has created class interests in the rural areas which traverse caste frontiers. The extension of the co-operative movement. especially with carefully regulated state partnership, is another measure that is calculated to secure modernization without doing violence either to traditional values or the principles of sound organization. It would seem that there is gradually a wholesome tradition to modernity in which it has not been necessary to throw overboard some of the unique values of the Indian tradition, such as concern for the spiritual good, non-violent persuasion in the pursuit of betterment. There is, therefore, every possibility of bringing about a rural regeneration which, whilst maintaining the traditional ethical impulses, could be carried out on scientific lines. Here I am giving a gist of what has already been said, with which I agree, and which need not therefore be said by me.

The great difficulty about tradition is identification of values which are current. An attempt to identify and enumerate succinctly has been made by Dr. Sudhakar Chattopadhyay in a volume called "Traditional Values in Indian Life", prepared by him on behalf of the India International Centre for the use of Indian Commission for Co-operation with UNESCO. They are set out under the following heads : (1) Socio-Economic Life ; (2) Religion and Philosophy ; (3) Politics; (4) Law (5) Arts, (6) Science and (7) International Relations. A somewhat similar statement is available of Traditional Values in American Life. A juxtaposition of these two sets of values under the same or similar heads will furnish a measure of the gap between tradition and modernity, i.e., between current values in a still largely traditional society and an indubitably modern society. Thus under social values in India we have the institutions of caste and the joint family system in regard to which, out of the ancient heritage, the impact of modern trends and the bitter conflicts on the eve of independence the following values seem to have emerged. (i) That every individual in society must have equal rights or opportunities to whatever class or group he may belong, and (ii) that the evils of the joint family system should be removed. The corresponding American statement lists the following in this field : (i) dignity and importance of the individual ; (ii) freedom of the individual ; (iii) regard for the group and for group activity ; (iv) regard for the family as the basic social institution ; (v) regard for voluntary public service by free men, (vi) concern for physical and mental health ; (vii) regard for work leading to recognizable accomplishment—activities—as a normal aspect of the good life, and lastly, (viii) acceptance of change as a normal aspect of social life. It need not be assumed that these latter values have been or are entirely unknown in India. But the incidence and emphasis are much less and the former set, viz., caste and the joint family system still exercise dominant interest. It is this situation that needs deliberate but understanding and tactful correction. It cannot be said that even in urban areas caste is on the way out and in rural areas it is strongly entrenched, and the misuse for personal gain by political leaders has given a new lease of life to caste, notwithstanding professions to the contrary. By contrast, the joint family, except where it is consciously used by smart people as an instrument of tax-evasion, may be said to be crumbling fast as a result of the impact of modernity, which hardly any society in the world can escape today on account of the rapid improvement of communication, thanks to the advance of science and technology. What remains of the joint family system is in effect a defence against destitution, a sort of built-in social security device in the absence of an organized security system.

Coming to religion and philosophy, India is stated to have the following traditional concepts and goals :

(i) that every individual should be free to practise his own religion ;
(ii) that no one should be politically or socially disqualified for his religious views ;
(iii) that the State is not co-terminus with religion ;
(iv) that fanaticism has no place in true religion, which demands toleration ;
(v) that all religions are essentially the same ;
(vi) that the State should intervene whenever there is any communal discord ; and,
(vii) that ethical rules form an important part of spiritualism.

The corresponding values in Amrican life are stated to be :

(i) the separation of Church and State ;
(ii) freedom of worship, barring practices that debase the eommunity ;
(iii) Church as a free association of believers who assume responsibility for its support ;
(iv) widespread but not universal emphasis on some form of theism as a frame for explaining the meaning of human life ;
(v) the idea, widely but not universally held, that ethical standards spring from religion ;
(vi) church missions to assist social evolution toward a better life and for mutual co-operation among all people ;
(vii) Merit can be acquired by performance of acts contributing to the well-being of individual persons and of society; and,
(viii) Pacificism justifiable, subject to State's right to demand special service of a non-violent character in times of emergency.

The things will be noticed at once, (one), that religious values have a place even in modernity and, (two), that there is a remarkable similarity between Indian and American values. The essential difference would seem to lie in weight of or freedom from trappings of dogma. Superstition and futile practices, which dominate the Indian scene (e.g., cow-worship) but seem to be under control and in balance with other elements in America.

In this context, I am not sure that the trend of thought developed in the basic paper on science and Indian Culture does not under-estimate the importance of religious values. I doubt if there will be general agreement with the view which is stated therein, that religion is only a phase in man's progressively self-liberation and that science is the last step in man's mental development. Whilst there is undoubtedly a great deal of room for throwing overboard a great deal of esoteric, dogmatic, and superstitious body of thought which has encrusted religion in India, I think it would be wise as well as rational to recognise the importance of religious values in human life and it would be unwise to equate religion with spiritual liberation attainable by discarding the various notions and prejudices which are supposed to have weighed down the human spirit since time immemorial. In this context, I would recommend for careful study Dr. Paul Tillich's book "Love, Power, and Justice", which seems to me to contain a remarkably perspicacious statement of individual, social and religious relationships. In the concluding chapter he says "that justice, power and love towards oneself is rooted in the justice, power and love which we receive from that which transcends us and affirms us. The relation to ourselves is a function of our relation to God. Indeed, if this relation is left out of account human race would seem to have no way of resolving the armed conflicts of power groups. It is clear that one should take note of the fact that Communist theory is definitely and uncompromisingly opposed to religion. The new Soviet Communist Party programme, indeed, calls for further efforts to overcome religious beliefs in the Soviet Union as a rival ideology or doctrine of judgment after death and ideas of Heaven and Hell. But it seems that the religious man and the religious institution will survive even in the U.S.S.R. Militant atheism seems to be out of place in the society of equals which is the ultimate programme of communism. If militant atheism is given up then communism will cease to be communism in the sense in which this term is commonly understood in the world today."

Taking Traditional Values in Science next, the Indian statement enumerates the desired concepts and goals as follows:

(i) That the power of nature should be harnessed for improving the general living conditions of mankind;

(ii) that the use of science for destructive purposes must be restrained in every way, and,

(iii) that proper facility should be given to the rising generation for getting adequate training in science and technology.

Now it will be noticed that this has a new ring, but obviously these age traditional values which have been handed down but which are nevertheless already adapted to the modern environment and which hold the field in India today.

The corresponding American statement gives the following:

(i) regard for rationality;

(ii) the conviction that man must dare to unlock the secrets of nature to the extent that his abilities permit;

(iii) the conviction that the man must accept and not shirk the moral responsibility for the use of whatever new power, increased knowledge brings to him;

(iv) the understanding that the rational method of science can achieve new knowledge only when it conforms to an ethical code, a code that might almost be described as the Laws of Creative Thought;

(v) the scholar who seeks new knowledge must have freedom to explore, to reason on the basis of discovered fact and to express his conclusions;

(vi) in communicating what he has found, the scholar must be faithful to the truth he has discovered,

He must describe only what he has discovered or found by calculation.

(vii) the scholar should approach the solution of problems with complete objectivity, willingness to accept evidence and to reject disproved hypothesis, no matter what the conclusions.

It will be seen that there is hardly anything in the American statement, embodying modernity, which is inconsistent with the currently accepted Indian point of view and it would appear as if in this field the traditional values in Indian life will not prove to be an impedient in the way of the march of science and technology to the levels felt to be necessary from time to time for improving the standards of living as well as for participating in the universal pursuit of learning. The apparent inconsistency between values in science and values in the field of humanity and sociology would also seem to be on the way to diminution in all countries, and in the advanced countries there is a new trend of thought which would make science responsible for using scientific methods to manage the use of the new radical powers given by science itself. Especially with the recognition that science involves team work, and social responsibility, and apart from qualities such as foresight, experimentation and verification by measurement and observation of hypothesis, depends on its success on intuitive thought. It is common ground between the two cultures that science gives no guarantee of wisdom in judging the wider problems of life and faith in co-operation or altruism is not amongst the usually accepted scientific values. Nevertheless there is a possibility of employing science to influence affairs by applying it to everyday problems of society. It could discharge the special duties which has to serve the community by influencing children in their formative years. Maybe science is on the eve of demonstrating that the whole of human behaviour was like a game, the mathematics of which could be worked out, as has been done in a book published by John Von Neumann and Oskar Morgensterny in 1944 entitled the 'Theory of Games and Economic Behaviour'. Maybe that investigation of conflicts and tensions would yield to mathematical treatment and in some of the advanced countries teaching machines are already being manufactured which seem to improve on the teacher.

On the Indian scene, whilst scientific values are recognized and to a certain extent realized by the elite, because of the inadequacy of education they do not yet permeate the lives of the masses. Added to this is the complication created by a false sense of pride which induces the belief that even in scientific matter like medicine what Indians discovered or propounded a thousand or two thousand years ago is for the best part still valid. The result of these factors is the exaggerated importance given to the outmoded system of medicine such as Ayurved, which was entirely empirical and which can in the modern environment be no longer regarded as science of any kind, in spite of the occurrence there of many hints of the utility of plants, drugs and other substances for the curing of diseases. What is obviously needed is a rigidly realistic approach to this matter which would help to salvage and develop so as to supplement the findings of the modern medical science by the analysis and standardization of Indian Pharmacopoeia.

Lastly, the Indian statement lists the following new concepts of Politics as now current in India, viz.,

(1) the rules of law;
(2) equality before the law; and,
(3) the concept of a democratic government.

While the concepts of liberty, equality and fraternity mentioned in the preamble to the Constitution of India can be traced to western political thought, the concepts of justice as well as perhaps, the unity of the nation can be traced back to ancient Indian culture. The dignity of the individual is assured by the Constitution, thus imparting a new element. Here again whilst the current accepted values are such as to be consistent with modernity, it is doubtful if beneath the surface there do not yet linger traces of a society only recently governed by feudalism and authority. Much of the apparent failure of democracy in the country reflected in the apprehensions in regard to national unity and disintegration can be traced to this lack of accord between the ideal and the actual practice in regard to politics. It is for the leaders in this field as well as the intellectuals to strive for an improvement of the moress of conduct or the ethos of Indian society, and in this connection even to reflect whether some modification of the type of democracy that is to be in operation is not needed so as to make the transition of a truly operative parliamentary democracy more assured. Thoughtful people have from time to time indicated the lines of such possible modification, as for instance, that the type of Constitution best suited for India would be the Swiss rather than the British type, or that an entirely new model should be evolved which discards the party system and evolve a new type of democracy more directly dependent on representative institutions of the people at the village and block levels. In any case, the principal problem in India is not so much the choice of a type of democracy as the spread of education which will gradually remove ignorance, backwardness and apathy of the people as a whole.

The progress of education is bound up with the economic progress of the country, and the latter in its turn is dependent on the progress of education. It is my belief that by means of judiciously enlarged education, India will be able to accelerate its progress on the economic front and achieve modernity without the sacrifice of any worthwhile traditional value, such as toleration. Indeed, it is my belief that as countries develop, through a process of give and take, the world will advance to a set of values, though not achievement, which will possess universal validity.

NUCLEAR TESTS AND DISARMAMENT

A recent press-report relating to the U.S. High Altitude test quotes an official announcement thus : 'There was no danger to human life or hazardous levels of radio-activity in the ocean'. This is the crux of the current controversy in the world regarding the cessation or continuation of nuclear tests. While there is an impressive body of scientific opinion, substantiated by detailed descriptions of possible hazards to mankind, from any further nuclear tests, the official view. possibly supported by equally weighty opinion of scientists, still seems to be similar to the one quoted above. In these circumstances it is obvious that no further step towards putting a stop to nuclear tests, whether underground, on land or sea, in the air and in outer space, can be taken unless there is general agreement in regard to the hazard to mankind from any further addition to the existing levels of radio-activity. This involves issues entirely beyond the competence of laymen. Since experts notoriously disagree, the world would, also, have to rely on a majority view. Moreover, the possible consequences of excessive levels of radio-activity being admittedly ghastly and disastrous, even where there is a substantial minority view that further testing will be hazardous to man, the benefit of the doubt must be given to man, especially unborn generations who cannot speak for themselves.

A scientific verdict of the requisite authority can only be given by an International Commission of Scientists. The appointment of such a Commission, with comprehensive terms of reference, by a body like the United Nations would appear to be the most essential measure needed if any progress is to be made towards the resolution of the present deadlock over nuclear tests. Pending the completion of the work of the Commission, the United Nations will have to place an embargo on nuclear tests by any of its member-countries. Since the present cold war situation is essentially one of a certain level of 'balance of terror', no country need experience any difficulty in agreeing to the suspension of further nuclear tests under the conditions stated above.

Governments, as trustees for their people, cannot reasonably be expected to take any risks in regard to the security of their charge in the shape of avoidably inferior armament. But no Government will take the risk of wholesale destruction of life and property within its jurisdiction as a result of the armament race. In the case of the use of poison gas or bacterial warfare hardly any difficulty was experienced in securing an international agreement totally barring their use. This was because of the relative ease with which even less affluent nations could resort to effective reprisals. Nuclear warfare has many more complicating elements, but there is a conceivable level at which the balance of terror could be established, where the possessors of nuclear weapons are bound to shrink from using them. With the breath-taking advance that science and technology are making, such a stage will be reached sooner rather than later. The folly of waiting for such a development is obvious.

According to press reports suits have been filed simultaneously in the appropriate courts in U.S.A. and the U.S.S.R., respectively, in order to obtain an injunction against nuclear tests. While this is one of the desirable alternative course of action, no judicial or political authority (i.e. in the United Nations) will have much force or effective sanction unless there is an authoritative scientific finding in regard to the hazards of nuclear tests and unless, in addition, the people everywhere are made fully aware of the finding. It should then be possible to mount a people's campaign everywhere against nuclear tests which no Government in power could afford to ignore. People will not be as foolish as the snakes of St. Nicholas, who committed suicide to save themselves from slaughter.

Since the principal countries involved continue with nuclear tests and other countries possessing the necessary means and skill are joining in the game, it would appear that current official scientific advice is to the effect that nuclear tests, whatever their hazards to other peoples, hold no dangers for the people of the countries concerned. But since there is some evidence of possible hazard for people in the regions closer to the testing areas, a question arises whether any Government, whatever the security considerations might be, has the right, in an international sense, to expose people outside their jurisdiction to the hazards of radio-activity. As was justly argued by Shri C. Rajagopalachari in the recent Convention held in Delhi under the auspices of the Gandhi Peace Foundation, no nation has the right to endanger the life and health of the present and future generations in other nations for the sake of its own fancied security or even to expose those others to incalculable risks from radio-active fallouts and concentrations. That is indeed a fit issue to be taken to the United Nations for obtaining a prohibitory decision from that world body.

In this context it is as well to debunk the theory of the 'clean bomb'. With the equivalent of 500 T.N.T. per person on the earth available in the nuclear bomb stockpiles of the nations concerned (and a recent addition has been announced to the ranks of these nations), clean bombs contain no element of solace for the present generation, whatever the respite and grace vouchsafed to unborn generations as a result of accumulating radio-activity. The destruction of life and property, plant and amenities and shelter and transport, as also the balance of economic and social life will be so devastating as to make life on this globe barely sustainable. It would not make much difference that with clean bombs these ravages will be confined to the combatants. Modern life is so integrated economically that paralysis of the productive activity in the territories of the combatants will inevitably spell disaster in scores of ways for the non-combatant nations as well.

The possible use of outer space for warlike purposes poses a new hazard for mankind in regard to which there is even less enlightenment and definitive information available than in regard to nuclear tests on or near the earth's surface or underground. It would seem to be obvious to everyone except those in charge of Governments that no liberties whatever should be taken with the stability of the physical conditions in outer space for any purpose without first undertaking a vast amount of internationally integrated research. It would be unrealistic to expect scientists and technologists to decline to co-operate in any project avowedly directed towards enhancing national security. But scientists and technologists could fruitfully collaborate in research aimed at throwing the maximum possible light on the hazards of nuclear tests anywhere.

In the nations' armament race there can be, in the nature of things, no static position. If the movement is not forward, it must take the reverse direction. Therefore, once nuclear tests are put a stop to—and this seems very probable in the near future—gradual disarmament, except for internal policing purposes, is bound to follow. It should also be possible for sovereign States to think more favourably than at present of the desirability of forming a world federation, in which keeping the peace between member-States would be the constitutional function of the Federation.

If the pace of scientific and technological advance is fast tending to lead the argument by arms to a *reductio ad absurdum*, it is also holding out the hope of a rapidly contracting area of disagreement over material welfare. Levels of living are already sufficiently high in many parts of the world to induce a more altruistic attitude towards the less favoured nations. This, with a World Federation, could before long grow into a more positive policy, viz., a purposeful and deliberate resolve to organize international collaboration for raising the standards of living of the less developed countries. In such an environment the current antitheses between political ideologies are bound to soften, if not become insignificant. As standards of life rise, in particular, in communistic countries, the *raison d'etre* for communism itself might conceivably grow feebler. In concrete terms, where the standards of life in U.S.S.R. to rise to the level prevailing in U.S.A.—which is possible, although not very probable—the communistic philosophy of life and organization of polity will in all likelihood lose their edge and their essential justification in the eyes of their protagonists. The success of communism might, paradoxically, deal it its *coup de grace.*

In any case, where there is great material achievement, causes for hostility or dispute should be few and far between and capable of being settled by peaceful means. Fancied threats to national security should diminish in frequency and gravity and where they arise international action should encounter little difficulty in removing them.

In more senses than one, then, the future of the world hangs on the cessation or continuance of nuclear tests. The latter almost indubitably holds the menace of annihilation for mankind. The former would set the world unfailingly on the path of prosperity and peace for all.

SOCIAL RESPONSIBILITY OF THE MEDICAL PROFESSION*

Madame President, members, Director, Dean and Staff, graduand and distinguished guests,

I am grateful to Madame President for her kind words of welcome. It has been a real pleasure to assist in the work of the Institute. I feel highly honoured and indeed touched by the invitation of the Institute to deliver the Convocation Address this year. In a sense this marks the end of my long association with the Institute, which began some 12 years ago, when I was Finance Minister of the Union and my esteemed colleague, the late Rajkumari Amrit Kaur negotiated the initial aid from New Zcaland, under the Colombo Plan, which enabled a start to be made with the establishment of the Institute. As Vice-Chancellor of the University of Delhi (1962-1967) I have been ex-officio member of the Institute and the Governing Body, an association which I have much valued. I have watched the growth cf the Institute and have had the opportunity of assisting the attempts being made to ensure for it the academic freedom that is so necessary for its optimum development. The Act which regulates its operations and the body of subsidiary legislation under it have many flaws which are not being removed, in my opinion, fast enough,

The Institute is a University-like body, but has fetters in the shape of many provisions of the Act and the Rules which would be quite intolerable in the case of a University proper and would ultimately prove to be serious obstacles in the way of its development to its full stature.

That the Institute has made so much progress, nevertheless, is a tribute to all concerned, particularly the first Director and his present successor and their academic colleagues, guided and assisted by the occupants of the high offices of President or Chairman and their colleagues from time to time. The alumni of the Institute have every reason to be proud of their *alma mater*. Whilst I congratulate

*Address at the fifth Convocation of the All-India Institute of Medical Sciences 1967.

them heartily, I would exhort them to be fully worthy of her in their life and conduct.

I imagine the graduands have a perspective of the over-all situation in our country in regard to Health and Family Planning. An idea of this can be had from the Draft Outline of India's Fourth Five Year Plan presented to Parliament in August last year. The general picture is that of continued inadequacy, imbalance and desperate effort to make up sub-standard conditions. To cite a few instances, the number of hospital beds, which should be, at 1 per 1,000 of population, 500,000 was less than half of this figure last year. Assuming that each bed costs Rs. 10,000 on an average we are short by Rs. 250 crores worth of hospital beds. As regards the number of doctors, we have one for a little under 6,000 of population, as against one for a little over 6,000 five years ago, which means that what little improvement takes place helps only to keep pace with the growth of population. It should be borne in mind that the desirable standard is one doctor for every 1,000 of population, as in the developed countries. The situation is worse in regard to nurses, even after taking into account auxiliary nurse-midwives, their total number being less than that of doctors, which is abnormal. There are a number of dais but it is doubtful if in the context of family planning their presence is an unmixed blessing, as I have heard complaints that for a small consideration they take out the loop, the insertion of which takes away a part of their business. The number of health visitors and family planning advisers with special training is totally inadequate, and all kinds of beneficent promotional work suffers grievously.

The projected number of primary health centres is very nearly attained, but it is doubtful if the necessary medical and para-medical personnel are available for the centres already established or the sub-centres found to be essential.

It is notorious that macro-averages conceal a great many disparities on a micro-scale in this country. The basic disparities in regard to availability of medical aid as between the cities and the rest of the country persist. A city like Calcutta, would, it is believed, have a Doctor per 1,000 inhabitants, but the typical Indian countryside would have a ratio of 1 doctor to 20,000 inhabitants and worse in outlying and less accessible places.

Currently it is in regard to family planning that the shortage of medical and para-medical personnel is mostly acutely felt. This has been the biggest bottleneck on the organizational side, although it must be added that efforts to provide workers with the appropriate training have been belated and half-hearted, as field experience in the Ballabhgarh block by the All-India Institute of Medical Sciences workers themselves supported by the Rockefeller Foundation demonstrates. In my opinion, the national family planning effort has so far failed to make any appreiable impact on the rate of growth of India's population and I would not be surprised if in the 1971 census population is found to have grown at a rate exceeding that recorded in 1961.

It is against this background that the new recruits to the medical profession have to form concepts of their duties to the nation and their philosophy of life. Some rethinking is called for as I have reason to believe that the enforced sojourn in a rural area before the conferral of the practitioner's status or the degree is accepted with an ill grace.

The conditions of work are admittedly uninspiring in the rural setting, although the augmentation of communieation and transport and the spreading of rural electrification are serving to mitigate some of the felt privations. But I believe that lack of professional facilities, in which teamwork plays an important part, has a great deal to contribute to the unattractiveness of medical practice in the rural areas for a practitioner with only average motivation and moderate urges from service of his fellow-beings.

In regard to specialized work, teams of doctors from the nearest district or large-town centre would probably be prepared to assist on a voluntary basis and in rotation if transport were to be made available. Recently it was brought to my notice that non-official practitioners in Ghaziabad had very imperfect information in regard to the family planning

*The provisional population total published by the census of India 1971 (Paper I of 1971) bear this out (percentage). The decennial growth rate for 1961-71 is 24.57 against 21.64 for 1951-61.

work organized by Government in the surrounding rural areas. In the cities and larger towns problems of a different character are emerging. One such arises out of increasing specialisation utilised below capacity and therefore soon obliterated. An idea is being worked out in Bombay to counter this difficulty through a cooperative hospital which would rationalise the services of specialists and reduce frustration as well as improve the quality and appropriateness of medical aid.

The social responsibility of medical practitioners is a relatively new concept in the world of medical education and medical practice, as indeed it is in regard to other vocations and professions, e.g., the businessman, the lawyer and the academician. Social and preventive medicine is now a well-established part of the medical curriculum. The Third World Conference on Medical Education recently supported the philosophy to relate medical education realistically to the world in which it must work effectively.

In this context it is the experience of some countries that in University Departments, although they are hospital-based, there is full integration in the courses of pre-clinical and para-clinical disciplines, as also an extended field of interest and influence beyond the immediate administration to patients in the wards, often taking the form of expanding research programmes mainly as laboratory-oriented clinical investigations. It is indeed, reportedly, widely admitted that research either directly or indirectly contributes greatly to the worth of a teaching department provided that its incorporation within a teaching programme is balanced.

Apart from research, I have recently come across thoughts about concepts about education, particularly about medical education of Dr. Marshall, Emeritus Professor of Microbiology at the University of California Medical Centre, which I consider it worthwhile bringing to your notice. I quote :

....."To require students to begin from scratch, bringing items together in their own individual and inexperienced ways seems cumbrous, expensive, slow, wasteful, and inefficient. Let us call this aggregate basic education. It is a loose assemblage tied together by the individual as best he can. In contrast, specialised training is really prefabricated education. It has been with us ever since agriculture became a subject taught in college.

......"Medicine is not itself a component of education, one which can be put together with other basic topics to compose what we call an education. Medicine is an art and a vocation, an organized collection of many skills backed and preceded by basic education. The art of medicine is a composite of many facets of men's total understanding. The process of assembling the whole training into a practised art comes after class rooms are left behind.

......"The early part of medical school consists of a series of bridges, leading from preliminary basic academic studies to the correlative processes of the clinic. The main bridges are anatomy or the study of the physical structure of patients, physiology or the dynamic functioning of the anatomic parts, biochemistry or the chemical reactions of life, pathology or the abnormalities which can arise, microbiology or the study of small forms of life which can play a significant role in normal life or illness, and pharmacology or the action of drugs on active parts. By means of these saparate bridges students reach the clinic where they will put all preceding subjects to work. Medical schools call these basic sciences. They should call them bridge sciences, because they lead from basic education to professional practice".

He goes on to point out that a beginning medical student tries to master each separate bridge subject so that his future organised resources may be composed of solid elements. Put together by the student, the result constitutes his total formal education, and he is now ready to practise the art of medicine.

A wide choice of courses, however, is often more indicative of academic poverty than of academic richness. Unable to provide basic educational elements which have conceptual breadth and depth, which are challenging and alive, they seek to impress by offering every possible combination of specialities—which remain just mixtures, or sometimes indigestible concotions.

Dr. Marshall holds that predigested compilations can be provided only at the expense of teaching students how to use the more fundamental elements of education for their own needs. Teachers who do the assembling for their students, whether in texts, subjects, curricula or day-by-day instruction, are prejudging the future and denigrating their students. This, he says, is more than improper ; it is presumptuous.

As in regard to other streams of higher education, the country's journey on the path of economic and social development in a well-planned manner is a matter of growing concern curriculum wise, for the obvious reason that it will, more and more obviously as time goes on, influence the environment in which professions are to be practised as also affect critical decisions in regard to general practice, specialization, choice of place and institutional participation. Since the health status and health policy of a country are vital factors in development, medical practitioners are bound to be involved in the process, not only as official health workers, but also as non-official professionals.

A faculty of medicine is powerless by itself to change the environment, but it can certainly imbue its students with a sense of social purpose and leadership through exposure to the realities of the national life. One of the most effective ways to accomplish this, indeed in the case of all students, is the compulsory national service, advocated by me some years ago as Chairman of a Committee appointed by Government to go into the matter. The Report of the Committee was burried, though still with a spark of life, in the graveyard of all good causes, the Government shelves of files. But it appears that the recent student unrest has led to its resuscitation at the instance of the Prime Minister. I may add that in 1959 or 1960 the Vice-Chancellors of India's Universities had unanimously supported the Committee's recommendation. I have no doubt that in accordance with our cultivated obliviousness of the past whenever convenient if and when the cadaver is revived it will be called a new creation of the present Government.

It is in the context of socio-economic national needs

that one may pause to take note of the current debate in regard to brain-drain from the country in so far as trained medical manpower is concerned. It is generally believed that with the facilities for gainful work that are so easily accessible abroad to medical practitioners, their contribution to the brain-drain is more than proportionate. No exact statistics are available, to my knowledge, but I should imagine that the register of medical practitioners, of modern medicine, would be enriched by some 10 per cent if our medical practitioners who have elected to settle abroad were to return. It is no one's view that they could be lured back by our offering better financial prospects to them for that would be beyond the nation's resources and norms of emoluments. Social pressures are becoming increasingly weaker. But something can be done to improve working conditions in areas where there are inadequate facilities, at least in urban areas. However, the most potent factor which could bring back an appreciable per-centage of the lost tribes would be a newly awakened sense of social responsibility. This can only be patiently built into the national system of medical education.

In most countries the fundamental responsibilities of the medical profession are undergoing change. While the general practitioner continues to be in demand for domiciliary medical aid and psychosomatic comfort, hospital staffs provide a complex of therapists and specialists, as well as an increasing number of para-medical personnel and even expensive facilities. A growing number of medical personnel are being equipped to prevent disease. With growing specialisation the general practitioner would, like all generalists, know less and less of more and more branches of his profession, and must therefore look for and have frequent opportunities of re-training.

In the U.S.A. the importance of the General Practitioner, termed the Personal Physician, is well-recognised. He is responsible for all facets of the individuals' health care-preventive, diagnostic, therapeutic, convalescent and rehabilitative. He is thus the central point for integration and continuity of all medically related service for his patient. He must therefore have a broad knowledge of all the elements that make up a comprehensive health service.

The WHO Eleventh Report of the Expert Committee on professional and Technical Education of Medical and Auxiliary Personnel entitled training of the Physician for Family Practice (September 1963) made some important recommendations which seem to be largely valid today. An interesting fact which the Committee noticed was that in every country in the world there appeared to be a dearth of family physicians, irrespective of their stage of development. The recommendations were :

1. Every medical school should provide opportunities for its under-graduates to receive some of their training in the setting of family practice ;
2. All graduates who choose family practice as their future work should undergo a period of post-graduate study and preparation specially designed to meet their needs in the field of medicine ;
3. Whatever the basis of his under-graduate and post-graduate training the family doctor ought to be a 'perpetual student' throughout his professional life ;
4. More research should be undertaken in this field of medicine, e.g., morbidity studies to decide priorities in under-graduate and post-graduate teaching programmes. Research should also encompass evaluation of different methods of training, both under-graduate and post-graduate ;
5. The need for family physicians to participate in the teaching of students has been emphasised :
6. At all stages in the training of the family doctor increasing attention should be paid to the development of the skill of with auxiliary and para-medical personnel, so as to increase the effectiveness of his work and to strike a balance between preventive and community action on one hand and the offering of personal curative services on the other.

There is much food for thought, not only for the medical

educators and trainees, but also for prospective general practitioners.

The Indian Medical Association has recommended the eventual merger of rural and urban health services and has set its face against coercion, especially of young doctors to serve in rural areas. Inexperience will be a handicap to them and a discouragement to the population served. A judicious taking of turns at the somewhat difficult environment of rural areas, not confined to ill-equipped and under-staffed Health Centres, with establishment of a group-system aimed at tempering professional and social isolation, is recommended by the Association and in my opinion wisely, for the gradual improvement of medical aid and health advice to rural areas.

However, as already stated the most powerful lever could only be the moral one, viz. the awakening of a sense of social responsibility.

I have no doubt that the graduands of this great Institution are fully aware of the ethical code of their profession, as subscribed to and followed in thought, spirit and deed by the members of the Indian Medical Association. But the very succinct first article, 'I solemnly pledge myself to consecrate my life to the service of humanity,' is so wide and general in its terms that there could be no reliable measure of observance and all kinds of passivity could be tolerated in adhering to it.

The concept of social responsibility has three main aspects, viz., (1) work for a patient on other than a strictly contractual basis, embodying the principle of philanthrophy, (2) work for the less privileged groups of the professionals fellow-citizens on an honorary or reduced charge basis, extending the principle of philanthropy from an individual to a class and (3) engage in work on a voluntary basis that will contribute to the betterment of the community at large within the sphere of one's competence, on a voluntary basis—i.e., undertake social work in one's spare time and with one's spare energy, embodying the idea of service to one's fellow-beings as a fulfilment of one's own personality. Voluntary work as a member of a professional or a non-professional body, free of charge, falls into this last category. This sort of work has to be sought for and the motivation for it can be cultivated. It is easily provided for occasional spells of social service by calamities like, accidents, epidemics, floods et cetera.

Apart from the time-honoured oath, the following fundamental observations are worthy of being constantly borne in mind.

"Medicine arose out of the primaeval sympathy with man, out of the desire to help those in sorrow, need and sickness" (Oslar).

"The basis of medicine is sympathy and the desire to help others and whatever is done with this end must be called medicine". (Payne)

Much care and thought has been devoted to the training of those who will be receiving their degrees and diplomas today. The aim and object of this Institute is to turn out trained medical personnel that will uphold the highest traditions of their exalted profession. It is my earnest hope that all our expectations of this year's crop of alumni will be triumphantly fulfilled.

DEVELOPMENT AND ADMINISTRATION*

Principal and staff and members of the Staff Training College of the State Bank of India, Hyderabad :

Thank you very much, Mr. Principal, for the very kind words of welcome that you have uttered. I am very pleased to be here with you this morning. I think it is about ten years ago perhaps that the old Imperial Bank was nationalised ; and yet so curious is the course of events that I imagine this is my first visit to any institution directly connected with the State Bank (cheers). Of course, many of the people who are working there have been friends and colleagues of mine and indeed some who worked there have departed from the scene, including John Mathai, who was immediate predecessor as Union Finance Minister and whom I persuaded to take over as the first Chairman of the nationalised State Bank. I mentioned ten years, which you will realise, is a very long period of time, and since I resigned in 1956 you can easily understand that I can no longer claim to be in very close touch with the sort of problems that are of immediate concern to you. Therefore, when I talk of Development and Administration, I shall not refer to matters in which I could not give you very much food for thought, as for instance, the taxation policy or the monetary policy, except perhaps to say in regard to the former that I believe it has become frightfully complicated and imposes an almost intolerable strain on everyone concerned.

When I talk of administration, of course, I talk of it in the special context of economic development and that, in turn, means planned economic development that is implicit in the somewhat brief title that I have given to the topic of this morning. It does not mean that economic development cannot take place otherwise than through a plan but experience has shown even developed countries or fairly

*Address to the trainees at the Staff Training College of the State Bank of India, Hyderabad, 1965.

advanced countries that the social cost involved in an unregulated economic development are so high as to put a very great strain on political tolerance ; therefore, one by one, gradually even those advanced countries which are not in the totalitarian sphere have taken to planning. For instance, France and Italy and even U.K.—I think about three years ago. There are a few countries which perhaps do not have anything obvious in the way of a plan, like Germany, but the conditions in which they made that choice were very special and there is no guarantee that in the future they could continue to run their economy without anything in the nature of some kind of planned regulation of the economic and social factors operating in their country. I suppose outside the field of socialised countries, that is to say totalitarian countries, France would be the oldest and perhaps the most illuminating example of economic planning and it has many features we in India could study with advantage after we make allowance for the disparities in their economic and social status and ours.

These are features in the French Plan which are common with the Indian Plan as, for instance, the concerted action that is taken by the private sector with the public sector. Indeed, the original Plan, may be, the second and even the third, depended very largely on concerted action determined as a result of common deliberations between the administration and the particular organs of public life involved, like representatives of the leading industries, representatives of labour and so on and so forth. As against this, for the fourth Plan, I believe they have now begun to realise that more concerted action is not enough—and that something more is needed which can more readily be identified as a Plan.

As against this, the U.K. tried to carry on for a long time without anything in the nature of a plan, with the result that their economy became a 'stop and go' economy. Sometimes they went ahead, then they reversed the engine, then they had to go ahead and soon, and about a few years ago they discovered that that was not good enough although they are enjoying a level of prosperity which they never had before.

Each country has its own special problems, and in U.K. too the Government have now set up a planning machinery. So far as these developed countries are concerned, they are also on the verge of a somewhat interesting situation, that is to say they are facing new problems arising out of the economic integration that is in progress now in Western Europe. That means the lowering of import barriers, the diminishing of the capacity therefore to regulate imports or to safeguard their balance of payments and they have to learn many new lessons. They have all elected to expose themselves to the whims of a competitive and an open economy to a larger extent. The result is that they have to pay very special attention to matters which reflect their relationship with the outside world, which means imports and balance of payments.

The major controversy in the field of planning is whether it should be total or global, that is to say, socialistic planning, or whether it should be planning which runs a mixed economy and, therefore, allows for some freedom of judgment and action. So far as historical record goes, I suppose this controversy will never be resolved. There are, of course, very brilliant examples of success as a result of both a socialistic, i.e., total planning as well partial planning as in France. We may include Japan in this category because Japan also has some kind of a planning machinery. The rates of growth that have been recorded by Japan are even more brilliant than those recorded elsewhere, except some of the totalitarian countries, although one cannot be too sure about the correctness of the statistics of some of the socialist countries. Nevertheless, when we consider countries which were backward or blocs of regions which were backward, perhaps for a generation ago, as the Central Republics of U.S.S.R., we have the testimony of people like Gunnar Myrdal, to say that within a period of 25 years, the comparability of these Central Republics has been brought nearer to that of some countries in Western Europe, say like Italy or France, rather than any country in South West or South East Asia. In other words the progress achieved is tremendous. Also historically it is almost impossible to prove what would have happened in any country if a particular course of economic action had not been resorted to. For instance, if France had not taken to planning, what would the conditions in France have been today? This sort of question is difficult to answer. There is a book by Dr. Hacquet on Economic Development in France, which some of you might have read, where he makes the point that at one time he devoted considerable attention to finding out whether the plan has made a difference and reached the conclusion that that was a wrong question to ask.

So I think this controversy has to be left where it is and whatever ones views or whatever ones impressions may be, the possibility of our evolving a good or bad plan cannot be a reason for selecting one or the other method for running governments. This I think is obvious, but it is just as well to state it, and that is that perhaps we could be just as happy running a sort of economy within the four corners of the western parliamentary democracy that we have undertaken. Nevertheless, it has to be added that India had very special difficulties in regard to her planning. For instance, when she began planned development there was no model of planning for a federal democracy. We had to evolve our own norms and our own techniques and, perhaps, we made confusion worse confounded by calling experts from all sorts of countries. I remember Lange came from Poland, Bettleheim came from France and Friedman came from U.S.A. (who was very very rightist) and Mrs. Robinson from the U.K. (somewhat leftist) and, I think, we got thoroughly confused. However, the first plan was a very modest kind of affair. That did not matter very much, since we were finding our feet, but the model that we began with has persisted and subsequent plans have only shown the result of attempts to rectify rather than to change the type of planning that we have undertaken.

The other difficulty that we have arises from the fact that not only are we operating within the four corners of western parliamentary democracy but we also have a nascent democracy, that is to say, a democracy which is untried both in respect of its franchise-holders and in respect of its leaders ;

and that has results which perhaps are not yet clearly seen in proper historical perspective. In the beginning, power fell as one would expect, into the hands of people who had given evidence certainly of their greatness and their integrity and their sense of service though one cannot necessarily say of experience of the management of men and affairs. In any case, they were great men and they were also modest enough to realise that they lacked practical experience and they took opportunities of rectifying the situation. Moreover, there is such a thing as confidence and the nation had very good confidence in them. There was also some kind of internal balance of opinion in the earlier cabinets and I do not think that India did badly under the sort of balanced leadership that it enjoyed between 1947 and 1951.

Then as successive elections took place, the electorate, like a new bride, found its power and discovered that they could make and unmake leaders and then they started to consider, ill informed and not very literate, what sort of leaders they should send, and obviously their horizon being very limited they sent the sort of leaders who could give small parochial benefits to them like a school or a dispensary or a road or a bit of a railway or an irrigation canal and so on. They were totally ignorant of the much larger horizons and issues before the nation and those that are have to be faced in the international community with the result, I think, that the people that have come to power now are people who are not necessarily very well-informed or of a very high calibre and they certainly have not passed through the ordeal of fire through which the earlier leaders passed. In other words their own horizons are also narrow reflecting the narrowness of the horizons of those that sent them to power. And in course of time, I think, the spirit of service has become somewhat dimmer and the spirit of keeping office and hanging on to authority has become stronger. The liability to pressure of this kind of people is of a different order, than that of people who were in power when independence first came to us. This difference has its own reaction on the bureaucracy, the permanent services, on the kind of influence and the pressures that Ministers exercise or the interference in the conduct of day to day affairs that they are often guilty of. In the total the result of their being in power is to demoralise the people under them. There is also another consideration that has to be borne in mind here and that is that soon after the advent of independence we lost about 50% of the topmost echelons of our civil services because they were aliens and had elected to leave, and their places were taken up by people prematurely promoted, and that this process of dilution stretched far downwards, with the result perhaps that, office for office, we do not have today the same sort of able people, with the same high general education and high calibre that we had, say, when independence first came. This, together with the weakness of the leadership, is probably responsible for many of the shortcomings which we notice. But apart from shortcomings, I think, India is facing circumstances tending to lead to a crisis of character. In other words, our scales of values seems to be imperceptibly altered : instead of that of service, of fellow feeling, fellowship and so on there is prevalent now a different and inferior criteria. Every one looks, after himself seeks to perpetuate his own power and tends to indulge in empire building. This situation has been aggravated by the mounting scarcities that are the results partially of the development process and partially I think of bad economic management, and that is the kind of picture that we generally seem to see in this country.

What are the symptoms of this nation-wide failure of good management? There are certain things which you will easily notice as for instance, that there is a great deal of uncertainty in regard to the planning machinery. I have some authority for referring to this because I was primarily responsible for organising the planning commission for the Prime Minister in the first quarter of 1950. At that time our idea was that it should be entirely an expert body of people who knew what they were talking about and that they should give completely objective advice both to the Central Government as well as the State Governments. In course of time, it has been noticed, I do not know what the impelling circumstances were, the planning commission contains largely people who are essentially politicians and not experts. The other factor that has loomed larger and larger is the worsening of relationship between the Planning Commission and the Ministries. The germ of this was present right in the beginning but as the plans proceeded and the power of the Planning Commission in the matter of giving definitive advice became more and more conspicuous, the jealousies, if that is the right word, of the Ministries grew, with the result that there were very serious internal tensions in the Governmental apparatus in regard to planned economic development. Another unfavourable development was that the Planning Commission itself was enlarged by ex-officio addition of a growing number of Ministers. In the original machinery there were only two Ministers—one was the Prime Minister who acted as the liaison between the Planning Commission and the Cabinet and the Finance Minister because for valid reasons or otherwise everybody thought that since he held the purse-strings he ought to be associated with the planning process right from the beginning and throughout.

I was particularly careful to ensure the fullest involvement in planning of the Union Finance Minister because the coming of a plan really means an imperceptible weakening of the influence of the Finance Ministry. No longer can you pretend to discuss every new expenditure on merits, since in the macro-planning for a period of years the merits are already pre-judged in the shape of a tentative or provisional budget for five years. There is therefore nothing much that can be carried out in the Finance Ministry by way of scrutiny of new expenditure a feature which used to be such a bugbear before the plan came. The Finance Ministry was then assisted by the standing Finance Committee of Parliament which the politicians have eliminated. As it happens this is the only Standing Committee that has not been resuscitated, the rest of the standing committees having come back in some fashion or the other. The point is that the Finance Minister had quite a distinct kind of responsibility in respect of the planning machinery that we had evolved. But there have been many other Ministers who have been made members since then, and recently we here that there is some idea that there should be an economic and social council for the country as a whole. In the meanwhile the State Governments have realised that the Centre of gravity of political power rests in the states because the elections are conducted on the same day for the Parliament as well as for the State Assemblies and psychologically a candidate cannot get elected to the Parliament unless he carries five or six of the local seats with him from the same party. Therefore it is quite clear that the local political organisations are very powerful and as plan succeeded plan the State Governments have tended to wield increasing influence. They deploy their influence in sending exaggerated plans and estimates. Often, I think, they have been guilty of diverting the provisions which are meant for one project to something else without even sending an intimation to the Planning Commission.

What are the symptoms of inadequate management? One perhaps is the vascillation in the monetary policy; but about this you would know better than I do. Then there is faltering in regard to controls, in regard to food policy. I am not quite sure that there has been a feeling of certainty or conviction in the minds of the Ministries concerned. Some of these failures of management became conspicuous in 1957 when we ran through our sterling balances, and, what is more, we failed to take prompt measures against the expansion of bank credit to correspond with the over-generous imports of machinery from outside. My reading of that situation was that the businessmen, being shrewd as he always is, realised that the one thing that was going to be in short supply during the second plan was foreign exchange, and therefore he started hoarding foreign exchange in the shape of imported goods, not for one year or two years as he could legitimately do, but for 4 or 5 years, whatever he could get hold of, with the result that the freedom to import was misused, and in about six months' time to Rs. 720 crores of foreign exchange which I left in March 1956 was reduced almost to within the minimum points permissible by the law.

Unfortunately that also happened to be a year in which our crops failed, so that we had to import for hard cash about 3 million tons of food grains—no arrangements for P.L. 480 was just then in force—and the plan and economy of the country suffered a set-back from which I do not think we have yet recovered.

As for the next period of 7 years, bringing the matter uptodate, I think the general conclusion would be that we have failed in the field of agricultural production, in the field of Community Development, may be, in the field of heavy industries in the sense that the actual cost had to be incurred has often been twice the estimate when you compare the original estimate for Rourkela which used to be Rs. 120/- or Rs. 130/- crores (with the actual figures you will probably find that the actual cost is about double thc estimate) and, again, I think there has been failure in the organisation of small scale industries, especially in thc country-side, although that was one of the main aims of planning from the Second Plan onwards. Here I think I must say this that although a good principle was recognised it was misapplied; the small scale industries were not indeed to be rural or village industries, but we pursued the will-o'-the-wisp of the Ambercharkha and some other things which were basically uneconomic, instead of viable units of small scale industries which run with the help of modern machinery.

These are some of the major areas, in which we have failed. Then, so far as the citizens relationships with the administrations are concerned, it seems to be the general verdict that red tape is probably more prevalent than it is to be, delays are more irritating and there is probably greater evidence of vasciliation and favouritism in the orders issued by Government. Vascillation in regard to the baby car is one instance. Again, I believe that there are over 50 licenses waiting for orders in regard so new cement factories of which only a few have so far been granted although cement is in woefully short supply. Why the remaining have not been granted, one cannot guess. There is a great deal of secretiveness in these matters, as well as perhaps toning down of the mistakes in the running of the Government machinery. There is another field in which we seem to have failed, but that does not concern planning, although it does concern the management of the nation and that is in regard to defence, but it is only necessary to mention it and I mention it for this reason that because of our failure, we have now to carry a very vast burden in regard to security. The total budget for defence now must be over Rs. 1,000/- crores, and that is very big chunk of the current efforts for raising and utilising public savings for planned development. What has had to be diverted to defences would have been available for expanding, shall we say, education, health services and many other matters which go under the heading 'development' as opposed to investment. Another field in which again we seem to have failed and it is the very critical field, is that of population control. This is very basic. When we examine the statistics, say, for France, we find that there also in the First and the Second Plans the gross national product went up by 4% as in our case after the First Plan; but when we reduce that in terms of per capita national income then we find that the result is quite different and that we have done badly as compared with France. Instead of the assumed rate of 1·46 increase in population rate we have a population growth rate that has varied between 2 and somewhere near 2·50 p. c. and no one is quite sure that it is the worst that we have seen. No economy can cope with a rate of growth of population of that order and yet hope to have national income so as to bring about a noticealle improvement in the standards of living of the people. You will realise the measure of this particular failure when the following figures are considered.

In the First Plan there was just a bare introduction of population control and a small provision of 50 lacs for a deliberative machinery, of which, unfortunately, the minister made herself the chairman. This is one of the bad habits which Government have viz. instead of having some one really competent and someone really interested, the minister always heads these supposedly autonomous bodies as chairman, because it becomes a small empire for herself as the case may be. Anyway very little was done during the First Plan.

For the Second Plan there was a provision of Rs. 6 crores, which later on were reduced to Rs. 5 crores, as all provisions were cut by 20%, but the actual expenditure incurred was about Rs. 1·2 crore. Now apart from the fact that Rs. 6 crores itself was not large enough to make any impact on the situation except a merely symbolic one. What little was spent was on imperfect and uncertain organisation. The provision for the Third Plan is Rs. 25 crores and another Rs. 25 crores has been promised if it can be utilised, I believe that during the last four years all that has been spent is about Rs. 7 crores out of Rs. 25 crores so that there is a very faint possibility of the expenditure exceeding, says, 50% of the original provision. When we consider all these figures we have to bear at the back of our minds that there has been a tremendous distortion of the economy and financial measures of expenditure incurred do not mean that we get in return for that money what we thought we were going to get when we planned. I should add in regard to population control that part of the handicap, of course is that of science. In other words, one was not quite sure what exactly one ought to advise the large rural population. I mean the appropriate age groups, or fertile groups of that population. If you are interested in that subject, I think there is now some evidence that both mechanical expedients as well as perhaps chemical expedients have been found, or have been perfected, which could be recommended without the fear that they would prove to be not safe or feasible in the rural environment. Currently in the University of Delhi we are carrying on research projects in regard to the physiology of reproduction in conjuction with the All-India Institute of Medical Sciences and I am myself hopeful that within 4 or 5 years we shall probably be armed with the necessary scientific knowledge which could lead us to almost foolproof methods of contraception. By that time it may be that on the industrial and on the commercial front the necessary agencies will have been perfected which could place within the reach of the people what they could safely be encouraged to do for limiting families. Fortunately there is no religious toboo in our country but I do not think that for future planners this is task number 1 for the nation. If the population continues to grow at this rate, no mātter what efforts we might make, we shall never be able to show that there has been any noticeable improvement in the standards of living. Indeed tnat has been illustrated by the sort of figures that were given out by the P. C. Mahalonobis Committee in regard to income distribution after completion of two Five Year Plans. We found that about 10 per cent at the top were better off, as they are always are, and about 10 per cent had more or less maintained their position, e.g., labour whose real wages were more or less maintained because they are a fairly well—organised body. But in between, and that means the middle classes in urban areas and the agricultural labour and the lower and the poorer agriculturists in the rural areas, the bulk of the population has heen badly hit by the distortions in our economy and they probably will be left poorer after the completion of three plans than they were before. It is hardly necessary for me to highlight the political danger that is implicit in a situation of this kind. A word about the Panchayati Raj in the context of the implementation of Plans. I am not quite sure, if institutionally a wrong decision has not been taken. It is all right to talk about democracy at the grass roots, but the real question is what does one entrust to what agency. We must entrust a task to an agency which that agency in our best judgment is capable of discharging. To transfer abruptly expenditures of the order of Rs. 10 or 12 lacs to Panchayat Samities is probably not a very wise thing. Also, the experience that we have had of local bodies like Municipalities, I think has been ignored in making this democratic decentralisation. The local bodies, mind you, had greater advantages in that after all they were an urban population with probably a greater possibility of finding more educated people to manage local affairs. Even so we found that generally all over India that was our experience in the last 30 or 40 years they have dismanaged their affairs unless there was an official in position who equivalent to a Municipal Commissioner. In the Panchayati Raj it is my fear that they have weakened the position of the Block

Development Officers or the District Officers. In some States they have been wise. In Maharashtra I think the power is concentrated in the District Parishad, not in the Village Panchayat, that is to say the Block Level Panchayat. But in many cases, I think, they have devolved power on instruments which really are not strong enough to be entrusted with the proper discharge of that kind of power.

Another instance of mismanagement or bad administration is the way land values are allowed to rise in cities say, like Delhi. Instances are not lacking where land is offered by Government itself at Rs. 300/- per sq. yard. In Bombay speculation is land values is explosive, but what happens in Bombay seems to be nobody's concern. There are all kinds of things going on under the counter. Anyway, in Bombay one can build tall multi-storeyed flats, but in other areas you do not go much beyond three storeyes, if cement is available. The point is that Government have probably a larger monopoly of land than almost anyone else, because they can acquire land and they can pay compensation to the agricultural people round about and they have command of resources which is far greater than that of any private real property speculator. In such circumstances what is the duty of Government? The duty of Government is to break that monopoly i.e., of the other chap, the private monopolist. Instead of that, they copy the private monopolist and inflate the prices which they charge based on the operations of that private speculator. In other words, Government itself becomes the biggest real property monopolist in the country, with the result that it has become almost impossible for middle class people to live in cities like Bombay and Delhi.

The position in regard to shelter is becoming very very difficult. As for other necessaries, cloth is not too bad and any way cloth is not priority number 1 in this country, excepting in the north in spell of cold weather but we cannot do without proper shelter. As it is, mankind has not succeeded in solving this problem of how to evolve a shelter at an economic cost to human beings. Added to that technical failure is the wrong economic policy followed by Government and the result is I think just chaos. One does not know where people would live or what they will have to pay. All that Government thinks of doing is to raise the dearness allowance—if you are in a big city—a special compensatory allowance, and as soon as that is given, those who supply shelter and goods grant the increase by raising their prices. This is what they did when the first compensatory allowance was given in Delhi. Nobody profited, I mean, except the purvey or of shelter or goods who has decided to exploit right from the beginning.

I have just put before you a mixed bag of these failures. Now, in general, what do you think is it due to. One reason I have suggested is that the guidance or direction right at the top is not as competent as it could be. Secondly, their example which is somewhat ego-oriented leads others to a sort of lack of fellow-feeling and everyone for himself and there is a noticeable lack of feeling for the other person—the citizen with whom you are dealing with. This may not be too dangerous, although it is very very harrassing at the moment, but when the situation will deteriorate and deteriorate into the law of the jungle one can never say. It all depends on how fast the general sense of the rule of law deteriorates as well as on the aggravation of the scarcities, which show no signs of diminishing. This I think constitutes a potential which is very dangerous.

There is a kind of administrative failure, apart from the failures in policy, which is most noticeable in the smaller official. If I might be pardoned, a generalisation and I hope I am not defaming the small official, I believe the small official is now far less conscientious than one expects him to be. Because he is a small person one would expect him to have some kind of a fellow feeling for another poor person. But often it is he who is found to be responsible either for dealy or for something worse. I believe that what is called the gazetted officer, I think still has a certain amount of conscience left. This leads me to suggest what perhaps could be done in order to improve the state of affairs. My suggestion is that many more things should be handled by the officer rather than be prepared for him by the official—in a chain of hierarchy and I believe that this is the system which exists in the more civilised countries. They don't have such hoards of noters and drafters and what is it called lower division clerks and upper division clerks and record keepers and so on and so forth. Everyone knows what exactly concerns him, he will handle the current correspondence, he will pass orders and he will be trusted probably to deal with the case. Here in India what comes up is only material perhaps poorly prepared on which an official cannot take a decision. The Under Secretary here does not have that kind of authority which he used to have in the old days. He must send up to the Minister. Now why? That leads me to another disadvantage of democracy. I am not against democracy, but there are things which we have to live through and that is the wave of nervousness, as Paul Appleby pointed out, that is communicated from the Parliament question hour or resolution or criticism all the way down the hierarchy of administration from the Minister to the Class III official.

I believe our Parliament has yet to learn that such excessive attention to the minutiae of administration is not the thing on which they should expand their time. They must trust the Executive, and not be tempted to take it to task for small errors of judgment. As Appleby pointed out and incidentally I was instrumental in having him as consultant on administration there is a kind of nervousness that is transmitted through the ministers, to the Secretary and down the line, as a result of Parliament's overscrutinising of details. Because the Secretary is trusted less he plays for safety and that communicates itself all down the line—so everybody becomes a happy file-pusher, and the final orders are reserved at the Minister's level and these are frequently delayed.

This is all very wrong. One cannot implement a plan by following this kind of a policy. The whole system has to be changed so that fixed points of accountability and responsibility lower down are located and they are easily identified, and if there is failure and probably you will find that there is less failure than in other circumstances, then one can take action, the severity of which will depend according to the enormity of the offence.

That is one of the changes that is badly required. What are the other remedies that have been suggested? One remedy which I have been suggesting but which as in the matter of corruption is not receiving attention is having some kind of real national leadership. What I have been advocating a national government. The Plan is a national Plan, and everybody is affected by it, is concerned with it. The Plan is passed by the Parliament as a whole. There is no point therefore in limiting the execution of it only to one party, if that party must have power, then it must strengthen its rank by the addition of a number of people who are either non-party or who belong to other parties. This is, precisely the course followed after the Republic was established. The cabinet which I joined had Prime Minister Nehru, Sardar Patel, Maulana Azad, Dr. B.R. Ambedkar and Shyama Prasad Mukherjee, Gopalswami Āiyangar and just before I went in John Mathai was there. These you will admit were very distinguished names, apart from myself. It was a pleasure to work as a member of this cabinet whether I agreed with them or not.

What I have just stated does bring out the point that Government must—both at the Centre and the State—reinforce itself with talent in order to have a level of competence at the highest levels of policy making and even excecution. The distinction in regard to policy making and execution as between Minister and Secretary is a false distinction. Policy certainly is fixed by Parliament. That certainly is an exclusive field of policy with which officials are not concerned. But so far as Ministers are concerned both with formulating policy and execution they are the executive of the Parliament, and certainly a good Secretary will help considerably in seeing that a proper policy is formulated, if he is allowed to advise without fear or favour and is implemented. I had been advising Prime Minister Nehru that we ought to have a national government. But this is a kind of a bee in my bonnet that nobody has ever taken any notice of. I believe that people in politics consider that party interests over-ride the running of a national plan properly. But I think that it is a very great mistake. I brought this matter up at the

Ooty Seminar on Planning held by the Congress in June 1959. This was before my ideas on corruption so they became well-known so that the powers that be were quite pleased with me. When I mentioned a national government in the final plenary session there was a sort of complete silence because nobody knew exactly what Prime Minister Nehru was going to say. Then he said 'Well I think there is something in it but the time is not now'. Well the time was not now because they were then trying to get the Communist Government of Kerala just out and much activity was in evidence from Ooty. I wish Prime Minister Nehru had kept that suggestion in his mind and done something about it, because he was the sort of person, who could have carried this thing through and not bothered whether a few party discontents had left the party and the Congress Government had instead of an 85% majority a majority of 75%. Actually what we have at present is not a proper form of democracy. As you know Mahatma Gandhi, when independence came, suggested that the first thing to do was to liquidate the Congress party and to form parties on ideological lines. Unfortunately that was never done because immediately everybody smelt the loaves and the fishes of the power that was coming. Also I fear that as the political game gets set principles are not so important as expediency. I firmly hold that there is a stage at which Government should say no we will not do it because it is against our principles. I don't think you have ever heard such a statement. What is the price that you have to pay for such an attitude ? the ruling party may have to pay for standing by principles? It may be that some people will walk out of the party. All right—what happens as a result of that? The majority is reduced from 85 to 75 per cent That is not a disaster in itself, but some person somewhere will lose his seat and that person is going to try his hardest that this does not happen. This has what has prevented their doing some of these right things that is to say strengthen the Government and giving better leadership to the permanent service.

I have already stated the other reform in administration called for, viz., that there should be an officer-based-administration instead of an official-based administration, so that there should be a greater concern for the citizens. This arrangement can only be followed successfully if there are good exemplars of this, and I think for that purpose, it may be necessary that we should have currently at any rate two kinds of studies—one study of grievances—the other a study in a sort of a research way—that is to say psychological, experimental psychological study, or a sociological study, to find out what exactly a citizen is thinking—what are his attitudes—what are his motivations—is he satisfied with the way things are happening—is there anything going wrong? There is not enough of these kinds of studies being carried out either by Government or by the Universities. Preferably it should be the latter rather than a former because if Government carries out studies we are not sure what finally will be disclosed. If it is an unfavourable study it might not see the light of the day. For instance, in regard to public ventures, I believe there is some kind of idea now that they will have a research section. We have suggested from the Administrative Staff College, Hyderabad, that we would study the working of public ventures—public enterprises, but I am afraid that there is some rival idea in the field, viz., a research section in the Ministry or Economic Affairs. I am convinced that this will be a wrong thing to do because people who are working directly under the shadow or the wing or whatever you prefer to call it of the Minister are not going to give you necessarily an objective view of things and that is why it is very necessary that such research should be entrusted to a separate non-official body. These problems of administration have been studied recently at the Indian Institute of Public Administration—I don't know if any one of you attended that Seminar.

The time is up now and I wouldn't take up your time except that it might be worth your while to get the records of that Seminar. There are three reports—one report on the study of administration which deals with the Secretariat, Management of Public enterprises, then routine administration, training, then the motivation of public service that is to say service and not career, then the question of delegation and review instead of checks and balances and inspections. Then procedure, a study of procedure, movement of files or the arrangements of hierarchy, the locating of accountability, then the appointment of an Ombudsman which is something which I would very strongly recommend for the redressal of grievances. I said there should be two kinds of studies—one is the general kind of studies and the other should be case studies of failures or of failures in administration. I am quite sure, that in the beginning probably the Ombudsman will have to go through a lot of chaff before he comes to the grain, but I am convinced that that would only be a transient state of affair and that in course of time only the worthwhile complaints will come up to him. Then there is another report on Industrial administration, which deals with the rigidity of financial control and otherwise itemised audit, then institutional changes such as unified recruitment or foundation training, followed by allotment to special institutions and special training and special courses in management skills, then flexible remuneration policy, then it deals with the question of whether there should be special cadres or specialists in administration or whether the administrator should be primarily an administrator who would be capable of picking up the specialities. This is again one of the perennial controversies which will never be resolved, but I am convinced that administration is a field by itself if one has a good speciatist one should not waste him, unless he is an outstanding administrator or unless he has really done so much work in his speciality that he can be spared for administration.

Then another suggested improvement is consultative machinery especially in regard to Development Councils; then better representation of small scale industry in the Development Council and then finally fixing a time limit for decision.

Then the most important thing that this particular report deals with is the status of the Cbairman of these Councils. He should have the following qualities. He should ensure freedom of opinion, he must have initiative, he must have imagination, he must have dynamism, personality, special knowledge and experience. One has only to survey the field of Ministers and Deputy Ministers to find out how many of them will have these qualities. If you come to the conclusion that they do not then you should give a proper Chairman to a Development Council. This is a matter in which I used to have a kind of running fight in the cabinet. I used to say that Ministers should not be the Chairman of semi-autonomous bodies. It must be some outsider. The Minister is not able to judge properly if he himself is the Chairman. Now what happens is the Minister is the Chairman, the Secretary is the Vice-Chairman, the Joint Secretary is the Deputy Chairman and the whole thing is an autonomous body but the Minister but without fianancial control. That was my quarrel in those days but it was a small quarrel, that did not lead to the final act of resignation. Then there is a report on Agriculture administration which makes various suggestions in regard to perspective planning for blocks, for enlargement of marketing opportunities, there ought to be about four times of markets that we have and that means more transport also— I mean better system of communication as well as transport then we have to decide which are the most effective levels of technical guidance at the block and district level—then village production plans, the position of Panchayats I have already mentioned. There are heaps of other things, but there is no time to deal with them. One lecture is not really sufficient to cover all the fields, but I have given you some idea. The position I think is not irretrievable. If only wisdom dawns on top leaders that the following things are required in order to bring about improvement, then I think the state of affairs can still be redeemed.

SWAMI VIVEKANANDA AND HIS CONTRIBUTION TO VEDANTA*

Swami Swahanandaji and ladies and gentlemen,

I am grateful for this invitation to speak on 'Swami Vivekenanda and his contribution to Vedanta'. Swami Swahananda has been kind enough to say that I have a little scholarship. Whether that is correct or not, I do not profess to be a scholar in relation to the writings and the contribution to thought of Swami Vivekananda, although like most of you I have read some of his writings and I have great regard and appreciation for him. It is possible that amongst you audience there are many who know much more about the subject than I do. But it is also possible that there may be a few who do not know so much and who might be prepared to listen to a learner like themselves. I shall confine myself to the subject and accordingly I would have to be largely factual and would have to give a larger number of quotations. I would not presume to have any special views in regard to the significance of Swami Vivekananda's contribution to Vedanta for the simple reason that as you listen to his words, what he meant will be crystal clear to you, as it was to hundreds of audiences all over the world, particularly in USA, UK, the Continent and then India.

We must first define our term. By Vedanta one should understand the speculation and philosophy that is contained in Upanishads, and more specifically, since there have been a large number of interpretations—we mean the authoritative interpretations given by Sankara. And I think in order to understand Swami Vivekanand's contribution to Vedanta, it is necessary to learn something about the nature of Vedanta as expounded by Sankara. For this part of my lecture I have drawn freely on Dr. N.K. Devaraja's book "Introduction to Sankara's Theory and Knowledge". He says : "The

*Lecture delivered on 31st March, 1963, at the Ramakrishna Mission, New-Delhi.

Advaita of Sankara generally considered to be the crowning achievement of the philosophical speculation of ancient Hindu India is well-known. Neither before Sankara nor after him did the Hindu mind, if not the Indian mind as a whole, create a system of philosophy which could be compared with the so-called orthodox Vedanta in boldness, deftness, and subtlety of speculation." Dr. Radhakrishnan characterised Sankara's Advaita Vedanta as complete in itself justifying the wholeness characteristic of a work of art. It has been held that Sankara was greatly indebted to Buddhist thinkers. But it has also to be recognised that his system as known today owes much to his successors. Sankara was able to discredit elements in the heterodox and rival systems of his time which he held to be opposed to the letter and spirit of the Srutis, and he welded into a coherent and powerful system the teachings of the Srutis. The first principle of Advaita is the establishment of the existence of the self-luminours 'chit' which is a deduction from experience. Since the world is non-eternal and the non-eternal is capable of annulment, the world is unreal. Sankara held that true knowledge should relate to an object which has a constant nature or an immutable essence, and according to him only the Atman qualifies to be called real. He held that the respects in which the effect differs from the cause are mere apperances just as Eddington has agreed that the table presented by the senses is but an unreal appearance of the real table which belongs to the shadow world of physics. Sankara emphasized the reality which is one without a second and believed that ultimate release can be brought about by right knowledge. He held the world to be phenomenal on moral and religious grounds. The actuality of realisation was as unquestionable a fact to Sankara and his contemporaries as the existence of the moral society to Plato and Aristotle. The highest goal of life, is, Sankara held, realisable here on the earth. It is an ideal which can be actualised and enjoyed by the individual in his own lifetime. The ideal is progressively realised through growing detachment towards earthly values. The highest work is contained in the mind that has achieved complete detachment.

The Sakshin or the witness Self is identical with Brahman, which is the metaphysical counterpart of the perception that highest work is contained in the mind that has achieved complete detachment.

This concept of freedom transcends the prevalent Western concept. According to Sankara, the individual could be completely free only through the conquest of the desires and thirsts associated with his animal nature and such freedom is enjoyed by *Sthita-Prajna* which is mentioned in the Gita as the saintly person whose wisdom is expressed in his serenity and balance. This is regarded in Advaita philosophy as the safeguard against pain and suffering. According to Vedanta the highest good of the Self is nothing extraneous to its essential nature. The Self's true nature is expressed by the phrase 'Sat Chit and Ananda' and the aim of man's life is to realise his nature concealed in his own being. The realisation can be achieved by the destruction of Adhyasa or the false identification of his true with the empirical sense. What needs to be accomplished is not the knowledge but the attainment of the self.

But this intuition is not absolute knowledge. It leads to it. Having destroyed other limitations the mental mood dies a natural death even as fire dies after consuming the fuel. According to the Upanishads, Sat existed before the beginning of cosmos. According to Sankara, Adhyasa or the duality of Self as agent and enjoyer is without beginning or end, and there never existed a time when Brahman existed apart from or without the World. Absolute consciousness emerges as the state in the World process itself. It is realised in the sages who have attained the lofty status of the Jivanmukta. This has great humanistic implications. Although there is self hidden in everything, owing to the gradual rise of the excellence of the physical conditions limiting it the self manifests itself in higher and higher forms in respect of power and splendour.

Neither the Vedanta of Sankara nor the previous Sunyavada of Buddhist does full justice—and that is the general verdict so to speak from the modern view—to the values other than religion. Both the systems fail to assign ultimate metaphysical values to the life of moral action nor do they express any solicitude for such human values as arts and literature, love and friendship. Whilst it is recommended that the aspiring Self should cultivate the virtues of compassion and general friendliness, he is not encouraged to develop loving attachment either to the beautiful or the virtuous. Not paying much attention to the duties involved in the communal life of man they seek to analyse or describe in detail the course of discipline which would lead to the flowering of saintly virtues in the life of the individual. And although they advocate a life devoted to the eradication of selfish and constrictive attachments to earthly values the greatest service which the unselfish individual can render to his fellow beings is the service involved in the dissemination of spiritual wisdom. But they seem to ignore spiritual and cultural activities which enrich (not only ennoble) life. They do not pay sufficient attention to the potentialities of man to rise spiritually higher on the plane of his specio-temporal or historical existence. Now I have referred to this because it is just these lacunae which were made up by Vivekananda. In other words his contribution to Vedanta may succinctly be said to be to fill up these gaps in the development of the Advaita Philosophy.

Coming back to Sankara, Sankara influenced the philosophies of the Bhagavatas, the Saktas and Saivas, etc., and the northern schools, influenced important writers on aesthetic, particularly of the Rasa school, the medieval poets and reformers like Kabir, Tulsidas and Nanak. Advaita Vedanta experienced a sort of renaissance during the later half of the 19th and the earlier half of the 20th century, when teachers and thinkers like Sri Ramakrishna Paramhansa, Vivekananda, Aurobindo, Tagore, Bhagavan Das, Radhakrishnan, etc., either interpreted or reformulated it so as to meet the requirements of the modern age.

Now, succinctly again, one would say that so far as Vivekananda was concerned, his contribution was the application of Vedanta to the theory of Vedanta. If the theory of Vedanta was formulated by Sankara, you might say that the amplitude of its application was the work of Swami Vivekananda. Here is a quotation from him regarding

Advaita in practical life—because he laid a very great emphasis on practice. "Believe, therefore, in yourselves and if you want material wealth, work it out ; it will come to you. If you want to be intellectual giants you shall be. And if you want to attain to freedom, work it out on the spiritual plane and free you shall be and shall enter into *Nirvana*, the Eternal Bliss." But one defect, he goes on to say, "which lay in the Advaita was its being worked out so long on the spiritual plane only and nowhere else. Now the time has come when you have to make it practical. It shall no more be a Rahasya, a secret, it shall no more live with monks in caves and forests and in the Himalayas. It must come down to the daily, everyday life of the people. It shall be worked out in the palace of the kings, in the cave of the recluse, it shall be worked out in the cottage of the poor, by the beggar in the street ; anywhere it can be worked out."

He has spoken and written so much on the principles of Vedanta that it is not easy to pick out what are the essential quotations, but here are a few which have been culled from a book by John Yale entitled "What Religion is." There is a section in it on the principles and the practices of Vedanta. One proposition is, when a man has reached the universal brotherhood, that man alone is Vedantic. The second, this Maya is everywhere, it is terrible: "At every step we are knocked down by Maya and it shows that we are bound and yet at the same moment together; with this blow comes the other feeling that we are free. The same world that was the ghastly battle-field of Maya is now changed into something good and beautiful". This is the gist of Vedantic morality, this sameness for all. Again, "the alpha and omega of Vedanta philosophy is to give up the world and to give up the unreal and take in the real. Each thought and deed lays up a store for you and bad thoughts and bad works are ready to spring upon you like tigers. So there is the inspiring hope that good thought and good deed are ready with the power of a hundred thousand angels to defend you. Lastly, Vedanta does not denounce the world. It, as we know it, as it appears to us. To know what it really is—deified it is God alone.

These are some quotations which would give an idea of what he thought were the principles or the doctrines of Vedanta. Some of you must be knowing that he delivered four lectures in London in November 1896 on "Practical Vedanta". I have no time to give you a summary of his exposition of Practical Vedanta in order that you may see, apply the principles of Vedanta to the problems of life which he even in his days describes as modern life and how he squared it with the tests that might be imposed by philosophy and science. And it is a fact that he was well-acquainted with writings in the modern philosophic field and he was generally aware of the advances of science in his days.

He began by saying that Vedanta as a religion must be intensely practical. He regarded the Bhagavad Gita as the best commentary on Vedanta whose message is Eternal Calmness in the midst of intense activity. Passion, he says, is not necessary for work because it dissipates energy. And there are two tendencies in human nature,—one is, harmonise the ideal with life and the other, elevate life to the ideal. Obviously he thought that what man should aim at is not the first one, make terms with whatever his inferiority was but to try to elevate life to the ideal. Then he describes what the ideal of Vedanta is. The ideal of Vedanta is *Tatvamasi* "Thou art That." Vedanta teaches man to have faith in themselves first. Vedanta recognizes no sin, only error. That is the essence of Vedanta. He had a lot to say about sin and its recognition because he was speaking to a predominantly Christian audience. Everything is ours already, he says, infinite purity, freedom, love and power but all this manifest, itself. It has to manifest itself. The scales must drop from our eyes and this can come by thinking in everyday life. The present life should be made to coincide with life Eternal.

The Central idea of Vedanta is oneness—in man, animal and all creation. And this is realised in varying degrees. If you believe there is a God, the animals, and the highest creatures, must be the same and he warns his fellow-beings that we have no right to look down with contempt upon those who have not developed exactly to the same degree as we are. Then he has a message of hope for mankind. "You can do anything and everything. You are All Mighty and religion must help man whatever his state of development. We have to have faith in ourselves. We must hear a voice in our ears day and night that we are Atman, the soul. Humbling yourselves, praying weeping to the imaginary beings—these are mere superstitions. You must tell that to others." "Show mankind their power" and that brings him to the subject of love for man which is a binding force because of this doctrine of Oneness and Ultimate Power and here he has a caveat to enter against intellectual preception. He says intellectual perception is not enough, and this is I think, where he elaborates what was not contained in the original formulation of Vendanta philosophy. We know that intellectuality is almost nothing for it is the heart that is of utmost importance. It is feeling that is the life. The strength—the vitality without which no amount of intellectual activity can reach God. Breathing is part of Brahman, sight is a part, feeling is a part, the mind is a part. There is a voice inside us to which we should listen. God is impersonal, a living God worshipped in the temple, the temple being the human body. "The moment" he says "I have realised God sitting in the temple of every human body, the moment I stated in reverence before every human being and see God in Him, that moment I am free from bondage. Everything that binds vanishes and I am free". Then he asks, "Do you feel for others?" "If you do, you are growing in oneness. If you do not feel for others, you may be the most intellectual giant ever born, but you will be nothing. You are but a dry intellect, you will remain so. Feeling is one of the most practical things in Vedantic morality for it is the teaching of the Vedanta that you are all prophets and all must be prophetic. The book is not the proof of your conduct, but you are the proof of the book. How do you know that the book teaches truth? Because you are truth and feel it—that is what the Vedanta says."

Then he refers to how this comes to you. He says "The voice of truth is inside ourselves. Understand and see the Lord in everything to see things in their real nature, not as they appear to be. But realisation must come to you. Religion is ever a practical science and there never was, nor will be a theological religion. Realising the truth means piercing the veil of Maya and recognising neither good nor bad, but knowing all as coming from the Self." The Self is in everything according to Vedanta. He said when a man has arrived at the perception that is neither good nor bad, neither life nor death, the one infinite Brahman, then man has become free. He says "I shall call you religious from the day you begin to see God in men and women. As our human relationships thus be made Divine, so our relationship with God. We can look upon Him then as Father, Mother, Friend and Beloved. But those who worship God through ceremonials and forms, however crude, we may think them, are not in error. It is the journey from truth to truth; from lower truth to higher truth."

And then he says: "What is darkness? Darkness means less light. What is evil? Evil is less good. What is impurity? Impurity is less pure. If you are free you must know that all will be so sooner or later, that is to say you will progress from step to step, will be more light, more good and will become purity.

Then he develops the philosophy of religion as a march from the particular to the general. There is one omnipresent ether and then from that he proceeds to postulate one all-embracing force which you call Prana. Then he says, "a theory of religion has to stand the test of the modern scientific mind. Is it sufficient generalisation'? And do we explain nature from nature? The idea of personal God, he says, does not stand these tests, but that of the impersonal God does. And the, impersonal being is in ourselves, Tat Twam Asi." This is the monism of the Vedanta.

We derive our ethics from monism only, especially ethics which are universally acceptable. According to him, the monistic theory has this merit that is the most rational of all the religious theories that we can conceive of, step by step, as realisation comes, infinite power and existence and blessedness are ours and we are not to acquire them. They are our own and we have only to manifest them. Then he develops his ideas, the Vedantic ideas in relation of the particular to the universal. It is true that we cannot think of the substance as separate from its quality and we cannot think of change and no change at the same time. It would be impossible, but the very thing which is substance is according to the Advaita, the quality. Substance and quality are not two things, it is the unchangeable that is appearing as changeable.

One of the remarkable features of the Advaita system of Vedanta is to harmonise the preceding systems. Dualism and all other systems that had preceded it are accepted by Advaita not in patronising way but with the conviction that they are the manifestations of the same truth and they all lead to the same conclusions as Advaita had reached. Thought—action, selfishness and unselfishness—have been two forces working side by side. Vivekananda asks "What right has any section of the community to base the whole work and evolution of the universe upon one of these two factors alone, upon competition and struggle. The motive power of the whole universe, in whatever way it manifests itself, is that wonderful thing—unselfishness, renunciation, love—the real, the only living force in existence. To reach the real basis of morality and ethics you must have the highest philosophical scientific conceptions. Human knowledge is not antagonistic to human well being. On the contrary it is knowledge alone that will save us in every department of life. In knowledge is worship. All truth is eternal, truth is nobody's property. No race, no individual can lay any exclusive claim to it. Truth is the nature of all souls who can lay any special claim to it, but it has to be made practical, to be made simple." And adds that the highest truths are always simple, so that it may penetrate every part of human society and become the property of the highest intellect and the commonest mind of the man, woman, child at the same time. "All these ratiocinations and logic, all these bundles of metaphysics, all these theologies and ceremonies may have been good in their own time, but let us try to make things simpler and to bring about the golden rays when every man will be worshipper and the Reality in every man will be the object of Worship".

This is the essense of the four lectures that he gave and I think I have quoted sufficiently—there is any amount one can go on quoting—but one would have realised that in applying the theory of Vedanta, is it something which had not been done before? It had been expounded on the religious plane, it had been expounded on the philosophical plane but Vivekananda also brought in the spiritual, social and moral content of life in a most practical way. And, as you have noticed he also reconciled all his thinking with the rigorous requirements of reason, came nearest to modern philosophy and science, and it seems to me that he has been successful in establishing or formulating the essentials of a Universal Religion which could be practised by high and low irrespective of time and space. His message seems to be particularly apt for the present day world with its emphasis on the oneness of everything and based on it, love, unselfishness, renunciation, fellowship and so on and so forth. And it seems to me that if this practical philosophy and religion is embraced by human beings, then the future of the world could be quite different from what one would be inclined to believe in one's pessimism from the modern developments in the world of international relations.

Thanking you.

Sd/-

C. D. Deshmukh

INDEX